To Michal from Serge

Letters from Charles Williams

To Michal

to His Wife, Florence, 1939–1945

from Serge

Edited by

Roma A. King, Jr.

The Kent State University Press

KENT & LONDON

Library of Congress Catalog Card Number 2001029896

ISBN 0-87338-712-0

Manufactured in the United States of America

07 06 05 04 03 02   5 4 3 2 1

Library of Congress Cataloging in Publication Data

Williams, Charles, 1886–1945

To Michal from Serge : letters from Charles Williams to his wife,
Florence, 1939–1945 / [edited by] Roma A. King, Jr.

p. cm.

Includes bibliographical references and index.

ISBN 0-87338-712-0 (alk. paper) ∞

1. Williams, Charles, 1886–1945—Correspondence.

2. Authors, English—20th century—Correspondence.

3. Williams, Florence Sarah Conway—Correspondence.

I. Williams, Florence Sarah Conway.

II. King, Roma A. (Roma Alvah), 1914– III. Title.

PR6045.I5 Z488 2001

828'.91209—dc21

2001029896

British Library Cataloging-in-Publication data are available.

Contents

Acknowledgments

I am especially grateful to Michael Williams, who owns the copyright on these letters, and to his agent, David Highman Associates, through whom arrangements were made for publishing the collection. Michael provided much information not available from any other source and continued to encourage me throughout the long process of transcribing and editing the letters.

I am grateful to the administration of the Marion E. Wade Center, Wheaton College, Wheaton, Illinois, which owns the letters as a part of its extensive collection of materials pertaining to that group of writers with whom Williams is most often associated. I especially thank Marjorie Lamp Mead, associate director, for her kindness in providing transcripts of the original letters and for her continuing help throughout the editing process. The days I have spent at Wheaton on this and other projects have been memorable.

I am deeply indebted to Anne and Ruth Spalding, who have shared their personal recollections of Charles Williams, who, during the period over which these letters were written, stayed in their home in Oxford. Ruth was active in the production of C.W.'s plays and provided interesting insight into what dramatic production could be like during those troubled years.

Anne Ridler has generously come to my assistance on several occasions, and to her I extend thanks.

I also acknowledge the encouragement I have received from the Charles Williams Society of London. It has been reassuring to know that I was working among and with the support of sympathetic scholars and critics.

To Lucille, my wife, I give loving thanks. I suspect that even she will never fully realize how much the completion of this task benefited from her continuous assistance and encouragement.

To Michal from Serge

Introduction

In late September 1939, the Oxford University Press, anticipating the outbreak of war, began moving its offices from London to Oxford. Charles Williams, who had been an employee of the firm since his early manhood, was, of course, forced to go along. Florence, or Michal, as he habitually called his wife, and his teen-age son, Michael, chose to remain in London. By September 7 Charles, along with an old friend and fellow worker at the Press, Gerard Hopkins, had taken up quarters at 9 South Parks Road in the comfortable home of Professor W. H. Spalding and his family. Professor Spalding, scholar, writer, and founder of the chair of Eastern Religion and Ethics at Oxford, was in America with his wife at the outbreak of the war. As part of their contribution to the war effort, the Spaldings opened their home to a few guests to help accommodate the huge influx of workers from London. As the situation developed, they were obliged to remain there until the war was over, leaving their house in the care of their two daughters, Anne and Ruth, and their son, John. Anne became largely responsible for the general management of the house. Ruth, the founding director of the Oxford Pilgrim Players, was frequently away from home touring through England with her company. John would later serve in the army.

Although the situation was as nearly ideal as circumstances permitted, C.W. (as Williams was called by his close friends, or Serge, as he was called by his wife) bitterly resented being separated from his wife, and in his letters we come to see how dependent he was on her not only as his wife and companion but also as critic and sustainer of his creative work. He returned to London for weekends as often as he could manage, and she occasionally came to Oxford for short visits. During a brief period when the bombing was particularly severe in London, she retreated to Lutterworth (Leicester) to be with her sister, who operated a boardinghouse there. But whether in London or Lutterworth, C.W. and Michal spent as much time together as possible.

Nevertheless, C.W. felt deeply the separation, and the two engaged in a prolific correspondence. His letters to her—all 680 of them, along with numerous other items of interest to readers of C.W.'s work—are now deposited in the Marion E. Wade Center at Wheaton College, Wheaton, Illinois. That he fully expected his correspondence to be published eventually is clearly indicated in the letters. In one, for example, he refers to the time when some "American Professor" would discover them and edit them. Most unfortunately, Michal destroyed her letters to him. (For her account, see the Appendix.)

The total number of letters would have composed a single volume of excessive length. Moreover, the letters are not all of equal importance. Many deal with practical matters, and some are repetitive. I chose to make a judicious selection that substantively represents the content of the whole in that it gives a full and honest representation of the man. I omitted nothing as a result of what might be called censorship—nothing in my selection itself or within the individual letters that I have chosen to include. I believe that my judgment fully represents an "uncensored" presentation of the entire collection. In the letters chosen, we see Williams at his very best and, on occasions, as something less—a man, however, honestly struggling toward light beyond the darkness.

What emerges is a look—sometimes painful, always sympathetic—into the man as husband and father and poet, one revealing as nearly as possible the vision he struggled to sustain during these years in spite of loneliness, near-poverty, ill health, and overwork.

Be it said immediately that there are no shocking revelations such as certain critics savor. Celia's story—which has already been told—was in the past, although her shadow continued to hover, as I shall suggest later: Charles remaining defensive and Michal remembering and cautious. Lois Lang-Sims is not mentioned—nor would we expect her to be. She was, after all, only a blip on the screen.

These letters were obviously written hurriedly and often under considerable stress. They are extremely colloquial and in their manner of expression suggest the intimate tone Charles Williams wished to express. The manner, thus, becomes part of the meaning. I have, therefore, retained the original, including the occasional slip in grammar or spelling. The only compromises I have made have been in his use of ellipsis and his way of indicating quotations. Williams habitually used two periods to indicate a break in thought or the omission of a word or words, and when the break came at the end of a sentence, he added an additional period. This I have regularized—three periods for an ellipsis, and an additional period when the ellipsis terminates a sentence. I have indicated quotations in the American manner.

Where to begin? At the beginning. C.W. was, first of all, a Christian and a poet. Although some would say he was a heretical Christian, I am more inclined to accept Charles Huttar's classification of his position as "Unorthodox Orthodoxy" (*Rhetoric of Vision*, 8–25). Or, I might say he was a skeptical Orthodox (in the classical sense) that left as much room as possible for honest doubt, sincere questioning. In his mind, all theological propositions were yoked together with their paradoxical opposites. He took very seriously his "mission" as a Christian poet—the word "mission" seems appropriately descriptive. For example, on December 27, 1940, he writes, "Do you not know that I am a poet by nature? and what does that mean? it means that my only faithful and certain devotion, made public to the world and private to you, is that announced in the early books of verse and in *Came Down from Heaven*; it means I live more by words than by blood. This is hard on you, but then, a thousand years ago, you would have it so." He is first of all a poet seeking identity, a vision, a voice, a style, a "communicating shape," a descriptive term by which he referred to the finished poem. His was a vision deeply rooted in the church and in the sacrament of marriage—marriage to Florence Conway, to whom he addressed his first book of poetry, *The Silver Stair*, and to whom he was married in 1917.

He muses about himself alternately in the persons of Taliessin, on the one hand, and Bors, on the other. On one level they represent opposites: body and soul, objective and subjective, doing and being. On March 16, 1943, he wrote: "In the poem you heard the Lord Bors said, or words to that effect about his own wife, who in the poem is a visible apparition of the Princess of the Grail Castle; for as for Taliessin himself wife he had none nor mistress nor love, except (as the old books teach) a mystical knowledge of an image of the Grail who was a nun, and anyhow Taliessin was only a voice and hardly human; but Bors a father and a husband and a quester of the Grail." Here he seems to stand apart from Taliessin and to identify more personally with Bors. Yet his view is ambivalent. Of his own work he writes, "Though there again—there are no *characters* in Taliessin; there are only functions and offices. All my work is, in a way, abstract; that is its difficulty, but perhaps its beauty (what it has!)" (May 12, 1943). Further probing, he says, "It's odd though. I'm a pattern, a voice, a name; not a person. I am Bach's *Ninth Symphony*, Shakespeare's *Tempest*, and Da Vinci's *Madonna of the Rocks*; one artistic vision, not a human being" (September 7, 1944). Still, he was appalled by Michal's criticism that all the women in his novels represented "a man's image of a woman."

No doubt he would have preferred yoking the apparent opposites into a single vision, each part highlighting and supplementing the other. The Taliessin cycle, when it was completed, was to have brought his poetic vision into sharp focus giving it symbolic "shape." We are concerned about the quality in C.W.'s poetry that David Jones points out as a weakness. He describes it as something "wholly to do with time—with now-ness. Somehow, somewhere, between content and form, concept and image, sign and what is signified, a sense of the contemporary escapes, or rather appears to me to escape. I know it is there in *idea*; I don't doubt but what the characters and situations were linked up in Williams's mind with now: but I do not often feel this now-ness in the words and images, or rather I feel it does not inform and pervade the poems as a whole" (Horne, *Charles Williams*, 214–15).

3

Primarily, however, these are love letters. Certainly one of the most vivid impressions they convey is the importance Williams attached to his wife's part in the formation of his poetry and consequently her contribution to his literary career, emotionally and critically. In his relationship with others he appears as father-confessor and counselor. During his stay in Oxford, many (including Robin Milford, Hurbert Foss, and Montgomery Belgion) sought his help. He also carried on a voluminous correspondence with friends and acquaintances, often in response to their emotional and spiritual needs. Obviously he was a sympathetic counselor.

These letters to Michal, however, present him in the reverse role. Here he is clearly the suppliant. There is often a defensiveness in his tone. Unfortunately, we do not have her letters to him and can only infer her part in the ongoing dialogue. On July 15, 1941, he complains, "You do not altogether believe that the only place where I have ever found rest is lying against you, but it is; always so and now that I don't find that primeval and original peace, I begin to feel myself losing hold. No doubt a Christian should not, but no doubt your husband does. These things are so much facts that they can hardly be expressed, even by me, in words. You are the absolute Fact of my life; consider if I miss *that*—flesh, mind, & soul. I always needed—& now always. There is not even a choice; it is merely *so*."

Shortly thereafter, on July 29, 1941, he laments, "Our labour to convince you is more than we ever have taken or could or would take over anyone else for anything at all." And on July 25, 1943:

How astonishing it seems to me that Your Sublime Serenity should ever have doubted that unceasing cry! What is the intellect (admirable as yours & mine is!), what is this or that, what is happiness itself, compared to that intuitive knowledge? That—which is never clouded by disputes or by the years; that—which is apt to gleam as brightly from your smile or your wit, your head or your hand, as ever it did; that—to which I have never, never, been false—not though the whole great creation had, & has, to be its balance and compeer; that—to which you and (one must certainly add) Beatrice are the only public witnesses in 600 years . . . O I could add "that" to "that" & never stop! Why, to send you money (poor as it is) is not, & never has been, merely to send money to one's wife; it is to maintain in action that transluscent thing, it is to serve a demi-goddess ("she seemed to him the daughter of a god"), to bear witness to a Fact as fixed as breath itself. Live up to it?—can you? can I?—but lose it ever? never you, never I.

One can hardly question the depth of emotion or the sincerity of the statement. Yet there is something in the language—a heightening of the style—which is characteristic of that quality Michal found excessive in his treatment of the women characters in his novels, a quality she called "a man's image of a woman." "I have always," he wrote, "kept in mind the knowing of you in God . . . . By the end of our lives, dearest pet, you will no doubt have understood my use of words; *or*, more likely, I shall have used words as you approve" (August 5, 1941). "There was in the Middle Ages," he explains, "a phrase—*amor intellectualis*, intellectual love, and for that matter there still is; the philosophers use it; but that is the way in which I look at you. For, as I have always said and shall always say, the speed of your motion is a thing to be studied carefully. . . . I think any speed in the present verse is due to your own physical. *Amor intellectualis*—I love you with vision, but though the vision is mine the spectacle is yours; that is, you provide it" (August 11, 1941).

As idealistic as his theology of marriage was, however, he never forgot that marriage itself was a sacrament of the church and that the sacramental involves body as well as spirit. "Perhaps, with you at hand, I might feel differently," he muses, "because you always have that kind of sub-driving effect on my genius and (so to speak) wake it up. If I could ever be persuaded that genius was related to sex, I should think that helped to prove it" (May 23, 1944).

Michal was, however, not only his inspiration, his Beatrice, she was also, on the very practical level, his severest and most heeded critic. In an early letter he writes: "Lewis says it would be fatal for a great man's wife to read him; I said that you, as unique in that as in all, read, admired, mocked, and left me free to play at my own job" (October 25, 1939). The words "mocked" and "play" may be misleading if they suggest that he took her criticism lightly. He did not. In response to her objection to his portrayal of women in his novels, he responded, "You are right—yes; yes. If I ever demurred, it was not at the fact but, might I say so, at your slightly surgical knife-way of putting it" (June 10, 1943). She might have been protesting on behalf of both Beatrice and herself. On September 25, 1940, he wrote, "I do not know that you can very well complain if you are the cause of poems on marriage as the Good Life instead of on yourself directly: no, I do not. Everyone else observes the relation. Another poet might have done it another way; he would have been a lesser. So that if you become a Doctrine, well, it cannot be helped."

The subject continued to be one for discussion. As late as October 7, 1943, he admitted: "I at moments realize that I may, all along, have treated even you rather too much like a man's image of a woman! This is a very shattering thought, and arises entirely out of your criticism of the women in the novels. . . . And long meditation on your remarks, & how it explains everything that is wrong with those books, arouses in me a deep suspicion of my capacity."

He was apparently disconcerted also by her suggestion that his work lacked in moral teaching and that his doctrine was dangerous. Again, it would be helpful if we had her letters to tell us, in this case, what the nature of that lack was and where it occurred in his work. In a letter dated June 9, 1940, ambiguously expressing triumph and deference, he wrote, "By the way you have sometimes blamed me for not being moral enough! but a strange man in *Theology* says that *D. into Hell* is 'the most virulent moral invective of our generation.' This, he said hastily, is *not* a modification of your judgement!—no, no, no." On the basis of these words we can only speculate that she in general would have preferred a more explicit statement where he chooses implication. Perhaps his comparison of his own technique with those of Bach, Shakespeare, and Da Vinci suggests that he preferred the spirit of a moral order, a symbolic vision that informed the whole work, to more explicit statements. Her reservation about his doctrine may refer to his "romantic theology" with which she was apparently never comfortable.

Perhaps this description of himself has to do with what he also calls his "detachment," his "remoteness": "I'm even more of a . . . prophet? priest? something—more of a Voice and less of a man . . . a slightly non-personal figure, and all my 'interests' rather in figures than in people" (February 17, 1945).

In spite of his tendency to idealize her and she to protest, however, she remained the stabilizing force in his life, the anchor that grounded him, that kept him in touch with the concrete, the world, the flesh (although theologically and rationally he himself affirmed them to be two modes of one substance, the Unity). She was the inspiration that kept him on course lest he ascend to heaven in a chariot of fire.

4

These letters also reveal a strange dichotomy between his private and public lives. Under the genial social exterior there lies a very dark underside. Shortly after his arrival in Oxford, he wrote in an undated letter to Michal: "I dislike people, & I hate being with them." This from the man who was known for his generosity and his willingness always to reach out to people in trouble is surprising. Nevertheless, this statement ("I dislike people") recurs throughout the letters. And so often, he appeals to Michal for help: "You'll have to keep me faced in the right direction as you have done so often. There are wells of hate in one which are terrifying, & wells of suspicion and even malice." And a little later: "You can't imagine how I dislike people's *faces*. Only the conventions of years of social behaviour stop me, I sometimes feel, shouting at them. . . . It is worse with the women than with the men, because every woman actually repels me, whereas the men are only passively unbearable" (October 15, 1943). Even more unexpected are his occasional outbursts against people with whom he has been long and affectionately associated. His respect and admiration for Sir Humphrey can hardly be questioned, but, still, when Sir H. finds himself deprived of his living quarters and with no others available, C.W. writes, "I must be allowed to repeat that this faintly amuses me. . . . The ungodly do not always flourish" (June 6, 1944). And of Geoffrey Cumberlege, his business associate, who is in the same situation: "Heard the sad sweet tale. Sad, no doubt, in itself, but sweet to me. I adore hearing of these people's difficulties" (May 17, 1944). About Gerry Hopkins, who was contemplating a new position that would take him from Oxford, C.W. wrote: "It's odd how I don't want him to. . . . O not because I want him here; simply because I don't want him to be able to do anything . . . . very shocking & shows what evil is in our nature" (December 9[10], 1949). Such admissions are usually accompanied by a show of remorse. C.W. had a tender conscience that gave him no end of trouble.

There were moments even in his relation with Michal when he seems to have momentarily lost control: "After my exhibition (between ourselves) at Paddington, I should spend a rotten night; which I found myself gloomily regarding as only too proper penance. If one allows one's temper to get twisted, it's hardly surprising that one's body should follow suit and one should have cramp and wakefulness. . . . Forgive it & me, & for yesterday. But I was very embittered, & I do hate people's faces . . . & I am unworthy your love. Still . . . continue" (June 1, 1944).

The vivid presence of evil in much of his work, particularly in the novels and the two plays *Frontiers of Evil* and *The House of the Octopus*, seems to reflect his personal heightened emotional and intellectual awareness of the darkness of the unregenerate human heart—a darkness that was intensified by the situation in which he found himself. He was separated from Michal, upon whom he clearly depended; he was a Londoner, like Dr. Johnson, who felt that to be tired of the city was to be tired of life; he was hounded by money problems and forced into doing hack work in order to make ends meet, feeling always that he was doing less than right by his wife and son; he was concerned for his son's future; he was handicapped by physical problems; and he was disturbed by the awareness that time was passing and his great work, which he felt lay ahead, might never be done. All these, and perhaps a natural inclination toward gloom and most certainly a tenderness of conscience, contributed to his continuing state of dissatisfaction during his Oxford years.

In spite of his insistence that he did not like people, C.W. was capable of forming and cherishing deep friendships. Throughout his life he spoke affectionately of Harold Eyers and Ernest Nottingham, the two literary companions with whom he spent many happy hours when he was a young and still-unpublished poet. Both were killed in World War I. There were also Daniel Nicholson and Henry Lee, editors of *The Oxford Book of Mystical Verse*, whom he met at the time their book was being prepared for printing. The Reverend Henry Lee, especially, remained a very close friend and confidant, and his death in 1941 caused C.W much grief. He also sustained an affectionate relationship with many of those who attended his classes in London, including, among others, Alice Mary Hadfield, Thelma Shuttleworth, John Topliss, Joan Wallis, and Raymond Hunt.

At the time these letters were written, the two literary figures with whom he enjoyed a close relationship were C. S. Lewis and T. S. Eliot. His close friendship with C. S. Lewis is well known, but the depth of his feeling for Eliot has not been fully recognized. In a letter to Michal written in February 1945, he said, "I've never been able to express this very well; but somehow except at home . . . and perhaps at Magdalen or with Eliot . . . I am always aware of a gulf."

It was Michal, however, who first captured his heart, awakened his poetic vision, and remained throughout his life his best friend and severest critic—his Beatrice.

5

Yes. The darkness is there. Yet its presence cannot be dismissed merely as an anomaly or as a contradiction. The light is also there and shines all the more brightly by being counterpointed, not contrasted, against its opposite. John Heath-Stubbs in his introduction to the *Collected Plays* writes, "Several interpreters of Charles Williams (including Mrs. Ridler, Mrs. Hadfield, and Brother George Every) have pointed out that the figure of Satan in this work [*The Rite of the Passion*] anticipates a series of figures in the later plays—the Skeleton in *Cranmer*, The Third King in *Seed of Adam*, the Accuser in *The Judgement at Chelmsford*. In all these, a figure apparently representing Evil or Death ultimately appears, in the light of eternity, as the instrument of Good." He continues by pointing out that the figure—the Flame in *The House of the*

Octopus—is eventually revealed as "the Holy Spirit guarding over and working in the Church" (Heath-Stubbs, *Collected Plays*, vii). We recall also the statement of The Skeleton in *Cranmer*:

> Where is your God?
> [After a pause]
> When you have lost him at last you shall come
> into God. (67)

The Skeleton was the backside of God who when he turned around revealed the face of Christ. C.W. followed Augustine in his understanding of evil. He contended that God was the sole creator of all things and that evil is merely the privation of some desirable good.

There can be, therefore, only the good and its absence—that absence is precisely the evil. The one defines the other. Failure to understand this metaphysical concept led F. L. Leavis to say, "Williams's preoccupation with the horror of evil is evidence of an arrest at the schoolboy (and schoolgirl) stage rather than that of spiritual maturity." I think that a careful and honest reading of what C.W. has said over and over on the subject would refute that statement. Nevertheless, the letters do provide further clarification for those who need it. Over against the imagined blackness—so intense that it becomes almost unbearable—the light shines clearly. C.W. was perhaps never able himself to achieve the serenity of Sybil, the saintly character in *The Greater Trumps*—or, if so, only in the rarest moments of vision—but he was able to imagine it and to embody it in language that communicates beyond its literal meaning.

6

In spite of the darkness (or as a correlative to the darkness), this was a period of rich achievements that must have provided some measure of self-satisfaction and joy to counterpoint the gloom. His bibliography during the period beginning in late 1939 is extensive, including such enduring works as *The Descent of the Dove*, *Witchcraft*, *The Forgiveness of Sins*, *What the Cross Means to Me*, *The Figure of Beatrice*, *All Hallows' Eve*, and *The Region of the Summer Stars*. This is admittedly the period also of the bitterly dark *Frontiers of Evil* and *The House of the Octopus*. Of the latter he wrote, "O encourage me, beloved! I shall make this play as bitter as I know how. I'll show them what I think of men" (June 2, 1944). To this list we might add his numerous lectures other than those sponsored by Oxford University and the many articles and reviews that he continued to write.

Oxford received him and honored him. Almost from the beginning he was on its schedule of lecturers and was received enthusiastically by the students. For the first time in his career he was surrounded by his intellectual and creative equals; he enjoyed the rich fellowship of the Inklings; he was awarded an honorary master of arts degree; and, moreover, at the time of his death a movement was under way to offer him a permanent position on the Oxford staff, a prospect to which both he and Michal looked forward.

7

It is generally lamented that Williams's death at age fifty-eight was untimely. Certainly he himself thought his greatest work lay in the future, although he did say on one of his darker days that he would rather earn a little money than to write the *Aeneid*—an exaggeration obviously. He rejoiced when the war was over and expressed eagerness to return to London, cherishing the possibility of eventually returning to Oxford, where he and Michal would live out their lives together. There is no certain indication in the letters of any premonition of what was at hand. On May 4, 1945, he wrote to Michal, "I feel as if I were ashamed to bring you so old a man; you should have something—no; perhaps not, & I may not really be so old presently."

He still had things he wanted to do and write. In February 1945 he wrote, "I do think that (religiously speaking) it's very important that I should finish my job, find my last style, make my last shapes in verse or prose or public comments. But that is all." In the same letter, he said, "I'm a little conscious myself of a certain new detachment. What you might call my 'field of operations' has widened, but it's more markably remote. Perhaps the people in my novels grow more real as my consciousness of actual people decreases" (February 17, 1945). One can only speculate about the meaning of "more real." Certainly more abstract.

His chief desire was to finish *The Figure of Arthur*, the unfinished version of which was published in 1948 by C. S. Lewis as part of the book *Arthurian Torso*. Perhaps most of all he wished to complete the Arthurian cycle of poems. He hoped to revise his Wordsworth lectures and publish them under the title "The Figure of Power." He had been asked by the BBC to write a short book on religious drama. At one time he expressed interest in writing a book on the lives of the saints. In his next to last letter he tells of a conversation he had with Gervase Mathew in which Williams seems to suggest that he is thinking about writing a life of Jesus, a thought to which Mathew said that he need only to copy the Gospel of Saint John and sign his name to it.

The next day, May 8, he penned his last lines to Michal: "The mourning & the burying are done. And presently . . . There couldn't have been a better Peace Sunday than last. I wish we were together, but that was very good. And now it is nice to be done. . . . It is lovely to feel it possible to be one with you over it, even if . . . We are, in a way, blessed. All my love and gratitude. Serge"

LETTERS

1939

My dearest love,

I have never known anything like it; I have found my way here; it is just outside Oxford beyond Magdalen Bridge. It is a rather large & pleasant house, in gardens occupied at present wholly by Sir Humphrey[1] & the Secretary:[2] we don't wander in them. Everything is, of course, in complete disorder; some sort of work is being done. But the corners & tables & boards & general absurdity is indescribable.

The train down was two hours late, but I did as was suggested, and went & had a shave, & sent the wire to you, & then took a taxi to the house. We are not all alone unhappy. Milford & his wife came down to Sisam's on Saturday, & found the Sisams still away in Sicily; no dark blinds; an empty house, & no *anything*. Similar things have been happening everywhere. I shan't get paid till we have heard again from N.Y. Still, I shall get it—so that's something, & it can hardly be less than £20, which will clear the insurance & leave a few pounds to catch up with.

Lewis has offered me the use of his rooms at Magdalen for the week-end, as he won't be there. So there, I think, I shall go on Sunday after breakfast, have lunch & tea out, & go back to dinner. I shall be all alone for the day. The Spaldings are taking on the two Milford children[3] for a fortnight, so as to let Mrs. M. get away with the new baby.

The weather is duller to-day, but keep the coat till I can come and fetch it. We can no longer sit in the gardens—partly because of the weather, but partly because we are now going all business-like & working. Cumberlege vaguely conveys a kind of military air into the house. On Friday I am to dine with Hubert[4] at his brother's house, who is a Major or a General in command of bits of this area.

The Spaldings[5] have been agitating the Press for me this morning: I had lunch with Hubert, & went round there afterwards. Ruth, Anne, & a brother

15

were there; they were all waiting, and we had a little discussion for three minutes. Anne (whom I don't remember) said she had mucked everything; Ruth said they "felt terrible." Nothing has been said about Miss Hill so far. I am going there to-night because the only alternative is to rush round Oxford to odd addresses, & I am very reluctant to do that. Also I wish to conserve my available cash. It is understood that the Press will pay a week's lodging; after that nothing has been said. With any luck I shall be able to send you a pound back some time: it weighs most of all on me that you should have so little, & I shall not be able to get any money from them here yet.

There is no sign of war except the usual gas masks & inconveniences. I am as inconveniently comfortable as I can be; there is no place for me but then that is generally true. Every room has six or seven people in it, & all crowded. Hubert has a room with a large bath, covered by boards & papers. The sanitary arrangements are (as regards men) for one Individual at a time.

I was terribly shaken at leaving you, and I wish only that all this was in London. I dislike people[6] anyhow, & I hate being with them. Here, at the moment, there is no getting away. If I could have found rooms for myself away from everyone it would have been more bearable. But that I dare not try for—not yet. So, most beloved, sympathize.

We are—it is odd—beginning to work. Gerry Hopkins is expected on Thursday; he is reported to be trying to get rid of children deposited on him by authority.

I shall remember your good-bye this morning for ever; dearest love, we are already each other's. I was unhappy coming down, you will believe. I read St John of the Cross[7]—who did not cheer me. I am sending this to be sure of the post. Heart of my heart, love me.

C

Southfield House
6 Sept./39

Darling,

There was an air-alarm here this morning, but I gather falsely. At the moment there is nothing more to report. I am sick at heart over everything, but we have put our own hearts together to do it, haven't we? I am determined to come up at the week end; I cannot say when: if you are out I will make tea for you.

I shall have to settle down to work soon; I saw the Professor of Poetry[8] at Magdalen this morning. Oxford is a mass—& more people are coming; Chatham House is descending complete—you wouldn't know it; never mind. Half the government offices are said to be here.

I think of you, and embrace you: you are my continuous centre; pray for me. My love to Michael—& ask him who wrote *Garbo & the Night Watchman:* I want to know.

My love. Till Saturday—probably.

C

Oxford
15 Sept/39.

My dearest,

I have been a little haunted by dreams of you being in—I can't say what difficulties because they were dreams, but I felt strongly that I ought to be doing something about them. I was glad to have your letter for that reason, apart from the fact that I always am. All the same, we mustn't write every day, or we shall get fussed if we don't hear. Or I shall!

The Mitre[9]—yes! I see myself. Not but what I find the Mitre has a room right at the back where one eats, drinks, & pays differently. Which brings me back to another subject. I haven't seen the Spalding girls alone to fix the money, but I hope to during the week-end. Gerry did during last week-end & settled, for the present, on 1/5/- inclusive of laundry. I expect I shall do the same. It may have to rise presently—if the war lasts; there is still a sense of hope here for a reasonably short business. Milford, I hear, has sacked several people—one or two I think it is very hard on. It gives one an awkward feeling to be paid an extra pound when they are flung out. But the official view is that the Press must retrench.

You were going to send me the exact amount of the Insurance payment, and the number of the policy. If you have one of those little green slips they forward to us, let me have that, & I will write to Edith.[10] It is the 28th we have to pay by normally; I am half a mind to write to them asking if the 30th will do. I should rather that than sending Edith's cheque. But I don't mind. Be at ease.

What is on my mind at present, and as much, is Michael's coat. You did tell me how much it was likely to be, but I forget. I realize the rent, the insurance, this month's Spalding bill, your next month's keep, & mine, have to come out of this end-of-the-month's cheque. But I wonder whether we could do something about it all the same. We know the American money[11] must come in a few weeks, & I am pretty certain that the counting-house can't afford to pay me till they get it themselves, so harried are we all. But tell me about Michael's coat, & we will see.

This is a dull letter; I apologize. Do not suppose I love you less for considering needs—you won't. Mrs. Oliver[12] is a marvel. I adore you.

C

Oxford

17 Septr/39

It is all very still. I have fled to Lewis's rooms; the College is silent all round me. I shall only go back to supper. He is great tea-drinker at any hour of night or day, and left a tray for me with milk & tea, & an electric kettle at hand. Sound man! You must come here one day and see my refuge.

Yesterday I went to the office—"the office!" dear God!—in the morning, had lunch, & went for a walk like Kipling's Cat[13] that walks by himself. To-day I went to church at 8, had breakfast, & came round here. It is a great relief, & I hope C.S.L. does it every week-end.

I have bought a tooth-brush, which I forgot; and I seem to have muddled my socks; anyway, I have but one clean pair after those I wear. Can you tell me my size? I had better buy a couple of pairs. Unless your Loveliness would like to do it—but I fear you have no money. (Everyone at the "office" is acutely aware of the expense of getting home!) Do you need more? I float cautiously towards the end of the month; I may have to come up then to get you and me some. But I shall know more, I hope, this week.

O sweet, how sweet you are! I do feel how difficult it must be for you—but you know that. It is now about three, & I have switched on C.S.L.'s electric kettle because I think I will have some tea.

My mind won't work properly yet—yet it must. The *Dove*[14] is to be published, they hope, on 16 October. That will clear the bank. Higham[15] has gone into the Army. The Bishop of Chichester[16] invites my help with prayers, but I think I cannot do much; he has Cranmer's.[17]

My love to Michael. I will write to him. But I always told you I needed you at my back to do anything. As at first at St. Albans.

C

Observe the arms on the envelope—Magdalen. C.S.L.'s envelope.

20 Septr /39

I couldn't not send a line on my birthday, so I do; to say thank-you. Ursula[18] sent me a book, but that is all—not that I wanted any. No, of course not; Isabel has sent socks. She & Margaret[19] are coming to Oxford; they have found rooms some quarter of an hour from me. And I am to call as soon as I can. Which I will do—but I am a little sorry. More than a little, in fact; poor dears.

The weather is very heavy here. I had meant to go to church this morning, but I didn't wake in time. Do you know from 8.15 A.M. to 10 P.M. I am hardly alone for a moment? It's incredible. This, really, is not grumbling; it is just stupefying.

This is a very stupid letter, but it shall go. All my love and all my blessings. And thank you still.

C

Oxford
3 Oct /39

You won't be sorry to hear that we are fixing up the *New Christian Year*[20] (which is the provisional title) as I proposed. I admit I could wish that things could be done *direct* with HSM instead of through Cumberlege—not that he is difficult, but it involves . . . . O well, it doesn't matter. Anyhow, as I told you, I have proposed to do it by next June, so as to clear off my indebtedness. I didn't put it like that, of course. Cumberlege wanted the book; and we are sending a note to the counting-house, cutting the present state by £25. Next June we shall have covered it all without more trouble than finding 500 or so quotations—so that is off our minds. Agree, darling, that is a pleasant thought!

At the same time, if you should need something (which you won't) to occupy you, and could look through any of the works of the Great—the religious Great—for quotations, it might help. You know the kind of thing in the *Passion of Christ*;[21] only this is for the whole year. But there is plenty of time; we will talk of sources presently.

There was a mass gathering last night at South Parks Rd: three young men and a foreign young woman. Very crowded and all, no doubt, very nice. *But* rather social. One of the young men had seen *Seed of Adam* at Sandwich, & admired it. Otherwise we talked about the war. G.H. says that this kind of thing can't go on, & I agree. But we neither of us quite see what to do about it; we don't like to retire to our funk-holes after dinner, & we can hardly object to people coming.

The foot is not too bad—a little uncomfortable, but that is all. I have bound it up, after a bath this morning, and I shall take a bus home before going to the Keays-Young woman.[22] Kiss me and love me. I have had no coffee since Monday morning!

C

Undated[23]

Dearest,

Heavens, last night! I realize that I must take care not to be simply difficult & hostile, and that, what with Oxford and Keays-Young and everything, I am in danger of becoming wholly resentful; still. . . . There were the Douglases & I and a Vicar and an undergraduate and Mrs. K.Y, & Mrs. K.Y.'s sister, & Mrs K.Y.'s daughter (an unfortunate sprawling semi-youthful creature of 35ish). And Mrs. K.Y's sister "can listen for hours to

Pat McCormick's voice"—so I said that an aesthetic pleasure of that kind was easily mistaken for religion. And then Isabel alluded to one of my books, and Miss K.Y. said: "O do you *write?*" and the sister said she must try & get hold of my novels; and in a fever of irritation I went home about 10 under a full moon. But what I did suddenly remember, as I went down the Banbury Rd., was meeting you in the dark nights of the last war.[24] So the evening was not lost—for the whole of my doctrine involves such fundamental recollections as power.

The Douglases are proposing to move to the Clarendon Hotel. This is in the Cornmarket, in the centre of the town. It will be (you may guess the deduction) easier for me to lunch. And they will have a sitting-room for me to work in, and they meanwhile "will be quite comfortable in their bedroom." Such a jolly prospect—me working at Witchcraft knowing that they are . . . . O well: I *am* unlike all other writers—I work best at home, in my own four walls.

Yes, I am irritable. I kiss your hand and control myself. I have a book to review for *Life & Letters*—Dylan Thomas's last.[25] Anne Spalding says that a girl who was at Downe, and admired me from afar there, is coming to dinner tonight, a Frances Murray, of whom I know and recollect absolutely nothing. O—and I have sent the rent. Positively the only gleam of light in the horizon outside London is the fact that we have settled the Press debt without having to pay any more. I have signed the agreement, and a note has gone to Merden to the Chief Cashier. Praise to the Holiest! If I get a small cheque from *Time & Tide*—no, give Miss Kinselle at least another pound of your five (which is certainly three now!) and tell her I will try & send the rest at the month's end. You will see that my economical life is urging me on to pay things off. There is £20 in the bank towards income tax, and America will provide another £20: we shall only need £20 more, I hope—perhaps less.[26]

You must forgive this. I wake up in the morning arranging my finance not unhopefully. Olive[27] has written saying I am difficult: I am tired of being told so. A man who used to be among my people has written asking me to go over to a place some miles out of here to lunch on Sunday, & I may go. There are buses, & one is back before the black-out, I understand.

Meanwhile I read out your remark about this war being arranged to crush the Cenotaph service. G.H. & everyone thought it a marvellous idea, and probably quite right. O buy another hat and content me more! The foot is no more than a little inconvenient at times. I bathe and bind it, as you said. This is almost the first time I have persevered steadily, but I trust the bandage as yours and take it seriously.

All my love. Ought I to write the doctor? perhaps I will. Thank you for buying something.

C

I seem to have left my pen in my dressing gown, as a result of doing some work last night. I hope to start again to-night! So you will excuse this brevity.

I cannot say how I wish I were being looked after by you, but you don't catch me moving nearer. I understand half a dozen of them—Page, Budgen, & others—went to the theatre last night; no, angel, let me know no-one in Oxford connected with the Press once I have left it. . . . Outside Lewis, I never want to see anyone of Oxford or in Oxford again! I was just saying to C.S.L. that I have a nostalgia for walking round the block in London—the City & the Dome;[28] the flat and you.

Time & Tide think they may have to suspend, but have sent me a book of 600 pages first. I shall be sorry if they do. One hears here of more & more dismissals in the publishing trade—not with us so much—& more people write asking if I know of jobs. A heart-breaking business!

The foot is, I think, improving slowly. I go on keeping it bound up.

All my love.

C

Oxford

6 Oct./39

My dearest,

I have just had a note from Anne,[29] saying that she had rung you up, and incidentally letting out that your back is bad. I have been afraid of that ever since Wednesday morning—and even before; I fear it was Monday night or Tuesday morning when it got worse. I am so sorry; that on top of everything else is double hell.

I think my foot shows a slight improvement; I wish I were coming up this weekend. As it is, I go to a dramatic reading of *George & Margaret* by the lesser staff on Saturday at 2.30; but I must leave the lodgings where they hold it in time to get to the Douglases by about five; I shall stop there till about 6:15 and then go back to dinner at South Parks Rd. This is what we call an unselfish day! On Sunday, if I don't go to my man to lunch—it depends how the busses are—I shall shut myself up in Magdalen. What with London and Magdalen I admit I have done pretty well for the week-ends.

Last night I did some more work: if this goes on I shall begin to see a kind of shape in the notes soon. You know that I was finding the act of writing a bore months ago, and it grows no less so. But there is no help for that; I couldn't dictate this kind of thing even if there were anyone to dictate to. Or talk to, for that matter. It is an odd thing that there is no-one here to whom I can talk about *Taliessin;* I had a faint idea yesterday of turning the Pope into a symbolical figure. Well, there aren't many in London, but Eliot[30] and Belgion[31] and

Raymond[32] and so on were there if I wanted them, which (in that way) I generally *didn't*. But it is one thing not to want anyone; and I considered how of all these people I have known so long—Gerry & Fred, & HSM & the rest—there isn't anyone who is capable of being talked to as I wish to talk. Nicholson[33] & Eliot are the only ones. . . . It was, I think, Anne[34] who said—years and years ago—that I was, in that way, alone enough not ever to need them; and it is true enough. As we said last Sunday, my domestic walls and an occasional man—'tis what I need; who would believe there was such difficulty in getting it?

There are, however, a few advantages: or at least Birmingham would be worse. G.H. & I, returning by Magdalen from a modest lunch (beer has gone up a penny, but bread & cheese remain the same), saw the Vice-Chancellor proceeding to a meeting—all in robes, with three beadles with maces preceding him along the pavement. He is G. S. Gordon, who admired Bacon & other things. So, as the etiquette apparently is, we solemnly raised our hats. The Vice-Chancellor touches his mortar-board and passes on. If this insane arrangement is to exist, I admit I would rather see the V.C. in semi-state than something less amusing.

To-night people are coming in from Balliol, that is, from Chatham House to sing madrigals. G.H. is to sing; I am not. Norrington[35] from the C.P. has been asked: it is not altogether displeasing to me that the C.P. should find me there rather than in a worse hole. This is snobbery; let it pass. I will not be tied up with the others as long as I can avoid it. I shall hand over my cash to-morrow morning, now I have paid up, & so in future; that will leave the end of the month clear. Send me the electric light & the telephone when they come and I will send cheques. By the way Parnwell,[36] for instance, talks about the income tax I feel quite cheery. But then, all being well, I hope now I have got a good bit of the January and some of the July arranged for; it will be tight, but not *too* tight.

We will go and stay, one day, (a) at Bath (b) at Canterbury (c) at Cambridge—this last merely to redeem the Universities of England. Since I recollected on Tuesday the black-outs of our high days I am more reconciled to those happening now: not that I am out in them. I feel that for once in my life I am being more economical than F.P.—but lunches, shaves, & cigarettes are my only expenses.

O and stamps and the paper. Could your most obedient servant do more? It was lovely of you to praise my letters—no, but to like them. They lack something of yours. O I must tell [incomplete]

Magdalen
8 Oct /39

Dearest,

This is only a short note, because I really have been working—certainly it was on the poem for *Theology*[37] but it was a little on magic too.[38] I had a note from my man saying he had to go away so would I put off coming. Which I, not unwillingly, did. And I came round here, & here I stuck; only crossing the road once for a brief lunch. It is now four and I have seen no-one since breakfast; I think I must have been asleep for the last half-hour—it's later than it ought to be.

Anyhow I have cleared the poem off. Which reminds me that your second book is coming out as a *Chameleon*[39] after all. They will send you four copies when it is ready, & give me two: is that all right? I thought I would give the Ss[40] one on your behalf & one I should like to have. I was shown an advance copy yesterday. I gave the copy of the third book to Karberry[41] some weeks ago for him to look through. (It occurs to me that we have never before published books at about the same time!)

I met the Vicar of St. Mary's on Friday who asked tentatively about a Passion Play; we will see about that. It might be amusing.

Meanwhile the *S. Times* has sent two books. At the moment I have four to review; one for *Life & Letters*,[42] one for *T&T*,[43] & two for the *S.T.*[44] (very uninteresting these). G.H. has another French book to translate, so, if the winter goes on, we shall both be settling down to our labours. Ursula's uncle has written asking me to call on him—which I shall do. I have been so pleased about clearing the O.U.P. up that I now yearn to make money wildly. By the way, do they owe you £10 for the Chameleon? if so, you shall have it (for almost the first time for years) ALL FOR YOURSELF.

Tell me about your guest. I'm glad M. was away. But you almost made me cry over your crime film, over your suggestion, I mean. All my love!

C

Oxford
13 Octr./39

I have decided, contemplating the whole canon of my work, and the immediate future ones, that I am the only writer in English who, now or hitherto, will have suggested what marriage is. This may surprise you, though I think it should not; but it arises because in the *Theology* poem[45] and the *Time & Tide* article,[46] and in my thoughts, I observe a new word creeping in, which is *substance*. It is clear to me that marriage is *substance*, a thing of solid existence, like very few other things; I should myself add religion & great art, but I do not press that. Anyhow the world into which we move is a world of reality and substance, and marriage is a way into it and an example of it.

This little essay, darling, is due, I repeat, to the work I have done this week, emphasized by a nostalgia which attacked me this morning. I wish I had said this weekend instead of next, but I am trying to serve you and my country with my pound notes, and husbanding them carefully. I take it you will be all right till next week-end at least for cash? but let me know if you are not. It is a pleasure to feel there are a few pounds in the bank; of course they are for income-tax—still, there for the moment they are. We haven't got the American money[47] yet, but I hardly expected it; no doubt the mails are going another route to avoid the German submarines.

I do not [know] why people have eiderdowns! I wake up three or four times each night because the thing has fallen off and my leg aches. However, it is a small thing. This week end I have no reading, but I shall spend extra time with the Douglases on Saturday. On Sunday Foss is taking me to Lincoln College to see some professor of music who wanted to set *Murder in the Cathedral* to music, and who, I understand, was then told by Hubert to consider *Cranmer*. Nothing, I suppose, will come of it,[48] but we may as well go and see him. I hope to return to Witchcraft during the week-end; the sudden rush of reviews is almost done, though I hope for more. *The Descent of the Dove*[49] still does not arrive; but down here everything takes twice as long to reach us. Of all the out-of-the-way, out-of-the-world places for a publishing house to be. . . .

O I *was* nostalgic this morning! I sighed for home and beauty—and let England look after itself. I walked to my barber's (it is the one quarter of an hour I get to myself, having parted from G.H. and let him go to the office, where I follow in ten minutes, until ten at night. But I don't so much mind, now my work has begun to begin again. However this morning I went all bitter along the High, & am still a little so. All this peace talk has made things worse, because it will come to nothing, unless indeed we all, including Germany, get too anxious about Russia.[50] But I see we are making trade agreements with her. I still think myself that there will be more of a chance in the spring. Thirty years as an *active* war is nonsense.

Well, but having gone all metaphysical I did not mean to go all political. There is no other news. There are to be more madrigals to-night; fortunately I don't sing, so I sit in a chair and think about witchcraft. The St. Pancras theatre[51] woman has returned the Passion play, & I shall think about that too.

I feel like a flower with its blossom buried and its roots in the air—waving rather uselessly, and with its small effectiveness stifled. But it is perhaps worse for some of our young typists than for me; they are dug out in lodgings, without friends and without their people, and not much amusement as the nights grow darker. HJF's[52] typist in this office—nay, bath-room, holding four people—put it into my mind from something she said to HJF's assistant.

I should like to go out with you and buy a dressing-gown; yes, faith. Lets. All love,

C

Oxford
[17?] Oct./39.

This ought to have come to you yesterday, but the rain and Lincoln College defeated me. Foss took me to see this Egon Vessley, a Hungarian, but born in Vienna, and a refugee & professor of music since the *Anschluss*[53] (the seizure of Austria). He had seen *Seed of Adam* & admired it. I hear that the response to it among the intellectual refugees, who did not even understand the language altogether, was more marked than among the English. Hubert explained to Vessley that I was the only person who could revive English opera by writing tolerable librettos. I have promised one day to revive English opera—one day. I told Ruth Spalding of this, & she said: "Yes, but we want you to revive English religious drama."

This for your amusement. I was very much afraid that the appalling rain would have made your week-end worse, and I was relieved, most noble lady, to get your letter. I fear Ursula will be done in because I shall come up to London next week-end—yes? Henry[54] has sent a p-c to ask if I shall be up on 29 Oct. or 5 Novr. I shall tell him not 29 but I can't say about 5 Novr.

The Douglases move next Friday. I called on Saturday & have promised to have dinner with them at the Clarendon on Tuesday week. Isabel—bless her—has produced more socks and writes an occasional letter. She says it is a very trying life for both of them. I have assured Margaret what a good work she is doing, and what a noble labour it is: which is true enough. They are both nice creatures, but it is an intolerable situation for them.

I haven't been to the cinema or the theatre at all; I don't feel sufficiently inclined to do so. The *Telegraph* this morning expected a crashing effort by the Germans soon which would fail, and then some sort of hasty peace against Russia. We live at the end of an age, and the re-ordination of the world, and very trying it all is. Vessley is an acquaintance of the Archduke Otto's, & has a photograph signed "Othon," the old Imperial name of the Hapsburgs. If anyone talks of the war, retaliate by saying that you think the Archduke is the solution. But don't mention that I would throw over Poland (I see the priests are being massacred) for the afternoon you describe—you, cinema, sherry, & tea.

You are a sweet. God bless you,

Serge[55]

Oxford

24 Oct./39

There seems, my angel, as we said, I think, little to relate; if I had not already thanked you for the week-end, I would do so now. But that apart, nothing has happened. Eliot has sent me his new book:[56] "For C—W—, with the humble respects of T. S. Eliot" . . . certainly the Great do better than the small! But I suppose this will mean a *Dove* sooner or later. Renée Haynes has written asking if she may bring a fellow named Peasey, who wrote a pamphlet in which he respectfully alluded to *Came Down from H.*—I meant to tell you—to lunch in Oxford with me next week: they are studying my *Time & Tide* article.[57] The

Dove does not much disagree with Eliot's book; we shall be starting a Movement between us.

There is a puppy at South Parks Rd. also a young man in uniform up for examinations. The *personnel* of the household is continually changing. G.H. is to review the *Dove* for the *Sunday Times*[58]—but only 300 words: Lakin has no room for more, which I can understand nowadays. He says he can't do it in that—which is quite true. Read it sometime & let us discuss. Every great man ought to be married to someone like you; it is always beautiful and always distracting: "the Incoherence," indeed!

This is a very stupid letter, & I apologize. But I am about to do some work; it is very dull; dull outwardly, I mean; and I am quite unworthy your Serenity. Sir Humphrey told G.H. yesterday that if he could choose he would never live in Oxford ("when I left it I swore I would never come back"—odd!) and never live in Epsom. He must have been unhappy most of his life. G.H. said that he & I agreed about Oxford.

O la, la! forgive me. Don't look for reviews yet—you know how these things are. Bless you.

C

Oxford

25 Oct/39.

Be at ease! It was a formal note saying that I was £15 overdrawn—but they were wrong! after the weekend it was £20—& did I know it? I was on the point of writing back rather peevishly to the effect that not only I but they knew it perfectly well, but this morning Longman's cheque[59] has come, so I am sending them that as well, thus leaving us £20 on the right side—or thereabouts. Longman's is £40—I feared it might be only £30, not exactly remembering what they paid as a first instalment. I now sit back with some pleasure, feeling that M. is clear, & there is £20 or £25 (including your £5) towards the devastating £60 or £70 income tax. God send the German submarines don't sink the sheets of the *Dove* on the way to America!

Budgen has just come in to say that Olive has been lunching with Sir H., & wants, if she can, to see me, & Lady Milford is supposed to be bringing her round this afternoon. I would give her the *Dove* if I had one, but my copy is at South Parks Rd. I fear I shall have to buy a few—Henry must have one, I suppose, & it would be kind to send Anne one. Raymond can have my proofs.

I dined at the Douglases' hotel last night, and am to go there to tea on Saturday. They want me to use their sitting room, but I should be driven to cart books round, & in any case . . . . Nor, though I admire the *Importance of Being Earnest*, will I go to see it here & now. I dance on the conversation like a tightrope walker; but if Margaret can read my writing, she shall type *Magic*. If she doesn't Ursula shall—bless them all!

Lewis was very good on Tasso & Milton this morning; it is years since I have heard anyone talk intelligently on poetry. Even T.S.E. is unsound on Milton. He asked how you were, & sent a message to say that he kissed your hand. You will observe that my distinguished admirers—from Alice Meynell[60] to C.S.L.—always admire you. Lewis says it would be fatal for a great man's wife to read him; I said that you, as unique in that as in all, read, admired, mocked, and left me free to play at my own job. This he highly approved—though in general he seems to think the minds of women not really meant for logic or great art.

Your letter about the key in the cage was delightful; I almost determined to write a novel with that title! And it was sweet of you to light a fire to read the *Dove* by; C.S.L. said this morning that we should put on evening dress to read Milton . . . but you had done it first.

Eliot's book[61] is very good—if anyone asks you. I have written to him saying I may be up in ten days if anything can be done. I will write to Anne to-morrow to the same effect. Lunch on Saturday somewhere out for the four—you, me, A., V.[62]—& Henry for you & me on Sunday afternoon; T.S.E. & M.B. as & how—?

Bless you. I shall let you know to-morrow if Olive turns up.

Serge

Oxford

26 Oct/39

Well, I saw Olive. At tea, with Sir Humphrey & Lady M. In their small house—the back drawing room. And the conversation was largely about all sorts of people who had or had not jobs under Government or in the Services. So it was not all that exciting. She asked after you & Michael. And I have—rashly—promised her the *Dove,* & have ordered it to go to her and Henry & Eliot & Anne. All very expensive, but unavoidable.

However, that, angel, is of no importance. What did amuse me, & what I thought would amuse & not displease you was that I met Lady Milford to-day in the lane as I was going to lunch. So we stopped & conversed, & she asked me if I was bored, & I said: "No, but apt to be irritated." And she said: "I said to my husband yesterday that I could not think how you remained so good-tempered." It seems that Robin Milford is so upset & disturbed and irritable that, he being a bit of a genius, his mother could not believe that I, being more of the same, would not also be almost intolerable. So I said no-one but you (meaning you) knew if I was irritable or not, but that, under God, I hoped I might by His grace be bearable. It is, of course, largely that Whig and moral—though in my own sense almost immoral—atmosphere that provokes Robin. My own doctrine may be, as you have sometimes thought it, most princely lady, dangerous, but, by God's splendour, it is so in a lordlier way than theirs. And a more religious.

However, my sweet ("she is the darling of my heart and she lived in our alley"),[63] this is only the equivalent of the key in the cage (What *does* that mean?)—to amuse you if it is fortunate. We are to-night, with a number of other people, to read aloud I Henry IV; not a bad notion. The war (we gather) may start at any time; everyone seems to be leaving off gas-masks. I carry mine with devotion.

If I wrote as large as you I should fill more paper. Consider this, and believe me your most humble, most devoted servant.

Serge

Oxford
29 Oct/39

Beloved,

Eliot has written about two or three things; he is going to review the *Dove* in the *New Statesman*,[63] & admires it, though it is "difficult & profound." He wants to know how *Magic* is getting on, and asks if we can dine on Friday, because he is going away for the week-end. I am rather anxious to explain to him that I am getting on with it & have an understanding about dates. So I think I shall come up on Friday afternoon, come home, then go & dine with E & MB[64]—I expect at E's club. And on Saturday morning possibly go in to the *Sunday Times*, & then we might lunch with Anne & Vivian[65] somewhere? and go to Henry's[66] on Sunday afternoon. This will deal with several things & then either the next week end or the one after I shall come up again & we will tell no-one. Will that be convenient? I shall send some money at the end of the month.

The weather has been horrible. I had tea with Isabel yesterday; her address is The Clarendon Hotel, Oxford. Margaret, very nobly, went out so as to give her mother an hour. But I have been most wondering about you, & the weather, & if in this cold you found our flat at all warmer than our past.

In fact I have been in to-day, for the first time since I have been down. I heard by accident Anne telling someone—there were people to lunch—that their parents[67] were stopping in America for the duration. So that is that. I have done some more Magic, and played with drama for St. Mary's for Christmas.[68] Other people are now arriving for tea. I found myself looking at the fire just now and thinking how I wished I was at home. So I felt rather ungrateful, but alas I thought it was very proper, and I forgave myself at once.

I shall now be polite at tea & then go out and post this letter. Your letters have been a perpetual joy all the week. It is sweet of you to be so kind to my finance, but it's nice to feel we are now straighter in spite of everything. I am anxious to fix Fabers on Magic, so as to have something clear for August income-tax; & then get Longmans going again. It's all a scamper, isn't it? But we haven't done too badly so far. All my love & kisses & goodwishes. Tell me how you are. Love.

Serge

My poor darling! it is a shame for you. I don't know how you manage to write as nobly as you do, and it is doubly hard on you that I shouldn't be about—not that I can do much but at least there is someone *there*. I was glad you didn't have to read to the Mothers; postpone it as long as you can!

There is little to report here. We are waiting for the Germans to invade Holland[70] in general; in particular I have plenty of work to do at the office—so to call it. There is, it amuses me to tell you, a certain vague consciousness of me in Oxford. One of the South Parks Rd. women, who came in late last night, told me she had passed a group of people in the street who were saying: "O yes, he wrote *Seed of Adam*," & to-day just before Lewis began his lecture a young undergraduate sitting near me said to a companion: "We've got a good man for the English Society next week—Charles Williams," & the other said; "O yes, I've heard he's brilliant, & I tried to get one of his books, but I couldn't." So I delicately shifted a little away, in case when they do see me they should be embarrassed.

An anecdote which will please you even more, considering how you made me bring my other coat down, is that when I came in from dining with the Douglases last night—and was it dark!—the actor-producer who is stopping with us, meeting me, said to Ruth: "How elegant & *soignée* he looks!" So (all right! I know he was jesting, but he was jesting accurately, if you follow me!) I suppose you were justified.

The Douglases are much the same. They have met people, & are really very reasonably fit.

And there we are. More (as they say) to-morrow. I would abandon all such trifles if they could give you a minute's ease. But I will tell you that on Sunday.

Serge

Oxford

8 Novr./39

Dearest, I am most worried about you. The Plays[71] I don't much mind about, though I shall think of you when I go to them. It has been pouring steadily all day so far, & unless it clears up I should think the congregational audience would be pretty small. But the church was freezing last night when I went round to encourage a rehearsal, & the cold & the rain together would depress any one—quite without my own particular genius for gloom in plays. Oxford will be in the depths of despair during the week-end.

Eliot's very nice & very long review of the *Dove* appears in this week's *New Statesman*. I shall bring it when I come. It is not that it is wildly laudatory, but it has a seriousness about my work, & it talks of the novels and the poetry also seriously. However, you shall see.

I am worried a little about Pitman's, but I can't promise anything till we see how things go.

O—& Bristol has written, asking me if I will go next term instead of this. I am very glad, & have replied putting them off till the *end* of next term. Lewis has rung up about my Milton lectures[72] here but nothing has been settled. I wouldn't mind if they didn't happen. However, I add a few fragments to my general work.

Gosh, angel, it *is* cold, & this room, though warm, isn't *all* that warm—or else I am chilly. I have put on the new shirt & it looks very nice. Also the tie. Ready for the diplomatic business of sitting by, near, or remote from Isabel. (I hope she won't *tell* you if she sees me speaking to Ruth, because of course you might get a Wrong Impression. Anyone listening to Isabel would get millions of Impressions!)

Thank you. And thank you. I shall think of you, & we will see them happily together one day. Till then! be blessed. All my love & gratitude.

Serge

10 Nov./39

You are undoubtedly very sweet to me—which is certainly what you are to everyone in their proper manner—Mrs. Oliver, say, & Henry, & all. I have had a Latin creed from Henry this morning, all about the Order,[73] signed by him & Lester: fantastic creatures! Still it *does* move, as Galileo did *not* say about the sun.

The only other thing that came was yesterday, & gave me a mild start. I had, it seems, when I borrowed from J.S.[74] early in the year, said something about repaying, if I was lucky, before the year's end, & this was a gentle enquiry whether I thought I should be able to do anything, put (in her own words) "objectively." So I took a night to meditate, & I thought the best thing was to *do* something. Which I proceeded to do—sending her £15 by return, as it were, & saying that I hoped to send more when the American money came. This still leaves me with £10 in the bank, & now I have seen Eliot I feel easier about Magic & *that* payment when it is done. At first I was a little ruffled, but I considered the nature of God, & decided that I need not be. And to-day I am rather pleased. In the first three months of our War, you & I have cleared the bank, cleared HSM., & reduced J.S. by 25%. Besides, it is lovely to have sent a cheque & have a few pounds left. As if in reply the *Sunday Times* sent all 3 books I picked out; they only want tiny reviews, still they do want them. It is, of course, mostly your doings. Because if you were not what you are I could never be comfortable—over money or anything. Coming down from London, I began some lines

> Ah still the Promulgation knows
> the first context from which it rose,
> when, are the doctrines of exchange

England's aspiring hearts could range,
and all my genius was as dull
as you were rarely beautiful,
your supernatural light betrayed
the heavenly crevice that you made
in earth's too-heavy walls; and run,
since my more wide career begun,
who study me could e'er mistake
that first incalculable break
of glory, when Saint Peter's Street
enharmonized with your young feet
itself and all the town, your head
a double weight of glory shed:
thence, O unknown! my future sprang
and knew not yet how much it sang.

Besides it owes through all the years
its energy to you, whose cares
provided it with freedom, peace,
and room for doctrine to increase.
Therefore the first that held it even
and swore that it *came down from heaven*
I with your name sealed to the earth
since once from you it had its birth,
madonna; and your first-born Son
was Love, and that your youngest one—
threefold a mother! Look and see—
God, Michael, my capacity.
Few, blessed one, the women are
who wear so sharp a triple star:
much, as I know, though you have spent,
behold the spreading increment!

The awful glory opens wide
about you; did your earlier pride
disdain a little tribute thus?
forgive it; it was rendered us;
our great vocation, still unknown,
opened—through *whom?*—through you alone.

———————————

———————————

I do not quite know when I shall be up on Saturday. I will try for lunch, but I may not make it. But I shall come.

Serge

Oxford
14 Nov./39

As I had hoped something more exciting than Olive! if one may say so to you—secretly—she is less interesting as she gets older: perhaps we shall do the same, but I hope not for myself & I think not for you.

Jean must have needed the £15, I think. I had a warm letter from her to-day, thanking me, & saying that if I could pay the other £20 I had mentioned, couldn't we call it all square? I haven't answered this yet; I shall be tactful to-morrow. It would be beautiful to be quite clear of everything by next June or so—allowing for Sir John Simon. To-night I speak at the English Club; after that I really shall get down to Magic.

To-day Renée[75] Haynes rang up; she was in Oxford & we had lunch. She told me that she met Eliot some days ago, and rather touched me by saying how fond of me he seemed to be—he had spoken of me so much. I must say that, after you, I do like my peers to like me. But this is only a whisper in your ear.

Nothing of interest has happened otherwise. It was delightful to have you at Paddington—it would be worth while (sorry! Hubert is dictating!) to come up for that alone. But it was a beautiful time.

The Douglases go to London to-day: expect the telephone. Bless you.

C

16 Novr./39

I send you your two pounds, which I am sure is better than splitting one: when I have 10/- I will put it back for you, so you can take the extra now as a salu-tation from me. Miss Peacock this morning seems to think that there is a faint possibility that, if nothing happens,[76] we might be returning to London in the spring. Sir Humphrey, she says, has been moved by appeals in the *Times* & the *Publisher's Circular,* and she hopes he may go on being moved. G.H.[77] has been trying to drop hints to the Delegates[78] . . . it may come to nothing but it cheered me even to play with the idea. Of course the inconveniences of our present communications with London become greater every week. I suppose the Fire Station would have to remain in the City, but then . . . however, I need not worry you with details. But, without expecting it, I thought you might like to dream of it; or at least think that the curtains may be more useful than it at present seems?

It is clear, however, if and when that happens, that you will have to go on writing letters. I had to nurse a solitary pleasure at the account of the Douglas telephone. Isabel wrote to me before she left asking me not to forget Saturday—do I ever forget? the answer is "yes, but rarely." Also at the kings and earls of Taunton.[79] But, my dear! do you mean he is *really* called "Taunton Oliver"—what a name!

A Russian doctor has now arrived for a few days at South Parks Rd. The Austrian female refugee is in a Retreat somewhere. Discussion at dinner on the Byzantine Church and architecture in Europe. Doctor (as you would say) given, after dinner, copy of the *Dove* by the Spaldings & left to read it. Cross-examines me on problems of history of Eastern Churches; brilliant evasions by me. Doctor finally says I have said all the right things but points out a chronological error[80]—ascribed by me to the printer. All snags successfully passed.

I then went to my room & thought of you. Also of Magic. Also of Taliessin. Also of you again.

Which doing still, believe me your servant still & always.

Serge

Oxford

17 Novr/39.

Dearest,

I agree about the fire. I don't see why you should have a fire when I'm not there. Or indeed food. Or indeed—considering everything—a bed! I always feel this strongly at the end of a week; to-morrow morning I shall feel gloomy, I know. I have observed that before on Saturday mornings—though, in fact, I do realize I have spent reasonably few Saturday mornings here!

I also agree about Phyllis & the Douglases.[81] But if anything is said to *me*, I shall be firm, cool, and fixed. Thank you for telling me about it.—By the way, you never . . . we never . . . mentioned the poem I sent you:[82] did you like it? Outside Nativities it is the only poem I have done since I was deflected here. *Taliessin* remains silent.

Last night I was asked at Magdalen if I would go & speak at Bristol, to that part of London University which is now there. So—I said I would: they will put me up, so I shan't be travelling in the dark—& anyhow it won't presumably be till next term.

The Russian has disappeared. Robin Milford is being kept between the army & civil life. No-one understands—at least, I do [don't?]—why he ever let himself in. Goffin remains in, & no-one has yet been able to get him out; hope springs still in them. But it has been a dull week since Monday morning. It rains heavily and continually. Oxford, they say, is like this all through the winter.

You will believe how often you are present to me, but your last paragraph was beautiful. I admit, as I plunge through the rain, I am *almost* glad you are not here. Rain in London is bad; rain in Oxford——. Give Michael my love and tell him, if he has time, to write. I like his letters. But not to worry him. I am anxious about you physically; I rest on you spiritually. Bless you for ever.

Serge

Oxford
27 Novr./39

Dearest,

Only a line to thank you. I am afraid you were caught badly in the rain on your way back. Here it was fine, but I was very dull—"and went upstairs and cried" as one of Patmore's young women said. I found here a note from Topliss[83] saying he was being moved & couldn't be here—come to Hampstead, I mean, on Saturday, but would write if he could get to Oxford later. So we will have a peaceful afternoon before the ladies in the evening.

Also Dean Inge's new book from *T&T*.[84] But it is a poor book—reprinted articles. However it means 900 words & £4. Only I wish I had something pleasanter to read!

Also a letter from *Vidler*[85] asking me to go to a Conference at Old Jordans in Bucks in January. Eliot & others are to be there, & I think I may go. It is from Friday to Monday, 5–8 Jan. and it is all about presenting the Xtn. faith to "the contemporary social environment." Am I a Christian? I don't know, but I know what Christianity possibly may be.

Bless you! The Peace be with you.

C

Oxford
28 Novr./39

Well, I have been lunching with Robin Milford; he is a nice creature really, and our separate youth has—or had—much in common, such as a kind of nervousness & so on. Only, of course, now I am—what I am, and he isn't—yet. I think you were more right than you altogether knew when you talked of perverted substitution . . . he is a little inclined to be obsessed by other people's troubles, which, of course, make him all the more of a trouble himself. I have delivered no monologues, & he is, naturally, worried by his Medical Board . . . so should I be, but I forebear to point out that he needn't have joined the army at all! However . . . .

I had a note from Raymond[86] this morning. He has had much to contend with . . . "Jewish evacuees (I had forgotten how badly children could be brought up)," extra work, colds, & so on. But it seems a little hard to have children in their rather limited house! The *Dove* has cheered him, he says. But I imagine Ruth must find it a bit of a trial.

I have had the Income Tax assessment: it comes out at 46/18/- in January & the same in July—which is less than I feared it might be. It means roughly

£50 twice in next year. But *if* O—*if* I can get Magic done in time, that will mean £35 out of the first £50, & I hope the new Christian quotation book[87] will be £25 out of the second! So we shan't be too bad, after all! at least, I mean it is a possible business. Thanks of course to your care largely. Anyhow we needn't worry yet, praise to God!

O bless you! I hope you aren't feeling too bad: I have written to Henry[88] to say I shan't be over on Sunday. To-night I go to Isabel; I had a depressed note from her last night.

It is, my sweet angel, all very difficult!!!

Serge.

Oxford

30 Nov./39

Dearest,

I send you a pound note in case you would like it for the week-end (till Saturday). You will forgive my sending a line to Michael yesterday.

To-day I have been trying to quiet the aggravated nerves of Hubert & Miss Sangston who have been in a state of high contrariness over the reading of the *Doctor's Dilemma*[89] to-night. By the frustrated Dramatic Society. And to which I must go & read a part. And if anyone thinks I want to——!

I should love you to be at Paddington, but I am afraid of the trains. Mine— if I catch the one I hope to—will get in somewhere about four, I think. But it was late—but late!—last week, and I don't want you to have to hang about for three-quarters of an hour! Have tea ready for me, and let us go for a small wander afterwards—black-out or no. You are in all things a dear!

I have just lunched with Margaret & tried to cheer her up. She said I was very kind to her, so I did not entirely fail. O and I meant to tell you I gurgled at breakfast over your letter about corsets, & someone said something about gurgling—so I read out that bit (changing corsets to stockings!) and everyone highly approved & admired.

Well, pass: this is not a letter; it is a cover for the enclosure which is of more importance! Bless you.

C .

Oxford

4 Dec./39

It was all very lovely, dearest, and I hope you were not worse for coming to Paddington. I realize now that so long as one can accept Oxford as exile, it is bearable; it is only if one tries to be at home in it that it fails. Do you remember Macaulay's "and pined by Arno for my lovelier Tees";[90] I altered that to "and pine by Isis for my lovelier Thames."

I realize too, as I wrote to Michael yesterday, that to write prose is the difficulty. The war & Oxford make it impossible to *settle*. Poetry is different; poetry is still more me than I am; and the coming of the great lines is less one's own work than—something. If I could do as I chose and yet had to be down here, I would do nothing but think of the next *Taliessin* group. However—"all luck is good";[91] I think it even if I have not felt it—not habitually. Let us determine to believe it; you, in fact, have done, for you have always said that if things went wrong, it was not without direction?

However, leave that. T's play was in the tiniest room, with 17th century wall-decorations, & it is very possible that Shakespeare walked in it. Between Shakespeare & I there is no record of anything important happening there! The performance was better than I expected, but the central character lacks a good deal, & one or two of the others are not striking. With a better show in that matter it would grip from the beginning; as it is, it seems a little dull there. If I can do anything, I shall; I have exhorted them, but I fear uselessly! Still, it almost got the famous C.W. moment—almost the tension!

I have had a charming letter from Fr. Patrick McLaughlin who was to have taken Cedd in the Pageant. He lives at Bishop's Stortford; when the war is over we will both go & see him there. He has asked me to dine with him and a few others next Saturday—in London, of course: the *Pax* group[92] & the Faith press: I do not quite know what they are. I have told him where I am & asked him if I may do it another time. His letter, referring to Cedd, began: "Begetter of the image of my soul's beatitude" . . . and he is profoundly grateful for the *Dove*—"the Great," he says, "will have pursued you with laudations." *Te auxilio* (which means, "with you helping"). I shall convert the Church of England yet—secretly, & rather like a Dove.

There is no other news: I have seen no-one of interest since I left you. The sirens all had a practice at one o'clock, but we were told of it first. Topliss writes to say he may come to Oxford on Wednesday. With such absurd fragments I end, your most devoted,

Serge

Oxford
11 Decr./39

The London post failed us this morning, so if—as I dare not be certain but strongly hope—there was a letter from you, I have not yet seen it. So as I sent my last only last evening there is nothing to report. Except that the young man who turned up was a complete stranger at first to me, but after a little probing he turned out to be that rather young assistant lecturer from Paris.[93] He was most charming—he is now at Bristol, or rather at the University of London which at present lives in Bristol; says we are still talked of in Paris—"C.W. on the Romantic Poets" is still a kind of thrill, according to him, & he has written an essay on me which he is going to send. It seems we are beginning to be written about!

Otherwise—the *Stable*[94] is to be given at Southfields House at 9 to-night. This is not due to the Greats, but to one of our young men who has combined with Dr. Berkeley who owns (& lives in) the house & heard of the plays: I was told nothing of it until it was all settled—in fact, to-day. I don't know who will be here: nothing has been said. (Except that I have done what I should not have done for myself—excuse—& by a most delicate series of chats with Miss Peacock discovered that no-one[95] will be here about whom you might faintly be dubious. Apparently no-one is at present in Oxford—so that is that.) Lady Milford is reported to have taken a chill, so I don't expect either of them.

I have just parted from Isabel—no news there except what I can tell you . . . they are thinking of asking you to lunch on Friday week. I have promised to dine on Thursday. She said you had told her that I liked to have them in Oxford, & could relax with them, & was this honestly true? Loyal to you to the last, I said it was. But *relax—relax?* However—pass.

I love you, I bless you. It is cold & very dull. The war gets more remote except for inconvenience and horror. Telephones have now been put in here, and we have lived in a continual knocking for a day or two. I love you.

Serge

Oxford

12 Decr/39

Darling,

And is it cold! What you must be feeling!! And your last letters, ideal as they are, do not mention your back. I fear it must be devilish at times; I think of you & wonder & hope & fear. But I shall come up on Friday, all being well.

The posts are getting less certain. London posts don't seem to reach us first thing, & one of my business letters has gone astray. If anything urgent *should* happen, I begin to think Southfield House would be the best address. But only so. I had your week-end letter last night, & left it open in my bedroom all night so that you could wake me in the morning.

Last night went very well. Sir Humphrey came & about 30 of the staff. I think it was the best performance[96] so far. Dr. Berkeley, who owns the house & to whom I was introduced, was so impressed that he doubled his cheque & paid the actors at £3.3.0 instead of £1.10.6. They are, each of them, living on 25/- a week—not a great deal. They get some hospitality here & there. In the New Year it is hoped they will get more; it depends on takings. Ruth says she will be producing my 4/4/- soon. I don't quite like taking it, but I shall; I know, most dear lady, you would agree in taking or refusing.

More strange young men tell me they have always admired me. Lorna Davis has sent a nice little note of gratitude for her evening. And I shall have to give up a couple of hours to Belgion; his letters are too touching in their hopes of seeing me. But apart from that let us be quiet this week-end!

I am now going to do some of my own work in Sir H's time, before I send a book away for ever. Bless you.

S

Oxford
27 Decr./39

I do hope you didn't suffer for it—I felt you had the worst of it, especially when I found you had bought me both the *Telegraph* & the *Times*. That, I felt, was the final Christmas touch! We got down by 10, & I went round to South Parks Rd., where I ran into Anne who gave me a cup of tea. Then I went on my way, & ran into—of all people!—Hugh MacDonald[97] whose face I knew "but could not, for some time, recollect his name." He is in Cambridge, in a single room, with a gas fire—very gloomy. He asked after you. His wife is at Princess Risborough still, I gather. He is in Oxford from time to time and proposes to look me up when he next is. "Warm," as our Lord Tennyson said, "from a gracious parting with the Queen." I was almost gay; his lot, both in distance & lodging, seemed so much worse than mine.

A rumour here that Hitler ordered mass attacks on London & the East Coast to begin just before Christmas; if so, the German General Staff thought twice of it. Or it was too cold or something. I do not much believe it; if he did, it must have been frenzy.

I have sent off the Insurance—also 12/- as my subscription to *Theology*, which has forked out 4/4/- during the year, so we are 600 per cent up on the transaction. Also I have written most touchingly to Algernon Blackwood.[98] A Christmas Card from Viscountess Rhondda, with a small written note "especially from the Literary Editor"! One to Theodora.

And that, beloved, is all. It was a blessed Christmas & I loved the Communion. Be blessed as you are holy.

Serge

1940

Gosh! But I don't see what else you could have done. I do hope M. is not too upset, & I wish I could be there. It is NOBLE of you. You shall tell of it on Saturday.

Robin Milford[1] has apparently got his discharge—he returns to Guernsey to-morrow. This because he has just been round and we have had lunch together. To-morrow Hugh MacDonald[2] is to be in Oxford; he has sent on a card asking me to lunch, which I shall do. G.H. says that even for a free lunch he could not stand H.M., but I have a wider mind!

Well, till Saturday, my angel, & do *you* take care. Margaret has typed the first chapter of Magic, so something is done!

C

Walking back with G.H. from lunch I discovered some cows & sheep in a field, and thought for some reason suddenly of Greenwich Park and you—though to think of you is not so rare as to think of G.P.! However I decided that we would go there again one day—you and I, & have tea. There are, I think, no cows there, but some sort of animal life haunts me. Our last voyage there I remember very happily; were we doing something in the evening? Also we will go & have dinner out, not on the same day.

I have been wondering about last night; also I thought how true it was—what I said when you were talking about giving people tea, that you giving people tea always became the centre of the stage—the most important thing in the room, the still volcano, the eagle in repose. That your mountain is your own and no one else's does not make you less an eagle.

To-night I go to see my plays again[3]—with a more or less new cast, which is, I think, why Ruth asked me to go. It is at the Friends' Meeting House, in the High. But I am getting a little bored with these; they haven't the *Seed of Adam* stuff.

I shall continue to talk about myself. The *Dove* is in Mowbray's window here, just opposite my barber's & also in the High. Miss Kindersby,[4] who was producer of *Cranmer* at St. Pancras, wants to do the *Rite* somewhere near by there; that little theatre is shut. I have written to Lorna about it, saying I don't wish to hamper her or St. Anne's, otherwise. . . . The idea is Sunday afternoon performances; I suppose in Lent probably.

I am still very pleased about M's eyes; I could forgive the universe a good deal for that. I keep on remembering our first experience. You & I have certainly pulled him—& ourselves—through a good deal.

You will have pyjamas for Essex?[5] I shall take a clean pair this weekend instead of waiting. *Magic* plods on—but has got to lose this weekend while I draft my ten addresses for Essex.

All my love. Thank you, with kisses, for dealing with the suit. The back goes reasonably well—and yours?

Serge

Oxford
12 January/40

Darling,

You relieve me very much! I had awful visions of difficulties. As some-one says somewhere to someone in my novels: "You are the rose-garden of the saints." You shall tell me all about it—M.B. and P. and all; & I hope P. was grateful; not, of course, that Christians ought to want other people to be grateful, see the New Testament *passim*, but it would be nice if he were.

The rest of your letter (I maintain my view that you do write the most charming letters!) was equally pleasing—at least in one way or another! The E.L. is wonderful; I will send a cheque to them when I am up & clear it. It was rash but marvellous of you to pay the 7/6; will you be all right yet awhile? I am waiting for money to come in, but it hasn't come. I am sending Michael 10/- by this post & telling him to split it which will 2/3 pay for the suit.

As for Gollancz[6] we shall see. I have accepted provisionally for both of us, but I shan't go unless you can, & I do understand you mightn't. But if you would, it might be fun to have done for an hour or two. It is perhaps worth doing all such things that we can in this war—after all we did get married in the middle of the last. And when my biography is written your war letters[7]—then & now—will be the chief part.

My Nativities[8] are to be done in Salisbury Cathedral & Ruth is going to write to someone she knows at St. Albans. Olive has just sent me a note to say she meant to write at Christmas & I am to remember "how desperately important" I am. Sez you!

All my love. It is a shame not to be coming up, but I am clinging to my last two or three pounds in my pocket. Consider that I serve you always—though you mightn't think it sometimes. But yes!

Serge

Oxford
15 Jan./40

Dearest,

I think there is no more news since yesterday—in fact, I am sure there isn't. But I am anxious about you in this weather, so I am making that an excuse for writing, because I am afraid this dreadful cold may be giving your back hell. Mine I can't grumble at (this to re-assure you); I feel it occasionally, without any special reason, but that is all.

Phyllis Potter, I find, has been in bed at Victoria (or thereabouts—her London address) & is only to come to Pleshey during the days; she has had a good deal of pain but that seems better now. It's most unfortunate—but perhaps the postponing of the Pageant[9] was a good thing for her in one way; she might have cracked in the middle.

No American cheque[10]—blast them! I have written to Nancy Pearn.[11] And no books from anywhere for review. *Time & Tide* have sent 3/3/- instead of the 4/4/- I expected; it looks to me as if they were reducing their payments. Thank God, Fabers' can't cut their agreement.

A small pleasantness—I was told yesterday that David Matthew (you will remember—the Archbishop-Coadjutor of Westminster) had said to someone that it was clear that, with my reputation growing everywhere, my own people would be the last to recognize me. He meant Anglicans, I think; though it applies a little to other places—say, . . . no, don't say.

Excuse—I tell you only for the pleasure of kissing your hand and saying that it seems that Roman Archbishops recognize their primal debt to You. St. Peter's Street, and your wedding-helmet of a hat—and the Ver[12]—and all that.

God bless you!

C.W.
Serge
Charly
—there!

Oxford
28 Jan./40

Sunday afternoon, Anne, John, & I are in the drawing room. G.H. has gone out to lunch; all the others are away. I have done the notes for the lectures to-morrow, & I have read the dreadful Vera Britten[13] life of W. Holtby, but I don't think I can review it . . . however, we shall see. I am about to turn to Magic, but I shall write to you first.

Yesterday was the worst night ever—as far as cold and snow went; this morning at 8 it was frosty on top of the snow. After church we went & bought a *S. Times,* which had put in my review.[14] But breakfast (hush!) is not till 9.20 on Sundays. I feel I could do with a cup of tea long before then. The staff have to get here from distances, which explains.

To-morrow I go to Magdalen at 10.45, where Lewis & Tolkien will put on their gowns and take me to the Divinity School. Of course there may be no-one there! but I suppose, in the grand Oxford Tradition, one lectures anyhow.[15]

Sisam sent me round an abstract from a letter from some big noise in the Office of Works (now in Wales) asking if there was a collected edition of me— the poems—because he wanted the London Library to have it. "Williams," wrote the man, "has many admirers . . . we will do what we can to see that he shall not be forgotten in the years that are to come." Sweet!

I was thinking that, if I do as I propose with the money, I might have my other suit cleaned. We will talk on Thursday about what we can do about something for you. I shall send a hasty line to-morrow after the lecture.

Yesterday it occurred to me that I like being looked after, and the more the better. And God bless you for all the times you have done it.

C

A mournful Pole to tea!

Oxford
29 Jan/40

Dearest,

Thank you for this morning's letter; it was a Sweet, & sent me off well & truly for the Divinity School, where I delivered my first lecture—hardly two hours ago. Lewis & Tolkien came, & G.H. from the Press. A reasonably large audience of undergraduates, &c. Probably there will be fewer next time, but that always happens! It is thought that, in the second term, there would hardly be so many if it had not been for me personally, because everyone is sick of lectures by then.

So that is that. Next week will be more testing because I shall be getting down to Milton,[16] & the first titillation will be gone. We shall see.

It is cold, a foot deep in snow, & still snowing here. This is but a note because I am only just at the house & must work. But I adored your letter & you.

C

Oxford
7 Feb./40

Dearest,

Well, what about it? But won't you want some things or something? I mean—tell me, and let us see. Michael could come down here or I could come to London—whichever he would like—for the week end, and he could come here for the rest of the few days. I will fit in with anything. Have you fixed a provisional date?[17] let me know all; I am very anxious for it to be arranged, because it may not be very thrilling, but it will be a Change. (My mother used to say that everyone needed a Change; in fact, she said a holiday. Did she ever mention it to you?)

I am feeling better to-day; indeed, apart from my thought, which is a little tiresome still (So it is—but I meant "throat"), I am practically all right. The only thing is that I didn't sleep well last night, & then woke up at 7.30 this morning, so there was no excuse for going to sleep again instead of to Church. So off I went—intending well, under God, for this Lent. If it wasn't for being feverish over Magic[18] I should be reasonably content to-day: I am sending off two reviews[19] (*T&T* & (*S.T*) & have only one more for *Theology.*[20]

Isabel very grateful, & nice. I delivered addresses on the nature of everything which she took lamb-like. Edith Sitwell has sent me a copy of her anthology[21]—"to C.W. with admiration & great gratitude." But no other excitement of any kind!

All my love.

C

Oxford
8 Feb/40

Dearest love,

As I have so often said, I don't know what I should do without your letters; their tenderness & gaiety go on being quite remarkable. I have said something yesterday about Michael; if we could put him up at South Parks Rd., that would be best, wouldn't it? What I mean is—he would like that? Otherwise, if he didn't, I could take a room at a hotel; this is only to fall in with his wishes. But, as you so sweetly said, my brain is not at its best these days. I seem more stupid than is, I hope, usual.

I am told the Salisbury shows[22] were quite successful. The Dean spoke so highly of my sister that Ruth & the rest came back with the impression that she must be a remarkable person; & he was very nice about the plays, I gather. Ruth says that Salisbury is stiff with the *Dove.* If I will do them a play for Pentecost,[23] they can probably produce it here in St. Mary's, in Salisbury Cathedral, Romsey Abbey, & some other places. I should very much like to, but I am not even thinking of it yet.

It's colder here to-day, but pleasant. I slept well except for a nightmare about you & Michael; don't ask me what, for I have forgotten. But I woke in some fear worry.

How sweet you are to the clergy! In our various ways, you & I are both positively nutritious for them! And I would much rather be quiet at home when I come up—Friday week, I hope!

This is a poor note. Excuse it & love me.

C

Oxford
9 Feb/40

Have I any news? Sez you. You are thinking of going to Fr. Clare's,[24] & you will have said all the right things for me. It has gone all cold again here, & is one degree (I am told) of frost. My throat, however, is getting slowly better, & I have little fear of appearing as cast down as I was the last time I fell into your sovereign arms. Still, be there and be going on catching me; your kisses at Paddington are the softest charms in existence. They explain all the better kind of witchcraft.

I read an odd review of the *Dove* which may amuse you for a moment: there will be one in *Christendom* which may amuse us both—I haven't seen it yet, but I am told it is good. Referring again to Clare, I know they must be suffering badly in their finance: we are re-arranging everything for the last time in our lifetime. I have been very much moved by the prospective Russian break-through[25] in Finland; it shook me very much when it appeared in the papers. God knows I don't shout politics, but unless we win this war life would be unendurable in Europe. It is very rough on people like you & me & M, & the rest of them—the Clares, for instance; but I shall never pay any taxes more willingly. To lose would mean, sooner or later, directly or indirectly, that all our lives would be dictated from Berlin—our *kind* of lives: what I say on Milton in Oxford and how you pray in S. Saviour's. They are stamping out. . . .

This is ridiculous; I didn't mean to begin writing so, but the Finnish news did shake me. Forgive me. Lewis says that my last Monday's address on the Comus-Chastity was "the most important thing that has happened in the Divinity Schools for a hundred years, or is likely to happen for the next hundred." I tell you for love's sake & laughter's.

Be assured of gratitude & love.

C

Oxford
12 Feb/40

Dearest,

Well, we go on lecturing still to about a hundred people. It isn't too bad to keep as many over these weeks. Apart from that, there is nothing to report since yesterday. I shall see you on Friday, and then we can talk.

It's a mad world, and all I can say is that I love you and you grow more a fundamental of existence to me every day. Have you any definite date[26] fixed with Phyllis? I was thinking that if the 3rd—sorry, the 2nd March suited, that would be convenient, financially & otherwise. But that we could discuss.

All love. I have just got back from lecturing and must work. God bless you.

Serge

Oxford
13 Feb/40

Dearest,

I only got your Sunday letter by Monday night & it quite worried me. It is most frightfully difficult for you—and for Michael. You know I don't lose any opportunity for "watching out" for him. I'm so sorry that Fr. Clare got on to the subject; as for the 1/1/. I shall give you that in April; you shan't go without things more than you have to.

All being well, I shall be up on Friday, as I said; I don't quite know when, but some time, and we will talk of things. It is bitterly cold and snowing here. I keep on—no; I mean I have just been with Christopher Fry who wrote a Tewksbury pageant and is now wanting to find a job. He thinks that someone turns up at the last minute, so I quoted your "fish's mouth."[27]

Tonight I go to the Randolph. I shall do a little witchcraft[28] here this afternoon to make up the time. Meanwhile I send you two *Observer* cuttings which will amuse you; Sunday seems to have been our lucky day—mine rather; it was bad enough for you, poor dear! *I* never wept over Mrs. Henry Wood.[29]

Till to-morrow. With all my love.

Serge

Oxford
14 Feb./40

"Will you be my Valentine?" Tell me on Friday; St. Valentine is covered with snow here, though the sun has looked out a little mid-day.

I have asked the Spaldings about Michael and they will be delighted; all the Williamses, they say, have a kind of prior right to entry, which is a very nice way of putting it. Tell him also, if you will, that I have had a charming note from Dilys Powell saying she would like to have lunch with him, but she cannot manage Saturdays. I have written to say that as soon as I can spare a Monday—after Milton[30] is finished—perhaps we could fix it then. Our *Economist* lady, who is being put through a course of me by the Spaldings, says that they are re-organizing there and if there is any chance of a job she will let me know. This only to show that I do go on.

I send you the two Church Times cuttings about our famous Thursday meeting.[31] I also have a cheque for 10/- towards expenses.

I shan't (he said, kissing her hands) write to-morrow. On Friday morning I think I shall have to go to a celebration of the Greek Liturgy at St. Mary's; Anne Spalding has been mixed up with the arrangements and I can hardly do less. In the afternoon I shall come up—as and how, & get home as soon as I can: God send the cold eases.

Always your most devoted

Serge

Oxford
27[24?] Feb/40[32]

Dearest,

Ursula has just been in here. Our relation—yours & mine—overwhelms her with a sense of marriage. My trying to rake up 10/- for you and putting it in an envelope at the moment when you were ringing up to say you were sending me 10/- was a great example. I was so moved that I told G.H. who said with some feeling that that was the sort of wife to have.

I shall ring you up to-morrow. It was so good of you to do so this morning—there again I had given instructions that the call was to be put through. But I was very much relieved—even to hear you were a little better. As a matter of fact, I had rather you didn't go down[33] till the weather is a little better!

I shall spend the week-end in work; I have two reviews, a lecture, another lecture to the Oxford International Society, & *Witchcraft* to get on with! so you will see I shan't be idle.

I shall talk to Basil[34] on Monday, & then we will talk. I don't quite know what ought to be done, or if he really means it; however, don't let us worry till you & I can talk! I only told you to show I was keeping up. I did write to Edgcumbe but have heard nothing yet.

I shall ring up to-morrow—probably about half-past ten. All my love.

Serge

Oxford
27[25?] Feb/40[35]

I hope, dearest pet, my letter brooding over you has reached you by now. It is— you will have observed—you that I have been worried about . . . love, my angel. . . . I know all about everything else. It should be crystal clear that I am preoccupied with you—one might almost say from morning to night, say from day to day. I rush round like a . . . white mouse (and praise be that you have caught yours), and as [for] God hating you, one might just as well say He hates me; quite apart from the fact that neither God nor man (neither) could feel anything but love & admiration for you. I send you another pound note containing 240 kisses.

It is snowing here, drivingly & madly. I know *exactly* what you feel about having someone else; everyone will say so, & everyone will be stupid. I shouldn't do it myself. But it worries me a good deal. However, nothing is settled, and we will talk. Either it will be for a short time, *or* we shall be able to make fresh arrangements: after all, by the end of this month a year will be nearly gone! Yet for you to be alone & in pain—

O I don't know! it's all very difficult. No doubt our sacred Lord will be of use, and . . . so on. He is producing in a few days from Fabers another advance payment to clear off the rest of the income tax which is something. (After you— a long way after—shall I tell you what I miss most? Novels. I never read a novel; that's not quite true, but you know what I mean.)

No, madonna; if I did not love you, I should not be proposing to lecture on you to the s.c.m.[36] Other people might—but not I. I am going more intellectual than ever; I shall be a physical wraith presently; but while this organism lasts it beams toward you & kisses you. So there!

Serge

Oxford
27[26?] Feb/40

So after ringing you up I read a rehearsal of *George & Margaret;* it may have been amusing on the stage, but it grows tiresome when one has to go on with it! And I went back to South Parks Rd by 10 and had some supper, & then I did a draft of a lecture to the Oxford International Society for to-night. To-morrow we read *G&M;* also I have lunch with Margaret.[37] But not with George.

I send you some money; I will send more on Thursday; you have been noble. *Time & Tide* doesn't pay, but it goes on sending books. Eliot hasn't answered; I think he must be waiting to talk to his Wednesday Committee.

It is mild & raining here to-day. Robin Milford has dedicated a Song to me— a setting of Hardy's *Wintertime Highs,* which HJF[38] says is rather good. I have just shown it to Sir Humphrey, being in duty bound so to do!

I think I have nothing more of interest—and I PUT IN THE TWO POUNDS! God bless you

Serge

Oxford
27 Feb/40

Dearest,

I left home to-day before your letter reached me, but that often happens on Mondays. I came to the office, looked at my letters, went back to the town to lecture, had a hasty lunch with Ursula, came back to the office, dictated letters, went off to Blackwell's in the Broad, came back to the office, & it is nearly 4 and I am writing to you in haste.

I will talk about B.B.[39] when I see you—next week-end, I hope. I am probably giving a last lecture next week, so it will be Saturday to Sunday. But the gist is that he would be quite willing to take Michael on a kind of "apprenticeship" (in the old sense) scheme. He has a Deed made out—which can be "broken"— lasting for 4 years, and when the "apprentice" leaves, it shows, as Basil says, "the stable he comes from." But at the end of the time, if he had made good, they might "as he is your son" to work him in there if we wanted. Pay of course formal—15/-, 20/-, 25/-, 30/- in the four years, but we could consider trying to start in the second year. Conviction that Michael would be specially good.

No hurry; if it comes to anything, the end of the month—March—or after Easter anyhow—would do. I can see the disadvantages—also the advantages. Blackwell, of course, is a very good name indeed, & he is a publisher as well as a bookseller, which is all to the good. It would be an absolutely right start— much better than I had—but . . . we will talk.

Edgcumbe at first wrote saying he feared there was nothing, but this morning I got the enclosed note. It *might* be worth while doing, though I fear the hiatus or what not puts it rather down. However, Hampstead & I might help. It will wait also.

I wrote a hasty sermon for the Pilgrim Players last night—no, Friday, & last night [page missing]

Oxford

28 Feb/40

Dearest,

Yes; I think so—about B.B.[40] But I have not made clear that it is you I am thinking of chiefly. Say I oughtn't to, if you like, but I am. It is all so sudden & unexpected that I haven't had time to make that clear. I know it's a very good chance for him—as good probably as he would have got anyway. And we could feel that, if anything happened to us, he was with someone who would be intelligent & sympathetic with & for him. But that doesn't alter my meditations on *you, you,* YOU.

I shall come up on Saturday, & go back on Sunday. It seems a Greek priest is anxious to come the Sunday after to talk about "my writings & the Russian Church." Meanwhile another 3½ chapters of Witchcraft will finish *that.*

Michael has written charmingly; pray thank him. And with all love,

Serge

[Undated]

[page missing][41]

. . . but; looking back over 23 years, I never—it is honestly true—wished I wasn't a husband. I don't know that I ever really wished I wasn't a father, but (if you understand me) I have come nearer it—at moments of great strain. But the experience which is you has about it (I am becoming all metaphysical) something that cannot contradict itself; perhaps that is what they mean by saying that marriage is a sacrament. It is why, from my own experience, as well as from the teaching of the Church, I have always looked askance at divorce-— here a real marriage existed. However, we have said all this before, but reading Your Loveliness's note this morning, I realized once again how true it is that you are all unique.

(Not that I should describe the Randolph as relaxation quite: the drink is, I admit[)]. It is odd how soon things pass—it never occurs to me to go in for a sherry now by myself, & there is no-one to have me in. What I mean—for the first five months it did, but "one forgets so soon." It is only when I am up for weekends that I want to. It is oddly true that relaxation is the one impossible thing in Oxford; some muscle or nerve, of body or mind, is always taut. Antrim Rd[42] is the only place where it loosens. I could have believed it, no doubt, once, "but now the time gives it proof." And proof, let me tell you, Madonna, of a thing within you, is all very, very odd.

Well, let us hope it serves the country & the Church. I have finished Milton;[43] & now I have only to rewrite the Courage pamphlet,[44] and finish the anthology,[45] & perhaps we can begin to think of something really new. Like your knitting, what fascinates me: I kind of feel like Cortes staring at the Pacific— which was a lovely sight, so you need not take it WRONG. O I love you, & you are sweet; & I will try & send you some money to-morrow or the day after. If I can't get you to love me without ten shillings, well, I must do it with—that's all; even in the present state of things. (The *Evening News* says that Hitler made his speech because the very heavy bombing of convoys have failed—& now he must go on. I am glad we are increasing exports again—Political Notes, no 259.)

Serge

Oxford
[Undated; found
between Feb. 28
and March 4 in
original file]

Dearest,

This is a short note because Sir Humphrey has been wandering querulously around, more or less complaining that no-one has been here since Friday noon. But I have gone & dared "the Douglas in his hall"[46] & asked him if he wanted me, so he was quite charming. There is a good deal in this matter of taking the bull by the horns!

However . . . Michael was quite charming and beautiful to me on Sunday, and we were right to let him come. The Spaldings will be delighted to see him on Friday morning to lunch, and if he wishes Lewis will be delighted for him to come to Magdalen before the lecture, & to be with us afterwards. I think it may be the last lecture.

It is warmer here to-day; a cold rain & a slow thaw. The train down was full with military; we were half an hour late, and the roads when we did get in were like nothing on earth. I only hope your back has not got worse since I left.

I shall write to Edgcumbe to-morrow. To-day brings a letter from my Mirfield father[47] and a *C.T.* cutting which I enclose. Also the United States Treasury saying that my literary agents haven't written to them about the money they say I owe them. We men of affairs!

All my love.

C

Oxford

4 March/40

It was a happy time, wasn't it? I always feel a little like an exile when I get back to South Parks Rd. again, pleasant & comfortable, as it is. Anne was alone till the Players returned about two; I spoke about Michael & she created the impression she was quite looking forward to it. I shall write to B.B.[48]

On the way down, in a full compartment, I turned to thinking of the Whitsun play,[49] & I thought, if it is done and when I print, it had better be dedicated to Michael "from both of us," as a memory of this year. I finished the Sitwell review[50] last night; & this morning paid in my Faber cheque; tomorrow the Revenue cheque shall go. What a world!

You were sweet all the time. No reviews or anything of interest here; only Brother George Every's[51] poems, which you may remember that woman speaking of at the Cumberland. Odd! I had been waiting for them because I meant to try out the Dacre Press office for M., though I felt that religious line was not meant for him. But now I shall do nothing.

It is warm here, after a cold morning. I have, it occurs to me, been thinking more of your sweetness than your pain. Yet you would perhaps have it so; it is more you. God bless!

Serge

Oxford

5 March/40

Thank you for the cheque book. I have sent my last in the old book to the Inland Revenue, thus finishing *that* (till June). I have also written to B.B.

But you forget, loveliest, the men. Am I only to be followed by the feminine? No; you will be attended—you—by the masculine minds: great minds, strong males, brothers of our energy—those who know our work—Lewis &

Eliot & Raymond & Tolkien & the young males; and they, having read me, will look for You, & walk round you, & admire, & say "This was the Origin of all, and the continual Friend and Supporter." And they will never leave you, so you will have no chance of getting to anyone else. So there!

By the way—Isabel is looking forward to you as much as to me, I may say. I have—*faute de mieux*[52]—been talking to them about Raymond's proposed book[53] on me, and lent them some of his letters. This only to inform you. Last night we went to Priestly;[54] I had a comfortable seat in the front row and I could smoke, so it was quite pleasant. But the play was all pseudo-intellectual. "I have thought" said someone, "that life is very strange." . . . Gawd!

I have told Isabel. I have told you about the radio. And now I shall read poems by Redwood Anderson, who goes on writing! So do I, but then. . . .

O what more? love, & love, & then love. I lecture on you to-morrow. Doctrinally—which is no use to you. But some to the world!

Serge

Oxford

6 March/40

Dearest,

Basil has just rung up to say he couldn't lunch to-day, but that 1 April would do splendidly. I said it was very good of him, & he said he thought he had probably done himself a very good turn. Which is a charming way of putting it, & I hope true. I have said that Michael will be down on the Tuesday before Easter; B. is a little full next week, & I go to Bristol, & so on. That is the 19th. I don't suggest his stopping the night, but we can settle trains later. At the moment I am a little agitated by the actual prospect of it happening, so suddenly like this, & not writing very well.

I know *exactly* what you mean about Isabel—exactly. It's not at all the arrangement I should have made, but . . . however you & I understand it all; and O darling, to have him actually in a proper job . . . and starting in a place no-one is—I won't say "ashamed of" but you know what I mean. . . .

I am sending the gas money to-day. But I don't understand how—or rather I am ashamed that you should do the rest. I shall give you the Central Fund money back as soon as I draw any more. I get fussed about your doing so much, & I am *terribly* worried over you—& when I say terribly, I mean *terribly*. It distresses me that I haven't been able to arrange better, but I have fought for the best. God willing, once we have dealt with not so long a time now, we may be able to make our last start in more peace. After all we *might* have been dealing with a half-blind nerve-ridden boy . . . I have, once or twice, wondered if your back[55] might not have saved his eyes; I am quite serious about that—just as your being alone does mean he has a job. It *is* exchange, after all; though only I shall see it that way. But do I!

And now I have begun a new sheet, and have nothing with which to fill it. Only that you will know that we are still and always working together, and doing what we can. Be blessed! I am sure you deserve to be. And (if you are able to sleep) do not wake to worry over his future. Of course there is much to be done still—I know, I know. But your famous Fish[56] has swum up once more—like when we first met, & ever since.

Ever,

Serge

Oxford

12 March/40

No: I never have, I never could, I never could begin to imagine myself under any circumstances making any suggestion about your most princely Highness except to you, about *anything*. I do not do these things. You are the only person I have never criticized to others; damn it, my wife is my wife. I do not permit anyone, anyone, to suggest to my wife what she shall do. Nor do I— except to her. I have always been much more fixed on you than, I think, you always believe. But pass that. And that I should begin to think of—no, darling, it just could not happen.

I am sick at heart about everything, and (as they say) "living on my nerves." And my nerves are prickly. I repeat what I said at the beginning of these months—I have no-one to talk to in Oxford and no-one to keep me happy. Nor could I be happy unless you and I . . . . I can go on as long as you and I are in union, whether we are together or not. I can do without all the rest of the world, but not without you behind me. And that is that. If ever I needed your support it is now.

Incidentally, I had an extraordinarily moving note from W. H. Auden[57] in America. He said he just wanted to tell me how moved he was by the *Dove* (& he no Christian) & he was sending me his new book "as a poor return." He adds that he was reminded once again "of a curious fact that though I've only met you twice, in times of difficulty and doubt, recalling you has been of great help to me." And he is ever mine Wystan Auden.

I can't think why it should be—but at least he is no woman and he is in America. But it does seem you and I have not been without a result. I begin to believe I am a genius—& we all know how the wives of geniuses have to put up with . . . but not women; no. O my heart, it is all a very odd life. [page missing, or end of unsigned letter]

Oxford

14 March/40

Darling, you have been too sweet to me, and I am a pig. I shall, no doubt, continue at intervals to be a pig, but I allow that your letters make me realize the piggishness. I thought your letter about shocks and thankfulness[58] very great and wise, though the shock wakes me at night still! Though I expect I sleep more than you do even so.

If Michael comes down next Tuesday, I see there is a train down at 9.45 which gets in at 11.25. I will find out from B.B. when we—when he had better see him. I shan't go in; much better let them start together. But of course I will meet him. We could lunch at South Parks Rd. or not, as he liked. I don't think I suggest his stopping too long this time, but we can't decide the train back until I have settled B.B. Does that strike you as sound?

No other news. References to the *Dove* continue; I send you one. And my profoundest gratitude.

Serge

Oxford

15 March/40

I forgot to say that Margaret is dashing up for the Rite[59] as you suggested, though it was also in her own mind. She suggested I should come too as her guest, but I declined; she has to go down early Sunday, & I should have to go too; and I am determined to stick at Magic. There are five separate half-chapters to do, & the Conclusion; but at least that looks like an end reasonably soon. With any luck. . . . So I shan't waste precious time on the Rite.

A thing called the *St. Martin's Review*[60]—edited by that nincompoop Eric Gillett—suggests I shall do an article on *The Church Looks Forward* for three guineas; so I probably shall; though what the Church is looking forward to, I don't know. But I daresay I shall discover three guineas' worth of prophesy.

The Expository Times alludes to the *Dove* in a long article on Sanctification, and rather supports my dear little Co-inherence. Otherwise, nothing of interest. I had hoped to send you a pound or so to-day, but nothing has come, and though I shall get my railway fare from the Bristol people, because Wrenn said they would write, I haven't got it yet. The hotel and the dinner they did, but I am 15/- down at the moment. And *T&T* who now must owe me about seven pounds altogether don't send it; Theodora said she hoped some for this week.

Yesterday I heard from Hubert it snowed in London; it did here, detestably. By the way, Hubert is losing his house; the people who own it have decided to return, so he is pushing his wife, &c, back to Golders Green. Having thus spent money for nothing. He is proposing to try & get Sir Humphrey to let him re-open the music side of Amen House. I wish he succeeds: it would be something.

Best-beloved, all my love. And all my gratitude. And kisses.

Serge

Oxford

29 March/40

Dearest,

I don't know whether you will get this before you go to the station; if you do, think that I embrace you there; if you don't, think I embrace you when you get back. I feel that this Saturday–Monday is a point quite unique in our existence, being, we may hope, the beginning of so much—so much beyond us. If it all goes well—& it may—it will be a real opening[61] on Michael's life: if not—but I think that unlikely—we will find something else. I wish we had been together for it, but it is European wars that are responsible for separation, not us. But I should have liked us to have had lunch on Monday. However, we will do it one Saturday instead.

I have just been having lunch with Hugh MacDonald, who has been over here from Cambridge, which (he says) is likely one of these days to offer me a D.Litt. Sez you! but it is amusing to hear such talk. He admires *Taliessin* very much; the *Dove* he doesn't know.

Isabel & Margaret have handed over the money for M's radio. I demurred—& took it. They were very nice about it, & it certainly will help. Anne is expecting him to-morrow, & I shall be there.

And now I shall leave everything to God. I am glad we went to church together on Easter evening. It was quite like old times—our very old times. And nothing could be better at the present time. I shall think of you to-night.

Serge

Oxford

3 April/40

It seems odd to think this is the third day of his earning money! He went off at 8.30 this morning, after dealing with what looked like a perfectly good breakfast. I had gone up and woke him at 7.30, so he has good nights. He says he sleeps well, & he doesn't seem too tired at night when he comes in—he is quite bright. I watch him like a . . . father. In fact he still pre-occupies most of my attention at odd times & at all times. We are to call on Hubert[62] to-morrow evening; it became necessary, owing to the publicity of all telephones here, to mention to H. what had happened. I have no business on going but as H. goes back to London soon it doesn't involve the future. All these letters are more Reports than letters: but you will understand how like a hen I have been this week! No doubt I shall become used to the feeling soon, or it will fade. As it is I cast myself on your mercy.

I am now about to write another review for *T.&T*,[63] insuring an extra £2 in May! I am going to send his 10/- this week back to you, but he doesn't know that yet. It shall come to you from him through me, and from me by means of him. There!

I love you. We do manage the best we can, don't we?

Serge

Oxford

8 April/40

Blast! (he said warmly.) Need we ask Ursula this time? I may have to see Alexander Dru,[64] who is over from Paris, on business, but I hope not, & I shall let you know. But I don't want anyone else. Why don't you come to Paddington & we can have a sherry & a sandwich there, & perhaps go straight to the pictures or something? Or anything else. Anyhow don't ask anyone unless you have to. If Ursula[65] is going to be a Christian, she can start straight away practicing. She can't be longing all that—two or three weeks won't make any difference.

Michael got back safely; I was so glad you thought he looked all right; I did myself. He spent the evening watching Walter Douglas[66] paint, & went off this morning very cheerful & in good time. All very satisfactory.

I have put on the clean things: thank you. And thank you. I am now about to touch up a few slips of Magic for Margaret to type.

God bless!

Serge

Oxford

9 April/40

Blessed one,

What with all the news to-day[67] I have been a little distracted, but it needn't prevent me thanking you for your letter. I didn't mean to worry you with M's pay; I only mentioned it en passant. I shall try & let you have another pound next week with any luck. Michael says Blackwell asked him if he wanted his money urgently—or words to that effect—and he said no; which I said was quite right. I never thanked you for paying the other things, which I meant to do!

Basil was at the Eastgate to-day & said: "What an engaging fellow Michael is!" and asked me, very nicely, if he was contented with things; he said M. seemed happy. I said he was, & murmured something polite, but B. was equal to this & said he thought M. would be very useful. So all is going well at present, & looks like going on doing so. It is good of you. But I do feel pleased at last; when I come up on Saturday we shall feel that something is done!

All the news is the public news. In one way it is bad, but I think it will quicken things & shorten the war. We shall be able to do something now, & I almost felt that perhaps this or next year might see it over.

All my love.

Serge

Oxford

18 April/40

Dearest,

I hope you got to Lutterworth;[68] I have been anxious about your journey—
& to-day is so horribly cold with the wind that I can only hope you are there
& *warm*.

I am very glad indeed you fell into some doctor's arms like that: you shall
tell me who it was whose voice drove you in. We ought to know someone,
and you ought to have someone you can ring up—and that quite apart from
my relief that you are "under treatment." Thank you for telling me. (I remember
all about the fibroid.) My poor love! but we shall get this and that over, under
God, and have a pleasant time yet!

And incidentally I write because I like to send you a line most days—not
from "necessity": so there! It never occurred to me that I "had to," nor have
I: but it pleases me, and I hope you, if I do it—just as it pleases me to post letters to you. Though Michael has gone out himself these last two nights. He
is waking very well in the mornings—to-day he was in my room before I had
gone up. He doesn't seem to me to leave the house before 8.30, but that I leave
to him; he will find his feet in time no doubt, and Blackwell's will hasten him
if need be. He says he likes the Foreign Book section best, & he *says* he is beginning to pick up German from the titles. He was talking about New York[69]
last night, & it occurred to me that I might try our New York Branch in time
to come, after he has finished his apprenticeship: Blackwell's would be a
good start for that, & the staff is not run from England. We shall see.

Business is being hellishly difficult nowadays. No review books have come
this week, alas! I have got on with the play a little. O and as for . . . no, I shan't
embark on discussions of our Lord now. It was Anne,[70] I think, who once wrote
that I was about as aware of women as Jesus Christ: it is (omitting the comparison) largely true. It is so odd, my sweet, that you, of whom the effect of
Our teaching has sprung, and whom We promulgate everywhere, should
scorn your own children, as it were. But leave that. I think of you continuously. Be as restful as you can at Lutterworth; it is a poor change, but it is a
little break: or I hope so. God bless you, & thank you for the doctor.

Serge

Oxford

23 April/40

Of course I shall come: what do you think?! It will be next Wednesday or
Thursday—yes? but Michael will be up on Saturday & you can let me know
perhaps by him.

He wrote the enclosed letter to be posted, but it had better come under cover
to Hampstead. I should love to meet your Mrs. Wallace;[71] I feel she would suit

Jock here. Not that he is religious, but he has been making me help him to compose publicity—all about our National Heritage and Separated Friends. God! what I suffer! and when I make suggestions he says that of course we must be rather sloppy for this kind of thing & these kind of people. The Press is becoming more banal every day.

Well, but so were Moody & Sankey,[72] & they did some good? I wonder if the great Apostles had style: they say St. Paul's Greek was not too good. But Jock is not St. Paul.

I hear that Burns[73] says he is hoping to do another book by me; thank God! In a week or so I must write to him. I keep as many balls in the air as I can, though with you away I seem to have one arm amputated!

All love,

Serge

South Parks Rd.
28 April/40

Dearest,

It will be adorable if you and I can be together at the play[74]—anyhow I shan't be there if you aren't. I have been trying to finish it this weekend. TSE. has written to say he has been reading *Witchcraft* "with the interest & attention that anything you write commands," & is discussing it with his committee on Wednesday, but he doesn't suggest he wants much altered. I am starting on the Christian anthology[75]—if (did I ask you?) you have any time, it would be kind of you to make any suggestions. If the Library——

Michael has just arrived here: not bringing any better report of you than I feared. I knew it before he spoke; and I am very unhappy about it, and anxious to get something done. You & I will talk next weekend. I shall be up on Friday.

Meanwhile—but there is no meanwhile. We shall have to make some better arrangement. I was uncertain, as you know, about Michael at Blackwell's from the beginning, but it seemed the best thing. And we didn't see how we could manage otherwise at first, did we? Michael, without meaning to, does manage to suggest to me that of all selfish husbands I am the worst, though I don't think that I have passed a period of pure pleasure down here. But I may have been—one so often is—more selfish than I had thought: if so, you must try and forgive me. I do the best I can to keep everything going under all difficulties—

This is a silly letter. I know we understand each other. It is only that I am exacerbated by conditions and not working very well and not at ease and worried over you. M. tells me you would rather have a cheque than pound notes, so I send it herewith. It will be cashable on Tuesday, not to-morrow. I shall send the gas and telephone on Tuesday; the rent I will send when I come. I do not forget Edith.

I do want to do what is best for us all. What I should like is simple—to be back with you in London. Love me and keep me: as I you.

Serge

I have endorsed the cheque & everything; you have only to push it in & take the money.

29 April/40

Dearest,

I remember you asked me for the review, but I had neglected to hunt it out. Michael thought I should send the whole number, and so I do; but if you like to tear out p. 319 which has the review[76] in question, do, and send it away. There is another notice[77] by me on p. 311 which you may care to look at. Unfortunately they brought in no cash; but we must do what we can for the Church! Though I admit when I wrote them I thought I was going to be paid.

It is cold here today. I have had a charming letter from a priest[78] who reviewed the *Dove* in *Christendom*, to whom I wrote a line of thanks. He lives at Pusey House here, & has asked me to dinner: I have told him after Whitsun I should like to go. There are moments when, what with promising to speak for the Greek Orthodox Church, and promising to write an article for the Roman *Tablet* on Chaucer (if formally asked), and doing reviews for the Anglican *Theology*, I feel like a little Reunion of Christendom. It seems likely I may be asked to do some work for the Roman *Dublin*;[79] which will pay. I hear also, indirectly, that Burns[80] of Longman's is still anxious to publish another book by me, and I shall write in a week or two.

In fact, I don't want to write any more for a little; as I keep on saying, my mind is clouded, and it needs a little more reading and a little laziness. As you used to say about Religion: "I am living on my past." But I shall improve.

I spent Saturday afternoon being "kind" to Margaret—which appears to be one of my jobs. Isabel went to rest; and I talked of this & that & got M. to talk as much as possible. I have a very great respect for Margaret, and a certain tenderness. You will not be able to think there is any other feeling *there!* and yet, on my honour, madonna, I think that is like all others or any other. Physically Margaret & Ursula & any leave me so remote you wouldn't believe. Of course, if this were not so, I should have been incapable of being of use to any: as it is I would, in that sense, as soon be with Margaret as with, say, Ursula. She rang up to say was either of us going up, so I said Michael was and could she meet me in the Broad? Having had tea with the Ds, I went off & collected Ursula complete with car and made her drive to the station where I was to meet Michael. And how any man could be attracted by Ursula or

Margaret (or the Spalding girls) any more than by—Miss Sangston or Ms. Couchman, I simply cannot understand.

Well—I didn't mean to break into that monologue; it was our poor Margaret that started me on it. Add Father Thomas M. Parker of Pusey House[81] to the list of my conquests. As I have had the honour to say before—they are not *all* women or *all* fools.

Milford has gone very humpy again—naturally now. I have asked F.P. to come to my nice empty office—which is NOBLE of me. Hubert comes down for a day or two this week; & Parnwell is seeing two men in it to-morrow morning. So the emptiness, after a day or two, is fading.

After to-morrow we pay 2½ for letters; so I shall try & manage to enclose Michael's. If we miss a post or so you will understand. But he writes his letter & insists that it must go that night, so either he or I trot round with it.

Jock has just been in & I asked him about Lutterworth. He was very interested; said his people did come from all round the Midlands and he would love to know some of the dates. He sent his regards to you & thanks you for seeing them.

I must sign letters. All my love.

Serge

You signed one letter—"Florence." Did it make me gaze! Bless you.

I'm writing to you, but Father wants to post this. I don't know when mine'll come. All my love, M.

Oxford

8 May/40

Love,

Thank *you.* I like Edith's phrase "once we had got used to the shock"—though I darkly suspect her of being facetious, as you would call it. However I approve of Canon Hardson; in the dim future St. Albans will know me.

I am sorry the pain is worse, but I do hope the doctor will be useful—it would be good to get something really done. I shall think of you to-night: and look forward to Saturday. M. has told you the aunt stayed last night. Anne told her she couldn't come for Whitsun, and Gerry said this morning as we left after breakfast that if she ever came there permanently he should leave, whatever it meant. The girls sit trying to be nice—& it's all very trying. However she will be gone to-night, I suppose.

I hear that Burns is going to write to me about a possible book—good. *T&T* rang up to say they would like 500 words on *Terror of Light* if it could be sent. I have to get some-one to do it; if I can catch the Professor of Poetry[82] I shall ask him—it would be a name. If not, someone else. It would hardly do for you to do it which is what came into my mind—but it would be awkward for us to waffle the guinea.

I shall write to-morrow, & meet you on Saturday. I enclose M's letter; the 2½'s are making him willing to enclose his in the same envelope. An awful thing has happened! I have left it behind at the office. Forgive me; it shall come to-morrow.

It is heavy and tiring to-day, & I have a slight headache in the back of my head—like some weeks ago when it went all tender there. Brain, brain! I love you very much.

Serge

Oxford
9 May/40

Dear one,

Michael has written another letter instead, which he posted last night. So his original is to be set aside. It was sweet of you to write, and I shall look forward to meeting you at 11.25 on Saturday. This is but an interim note. I will tell Anne about the Orange. And I loved your comments about *T. of L.*[83]—don't think anything else. But it was a shame about your dreams, and your bad night. I have lost count: was it Tuesday? Because if so I was awake, but I spent 2.30–3.45 writing an oration about the Holy Ghost, for possible inclusion in the play.

No more developments anywhere. I was a little shaken by the official call-up of the 19s—or rather the proclamation that they would be. But there is more than a year[84] to go, during which anything may happen, and it would have worried me much, much more if he hadn't a job, because I should have felt he would have been in a more awkward position. With any luck his drawbacks in health may be useful yet. But you will tell me not to worry, & you will be right. One lobe of my brain thinks of you & one of him.

Till Saturday then, my own.

Serge

Oxford
14 May/40

Dearest,

It would hardly be decent for me not to write and be grateful. "I will . . ." What is it Simon Magus says?[85] something about being grateful enough and Peter says he can't be. But that was not between married people.

It was a very good time, and I write this from my Southfield House room. When I arrived this morning an undergraduate was waiting to ask me to speak to some study circle. I do become a public monument, but leave that now. I feel more friendly to Oxford now you have been there: it has been the first time we have been at all alone in it.

Schuler and F.P. are proposing to go to St. Mary's to-night[86]—not together. I am disappointed at having to be *aware* of Isabel to-night; it isn't her fault, but I have to be kind and it's very tiring. Margaret is different; I begin to respect her a good deal. But I suppose I shall be enveloped!

My thumb is not behaving too well, & you must excuse the writing. I can see I shall miss next month's St. Martin's with my article;[87] however it will come the month after. No sign of Chichester.[88]

God bless you. Thank you for everything. I will write a poem, one of these days, on you in Oxford. All love.

Serge

Oxford

15 May/40

Dearest,

I thought of you this morning and wondered how you were getting on—even amidst the mild shock of the Dutch surrender.[89] Mild because it was clear that the Allied High Command was not going to risk its armies in Holland, and that the last thing the French are going to do is to be found where the Germans hope.

Miss Peacock was asking after you. She had some story that at one place a motor-bus was stopped by the police and all passengers asked for their identity cards. I keep mine in my pocket-book; if one is anywhere except locally I think one should have it. It is clear that a strong movement against all doubtful characters may begin any day. There is a growing feeling here against refugees, and what is said to be the Government effort to force them on people. Miss P's office was seething about it—I don't quite know why!

Last night the play[90] went as well as Monday. I didn't escape a certain forceful attack myself from Isabel when (innocently enough) I said: "Well, as a play it's pretty bad, but it has its moments!" But I must tell you that when the lights went up afterwards—directly after the end—I happened to look across the aisle, and two ladies who had been sitting in the front row were discovered to have sunk to their [k]nees in prayer! They must have done it almost before the play stopped. John Trevor[91] & Ruth urge me if I am going to re-write it (which I must do; I couldn't pass it at present) to enlarge it to make a full two hour or so affair. It would be (like the *Rite* in another way) the only thing of its kind. And we would cut out the touch of facetiousness and improve the style. I think I may.

Meanwhile I have sent off *The Church looks Forward.*[92] The first review book has arrived from the *Dublin,* so apparently I am supposed to be writing for them. I must ring up Dawson to-morrow. I am particularly taken with the idea that the article on *The City in English Poetry*[93] will (a little late!) pay the last insurance almost exactly. Very useful!

There is no other news. Ruth said how nice you were & Anne how nice it was to have you. But I don't call that *news*—because I know that all along. John Trevor, speaking of a desirable alteration in the play, said that "was one we owed to Mrs. Williams." And G.H. said that he thought you were looking very charming.

I cannot help this little bouquet; the flowers of it grew spontaneously at different moments last night. But I think you should have them! I kiss your hands & your feet. Michael shall bring you some money.

God bless.

Serge

Oxford
17 May/40

I had intended to go to church this morning on your account—I mean in my own personal gratitude. But what with waking late and slipping up to M., though he was up, I didn't. I will either go to-morrow or remember on Sunday. However, there being no cooked food but only cold ham or something for breakfast, I kept the fast for once, not without reference to you. I really must do something about these things, and I could if I would only make the effort. But I was so relieved.

It was nice to hear you last night. I say "nice" because it is a tender intimate word, and I hope you don't think it too small. It was all very silly of me, but I am glad I rang up: to hear you, and to hear what you told me. To-day I have been more at peace. But I have *not* written to Ursula. It would be a precedent. Outside you & M—O and my mother and Edith—I do not write on birthdays; I do not even know what birthdays are. I don't know even Anne Ridler's. And I don't propose to begin. I will do something about Margaret if you remind me when it is, because I think she needs it. But otherwise—no. (And in any case not Ursula's this time!)

For the rest—be at ease. I know generally what is right and what is wrong, and I know a great deal that is wrong with our unfortunate P——. I could tell even you something!

I had thought of volunteering for the Parashooter boys, but I decided against. My old Volunteer experience[94] didn't convince me of my own vocation for the army, and my eyes wouldn't let me discern the parachutes! If they come. The danger of treachery is more depressing, but I still think that the English are more difficult to catch than our Mr. Hitler understands. I am delighted to see that the Americans are worried.[95]

Well . . . I adore you. I also love you. I also think you a sweet. And I am also your dearest love—whether you like it or not. And thank you for telling me.

I *shall* go to church for it. Also I shall do something about the cash. Kissing
you,

Serge

Oxford
20 May/40

Waking in the morning is not very cheery these days, is it? There emerges
slowly in the mind a kind of consciousness of you and of the war, and of the
need for being iron, so to speak, and of all the things depending on it, such
as work and money. I won't again bore you by saying how difficult I find it to
work or you will say with some justice that you have heard it all before. I read
half the Bishop's MS.[96] yesterday during the late afternoon & evening: myself, I think it's rather dull, but I can't improve it there. And I sketched a review for *T&T.*: unfortunately *T&T* is also beginning to fall in the review-pages—
I fear I shall only get one in this month. It's perhaps a little-heaviness that makes
quick writing impossible. But not altogether; the paper is partly responsible.

I think perhaps I shall do better if I eat less breakfast. I am sure two heavy
meals are not good for me as a regular thing; and if there are no specially cooked
things I shan't have to eat them. I haven't liked to eat out, partly because of
G.H.; it looks so awkward to leave him to be alone in having things cooked.
But this morning I had only a little porridge & a little toast—much better! But,
of course, one can't, as it were, *sometimes* have things: one can't say, "well, let's
have an egg!" or, alternatively, "*don't* let's have an egg." However it is a great
thing that M. goes on being fed at breakfast!

I suppose one day I shall have odd coffees and bread and dripping and what
nots again? One must work for one's pleasures! So I did, a little. But if here
on Thursday evenings I come in late from Magdalen, do you say: "What about
a cup of tea?" (Angel sweet, do you remember our first tea & cake at eleven
or so? a long time ago but vivid. There are a hundred vignettes of you still in
my mind—& that is one. I will tell you the others one day. Or some of them,
as occasion serves: they crop up from time to time.) No; you do not.

Get Michael to the end of this month,[97] & I shall feel more certain that he
is settled; he tells me B.B. will have the indentures made out soon. This, M.
[incomplete]

Oxford
21 May/40

I shall wish you many happy returns now (a) in case the post is delayed
to-morrow (b) because I like to be in time (c) because I should like you to
hear the first wish on a day apart from the doctor. But I will write again
to-morrow and send you the pound for her: not my ideal birthday present,
but we will do better sometime.

I have had the *Dove* statement this morning. We have sold (besides the 5000 Religious Book Club) 500 copies. This, of course, excludes America. I asked Basil what he thought the R.B. Club sales were equal to in ordinary sales, & he said about a fifth: which would give us about 1500. Not too bad, though I had, after the general reception, hope for more. Tributes still wander in. I am to dine at Keble to meet the Warden who has read it; & George Every tells me an old invalid in Cumberland has a great admiration for that & *Taliessin*— which touched me.

I shall write to Phyllis—she certainly can't have *the Play*.[98] They asked me about it at Pusey House last night, & I said firmly that no-one was going to see it till I had rewritten it.[99] Which I shall do as soon as I can. Adam Fox[100] in *T&T* was agreeable but hesitant. When I have finished with it, everyone will know the difference between good & bad.

Your description of belief in the Trinity charmed me. Also your nobility in going at all—Which reminds me to ask, rather plaintively, *need* we ask Ursula in this time? I'm sure it's very good for her and I'm sure she would like it, but it does hamper our movements. I have a good mind to write myself. I know—poor darling!—you have to have her, & I feel I ought to help. But, for once, as it's practically your birthday, *need* we?

We hear the Archbishops are to be asked to press the government about paper. We also hear that the amount licensed is to cut down from 30% of our usual amount to 10%. Jolly! We also hear that lists are in existence containing names of firms and periodicals to be suppressed altogether if necessary! Thank God the O.U.P. is likely to be left out of *that*. —I gather that the news is regarded as not too bad. Churchill's speech was partly for Hitler and partly for the U.S.A.—O well, I shall see you on Friday.

God bless.

Serge

Not having now at hand[101]
my genius, as I was wont,
but finding desert sand
rough on my spirit's front;
between a time and a time,
in a crack between ages,
I will add this colophon of rhyme
to my printed pages.
It shall be as a flame that burns
on some statue's front; it shall say
"Many happy returns,
many happy returns to-day."

A poet does not know,
more than others, what his life means,
nor, more than others, what glow
a body lets through or screens:
but, more than others, he knows
what he has thought or said,
and whether his verse shows
one other praised head:
therefore because mine learns
the knowledge of yours, I will say
"Many happy returns,
many happy returns to-day."

Images, now or then,
are often strange fictions
and greatly deceive men,
if they hold not their contradictions:
but when thine are showed
early love is made new,
after a great mode
which shall rest all-through.
So while the world burns,
by the passion of Christ, it shall say:
to you: "Many happy returns,
many happy returns to-day"

23 May 1940
C.W.
(being of Our tribute,
but the rest I will
tell you—
privately)

Oxford
27 May/40

There wasn't a cheque so I can't send you anything! If it should come to-mor-row I shall post it. But I begin to wonder if *T&T* is smashing up on the quiet.

However, that was not what I was going to say! Which was that I was re-minded, on my way to Oxford, of the evenings in the hospital when you had been to see me—for the first week—& disappeared round about eight o'clock—or half-past, was it? Something of the same *substance* disappeared with your bus, & I looked at Oxford as I looked at the ward. You will know that odd sensation: it is not "missing" anyone; it is the disappearance of a solid, almost of the floor. One does not "miss" the floor; one misses a chair or a desk or a table, but not the solid existence. When that goes, one is left dancing in the air—uncertain, heavy, lost.[102] That is how I felt in the hospital and that is how I felt to-day.

And it is worth 2½ to tell you so!

Serge

Oxford
29 May/40.

You might, my dearest love, notice the date. For this very morning I have signed the Indentures. And Basil Blackwell has signed. And Michael has signed. And Mr. Henry Shullich—B.B.'s partner—has signed as a witness. It is, strictly, not legal; for it has not been stamped & registered at Somerset House. But it is unlikely we should ever want to sue B.B.: and anyhow legality would pin *us!* But short of that all is settled—until 1 June 1943. M. Starts getting a pound a week on 18 June, or as near as possible: say the first of July, and rises to 25/- and 30/- on the next two Firsts of July. On 1 June 1943 he is a man and free (at least, the 18th strictly) of his indentures—a settled bookseller! If he wants. Anyhow it will be a certificate for him everywhere through the world—and we can begin to worry about his next Job in 1943. So no more worry about School Leaving Certificates & so on; there is now a document which will re-place all that. B.B. is keeping it in his iron box till 1943, or you should have it. It was all rather amusing. BB sat at his desk & filled in the form making small jokes; and I lay in a chair; and Michael stood by BB, and Mr. Shullich busy behind. All too sweet! It was only ten or I would have stood BB a drink. I will not say *nothing* could have been better, but I cannot think of anything, because nothing else would have given him the formal record, and so much of likeli-hood of certainty. I was rather glad the partner was in on it for that reason. And he is not yet 18, so we haven't done too badly. "It is the Lord's doing and it is marvellous in our eyes."[103] Later on, when the troubles are over, I will begin to think what had better be done in the future. If HSM retires & Cum-berlege succeeds I shall tackle him. Or I have even thought, later, of trying the New York branch.[104] But that we shall see. Let us congratulate each other. He is no longer without a background and a name—as it were. B.B. would nurse him a little if we were killed, and it's all much better than we thought three months ago: only three!

I shall send this just as it is; with my love & gratitude.

Serge

Dearest,

Your letter this morning made me feel as if I had been so taken up by my own needs & desires—in the matter of having you here—that I was neglecting more important things. I was extremely moved by your last sentence especially about the hostages and the voluntary offer. It is a little crushing (if wonderfully so!) to be offered what I do most firmly believe to be a principle of the world in answer to one's own pleas, and I am not giving in to it yet. But I will waive it till I am up. I haven't heard from Burns yet, but I will send word as soon as I do. My heart stands still for you—because of you, I mean, as it always has done.

There is no particular news—in fact there is none. I look out of the window and think that this is a dashed exposed position, but I also think that (and more than ever after your letter, which I have put in my pocket-book to keep as courage) that what we can do we will. It is dreadful for those whose sons are in the Army in Belgium;[105] Lewis pointed a man out to me whose son was there—& all news cut off. I do feel we are lucky that Michael is not there as an R.A.M.C.[106] orderly or something: he is as safe as anyone nowadays for the next couple of years.

I am repeating myself. I shall go back to making up a small catalogue of "Theological & Philosophical Works" published by the Press; we are saving all big catalogues and shortening everything to save paper. Bless you, and thank you for this last goodness, as for all and for all.

Serge

Oxford

31 May/40

I have thought a good deal about your profound sentence about voluntary sacrifice, but perhaps I will not write about it now; we can talk about it when I come up. I have promised—all being well—to lunch with Burns, picking him up at the Ministry of Information, on Tuesday next; & I have promised HSM to try & find at Amen House an article I wrote on Browning years ago[107]— and I shall probably see one of our authors there: Also our Miss Pearn in the afternoon. What I think of doing is to come up by the train on Monday evening; do the jobs on Tuesday; meet you, have a meal about 6 on Tuesday evening & catch the 7.40 down. How does that strike you? I wish I could stay the Tuesday night but I think I had better not make it too late before I arrive here on Wednesday.

Everyone here is more cheerful about the news now:[108] there seems to be no doubt about the winning, though there is a distance to go! But the evacuation of even part of the B.E.F. has done wonders, it seems, among ordinary people.

I want to hear about Chelmsford, & I am glad you saw Pleshey.[109] Let's hope we shall both be comfortably there next May. I have been asked to attend the SCM[110] meeting down here in July, but it comes directly after the Anglo-Orthodox conference in London and I think I shall decline. No other news. I am too relieved about (i) Michael (ii) Longmans to mind anything—only I wish I worked better. I shall try & get down to it during the weekend.

Michael's letter enclosed. Adieu, my sweet love.

Serge

Oxford
5 June/40

Darling,

I seem to have been fiddling about with my own articles to-day, & I have been trying to write a letter to *Time & Tide* which they have written asking me to do about another article.[111] (This sounds very complicated!) It was to be all about the Peace—when it comes. But I do not feel inspired about the Peace.

It was lovely yesterday and I felt more like writing again as I went down to Oxford than I have done ever since I was there. The combination (after you) of Eliot and our drinks: and perhaps a little the talking of things as if the poets still wrote! But, as I said before, the quality of our interviews—yours & mine—almost makes up for the quantity: is perhaps a compensation!

There is no news here. The Germans, we hear, have begun an offensive towards Paris.[112] God send the Somme line holds! If it does, the raids here may likely be postponed a little.

God bless you.

Serge

Oxford
7 June/40

Dearest,

If you could bring yourself to look again at the last few pages[113] of the last chapter of the *Dove* you will see what I have *said* about the Germans. And if you read *Taliessin*, thinking of the pirates & the barbarians as (on that level) the Prussians, you will see what I have *said*. Or if you look over any of my public statements. I have done all that I could, even at the conclusion of my Sorbonne lecture, to unite the European cultures. I was in favor of the Hoare-Laval peace terms[114] precisely because they gathered the non-German nations together. And if my reputation were higher and the Gestapo got here, I should be certainly shot.

This merely in mild defense. I would not even bother to defend myself against anyone but you; it would be too silly. Why, you have thought me too severe on the Germans for their treatment of the Jews! I have talked European politics on & off for twenty years. I have even quoted GKC against the Germans—"the barbarians come again." I shall agree I did not fully realize the consequences of the disappearance of Austria.[115] I shall agree that when people talked of Hitler as a maniac gangster I thought they underrated him, and I am quite sure they underrated the Italian feeling. But I have done as much for the maintenance of England in Europe and of Europe against the Prussians as any private literary man.

Leave it. But I was a little startled to find myself suspected of improper affiliation in politics as well! (I shouldn't have been surprised to find the Ds. telling me off; they used to think me remote. But then they knew nothing & talked nonsense—being imbecilely abusive!) But in my own heart! Love, you ought to hear its beatings better! I give you leave to hew it if you ever find the Prussian colours there—any time these twenty years!!

All love.

Serge

Oxford
9 June, 40

Enclosed is One Pound. This is from the last Witchcraft payment which TSE thoughtfully sent on. I have unfortunately disposed of half of it to Jean Smith who turned up yesterday morning. She was anxious for me to agree to forget the other £4.0—to offer it, she said, as a small contribution to M's start in life. If I didn't mind & it wouldn't spoil a friendship. It occurred to me fleetingly that the other way round would be much more likely to spoil a friendship—but I didn't say so: I was the English gentleman complete. And I said all the right things. After the war if I can do something, I will. It is really very nice of her—and she got the *Dove* and lent it & hasn't read it, so I promised her another copy of that . . . as a makewright. "If we have sown unto you spiritual things. . . ."[116] But as I knew she was coming when the Faber cheque arrived I thought I had better give her something, and did before the Conversation took place. However, you will not despise the pound as a temporary aid!

Yesterday evening Christopher Dawson[117] came round to see me. He was very pleased with the *Dublin* article[118] & I exerted myself to be agreeable, having an eye on future *Dublins*. I am especially pleased to have that for the insurance. I have written a synopsis of the *Courage*[119] pamphlet & sent it to Graham Greene;[120] of course he may not take it, but he might suggest something else. In a way I should rather like to do something for the Ministry. Also I have written to Burns, & promised him a synopsis of a book in case Longmans would like it. I have a kind of yearning towards a novel, but I don't see my way yet. However, if I do think of anything, I will promise you that Lord Arglay[121] shall NOT come in. I think, turning it over in my mind that you are right. By the way you have sometimes blamed me for not being moral enough! but a strange man in *Theology* says that *D. into Hell* is "the most virulent moral invective of our generation." This, he said hastily, is *not* a modification of your judgement!— no, no, no.

I loved your gardener. O and I loved your invention of the Archbishop! it was exactly like. Anne Ridler & her husband came here to tea to-day. She thinks she may be going to have a baby, but doesn't know yet. She has been very upset and frightened by the war: V. expects to be called up any time, & I rather gathered that she has not felt brave enough to ring anyone up or get into touch. Which explains why I have heard scarcely anything and you nothing. But there was no convenient opportunity for any but general talk except for a few moments. G.H. is away & so are the Players. But a young Hungarian girl has been dropped here for the weekend.

I love you, and I shall see you on Friday. If you were very sweet to me I might find you another pound—with luck. My anthology[122] is now weighing on my mind, but I have done something towards it to-day. I went to church with Anne (S. not R) at 11 because I didn't wake at 8. When I did I was holding your hand— so there!

This is an account of others, but it brings you up-to-date. Anne said you had written her a sweet letter. She hasn't liked to go round to the Milfords. She did wonder if you could come for M's birthday and call, staying as long or as little as you chose. We will talk on Friday—it might be an idea? Or you might come back with me on Monday?

The parents here—did I tell you?—have decided to stay where they are; they think they can be more use to the world. I gather that Anne's view is that if the father was going to be ill, when he got home, it would be much better if they did.

Dinner! God bless you; till Friday!

Serge

Oxford

11 June/40

I quite see that you were right—as far as the fall of Paris goes—or so it seems; fortunately I did not deny it. But I promise you I find myself thinking occasionally of those pages[123] in the *Dove* with the faintest anxiety! and at that half seriously, too. I go on feeling I need you very much. I could have cried ten minutes ago when I thought of how we were looking forward to a little peace— though as a general rule I try & remember those people whose sons were *not* evacuated from Dunkirk or Calais. One hears of more of them every day—

though I know the numbers were few. I thought of you and me as I read about the smoke over the bridges of the Seine and the Place de la Concorde—rolling all down the Rue de Rivoli and over the little place opposite the Madeleine.[124] You will not think this sentimentalism.

G.H. & I stayed up to listen to Roosevelt.[125] I am told the military authorities are still cheerful. But it is a long long way to October & the winter. I do think that *Tenez bon*[126] is still the cry, but—O if we come through this, you & I, we will settle down and do nothing except go to church, bus rides, & the cinema for the small rest of our lives.

Graham Greene has thanked me for the synopsis[127] & says it might fit in another series better, but he will talk to his committee and write in a few days. I am trying to push ahead with the anthology.[128] Friday will be soon; my heart aches for it. Sweet, sweet, you are: the darker the world the sweeter you!

Serge

Oxford

12 June/40

I am afraid yesterday's letter was a little glum. Except, as I remember, about you; & I was doubly sorry when I had your scintillating note. But I am anxious about your leg—especially when you wrote of taking Eve to Mistenton. Ought you? I know your habit of doing things for others, but do rest it. I'm not going to have you walking with other people and then not being able to walk with me!

Gerry & Michael are going out to dinner together to-night! To Mr. New of the Clarendon Press, who has the great cinema collection. Will you hear of it! I should say you would. But it is all good for M., & though Mr. New is not, as one may say, of the High Command, one never knows how useful people may be. Next week, it occurs to me, M. will be officially getting a pound a week! Lor'!

I was reading Leon Bloy for my anthology when I came across something which made me think of you: "Let us love each other in the way that God wishes and then let us courageously await the will of Him who made us for His glory."[129] While you do better than I, but I make efforts—towards the second part, I mean. The first is natural!

A note from Anne sending a book says: "The baby is certain, bombs permitting." I should suppose she would go to Berkhampstead reasonably soon—if that is safer, which I doubt! Have I told you we have guards opposite us at the Pathological Laboratory, who also awake me? It is, I am told, where all the bacilli were, and if they got out, 9 South Parks Rd would be, I should think, a touch unhealthy. At present the guards shout to each other about midnight, & at intervals, in highly cultured voices: Oxford at war, & all that.

Everyone is peeved about Italy[130] in a slightly contemptuous way. However, we can talk of that on Friday. I will not write to-morrow, but I will see you, I hope, by eight or so on Friday, & we will go for our little stroll (if your leg is all right)—yes? All my love.

Serge

Oxford
Sunday[131]

I have sent Martin & T's cheque—I tell you this first, because I thought you would like to know it had gone.

Week-ends down here are, I really think, the worst time. I have been work-ing almost all the time—I have done a review and about four thousand words of Magic, as you will see I have stuck at it, but I have been feeling so sick about everything you wouldn't believe. I was thinking yesterday how you used sometimes to propose my going away for a few days to write, and how I never did, for I am sure now that I knew better. As for the future—that makes me feel ill to think of; and I almost wish I had never spoken to B.B. I had no ex-pectations when I did, and it was all such a shock that . . . I suppose we did right, but I'm too miserable about it all—except his actually having the job—to think so.

This is not much of a letter, darling; but after all I do miss you—apart from worrying over you—out of bed as well as in it. And I am beginning to get bored with the food—there is some damn macaroni thing, or tuna, or something; and though of course it's all very good and Michael will have all he wants, and be satisfied—still, from my point of view, it isn't all the absurd *littlenesses:* the chipped potatoes, and the biscuits, and the bread and dripping with coffee brought in; we have dripping occasionally, but at table, which is not the same thing. You used to say I didn't take much interest in my food, but I always did with your "trifles," and I'm sure I don't now. I could scream at the sight of toast for breakfast, though there is always bread if one chooses to cut it. And people come to tea on Sundays, & anyhow I hate a formal tea on Sundays, and . . . and . . . no; it's no good; I'm thoroughly upset. It's very ungrateful, but there it is. I have never been nearer crying, and one can't ever cry. Except in one's own bedroom—bedroom, I ask you!

I went round to the Broad yesterday, & I see Blackwell's keeps open till six on Saturdays. I don't know if they leave at six, but if they do, Michael could sometimes, if he wanted, have dinner, & catch a train at eight—during the sum-mer. But that we shall see.

I shan't write any more, because I want to try & catch the post. Which I shall probably miss. God bless you; forgive me.

C

Oxford

21 June/40

I am what they call disgruntled to-day—why? I don't know that I have any particular reason to-day more than any day. I just agree with M. that it's all a filthy place and filthy people. All. Fortunately I said so long ago. I am in one of my periodical fits of loathing the food at South Parks Rd., which is unfair enough! but (as you very well know) I like snippets & things. And does anyone ever say, at 9.30, "wouldn't you like something to eat?" No. I daresay I shouldn't, but I miss the angelic voice proposing it. I miss any suggestion that I might finish up the . . . apple pie, or that there is another custard. I miss angelic hands putting out shirts for me. I even miss working to the sound of someone doing things about the place, and even being interrupted by a voice saying: "Darling, what about a cup of tea?" I am not quite sure that I don't miss taking a small parcel of leavings down to the dustbin!

There is an outburst for you! But these things have been nine-tenths of my life. Thank God I have always known so and said so. I attribute the fact that I may be a better poet than TSE entirely to the fact that he has never had, I suppose—at least, not for years—that kind of life. I attribute my undoubted success as a praiser of marriage entirely—no, largely—to that. The rest has to do with your face, arms, and figure: to say nothing of your walk. I always have thought your walk superb; it skims, as much now as ever—how right that doctor was!

Well, here is a couple of paragraphs about you, and I have written myself, so, into almost a good humour, but my thumb is a bit difficult, as you will see here & there. However, that is but one of our crosses! I have sent a message to Christopher Dawson, asking if (i) the *Dublin* goes on (ii) I finish a poem, whether he will put it in. Meanwhile think of a subject for a new novel, I beg you; let it be supernatural this time, because I am more certain there. I love you. I love you. I love you.

Serge

Oxford

25 June/40

Dear Love,

I suppose you were got up? I made some small effort to telephone, but the line was engaged, and they are so particular, that I abandoned the effort: feeling that we have agreed about that. We were shaken out of sleep at half past one; I was half dressed when M. arrived in my room, also half dressed—very good and nice. We both went down-stairs, and the others came presently. Beatrice sat darning socks; Anne & Gerry played patience. Michael, after trying to read *Wuthering Heights,* curled up under his raincoat and half dozed off. And I stroked his hair in an unobtrusive way, and patted his shoulder, and turned the pages of the *Three Musketeers*, and mentally said things to you. At half past two the all clear went and we went back to bed.

Michael, having got his steam out of him, was charming, both yesterday evening & in the night. He scored heavily at dinner with a comment on George, which G.H. supported; and in the night he was really lovely—making Beatrice laugh, being nice to me, &c. As all the curtains on all the landings had been taken down for the spring-cleaning we couldn't have any staircase lights on, which was inconvenient.

On the other hand, I don't quite like the idea of M. being without either you or me in a raid; I think he would be all right, but it would take it out of him more. He hasn't—no; what I mean is, that he is surer of himself if we are about. I may be wrong about that, but that is how it strikes me. I am quite sure you should be here—for his sake as well as mine. But I have urged my sake. Anne expects you whenever—; and especially when one of us goes to London. Anyhow, do come! M. is displaying some symptoms of suggesting sleeping in my room: which I think would be a mistake. But I cannot, if he comes to it, very well refuse if you aren't in the bed! You see!

I loved your 5th columnist on the telephone, & his hissing! I hear to-day that the police are stopping people in the streets after 11 or so, & asking for their identity cards. This leaves me cold; the only time I was out after 11 was when I went to Magdalen, and Magdalen is off in the vacation unless occasionally.

To-day I raised the question—or rather Miss Peacock did—of my anthology[132] at our poor little shadow of a Publication Committee! It makes me smile & cry to see it functioning still in this bathroom. I have been a little uneasy in case paper or what not checked it—but GFJC swallowed it still quite naturally. And I said it would take a month to finish—which means 100 quotations a week, so for our dear Lord's sake find Something. Henry [133] has a number of Church writers—you couldn't spend a day with him copying out suitable bits from the right people, could you? "No," she said, "I couldn't. Mrs. C. would be coming in with confidential chat whenever H was out, & whenever he wasn't I should be being nice to him." O well, madonna, if Mrs. C. puts you off more than I put you on! I am half serious; I do want help.

Repudiating (for financial reasons only) your remarks about Courage:[134] I have counted them—they take up 36 words. I think they are quite right—but I want 7000 words: which is almost exactly two hundred times as many. Your Gloriousness will perceive the difference! 7000−36=6964 words: or, roughly, each of your words has to be extended into 199. I will miss you as often—yes, indeed! But I shall try & make the extra money!

I liked the last war better: last night I thought of Haverstock Hill[135] and the "bombling." I admit to a gratitude that M. hasn't far to go between his work

& his lodging. For me, I can see I shall more & more willingly take a bus down or up the Cowley Rd!

Don't say I never write longer letters! They are not as amusing as yours can be, but I write from my heart. God bless you.

Serge

O darling I do miss you.

Oxford
4 July/40

This will be a shorter note because I have been reading a MS. for Sir Humphrey. Also because I am in a towering rage. The MS was about Milton and attacked Eliot. Sir H. remarks to Jock that he has given it me, & Jock says: "O he won't like it! Eliot is his great idol" & Sir H.: "Ah, but he is a great Miltonian too—& which will win?" Milford told me this and I said in extreme irritation: "I suppose it doesn't occur to either you or Jock that one might decide on purely critical principles, *not* on anything else?" And anyhow—Eliot my great idol! I admire him very much; I like him immensely; but my idol!! All these people pretend to be cultured & read criticism, & after three years they . . . it is unendurable. Yet I have said, exactly & carefully, in place after place, what I thought & what I meant. . . . One might as well talk to—Germans. Well . . . I am better now. But it *is* tiresome. If it had not been for our determination over the years, I should say I was misunderstood. But that is hell's own path—to indulge that kind of nonsense; I will die first. At the same time it would be nice to have a little accuracy even in a publishing house, even among the Whigs of a dying culture. Really, darling, in these things I *have* tried to be accurate & careful, & this blather of incompetent imbecility. . . .

No! I really am better-tempered. I have fought without allies in these things all my life, & I shall go on fighting—"I did say *this;* I did *not* say that." One would think it simple, but the Oxford Press are incapable of understanding it. All right, but I shan't compromise or retreat. As you have once or twice hinted with some justice—when I am arrogant, I am arrogant. Now you disagree with me over Eliot, but you don't say silly things about what I think about him. Idol, indeed! All that Jock knows of either of us would go on a pin's head and leave three-quarters of it empty.

Bless you for listening to that tirade. On the other hand Michael & I have been doing very well this week. He & I went together to the theatre last night to see the lady he met at lunch on Sunday act; & he has written her a note about it—very charming. To-night we are to talk about his doing some reading up. He thinks it would be a good idea if he came down by the earlier train on Sunday; this is your doing. A letter from Phyllis P., sending a book, says: "I *do* admire her, & am writing to tell her so." She is still working at *Taliessin*.

I think I must read some T. to you alone when I am up next: it would be fun—& then a bus to that charming Coventry St. place?

The Ministry of Information, per Mr. Graham Greene, are inquiring after me still. "What," they say, "has happened to the pamphlet?"[136] G.G. says he is very anxious to have "something from your pen." I have replied informatively and warmly. But I am glad—it soothes my conscience. I feel that both you & I have put ourselves at the Government's disposal as it were. Up to this morning I felt you were one up on me.

You are a sweet, & this is a mingy letter. But I loose myself to you—as so often. I could do it better by voice: however——. I will permit myself to remark that this correspondence is becoming very attractive—in a sort of a kind of a way; by which, I mean a different kind of attraction from that the *Song of Solomon* talks of: which is, as one might say, more accurately descriptive of you. Your balcony is a watch-tower of Jerusalem;[137] I begin to believe the war will be deeply decided there. Basil Blackwell's doctor tells us the German soldiers he saw in France (there were *some* prisoners) were drugged with heroin. I have heard this before, but never so directly. If it comes to heroin or prayer I would rather trust myself to your prayers.

Talking of the O.U.P., our Mr. Parnwell has changed his mind & now thinks London is preferable & that we ought to be there. I said I had thought so all along—which he admitted. Unfortunately our Mr. Parnwell cuts *no* ice with Sir Humphrey or Sisam except as a kind of third footman. I will say that they misunderstand me but do not treat me like that. God bless you—love keep you.

Serge

Oxford
6 July/40

Dearest

I am thrilled[138] beyond measure. I shall ring you up on Monday evening to hear. I am promised that my 7/7/- may arrive any day, so if you want any trifle and can get it I will send you your other £3.0.0 on as soon as I do. I realized on top of a bus this morning that if you do go my solitude is going to be—what I thought it could not be—increased. But that will be part of England now.

Curtis[139] thinks my past MS. on Courage wonderful, but not with "a sufficiently wide appeal." So I have sent it to the Ministry saying "& now what?" & more or less offering Sir H. to them instead: we shall see. Nancy Pearn is said to be lunching with Greene[140] on Tuesday & she is devoted to my interests. However I may be doing an introduction to Milton[141] in the World's Classics which we are re-setting; I was shown a specimen page & the Holy Ghost moved Us to say: "would you like an Introduction by Me?"—

very haughty like, and Jock said he thought it would be a *very* good idea. He may change his mind or Sir H. may feel he can't afford it. I shall only do it if they pay—ten or fifteen guineas for 5000 words. Spoiling the Egyptians.[142] I won't—I promise you—be wilful or facetious or intellectually proud. I abhor them all; I renounce and anathematize them. But my wilfulness is really only with people like Belgion or Jock or Isabel or the rest; I do but do what I can see and write as I can. But I will do better in future even—if we live & do well.

And now I am writing about myself when I am all of "a wonder & a wild surprise"[143] about you. Of course I shall be up. I shall think of you & pray for you; and I have always been proud of you & am almost wilful with pride & arrogance about you. But the real point was to promise you the 3 pounds as soon as I get it.

Serge

Oxford
8 July/40

I have been wondering, as you may well believe! and only hoping you didn't have to sit about too long. That is always the nuisance of such places. But I shall have spoken to you before you get this (how pleasant and how odd!), so I will say no more of it now.

I have talked about week-ends down here before. I do not exactly grudge Michael his—no, I don't at all, because I realize from my own feelings what he must feel—and more indeed because he has nothing that *must* be done. In fact his and my feelings are much the same—only I conceal mine. I went to meet him yesterday, and all went well. I never knew anyone who could be at once so quick and so slow as he can. He has decided that the washing ought to go off on Monday morning, but I refused this morning, when I wasn't ex-pecting to have it handed over at 8.15 to pack! I shall wait to see if he sends it off on Mondays when I am in London.

Milton is agreed on.[144] Another pleasant note from Greene, but he hasn't my last! However, something may be done about the Ministry & Milford:[145] I shall hear in a day or two. I do feel that both you and I are trying to do the jobs we can and ought to be doing. On Sunday I wondered if I ought to vol-unteer to dig trenches—*not* at Oxford; the volunteers went an hour's journey by special buses first; it was in the Oxford paper: and took your spade if you had one. But I didn't really think I should be very good at it. So I asked you, & you (I thought) didn't encourage me.

But I ask you many things: I may get the answers wrong sometimes, but I ask all right!

All love.

Serge

Oxford

9 July 1940

I don't know—no, that's untrue; I do know—whether I am most disappointed for you or relieved for myself.[146] It would have been madness to propose to undertake all the laundry for fifteen children; and indeed I can't imagine that anyone who undertakes it won't have their hands full! But it certainly isn't for *you*. But I was disappointed "in you & for you" because I know how you feel about doing something, though I won't pretend that a vision of submarines didn't haunt my waking sleep for a day or two. I reminded myself that submarines are less dangerous than air-raids probably, but they remained (especially after the refugee ship) a little uncertain.

About tea I say nothing. I will promise not to drink too much of your mingy allowance when I come up. But at the rate things are going—though I think the Government are right: rather bombs than tea—anyone living as you have to do. (Some I mean—anyone only drawing a single ration) will be in an unbearable position——

O I was all willing that you should go but I *am* glad you're not going. So there! A very proper feeling, and patriotic too!

It is so heavy here to-day you wouldn't believe! People assert they hear German aeroplanes, but I can't distinguish the difference—if there are any Germans—and anyhow I sleep heavily most of the night, though in spite of windows on the garden one wakes unrefreshed and heavy.

Bless you—ever so much—and thank you for stopping. (That is only my personal view; I agree about England!)

Serge

[Undated]

Dearest,

I have been trying to write the essay on Fear & Courage[147] for the—or rather on the chance that H&S[148] would take it. But it is very, very stiff going! I'm not used to writing encouraging studies of Fear, & so on, & it won't stretch out as long as I want it to. Still, I shall turn to it again when I have finished this, which I shall do before 5 so as to post it. It is cold and raining here. Christopher Dawson and Barbara Ward[149] have been here, & at lunch the conversation was all international; and Anne assured me I had saved the meal by talking! A completely strange woman, known to someone who is known to the Spaldings, has been expected all yesterday and to-day from Aldershot, but she has been ringing up at intervals to say she can't get a train, & won't come till to-morrow! This is the most extraordinary house for what one might call home refugees! Michael, as he will have told you, shared my room on Friday because his was being spring-cleaned. Anne & I put back the curtains before lunch;

that is, I held the ladder and she put them up. And then Anne & I & John S. (who is here for the day) & Beatrice all put the carpet down.

I am so sleepy you would hardly believe. Why anyone made Oxford a University town I can't think! one is *always* sleepy. But I had a restless night, thinking at intervals of the South Coast house where three people were killed, and wishing (he went on persistently) that we were together! All the authorities' "Stay Put" is in the event of invasion, & not about the present. And how—to recur to your letter—Finchley is better than Golder's Green I can't think. I gather that the East Coast is being more or less evacuated so far as possible, and I wish Phyllis Potter was rather farther in. Because I think her house might get caught now either by bombs, parachutists, or something.

This, most sweet lady, is a small letter; forgive it. My thumb has lasted very well but is going a bit screwy. I shall post this. I love you; and God willing I shall be up on Friday. God bless you, & kiss *me*.

Serge

Oxford
16 July/40

And did you go to church after all for the purpose you named? it was, I could almost think, enough for you to think so; only the real answer I wish I had made would have been to ask you to do it for me and in my place: and next time you go you shall. One gives thanks perhaps better in another even than in oneself;[150] yes—it will take generations to work the great problem out, but you should not despise my doctrine—it is not a small thing to be able to flourish in some other neighbourhood, and you are a Good Samaritan of the soul. I thought Ursula was right when she called you: "Honey"; I would have called you "Honey-sweet lady"[151] myself, if I had thought of the quotation; but I was dull at Paddington and I detested Oxford when I reached it. If we get to London again I will never come back[152] here except to see a play of my own or take a degree or something of that sort. Still, to complain or repine now would be ungrateful to you and God—whom, in your degree, you resemble more every day even in your slight extremities of language—to judge by the Old Testament; there, I am more like the New. But if we form the whole Bible between us, who is to complain?

I babble. It is heavy here to-day. Michael was charming when I returned, but went a little glum about Blackwell's later; George is coming back next week and M. thinks that he must speak to G. about his poor jokes. Also he hadn't realized that he was bound to Blackwell's; so I said of course he wasn't if a much better job came along. All was peaceable however, though George has rather taken Anne's place as the Chief Villain. And I wash in cold water when I ought to wash in hot, because it's better for the skin, and because then the water would be hotter for M. afterwards. But we got on very well.

No news elsewhere. I have almost finished my short Co-inherence pamphlet,[153] at which I wrote firmly last night. I shall take it to Margaret to be typed. Meanwhile I wake thinking of you. Especially about the way we agreed over the Church. Powers of Love keep you!

Oxford

17 July/40

Madonna,

You'll be relieved to know that the great George problem, is in a fair way to be settled. M. may have told you in the enclosed. Basil saw M. yesterday and said he shouldn't stop where he was, but should be moved soon. This relieved our son's feelings and he took a brighter view. It relieved mine too; I had been faintly alarmed at the prospect of either soothing M. or having to speak to Basil.

Tonight he and I—and G.H.—are going to Mr. New's to see his great collection of—things to do with cinemas & theatres. I am, happily, not supposed to be interested in the cinema, but the theatrical things are to be shown me. G.H. has seen them all twice, but he has to go because some-one he knows is staying with New. However, it had to be sooner or later, and I shall get it over. Afterwards I feel it will be a long time before I go again.

Raymond is delighted with Margaret's letter. He has replied joyously, but (as I foresaw) with every intention of seeing that she now does something more. I don't quite know what—but I suspect that he looks forward to having a collaborator in the great task of collating, editing, and generally preparing for posterity the whole Canon[154] of Our work. He assumes that she is quite right in collecting all she can in drafts and temporary versions: "any point in the advances of such minds is valuable." I think this has pleased her; I only hope it won't vaguely upset her mother. If it does, I shall correct it. "It is the voice of a god" (be it said with reverence) "Not of a man."[155] O darling, how fantastic the world! But I am honestly glad about M.D.; she needs some exterior cords, and the more she can feel she is *doing* something, the better.

Hubert[156] is down here to-day—AND talking, so that my hearing and my mind are a little distracted. (This is where we leave off writing [page missing]

Oxford

18 July/40

A little faint from doing the Income Tax Return—& hoping that the reduction in income will cancel the extra tax, which it certainly ought—I turn homeward, as it were, to you: contemplating your Goodness's goodness to the charwoman. How lovely for her that she met you! But indeed it is a sad story—especially the contrast between the two children. When I think of all your acts of this kind I see you entering heaven between two lines of candles, each candle a separate star of deeds, and all the angels humming a Gloria. All the same—must I part with my suit? it isn't split yet, and I have sometimes changed into it to save my others; not expecting ever to have any more suits at all. If you say so, I will be good of course . . . but. . . .

It is now the afternoon of the 18th. A month ago we all heard that the famous German entry into London was staged for the 20th.[157] Under God, it looks as if the time-table was getting a bit delayed. I think the same source that talks of Friday for the grand attack put the number at 600,000; if they can manage a million and a half of the English army—no; this is not optimism, because they can't surely wait long now. But I talk at random; let us leave it.

I hear that Dr. Barclay who owns this house has been trying to sell it to Sir H. as permanent quarters for us. I hear also that Sir H. has firmly refused: he will not come back till the war ends and he will not stop in Oxford when the war ends. It is a small mercy, but it is a mercy. You and I will dine out on the first evening of the Return and drink our first glass of wine in silence to the memory of our week-ends. I was thinking of them when I climbed our lane this morning. I was also thinking that I will send you by Michael a cheque made out for the end of the month for the £10 for next month; then I should know you had it and could change it if necessary. If not, you could give it back to me and I would change it myself. By "if necessary" I mean if posts *were* at all delayed.

Isabel has bought your two books to give to the Winifred Berry who was at lunch with them and Michael on Sunday and who is interested in children. Isabel wanted to send her something on the first night of the Revue and didn't want to send flowers because W.B. had brought flowers to *her*. So she went off to the Depot and bought the books and left them at the Playhouse. W.B. was very pleased. I. is writing to you to tell you, but I thought I would too!

We looked at the New collection last night—a curious devotion, all made up of pages torn from periodicals, about film-stars, & a few theatrical people. I got away, as it were, with Henry Irving, which was not too bad; and M. was satisfied with my behavior—praise God!

More important—I have done the pamphlet on the co-inherence,[158] and propose to do the Milton introduction[159] during the week-end, or most of it. Gillette has sent back *Courage*[160] saying they are most interested and will I finish it and let them see it, but (naturally) promising nothing—blast him! However I probably shall, but I *think* Milton had better be first, because I have GFJC's promise for that. Meanwhile I am getting slowly bored with the Christian doctors.[161]

And I love you, and you are sweet. I think I dislike Michael coming up—but he needs it, bless him! He has really been very nice—and he is always very nice when he wakes in the morning—and what with bubbling about this and the other I have never spoken about your agonizing back! It was such a shame! and I hate your suffering alone—& at all. It was good of it to let you carry me to St. Albans; I am glad we went, and I am glad you haven't to think of going on Saturday. It would have been too much anyhow with M. coming up.

It is suggested that we should have cocoa at 4 in the afternoon!

Serge

Oxford
19 July/40

Miss Peacock asserts that what I have just been drinking at 4 o'clock is *not* Camp Coffee, but Coffee Essence. It seems to me a pretty foul substitute for tea, & I think of you & your Mrs. O. with warm sympathy. I suppose I would rather have it than nothing; it is not so bad while one is actually drinking it—but afterwards the taste lingers on one's palate like a bad dream—the sweetened horror of something that is as unlike your coffee as it is diabolically *like*. Hitler has injured me up to now, but now he has insulted me. . . .

In the night I woke, or was awaked, about two, by a noise that sounded exactly like a bomb—a thud and a boom. I listened and wondered all in a breath if M. had heard it, and heard him stir, as I thought. So I opened the door into his room, but he was fast asleep, and there was no sound of planes or of guns, and silence in the house. After dithering round for a few minutes—not wanting to scare him and all being still still (if you follow me) I at last went back to bed. In the morning I found that G.H. had heard it too; and now we have found out what it was. A soda-water factory caught fire and had a few little explosions all to itself—compressed air, I should think! But quite harmless! I was very glad I hadn't disturbed M. Of course I should have done if I had heard anything more. Half the inhabitants of Oxford must have jumped. But we all Kept our Heads and Stayed Put.

I understand that every road into Oxford has been barricaded, with iron gates to go across the roads and concrete blocks, and the hedges partly cut down. Very proper, of course; but it makes me (if possible) yearn even more for home. Miss P., Mr. Budgen, & I have just been reciting a Psalm—"By the waters of Babylon we sat down and wept: when we remembered thee O Zion!"[162] Though, as I pointed out, I always use the plural Zions: one for the earthly Zion which is London, one for the heavenly Zion which is you. Mr. B. had not thought of saying that about *his* wife. Ha!

Love. And then Love. It is raining hard; & M. & I are going to see a tragic film. What fun we do have!!

Serge

Oxford

24 July/40

A long discussion here is just over on how we manage the Government's tax on books—all of us really brooding over the government's tax on ourselves. If they are going to cut at the source, it means that next year I shall get only £31 a month, under the present rate. There is something to be said for this method; it will leave us, when we have settled to it, without huge lumps to deal with twice a year: and we are doubly fortunate—thanks to you—that we don't run bills or have any other heavy payments. What no-one is clear about is whether this is in addition to the January payment of £50; whether the cutting is for the July payment. The government will want to get its money clear in advance; however. . . .

I didn't mean to break into that; praise God that, with all its faults, the O.U.P. has never gone in for cutting down its staff. There must be a number of oldish men in small publishers & booksellers wondering this morning if they ought to try munitions. And praise God—with all the difficulties—that M. *is* in a job, which he is at least holding down! And finally praise God that HSM won't stop here after the war! Get through the adjustments of next year, and I think we may be easier!

I shall send you a pound to-morrow; I am sure . . . there was an interruption there . . . they are going to move all the Barclays' furniture. This bathroom will look like a bare barn; & the gas-fire is going too! I suppose they will put another in. But I am not sure that I shan't move out on to the landing behind the curtain, and suggest that this room shall be given up to the typists out there. It would be too ridiculous for me to keep this to myself, & I would rather move than have someone else in. It is cold and horrid here to-day.

I am sorry I made the suggestion about M.; if anyone returns I should leave him to it (at least anyone but Anne!) But I don't feel safe at leaving him with G.H.! —which means alone most of the time. I have been contemplating it with uncertainty and gloom. Perhaps I will ring you up to-morrow—only to hear you. Anyhow the next week I shall come up on Friday, & we can have a few hours together on Saturday. I suppose M. & I must go back together on Monday: we are closing for the Bank Holiday here.

O this is so dull & fussed a letter—it is only a slight feeling of oppression and wondering what to do. And Budgets. And these defensive and valuable but recuring aeroplanes. And tiredness with everyone here. And not having you. I shall stop now or I shall make you miserable. But (as you say) it's nice to write and talk to you.

If M. does find it dull, & difficult, I don't wonder; I occasionally HATE the drawing-room!! But "time and the hour run through the roughest day."[163] Without you, how much more terrible it would all be!

Serge

29 July/40

I thought of your back & hoped it was not too painful. Saturday was nice.

Darling,

All went well. Michael was charming; he said at Paddington that it was nicer to go down with me than by himself, and quite lived up to this, all the way. I admit that by the time we got down it struck even me that a meal would not be a bad thing, but he was fed and talked to by the Ds, who urge him to go in whenever he comes down & they are there, whether I am there or not. I have promised to encourage him to this, because (it was put to me) you would like to know he was reasonably comfortable and because they like him. So he was very agreeable all the evening and went off to Gilbert Murray's happily this morning.

We hear that bombs were dropped near Woodstock last night. I was told that there was an explosion at 2.30 which I didn't hear, and there was an odd kind of continuous reverberation at a quarter to eight, which sounded like guns at a distance. I was in a bath, but it was too distant to be alarming. Nothing in the papers so far (3.30) about the Midlands: they may know more to-night.

The Players—as represented by Ruth & John—full of adoration for you. I have observed before that it is generally recognized in the England of to-day that the one practically certain way of getting me to do anything is to pray to God to move you to suggest it. I may do things you do not suggest, but certain publishers do, or indeed that I think of myself. But that I shall not accept your High Lordliness's suggestions or *dicta* is unheard-of. I regard this attitude on the part of what St. Paul would have called "the world" as very beautiful and quite accurate. Ever since I came home one Saturday, years ago, & told you I had been asked to do a play for Canterbury & they might not pay much, and you said that of course it must be done. Do you remember how you and Michael saw me off on my first visit from—Victoria, was it? The first morning of my Dramatic Career? Well, kiss me then!!!

I shall stop at that.

Serge

Oxford

7 August/40

Herewith, as one might say, an Instalment. I owe you the rest for the hat besides what I borrowed at Paddington. But that shall come later, when your need is greater: and that rhyme ought to belong to "Poems to an Insufficiently Supplied Wife"—a series contributed to by practically every English poet of standing, some time or other.

I have mentioned your coming. Anne thinks it would be delightful. On the Friday. She is going to ? Haynes, wherever that is, on the Sunday, but she is anxious that you shall forgive *that*. It also looks as if the P.P.[164] might be in

Cornwall and Gerry away. This would be marvellous; I would get some time, & we need do nothing!

The Ds. hope that you, or you & I, will dine, & also that you & M. & I will dine & go to the last night of the Revue on the Saturday. Isabel looks forward to seeing you; I have said that we bought you a hat, & she was very pleased. The only thing she wants me to buy for myself is a torch!!

Apropos—the Milford baby was received into the Mercy yesterday: may its soul find peace! So that question won't rise.

M. is rather glum again over George who has been heavily cultural. But otherwise well.

Your letter this morning was lovely!

Serge

8 August/40

Darling,

("And why is there not another pound note?" said she. And he could not think except that he had not got it in his pocket! But we will talk of *that* another time!)

I am sorting up all the extracts for the Xtn. anthology.[165] There are about 500 & I have a feeling I said 600. I have settled the Christian Year as far as Septuagesima, & I shall return to it soon, because it takes a long time, and it must be done by next week. (The curious look of this writing is due to the use of an ordinary pen with a thin nib, *and* an ink bottle.)

Tonight M. is going to the Randolph & the theatre. And I have agreed to go with Anne to Headington to see the new cast in *Terror.* I understand it is very good—or at least much better. But I still think it is *not*—so far—a very good play, and I want to rewrite it. I think I must dedicate that to you—for fun, pleasure, and to make everything perfect. Perfection, I realize, is not a thing one easily understands, though one thinks one does.

But does Madame agree to your dropping the treatment? and do you? Because I can produce the cash if we agree. I am glad we thought of holidays together— one of these days we will go again to (a) the sea (b) Bath (c) Chester (d) Cornwall (e) Canterbury (f) Rumford—or wherever it was we went on the famous bus journey where the bus conductor kept changing his mind about the fare!!

Serge

Oxford

9 Augt/40

Odd things happen! Sir Humphrey has just been talking to me about destroying his & his wife's letters to each other—he thought some thousands of them. He has had a lot of his furniture moved down here & there was a half-sackful of letters which he hadn't reached. It was when he was looking at the sack that I ran into him, and he began talking. He says he has still to deal with letters written by the children. I found myself feeling more tender towards him than usual. He says his wife & he had always talked about doing it and never done it.

Wardrobes & chests of drawers have gone out of my office, & some shelves & a better chair came in. But it still looks an odd BATHROOM & nothing else; you shall see it next week. Ruth babbled about paying me last night, but nothing has so far happened. It seems that in December (if all goes well!) they are coming to some church in London: if so, I will come up & we will go & see the two short plays. They would like *Good Fortune* lengthened by ten minutes. Abraham strikes Ruth as a very good idea—everyone is devoted to you. I keep on saying rather coldly that I had not had any serious idea of doing them *until* you spoke. But even now I am no nearer the Holy Ghost.

Then the idea is that if I choose to rewrite *Terror* in verse & longer they should aim at doing that in London, if at all possible, next Whitsun. That *would* be rather agreeable—if the war were going well! Re-organized & in verse, it might even be a mild religious success!!

And I think it is wonderful of you to drink that coffee. And I want to see the Hat. And I will send you another pound as soon as I can. I love you.

Serge

Oxford

14 Augt./40

The Professor of Poetry[166] invites us to sherry with him in his rooms at Magdalen on Friday at 6. I have accepted for both of us. Don't say that the officially great do not rush to welcome you! I am sorry not to have an invitation from the Chancellor of the University—but as he happens to be Lord Halifax,[167] and is presumably looking after the Foreign Office, you may excuse him! Anyhow I shall be at the station on Friday morning. We then go to S.P.Rd. & drop your things. We then go to the Randolph for lunch. We then go to Southfield House for Miss P.[168] & tea. We then go to Magdalen for sherry, & back to S.P.Rd for dinner. On Saturday you and I blow away quietly for awhile and we all go to the Revue in the evening.

John Spalding is back till Saturday. The Aunt is coming down to-day for the day. She is (did I tell you?) proposing to come for a week—the week M. is in town. Anne comes back to-day.

I loved your story about Madame. They say Portsmouth has suffered, but Bath only in the outskirts. It is credibly reported that the R.A.F. are yearning for mass attacks, and if they can keep up the proportion of 75 to 14 I don't wonder. The King ought to give your vest to the best R.A.F. fighter aircraft as a mascot: "the white plume of Navarre"[169] kind of thing.

No-one sends me any books or money or letters or praise. But you shall comfort me when you come. I shan't write to-morrow in case you have left home for our 9.45. Till then!!

Serge

Oxford
21 August/40

Dearest,

It is a shame you were not here to-day, because the cheque for £37 came, & it would have been amusing to have spent the odd 2/- —no, I think it is for 37/12/- —the odd 14/- —on a drink. I shall send £36.18 to the Inland Revenue; & I shall buy a pen with the odd. I am now bare, but all is settled until the month's end. If Chichester[170] pays we shall have the insurance, & *that* will be done.

A quotation from Housman's *Victoria Regina:*[171]

"The Prince Consort: The Prince is now eighteen—a difficult age.

Dr. Stanley: Yes, Sir, as those who have lived through it know.

The Prince: I lived through it without any difficulty, Dr. Stanley.

Dr. S.: Then your Highness was a happy exception.

The Queen: Of course he was, Dr. Stanley.["]

There! M. was quite agreeable on our way back. I went to my barber's, & then back to S.P.Rd. to get my umbrella & a book. I ran into Beatrice & gave her 5/- with your compliments, regards, & gratitude. On arriving at the office & finding the cheque, I decided that this had been Meant. We have never lost by being free-handed. When I think of how people have loved us, as it were, with money, I feel that we have done better, in freedom and friendship, than the more cautious kind of people—like the Pages (only he is in this Bathroom, & I feel a little awkward even writing it!!). Let us continue, my angel: we are Ourselves and have always lived, as far as we can, magnificently—we who write about our marriage for posterity and do things as We choose, you & I. We are Elizabethans, not Victorians!!

Well—it was a good time, in spite of everything. If you want to go to Madame, do! I shall [page missing]

22 Augt/40
Oxford

(A nice town, I am told, by people who have been there. I knew a woman once who found it bearable, but she had spent a week-end with her husband there, and he liked it better afterwards! You might tell her that sometime when you are looking in the glass.)

I shall send a cheque for the gas—exchange & so on—when I have paid the other cheques in. Very wonderful & good, *I* think, much less than I thought it might be. And convenient. Bless you!

I have arranged that M. is to go & see Hubert[172] next week (raids allowing) at 12.00 Tuesday at Amen House, the music door. M. has been talking of studying for film Publicity, as you know; and Hubert knows people. Be at ease; there is nothing immediately to be done, but a short chat about it with H.— or possibly with someone else—would cheer him by suggesting that I am not oblivious of his needs. M. wants to write to God knows who, but I do not really think that is a good idea, and if we can "substitute" some other movement, that may serve. He says he does not expect anything yet, and if he can be generally eased by *something* happening, it is all to the good. It will give you a couple of hours off anyhow! There was a difficulty with George yesterday, in which I really think M. was right. But he did not behave too badly, and the last thing he said this morning was: "ask God that I may do the right thing."

Miss Harris[173] & I conversed. She knows masses of people & was pleasant. She is obviously about to embark on a course of me. (Which reminds me that Auden[174] has written again. He says he is trying to learn more of practicing the Presence, but it is hard. He wishes I were there, & his day dream is that I shall be moved to the [page missing]

Oxford

23 Augt/40

We hear, Serene Angel, that you had an alarm[175] in the night—from 3.30 to 5. I cannot hear as yet that any damage was done, and our people report that trains are running regularly, so I hope it was no more than tiresome, and that you were not too tired . . . that it was not too cold and that you got a seat. Do go to Madame *whenever* you think well; I will send money at once.

All was quiet here, which in a way annoys me. I do not like being safe if you aren't!

I have heard from Phyllis that the Chingford Conference[176] is still on. She was asked to send me the subject which is "The Sovereignty of God." So I shall come up two Fridays running—the 6 and 13th—presumably; go to Chingford on the Saturday 14th, come up on Monday 16th. What about your coming? It will all be Religious, & I don't know where we are to be put up or if it will be comfortable. But what about it? Can you bear hearing me speak on Religion for (I think) three separate hours? It might—otherwise—be fun; and anyhow it would be another experience to add to our necklace. Do come!

I have almost finished the anthology,[177] and done the *Dublin* review.[178] Tonight I shall try & do the other *Time & Tide* one: on Sunday I shall attend to the poem; next week to the book I design for Burns and (I think) to *Magic;* then the plays. Which we might discuss again.

And I love you very much!

Serge

Oxford

29 Augt/40

I have given orders that efforts are to be made to get through to you later, & if it succeeds so much the better. But I shall write now. I have just heard that you had a seven-hours alarm.[179] You can't go on being exposed to this: if we were together in London it would be another thing, but you will have no sleep at all. I lay awake myself listening to the continual planes and wondering about you, but it is one thing to lay awake in a bed and another to sit in a shelter: and to be alone at these times is nerve-racking. Come down with M. on Sunday; come & listen to aeroplanes along o' me!

I send the 10/- h/w as a gesture of devotion. I shall be a little lost, it seems to me, as far as my own cash for the month goes, by Saturday, but the gas bill might have been another ten shillings, so you ought to have this—yes, I assure you. God knows what will happen—but we *have* got through a year, and God & the Fish's Mouth . . . .[180]

I am very glad M. is all cool during raids. I shall meet him on Sunday at 11.42 (Oxford) & I think he & I had better have a quiet lunch somewhere—all three of us, if you would do what I urge!

O it's all very strange! (But I am glad M. is seeing someone—& H again. It fills a little satisfaction for him.)

No personal news: no letters or reviews or books. Thoughts about you instead.

Serge

Oxford

30 Augt/40

Yes—as Sunday draws near I find myself a little inclined to determine to be "understanding." I hope I shall do better than only to determine so, but I feel that an "all-seeing Eye" will now be over me, and a courteously critical Voice about my path and (more especially) about my Bed. Still, I am relieved that M has not shown undue concern about the raids.

I was immensely touched by your saying that they did not worry you—which seemed to be merely a part of your general Virtue. But for you to be alone under the brutes does worry me; I go all of a dither thinking of you—& I wish to ring you up first thing every morning. This morning I woke at seven, & for some reason remembered that on Fridays St. Cross has a celebration at 7.30—so I thought I had better go . . . not, I mean, having any excuse not to. So I did. G.H. was on guard from 6–8 in the courtyard opposite!

I shall probably go to Magdalen to-night. I haven't seen Lewis for two weeks & shan't for the next two—fortunately. I shall be doing something better next week, I hope! They are good for my mind, I know, but I have always said that all enjoyments depend on your centredness, which, in fact, I *have* always said—in private and public. Dream of that over . . . what meal you have next!!

And I hope to-night you sleep—& Berlin is awake *all* night. I meant to kiss yesterday's ten shillings, but didn't. I will kiss this instead.

Serge

Oxford

1 Sept/40

M. arrived safely and full of pleasure in the air-raids! So far he has suppressed anti-Oxford except for announcing that if Oxford is raided he shall go back to London; he will not be raided down here dully. But that can wait. We had lunch at the George—he & I—& then we went to Blackwell's & it was shut! We hung about for an hour till 3, but it was still shut, so we came back and upstairs to go to sleep. I suppose they changed their arrangements. But it was just as well for him to be down, as even he thinks!

He said not to ring you up. I spent part of yesterday trying to get through and failed—and when the first half of his train came in without him I *was* a little anxious, especially as no letter arrived on Saturday. But I realize that we must put up with that sort of thing, & calmed my spirits; & then he arrived with your note (and the rent note! I have made out a cheque for Anne, leaving out this week for M., for £4—she won't let me pay anything for you being down— & for the I.T. £36, & for the rent £11. Oddly, there doesn't seem much left.) M. reminds me it is a year to-day[181] since he first saw South Parks Rd. and a year then on Wednesday since we thought we might be parting for ever. Well!

I have spent so much time on M that this is short. Two young Russian girls to tea; M. is having his at ease in my room! (He thinks Anne should have offered to send it up, but I solved the problem by taking it!!)

All love

Serge

Oxford

3 Sept/40

You, I fear, were up most of the night. We heard bombs in the near distance somewhere before twelve, & Michael said should we dress & go downstairs, but I discouraged it at least until a warning. We have heard enough sounds of bombs now to feel there is nothing much to be done about it. It still gives me a faintly odd feeling, & a kind of suspicion that the next may be nearer, but one can't dress every time: & so God take all.

I have heard nothing officially from the Diocesan Youth, but if it comes off I think that the thing to do would be to go to Phyllis on the Friday, and come back to London on the Sunday after Conferring.[182] It would suit her, and be as good as not for us. I shall write to her if I hear, & in a day or two if I don't.

I don't even know who the Chairman is! Nor do I know what the "Sovereignty of God" quite covers. It will be odd to go on talking through a raid.

It is very hot & close here, & I am tired and sleepy. Blackwell & G.H. & I have been talking about the future of bookselling & publishing—about which we were all pessimistic. It would be funny if M's passion for films really was of use to him, after all. But I still feel the Press in America is the ideal place for him.[183]

Your Friday's letter only reached—O I told you. I will probably do something about Fr. Clare. I must pull myself together & get on, but I may feel more like it after the next week-end. I shall bring—no, perhaps I shan't: *Witchcraft* I was going to say, but I think 3 days—or 2 days & 3 nights' laze—is what I need. With you. God bless you.

Serge

Oxford
13 September/40

Dearest,

I think I had better send you the other pound *now,* and so I do; I have ordered the bus services to be enquired after, and you shall have them as soon as I hear. I have also posted the insurance. This leaves Anne to be dealt with for 4 weeks at the end of the month, which will be £11, but the *Dublin* will, I hope, help there, and there will be a little from *T&T.* Anyhow everything will be clear.

I see there was another 8 hours last night, but I hope you slept. I was very much badgered with a mental picture of our beloved flat, and with a sense of guilt in leaving it. But one hears such tales of bodies found in ruins that, after my earlier experiences of you left in London, it is clear I could not have stood it.[184] Sir Humphrey was rung up from London to be told that the house where Pippa and her friend were living was débris, but that the two bodies brought out were not theirs. It seems they had gone to Kettering; he rushed over yesterday. He got back last night & came up to ask after you this morning. So I told him you were coming on here next week, but that you were safe so far.

Michael very good and intensely relieved in secret. On placable terms with the Aunt, & still very pleased with his desk and present work. I was so sorry to have disturbed you yesterday afternoon, my blessing, but when I heard the lines had been damaged I was frightfully anxious to know whether you had even got to Lutterworth. No telegram yet, so you can see I could not have heard otherwise!

The Woodford conference is cancelled; a telegram this morning—48 hours in delivery—to say so. Any more news? No, I think not. I am infinitely your servant and your devoted

Serge

Oxford

15 Sept/40

Blessed one

—that beginning is probably due to my just having been to church. I only woke at 8.20 so I have been to St. Cross by myself at 11. Fr. Curtis of Mirfield is coming in to see me at 3; he is taking a retreat at Oxford in the Banbury Rd., & coming to South Parks Rd this afternoon. (M. & I are dining with the Douglases to-night as it is Sunday evening!) Anne & the Aunt are cooking the dinner!

Speaking of the Ds. reminds me that Margaret is very anxious for me not to feel I must pay her back the £5. I told her we had gone in taxis & so on, and that you and I had been able to do a little quicker in getting round than otherwise. So she almost cried (poor darling!!) and said if she had been any use to you and me it was all she wanted, and if it had helped to take you out of danger it was more than she hoped. So I said you would say the same thing as soon as you saw her, and that might be next week.

Talking of danger reminds me that I seemed to think yesterday I hadn't seen Page about. So I made inquiries and gathered that he had been sent for to London because the house where his sister was living had been smashed—to do something. The sister, I gather, had rushed to Welwyn. Mrs. Budgen has, very reluctantly, come down here for a few days—until the raids ease up a bit. I haven't seen her, but Budgen told me. Only Miss Peacock goes on saying she would rather be back even now. From this morning's papers I am not clear whether they had an all night one last night. And in writing this I forgot the one o'clock news!!

I enclose a slip about the buses. But on looking at it I see that it only gives a morning bus; I think there must be an afternoon one from Leicester, & steps shall be taken to find out. If it is for the week-end one has to book 3 days in advance, but there is no reason why it should be week-end. I propose Thursday—if you can bear to travel again so soon. Anyhow you are always expected and wanted here—"at any hour of any day or any night," to use Anne's phrase.

[Unsigned]

Oxford

17 Sept/40

Lovely! as I remember the bus reaches Oxford at about 12.30. I will meet it then— but if the time is different you might have a heart & send me the actual time. I couldn't bear *not* to meet you. We will discuss everything then.[185]

Michael is very upset about going back to George & the old books. We spent an hour on the subject last night, but we got along very well, which was something, and he didn't behave at all badly. It is the dust and the running about and George's high-falutin' which worry him. He is going to write to you. He was (he says) just beginning to like Oxford & to feel good-tempered;

which is true enough—& now he feels thrown back again. However, he & I agreed we would try and deal with it together, and he asked about some prayers to say, & I promised that if it went on too many weeks I would speak to B.B. So I hope for the best.

We heard a bomb some distance off at 11.30 last night, but no alarms. I feel so tired & sleepy to-day you wouldn't believe. But you and I will have a pleasant time as we did before. Under present conditions I *should* like you with me on my Day.[186]

God bless.

Serge

Oxford
25 Sept /40

Dearest,

I have rarely been more relieved[187] than when I found it was you on the telephone this morning. I had had the darkest visions, and (as I said before) nightmares about you. This, one would think, one should not do about one's wife, though most people would say it was right and natural. But I (if you will forgive the phrase) "have not so learned Christ."[188] The more important the thing—the person—the image (in my own vocabulary) the nearer it must be to the idea of God, so that it should be easier to feel it there: in which case, though one might be anxious, one wouldn't have bad dreams. It ought to be easier to live from God or peace in marriage than anywhere else; and indeed I think we do live from a kind of peace: and the poem[189] I put in *Taliessin* about Bors & Elayne was a kind of suggestion of it—since Bors was the married Lord of the Quest; and her name is the same (without the symbolical aspirate) as that of the predestined Mother of Galahad.

All this, however, is only a meditation arising out of the week-end; and I do not know that you can very well complain if you are the cause of poems on marriage as the Good Life instead of on yourself directly: no, I do not. Everyone else observes the relation. Another poet might have done it another way; he would have been a lesser. So that if you become a Doctrine,[190] well, it cannot be helped.

I write at more ease than I could have done last night. I took M. to the pictures, as he seemed (like me) gloomy over you, & we came back, & God gave us sleep. London & Berlin seem to be hitting at each other. Ursula is now with her mother & sister at her uncle's- 1 Frognal[191] [page missing]

Oxford
27 Sept/40

What a morning! Your letter about your being bad—my poor love!—has been followed here by the Income Tax Assessment. This works out at £15 for each month from the end of November to the end of April; & £11 from May to October. Even I had not expected so much. I am going to write to them about one item, but I have no hope of it making any difference. But to have, so far as I can see, only £26 a month—£11 rent; £6 (say for the moment) you; £12 Anne—makes £29 less M's £2.10, which makes it almost equal. So my subsistence £1 a week & my reviews—say altogether an average of £6 a month will have to cover everything else, till the end of April. Not so good.

Don't think I am too depressed! I was a little shaken certainly, but I shall pull through somehow. There will be the Fish's mouth; someone will take a book, we will hope; and we will hope Ruth will pay something for the 3 plays if I do them; and the *Dublin* will take an article or two. But must we work! Thank God M. is in some sort of job, whether he likes it or not.

I have cheered up, having written it down. There will be no enormous sums to find, and if I am driven for a pound or so Margaret will always supply it, & the Insurance is there for the moving & to give us, as it were, a fresh start next September. There will be the club money between us at Christmas—and when you come here[192] for good you & I will manage our private expenses on the extras. So altogether I am still high, but I had to pour it out to you as I always have done. It doesn't begin the deductions till the end of November, so we have a few weeks to turn in.

Forgive this: and don't think I am overweighted. It will save much to have it vanish—though £26 instead of £41 rather hit me at first. But I love you and you love me and God is in his heaven.[193]

Serge

Oxford
8 October/40

I may ring you up to-morrow from here—because some-one else can do the getting-through—& see what you think. You do write the most delicious letters; I can't think how you manage it, nor why I can't. Each to his own genius and why don't you *now* consider, plan, & write the long-talked of novel? Do, sweet; it would be marvelous: why didn't I suggest it before?

Sir Humphrey has been up to say he joined the Press at Oxford 40 years ago to-day. We talked of his retiring, & he said at first that if it were not for a few of us he would, but he rather altered this afterwards, and wondered whether he would be happy if he did. He asked after you, (obviously touched to the heart by your sympathy with him).

The Aunt has gone back today. She told me when we were alone that she had never been frightened before, but she thought she ought to look after her two men there; the girls didn't need her, though two or three years ago they would have done. But obviously she feels the home runs itself, so to speak, and she isn't *needed*. I forbore to point out to her my profound conviction that only when one has left off demanding to be *needed* can one be profoundly useful. Anne attributes the success of this week-end to my "balm-in-Gilead,"[194] and both Anne and I attribute all to your sublime charity. So there.

We have instead one Russian serving in the Belgium forces now quartered in Britain, and are to have two German refugees working on the *Christian News-Letter*. All temporarily. The Russian left Tenby at 2.30 yesterday and reached Oxford at 5 this morning.

Michael sends his love and will write soon. So do I, and have written. Blessings.

Serge

Oxford
16 Oct /40

Darling,

It was not only because I was at dinner that I didn't speak last night; it was to give M. a free time. His financial difficulties are a little weighing on his mind: he is beginning to think in terms of paying "at the end of the month," & I have shyly pointed out that this will run away with most of his own money—which was so obvious that even M. could hardly deny it, and went off somewhat gloomily. The London visit has revived an anti-Oxford feeling. I really do think it's as well that you are *not* there,[195] even from that point of view!

Much more—O but much more!—from others. We hear that the last two nights have been the worst yet; I dare not dwell on them. The Mediterranean cheered me up a little. I am sure we are doing the right thing and the best thing, but it is difficult. I have refused Marylebone—but I should like some of our things. However, I think of how sweet and good you are being (O you are!) and that comforts me.

Another letter from our Mr. Auden,[196] who is now of the opinion that I "have a Divine gift as a teacher" and that "one day the *Dove* will be known for the great book it is." He has gone all Christian and is composing verse under your husband's influence—he sends me four poems and says so. Also he prays that I may be kept safe from bombs. I am quite moved by this. He is, I find, only 33; still he is a good poet and a well-known. Thus we—you & I—"move the minds that move the world." Like what Macaulay said of Francis Bacon.

I spent much of last night labouring on Witchcraft—the worst is that I must, I fear, write the last chapter again. But I have drafted most of it; tell Alicia so. Tell her that a firm offer for 250 copies would be a good idea!!

I love you. I love your letters. I love your lips.

Serge

Oxford

8 Nov./40

The great problem to-day is: what does C.W. do next? One of our people has
just been pushed out of the Army or something & has returned to us. He has
temporarily taken up the window table in my room. (And what will Hubert
say when he comes down?) Now—do I do nothing? No. Do I move? Yes, if I
can. I have my eye on Jock's old bathroom, and I propose, if nothing else happens, to make motions towards turning its present occupier out, and taking
that over. Its present occupier has it to himself. I would much rather have a
smaller room to myself than this room with the less distinguished. But soft
and gently! I remember there is a war on; I remember I must be abnegatory
(your word, madonna!) But I have every intention of abnegating across the
landing, if necessary, rather than here. That ought to be entirely adequate—
except to the fellow I turn out. But I don't see how he can very well shout—
he being obviously inferior to me in standing! and if I can snatch a room—
under present conditions—I shall.

Not that I will not still remain a little detached! I do try not to depend on
external things too much: not from pride, but from a sense of absurdity.
Also—& this is pride, I know—I do not move unless I am fairly sure to win!

I shall send you *He Came Down*, because I have my copy at S. Parks Rd, and
it is entirely at your disposal. The *Dove* I will see about sending for. Your Highness (I mean that, as I hope you know) has always been very sweet about that.
. . . I have sent a messenger round Oxford to warn them about Alicia's book.
BUT I have not yet read it myself—shall I, now?—Give Alicia my love and tell
her I am delighted that she and the author agree with the Holy Apostolic See
of Rome; for the Roman Church takes exactly the same view! I do myself agree
with you. I think the practice dubious but hardly Satanic—but say anything
you think will please her, and I will confirm it when I come.

We had several bombs last night, and a good deal of air activity, but no warning, & the bombs were at a distance. I am going with Michael to *Elizabeth and
Essex* to-night—I should rather like to see it—but early, and we shall be back
long before any raids begin. (Yes, indeed!)

I was distressed about the back—though after Tuesday I feel it was threat-
ening. It was a dreadful journey. I shall come to L. at the end of the month—
and with any luck I shall send you some money before then. And all my love!

Serge

Oxford
11 Nov./40
(Armistice Day—
coo!)

All your letters arrived this morning: now is not that agreeable for me? I am always anxious when I do not hear, though I know what chances there are against it!

I am causing my copy of *He Came Down* to be dispatched to you to-day; it has a little poem in the beginning, composed in this bath-room—the first, I see, is to be the last of mine in this room: Jock and I & everyone, by which I mean indeed only Miss P., for no-one else has been asked, have, it seems, decided that I shall abandon this to two or three lesser creatures, and I shall move to the smaller bathroom opposite. It will perhaps be warmer; this is chilly & rather draughty these days, and it looks out over the front door; so if there is any coming & going one may even see some of it. Contrariwise one hears more of the typists in other offices; & (a more serious matter!) I do not know where we shall wedge Sir Humphrey's chair, which to leave behind for the lesser ones would be unwise, for I should hardly be forgiven. I do not much mind the change, especially as I have always felt this was absurdly large when Hubert was *not* here. When he is, NOTHING is too large. But I do not know exactly *when* I shall go—All that is a parenthesis breaking in on the poem: 'tis but a small thing, but I hope you may do me the honour to like it. I will see about the *Dove,* if you would like that too.

Lincoln[197] has sent alternative ways; one goes, it seems, to Nottingham and then to Grantham and then to Lincoln; leaving Oxford at 11 and reaching Lincoln at 4.30 or so—this is a much better way. And one comes back, mysteriously, viâ Sheffield. So I shall embark rather gloomily, and eat & drink when & as possible. On Friday one leaves Sheffield apparently at 12.7 (if one does) & reaches Oxford at 4.33, so presumably one doesn't! Let us hope the ordinands will be grateful, & after congregations benefit.

The B.B.C.[198] have written inviting me to take part in a literary series they have on: it has involved, or will involve, TSE & Hugh Walpole[199] & L.A.G. Strong[200] [page missing]

Oxford
19 Nov/40

I have been delayed in writing because Sir Humphrey is going round in a series of private interviews, discovering our financial positions. Because if the war goes on too long "it may not be possible" to keep up the payments to everyone. All rather vague, but he hated the job! He feels that some people are doing better than others: he even mentioned F.P.[201] who, he said, had lost nothing by the situation, whereas obviously others had. So I went very frank, &

disclosed my all, as it were—flat and everything, including Michael at Blackwell's, who (he said) couldn't be getting anything appreciable yet. He asked if I were paying about two guineas at S.P.Rd., but I said no, because all my laundry was sent away and I had a number of meals out—rather exaggerating this because I said that if these things altered I might have to make other payments. (Which I hope not!)

I will say he was very nice, and thought you—after whom he particularly asked—and M had had a very rough turn. But he thought that you especially had been magnificent—that is my word, but he did say he thought you must have been an exceptionally unusual woman to have dealt with London and me so well, and he sent you his remembrances. I gather that nothing is expected to happen at present, and there will be no universally applied rule; he will do as he thinks wise in each case, if he has to. So I hope we are safe for our extra pound a week yet awhile. F.P. will lose his first anyhow, that is clear!! But he doesn't know.

To-morrow I am going to move across the landing into the other bathroom! It is a pity in some ways, but I think perhaps I may come to prefer the front of the house. There is a certain deadening monotony about my present outlook. The front may not be Haverstock Hill[202] but it is nearer it!

I was going to start about your fall, my poor blessing, but Sir Humphrey's finance distracted me. I was distressed to hear of it. All my love.

Serge

Oxford
25 Nov./40

Dearest,

It was very fortunate that we managed to get you yesterday[203]—both Michael & I thought of it! He will be writing to you, probably in much detail, and probably to-morrow. Everything went very well, as both of us agreed. We started from S.P.Rd. at 7 after tea and bread-and-butter on a tray, caught the 7.40, more than an hour late up—reaching a quiet London at 11.10, took a taxi, & swept into Antrim Rd—all secure—at 11.30. Then Michael got down to his jobs, and I went and found Wallis. His initials are—W.T.S. Wallis.[204] He had had your money, apologized for not acknowledging but had been very busy. I was so moved by the freshness of the air in the flat, and his taking the dressing table mirror down, and the fastening he had put on the French window when the catch and bolt had gone, that I forked out another 10/-. We had a little chat. He says that only six or eight people use the shelter; they have had electric light put in; it is cold, but they usually stop there only till 12 or 1, and then everyone except Mr. Lea goes home. Mr. L. being on a top floor generally sleeps there. No harm has been done to the Mansions[205] except for a dozen windows which they have boarded up with black—glass they can't get.

Their worst night was when a score of bombs were dropped in a circle round, of which afterwards we saw some signs. Wallis also says that if we are likely to be up and can let him know the time he will light the fire. I also saw Claude but I didn't give him anything!

Both Michael and I were agreeably surprised. We had expected the flat to seem stuffy or even worse, but it didn't. Of course I know that when one got down to it, it would probably seem filthy, but it didn't show so, and Michael thinks W. must even have dusted the bedroom. Anyhow there it all was, comfortable and appealing—if *not* safe—and I was far too enthralled to think of trying to get rid of it. I even had the fantastic feeling that, now we had gone and been nice to it, I didn't so much mind if it went up in fire: we had said goodbye friendlily. But I hope better things. Michael—much to my private surprise—suggested that we should say a blessing on it: so when we were ready to go, about 2.15, we went through it and into every room, and then we both knelt down by your bed, and we both said, out loud and together, the Lord's Prayer, and the Hail Mary, and I said might it and we (meaning you) and everyone all be blessed, and he said Amen, and we came away. But I feel much better about it now, and look forward to seeing it again soon: we will talk in a few days.

We rolled up the carpet and felt in paper, and M. went about with brooms and things. He would hardly let me move a chair, but he ordered me about in the most charming way and apologized and I said it was absolutely right and just what he ought to do. And we had tea when we arrived, and I got some milk from the Cakery; and presently we had tomato soup and biscuits and cheese, and cleared up, and I took the rubbish down, and he went and saw Mrs. Oliver, because he said that was his job and gave me something else to do meanwhile; I gather he saw Mrs. Palmer too, but otherwise—rather fortunately—we ran into no-one.

And then we went away and looked at Parkhill Rd. Collins' house and the one next it are merely a heap; 28 is badly damaged; the Wheelers's house is half-gone, and the room where Michael went to school. Michael with great restraint did *not* say it was a judgement on C., but we both just managed not to feel gratified. Two houses opposite Belsize Station are gone, and the back of the Odeon. Just there however we saw a taxi and took it back to Paddington, where we arrived soon after three—but we didn't want to be caught after the earlier alert. I thought it was so agreeable that the All Clear went JUST when I was talking to you: symbolical like. I could have done with some coffee at Paddington but M. thought if he drank it might make him uncomfortable for the journey, though he urged me to go. But we had got on so well from the first that I wouldn't disturb the harmony. The [page missing]

Banbury Station—
the place I write to
you from, and a
cold wind blowing!
27 Novr./40

I sometimes a little despair of the clergy. I have delivered a quite good address—wholly based on You: yes, it is no good denying it, even if you want to, but I hope you do not—and they say, of course it is all on a high and lofty level, and they hint that it is out of touch with the world. I define marriage for them, and they are vaguely uneasy. They were all very nice, but I *did* tell them what you were like; I talked of the light that You shed, and how I saw the virtues in You (and all), and they say I am a poet. By which they mean that I am inaccurate. But poets are always accurate and anyone who has known You must try & be accurate. For the glory in You of which I write is always accurate.

Well . . . they were very nice, nine priests. They laboured after me, I will say. And so I left and here I wait for the train, hoping one will come before the black-out. But it has given me some mild pleasure to hurl our St. Alban's days in their faces, and to say there is *no* disillusion, there is *never* disappointment, there is *no* bunk in that Mystery, because it is divine.

One priest says he & his wife are of one mind, so much that he thinks something sometimes, & then she says it. There! does that make you envious? I do not think I should like you always to forestall me so—though we have done it often. But that is not quite what *I* mean by one mind.

This is but to greet you and say I come on Friday. Time—as it happens. Bless you: I have just smiled at you on the platform. It is getting colder and duskier. I shall walk. Ever yours.

Serge

2 Dec./40

This is only to thank you for the week-end. I caught the bus from Banbury; it is only 2/6 and leaves at 10.30 and gets in at 12., or just before. So next time you come I shall meet you and we will come by that. Quite a pleasant ride!— and North Oxford is ridiculously large! I should think the chance in case of an attack, of a bomb hitting S.P.Rd. was small.

It *was* a good time, wasn't it? I am a little dashed by finding *T&T* have only sent a pound odd this month, but I shall check it! However, I expect they are right. But I was reckoning on £3. The b.b.c. propose to pay £8.0.0.+ expenses = £9. I had vaguely hoped for more . . . but still . . . ! They have sent a ticket to get into bbc House & a rigamarole of instructions.

Tell Alicia that Faber's are prepared to start setting up *Magic* as soon as they get the Preface. Also say, "My husband says '*Damn* the Preface.' I am bored with that book!!"

All love & gratitude.

Serge

Oxford

17 Decr./40

Having gone out to lunch to meet Basil, who turned up with a stranger—"Professor Edwards—Mr. C.W.—" "You are the editor of Gerard Hopkins, sir? I am right?" He was, of course; I restrained myself from pointing out that I had other claims, hoping Basil would do that, because they were going to a serious lunch & had come to have a drink first; so I declined B's invitation and fled back here to do one of the *Sunday Times* books. Which I have spent two hours reading and then writing about, so that it can go off to-morrow, in case there is a chance for it to go in this Sunday.

(I meant to say about the washing that perhaps we could take it back with us after Christmas; no need to post it—just as we can bring next week's. Parcels are delayed over Christmas, & I've no doubt we can borrow Anne's case. I shall bring the *Dove* with me, all being well.)

A charming letter from T.S.E. which I will show you some time, encouraging the novel[206] and saying that I am the only living person to talk intelligently about Milton[207] & the only one to observe what he has said—*exactly* what. He adds that I am in a direct course towards beatification——sez you!

There has been, I understand, a good deal of difficulty here about Christmas—Sir Humphrey has apparently decided that we can have 2 hours off on Tuesday, & half Friday, *but* that we shall all go in on Saturday afternoon. It seems a rather silly & unnecessary arrangement, but it makes no difference to me; I had as lief do it as not—perhaps I will write another review. To-night I shall go round to Magdalen[208] probably. One male and one female Russian are understood to be arriving for a couple of nights or so at S.P.Rd.

And so till to-morrow. Bless you! all my love.

Serge

Oxford

20 Dec./40

I am always 24 hours late in writing now, as it were, because your letters arrive during the day and not first thing. So if you get a bright letter when you are feeling depressed or the other way round you must forgive it.

I am sending on a letter from Phyllis Potter which she enclosed in one to me. She says she is generally in London now from Thursday to Saturday; so after Christmas if I go up one day to lunch with the B.B.C. Dr. Welch you might have another night up there with me, and we would see her in the afternoon. But not if the nights get bad again; then I shall only go up to lunch—expensive, but I don't intend to let Dr. W. slip in case he's useful.

It is only for me to repeat what I said yesterday—more strongly. I will not have you doing those kind of chores; to be useful in your best way is one thing—this is quite other. I will see that you have the money. (By the way, you don't want the things we bought for you brought over?) I will carry you off with me after Christmas and forbid you to go back if there is this arrangement pushed on to you; it is quite impossible.

Michael is getting a little tired with the Christmas rush, poor boy, & a little fractious. He got to bed early last night and I took him up first milk & then tea—and he had a good night. If I can wangle it I will take him his breakfast up on Sundays: especially if the Aunt is there. It will do her good to see it done. The girls—at least, Anne (Ruth is away) are gloomy about her coming. But last night M. & G.H. & I were alone: & G.H. is a little glum—over finance, I think; & it was *not* what you might call cheerful. I don't mean that M. is not very good; he is. We are cheering him up by having his shoes mended! and presently we will see what we can do about what else he wants.

But it is you who are on my mind! we will have Christmas & talk. Thank you for being so sweet.

Serge

Oxford
21 Dec./40

I must go on saying "my poor love" till I see you, and then I will say it to your face. I do feel the weight of your troubles lying heavy on us. It is a wearing-down world as things go at present, though I continue to believe in our star . . . largely because it has shone so beautifully in your eyes: and the later the more—so to put it. At least when they collect and read my letters,[209] every-one will know that you "grew in beauty."[210] But that is the sort of thing that one can say better than one can write. Tributes in separation are apt to sound a poor thing!

I think I had better post this to-day instead of to-morrow or it may not reach you. Except for the arrival of the gas-bill (£1.15.6), nothing has happened. I rather expected the Insurance bill, but it hasn't come: after Christmas I must send it, I think, anyhow. I don't want to run risks, especially with the Government scheme coming along soon: but that, I gather, is not likely to want payments till next July.

Leave such disgusting subjects. We had a warning last night, & I thought I heard something afterwards. But nothing seems to have happened this morning. Anne has sent a Christmas-card; Anne Ridler, I mean. And my sister sent a few cigarettes. I have written to her; & Michael is sending something from

Blackwell's—quite cheap. I was just going to say I was very dull when I re-read your letter for the third time, and found that you had said you were. So, as you obviously—I mean, the letter obviously—was *not* (it was a dear letter), I thought I wouldn't say so. But I think I *am* a little heavy all the same!

God bless you. I won't write next week. But we shall meet on Wednesday. Margaret would like to go to the midnight celebration, and I can see myself going too. I shall find out delicately what Michael would like to do and adjust everything. And then I shall hurl myself at you. Blessings

Serge

Oxford
27 Decr./40

You will like me to write to you before business, and I shall like it. Let us. Madonna, do you not know I am a poet by nature? and what does that mean? it means that my only faithful and certain devotion, made public to the world and private to you, is that announced in the early books of verse and in *Came Down from Heaven;* it means that I live more by words than by blood. This is hard on you, but then, a thousand years ago, you would have it so. Blame yourself as well as me, most excelling lady. I was never anything less than myself or concentred on anything but you.

That paragraph is largely due to the B.B.C. having paid up. I cannot change the cheque at the moment, but I shall send you the two pounds I talked of as soon as I do—some time next week. I am always more devoted to you when I have money to send you soon.

As for my contacts—I insist on being allowed to tell you. Dr. Welch[211] has been reading *Cranmer* "twice . . . immensely moved by its truth & beauty . . . only bright patches in a dreary week?" There's nothing else of interest.

The journey went very well; Michael very good & courteous all the way, & doing a cross-word most of it—rather well. I was here by two—there was a parcel of imbecile religious books from *T&T*: which I half-resent. I must get back to verse & critical stuff. We had lunch at the Randolph—rather hastily, for I was determined to be here as soon as anyone. Our Mr. Parnwell, into whom I ran, in a state of intense gloom at having lost £150 per annum altogether: the tenant of his London house has bolted and he has lost all the rent, though not (I gather) the furniture. But he is unexpectedly down not £50 but £100 on the year; the rest is I.T. Ha! We do well not to depend on such things.

Bless you! Anyhow it was a beautiful morning, & when I saw Oxford again I cursed. Which did not prevent me disliking to hear Michael cursing. But you are always good and Love, & so am I—yes, but I am. And I have been interrupted three times in writing this—so don't blame me. I love you. I am your servant.

Serge

And as happy and fortunate a year as one could wish! as you could wish!! or as I could wish for you!!! And I only hope that you are not in pain or wrestling with E. when this reaches you—because to be wished a happy new year in that case . . . yes, well, I do anyhow.

Things are a little gloomy here to-day because no-one knows whether any-thing of Amen House is left; no-one in fact knows anything. In fact when I had your letter about taxis & cinemas this morning *and* was thinking of A.H. being no more, I very nearly broke down altogether. Michael was very firm with me last night for being sentimental over "the place where I worked"; he thinks my family *are* sentimental whereas "mother's family go out and do things." However we soothed down afterwards; but obviously M. doesn't think much of me as a go-getter; and as for A.H. it is an old building and it would be, like every other old building, better if it were burned down. This, I admit, did rather stab me (you won't speak of it to him, of course! I'm only telling *you*.)—but it wasn't only A.H.; it was all my poor loved City! St. Bride's! & St. Andrew's by the Wardrobe & the Guildhall! O well—!

I send you a cutting which, if you haven't seen it, may amuse you: it is some-thing to be "in at the death" like that. And I take some pleasure in having been at least proposed to be active in the devastation. The bank was so full to-day that I didn't stop, but you shall have the cash soon. I have sent the telephone and the insurance off and paid Anne all up.

This morning I had a note from Ursula warning me that her uncle would probably be writing to me again. I quote—["?]warning Your Excellency that I did *not* do or say anything that you or I or the blessed Archangels could have thought might induce, provoke, or hint at it: you know what I mean.["?] But I now run the risk—"I was very sorry not to see Michal especially as she was up one night alone. I do miss seeing her as I [page missing]

1941

Oxford
1 Jan./41

I may repeat—a happy New Year! and at last I enclose the cash. Hoping that this reaches you safe. This is a short note, because I am between Dr. Oldham of the *Christian News-Letter* & Sir H. The Oldham would like me to write him a Supplement on Natural Goodness;[1] but as he won't—or can't—pay anything I have postponed him till March. And—except that he told me that his wife went into Blackwell's & lost her heart to Michael "a charming young man"— that courteous Dr. Oldham.

Amen House, it seems, is still erect—though the Square is choked with débris. But the Longman place is destroyed & so I think Amen Corner where we embraced in the last war.

And on that, most divine lady, I kiss your hands and bless you.

Serge

I have sent the rent.

Oxford
6 Jan/41

I have been reading a book for *T&T (Philosophy & History)*[2] & trying not to go to sleep over it for so long—having spent the morning with R.M.[3]—that now I am all jerky, & it's all but time for the post. Michael has gone to the Oldhams[4] to tea—rather dubiously, but Mrs. Oldham was so struck by his behaviour to her in Blackwell's that she sent him a note asking him, and he has actually gone! He and I last night were in to dinner alone—Anne away & G.H. out— and we had a very nice quiet evening without any difficulties at all. Warnings come regularly now about 10 or 11 at night, & there is a certain amount of distant noise. I gather that one or two batteries have been established in the neighbourhood. The "all clear" not till this morning at 7.

It seems to be certain that we shall establish fire watching turns at Southfield House; so I suppose sooner or later he and I will be trotting off in our different directions on the same night. I am proposing to take steps to find out what one does with a stirrup-pump—& to practice with the long-handled shovel thing for sand. If I am to be caught up in anything it had better be Southfield House—where no-one much can say anything.

To-day it is colder than ever, though windless. The fire scarce to be felt a couple of yards off. I am only afraid your pains may have returned. It was very good to know they were ever so little eased.

I am not taking up your wit to-day. "Witty, no doubt," as St. Sebastian said of the arrows. Anyhow I immediately subjected myself to the inconvenience of talking to my Producer[5] about the play without reference to the MS.: odd, but beautiful if it satisfies any slight preference of Your Exalted Highness! But I demur to your flights reaching me at 5 on a cold day without lunch to speak of, just when I have written a charming letter to you which I hope you have had. Not that I think my demurring will make any difference.

I am now going to catch the post. The distances I have walked to do that for YOU, when I would not have moved a step for any other living creature— O madonna, you underestimate my continued pre-occupation with you. God bless you.

Serge

Oxford
8 Jan/41.

It is now raining. It is also a week and two days, or less, to the time of my being at Lutterworth. It is also a fortnight since I ought to have had a cheque from *T&T*; however, I cannot ask for it till I send a review, to which (most excellent Theophila,[6] as St. Luke might have said—meaning "beloved by God") I shall turn, regardless of Sir H's business, when I have written this. I am thinking of sending them another old poem[7]—the discovery that I can make a guinea out of some of my abandoned MSS. "works like madness in the brain," as Coleridge[8]—at least, I hope it is Coleridge—says. I encourage Michael to know literature by giving him a penny whenever he knows a quotation; he does, sometimes.

We have 176 pages of *Witchcraft* proofs—I suppose the total will be some 288—& I have begun to read it as a book. A little jerky, I think, but sound in the main—lacking in epigram of the profounder sort; lacking in the kind of thing I said in

a bright eternal thing,
a landmark in our wayfaring.

Only the fact that it was about your profile reconciles me to those two lines— but I permit that to do so.

I could bear to be made "comfortable" in our sense of the word; or indeed to try and make you comfortable. We are sacrifices for the future—I could bear the future to look after itself, but it will not. The complete activity for which you are responsible and the complete comfort which you create are the poles of movement. Let us have no more nonsense, dearest, about my thinking you "inferior"—I have put off ever murmuring the offensive word, but if I do not, you will one day think I avoided it; yes, but you will. To think you inferior to any created being—well, let us allow the Blessed Virgin and the Archangels, who were, I suppose, *created*—is to think that plants can grow without the sun or the English make war without munitions. I am as lazy as the Sahara is dry, but I have never been too lazy to say so. Shakespeare (of course!) said it better—

> the odds is gone,
> And there is nothing left remarkable
> Beneath the visiting moon.[9]

See my comment on those lines in the *Poetic Mind:* Cleopatra does not say Antony is inferior or superior; no; she says he is the only means by which she knows that there is any measurement at all. He is the only test of proportion. He is incredibly and absolutely unique. So, most regarded lady, you. I have said all that a score of times.

Did I say this yesterday? I shall go on saying it till you believe. I can talk of it indefinitely—indeed, I do. And anyhow to-day there is nothing else to talk of; nothing has happened. We had a warning yesterday just before I left here at 5.30, but nothing happened. Personally I think that another couple of months, less or more, will see the Enemy's great effort. And I think it will be terrific, and will fail, as he has failed now three times at least against us. I wish, most of all human wishes, such as money, we could be together during it; let us see if we can. And then, after the failure, the real turn, and victory, and London—not any more disturbed till we settle where we shall spend out declining years. Do not call me optimistic—indeed I am a careful Realist. It is why I cling madly to what I *do* say and repudiate so strongly what I do *not*.

However . . . this is a letter about myself, I know, say, in my terms. I kiss your benign hands, the centre of my adoration: yes. If you are unhappy about—O I am being stupid; I mean, if there is clash and quarrelling at Lutterworth,[10] I think of you always with hope and belief and love. You are—you are—beautiful and good. And I love you. Love. By which, in spite of our vow, I do *not* mean sentimentality. Granite and perdurable power.[11]

I turn to *T&T.:* and—God help us—the six religious books. O lud!

Serge

Oxford

9 Jan./41

I have never known so long a time—at least, I have because I remember that I have, but it does not seem so now. I thought of you all the way from Southfield House to S.P. Rd.—except (to be quite honest) while in the gathering dusk I was looking at the headlines in the paper. But I would rather wait one more week now and not stretch the interval afterward still more interminably. I am holding on financially—as *I* think, fairly well—but only one Friday of 52 poundless ones has passed, and I am walking on eggshells, though so far without breaking any.

This is the second morning & no letter. I am hoping there may be one when I get home—so unwisely to call it—what I meant was *back*—because I fret without them: though nowadays they tend to come in little bunches. I have read in books of people who numbered their letters; the dates will number ours. To-day my slight bruises from the fall in Cowley Rd. have come out and I am a little stiff, but it will be better to-morrow. My loose tooth goes on getting looser, especially at night when I wake myself by working at it unconsciously with my tongue. I will promise you to have something done about all of us— but about the tooth—if possible when I am paid for the *Forgiveness* Book— whenever that is published!

G.H. & I spent a quiet evening last night—everyone else being out—& I finished the draft of Act I.[12] I am not frightfully keen—like the other stuff written since I left London, it is all in my second line, good enough and useful in its way. God help the writer who must have everything of the best: he lacks intelligence. I look forward to doing something better of my very own after Lutterworth. This, like the other plays, is good minor.—

Sir H. came in there to ask about R.M.[13] I considered asking about the £25, but it's a little awkward to, as it were, blackmail a man in his own office, & I desisted—postponing it till next week. I have very little doubt he'll agree. [page missing]

Oxford

14 Jan/41

Dearest,

I tried again at 8.45 this morning, but was foiled again. However, as we draw nearer to Friday, my resentment fades. M. is, I think, recovering; he says he feels better and is more amiable. To-day he has been to see Havard, the doctor you met—who is an R.C. & a friend of Lewis's & mine, so he is fairly sound on general matters. I tried to ring him up before M. got there but only managed it afterwards: however I rang up M. at lunch, while eating some cake; & M. seemed to be very contented with him. I shall see Havard to-morrow night at Magdalen, & shall have a small chat. I am rather glad that M. is in touch with H.—especially if he likes him; it is always useful to have a competent doctor about, and especially (for the 18 year old) a sincere Christian who is also a man of the world.

Michael will no doubt write to you all about it. Meanwhile I have preoccupied myself with the proofs of Magic. I *may* try & do the short index while with you, though I doubt if the proofs will be quite complete by then: we have reached p. 240, & I should think there must be 48 or 64 pp. to come. At any rate no-one has seen *them*—except indeed F.P. who has been reading them for misprints. Only I wish it was something better to show *you*.

What with Michael & Magic I have done little else lately. But after Monday I really will get on. The Blake article[14] will lead to the *Forgiveness of Sins* and that to the novel. But that we can talk about.

All my love!

Serge

Oxford

15 Jan/41

This is but a note to thank you. It is snowing here; if it is nasty on Friday don't wait in the cold for a possibly very late train: It will be worth more to me to have you as well and warm as possible. I incline to think it may do M. some good, or no harm, to have me out of the house for a day or two. However, I shall forget him for a few hours on Friday. I shall bring the proofs of *Magic* & as much of the play[15] as I've done, but this last week has knocked it silly.

All love. Forgive the brevity.

Serge

Oxford

21 Jan/41

I sat down in the Chair to write to you & appear to have gone to sleep; at least I was aroused from unconsciousness by the entrance of a Menial, or at least a Hireling. And this after a good night, for I put my light out at 10.15 after doing a little more of my Index.[16] Michael, for once in a way, was asleep already. I think it must be the weather, which is a cold thaw here of the kind in which you never know whether you are going to slip on the frost or crash in the slush. Unspeakable!

However, let us count our blessings! Anne told me, when he wasn't there, that he had been charming all the weekend, beautiful to everyone, G.H. & all, and that she thought he was charming. They are on the best terms apparently— he calls her "Heather" for some reason and she calls him "Stansby"—or at least they did once. Also he and I are going together to see *Hedda Gabler*—the film? no, my sweet, Ibsen's play. I had been asked to go elsewhere and had refused, not thinking I wanted to see it, but Michael wishes to go, so I warmly agreed that we two should trot off. The Lord direct me to say the right things! Ibsen may be a little out of date now, but to know about the Drama means knowing about him.

Also I went up into Oxford mid-day to-day and had a sandwich with B.B.[17] (Why does a sandwich leave you hungrier than nothing? Very odd; when I got back I was so hungry that I had to finish the old cake and begin the new; yet I can go comfortably without eating.) After talks of publishers, &c, I said just before parting that you & I were thinking of spending the next week-end but one in London, & it would be agreeable if Michael could come up a little earlier with me on this Saturday and go back on Monday morning—go back by train, I mean. B.B. was quite willing; "anything of the kind"—"very suitable" & so on. I said—what was not quite true—that I had not spoken of it till I had asked him, and I told him, on M's instructions, how much M. liked his new work. Anyhow, there we are. It can be adjusted as you think well; but he can get up in daylight and go back in daylight. (Though I fear it may have to be third class!)

This all cheered me a little, and I began to think—after your letter, too— and except when I think about your doing so much—that the world had its moments of kindness. . . . Anne has just rung up with a question about the Players, & I said I had just written to her what you said, to which she replied that it was all absolutely true. So you see! and so I see. And here's to you, and thank you. (And it would be nice to think I came to Lutterworth "all on your behalf"—go on saying it! But alas, I did it for my own joy. To my Joy, for my joy, as it were——

at the station, I said, "I should like to see her at the corner,"
picking and choosing my plumbs like little Jack Horner.
But, more fortunate than he, at the corner she came,
and every flake of snow reflected her Flame.

There!——

Serge

Oxford
5 Feb/41

You are the sweetest thing; yes. As I have ever said. And your letters improve, assuage, and generally heal my chest[18]—not that there is more wrong with it than a soreness, which is always most sore in the mornings, & stiff after the night. However, my head is all right though a little discoloured, so by next week I shall be all set again.

This is a rather short note because Sir H. has been talking to me about Robin.[19] Yes, I know, I know (In fact I am feeling a little sympathetic towards Robin.

Sir H. is—well, he is Winchester & New College, & the word "sin" revolts him. But it doesn't revolt Robin or me.) So after a long conversation—O & we were interrupted in the middle by the telephone announcing to him that Anne[20] produced a baby last night—a girl: "mother & child doing well"—I thought of my £25.16 Tax, & asked him for £25 in advance on some book or other—*any* book—which he consented to at once with every willingness. So that is that. My labours are useful sometimes, & I have been just a little anxious to have that cleared up. So now we have no more biggish sums till *next* February.

And I hope you sympathize with my slight relief in getting it settled; and you shall have your pound in a day or two. (Mrs. Travers was the woman we met at the Gloucester after our famous rush round London for my meeting.) And I love you and was thinking of you, at 1.30 this morning.

Serge

Oxford
11 Feb/41

This will be but a brief letter, because I returned here this morning to find a telegram from Fabers asking for the return of the Witchcraft Index "to-day if possible." So I shall rush that through this afternoon, & that will finish *that*. Also my electric fire has gone wrong, and the room is cold, and writing difficult!

I got back quite safely. But I did *not* get to the Church. I met Welch[21] at 1.15 & couldn't well rush off. He was very polite, & we have agreed that I will consider trying to do an air play[22] or something (a) for All Saints (b) for next Lent. Whether it will come off or not is another matter, but we can see. Welch is a nice fellow—he is living in Bristol; his wife in—I think—Devonshire; & their only child at school somewhere. But he is worse off even than this; he had just taken a London house near the B.B.C. for ten years, & spent money on it— and is now paying just like us, only more, for something he uses even less than we! I went to the flat & got 2 books; there wasn't time to make any (even milk-less) tea! and saw no-one. I had my hair cut at my own little man's, tried to get Nancy Pearn & failed, & returned by the 4.45 in profound gloom. I even walk better in London!!

I improve steadily, though my chest aches a little still. A letter from Lester about Henry[23]—he was in the Wimbledon Gen. Hospital soon after Xmas; pleurisy set in, & they had diagnosed a growth, & feared pneumonia. But they did not expect so sudden an end. I have written to Lester & to Miss Lee[24] (sending her letter under cover of L's to Clifford Gardens). All pretty glum!!

God bless. . . . The Index—

Serge

Oxford

13 Feb/41

I do hope the bad attack hasn't developed? It is like spring here to-day, though I find as I did last year that one's bones tend to prick and ache a little in the mornings.

But really to-day there is nothing to say! I stopped here till ten last night, but nothing—fortunately—happened, so I went back & went to bed, and to-day I have been working almost uninterruptedly at the Index (*not* my own) & seen no-one & heard nothing, as it were. No interesting letters either. And I have written often about love and I won't write about money, & I write no poetry to write about: who could in Oxford? Only the second-rate. That perhaps waits for me again in London.

Lester (not that I have heard again) hopes to see us in London; he says it is the end of a friendship of 40 years. I must have met Henry[25] first in 1917–18—which is only about 22. There are others I could have better spared!!

I do hope you are as well as may be. I hear nothing of the christening[26] and my purpose holds at present for the next week-end

.

.

.

Schuler has just been in and suggested lunching next Wednesday. As this means a free lunch I have accepted; he wants to discuss ideas. Will it be a little dull? it undoubtedly will. Still. . . .

O God bless you! I shall do some work. Your letters have been sweet.

Serge

Oxford

14 Feb/41

At Banbury I began to feel glum; at Oxford I was torpid with gloom. I go positively flat when I arrive at this town—by rail or road, and no wonder I stare at its difficulties with increased gloom. However, thank you for this morning and last night, which was the only thing that held me up when, opening my letters, I found that the I.T.[27] is £26.15 and not £25.15: lor'! So here I sit in my bathroom and write to you—hearing GFJC[28] wrangling with GH in the next room. It would be, I sometimes think, pleasant not to have to live perpetually in public. But no doubt God knows best.

Well, it was lovely of you. I have eaten some of the cake. O and I have had a note from Miss Lee asking me if I will write a notice of Henry[29] for the Diocesan Chronicle. I must, of course, but I am not very keen on it; I didn't have much to do with his parochial & diocesan sides, and I shall have to look up dates, yes, in Crockford. However . . . !

How did the doctors go?

And thank you again for all!

Serge

(and not so much Charles!)

Oxford

20 Feb./41

Dearest,

I am sending another pound in case you should be able to go to the doctor about the eye. Also instead of myself for twenty-four hours: let me think it an inadequate substitute, but it brings kisses & means love. It is horrid weather here; and either Oxford or my banging myself[30] is making my bones ache in the cold and the rain. Not like yours but enough. Oxford is a foul hole for the damp.

We have just been all having—here at s.h.—a fire-fighting Lecture, with a practice—bomb and everything complete. But it is clear we shall have to organize better. I don't feel that I and the two aging caretakers make much of a squad to hurl burning bombs through a window, or drop sandbags on them. However. . . .

I shall try to ring you up in the morning on the chance . . . the telephone being now restored. And in 48 hours, almost to the tick, I shall see you—delays and invasions excepted. That will be wonderful & good.

Serge

Oxford

28 Feb/41

Ough!—That means, as you might guess, cheques. I have sent £26.15.6 to the Inland Revenue—& no more direct payments to *them* till next February—cheers! and I have sent the rent—the slip arrived this morning & I think paying by direct return is jolly good. It was sweet of you to send the £1 to M., but you shouldn't have done; because I am anxious for you to have a few shillings always with you. However, I will do what I can presently. I am relieved to be clear up to now; & I wish we were going out—you & I—for the bus or the pictures. O I should like to go to the pictures with you again, but perhaps I may even not too far off. It has been the worst winter of all our lives, and there can hardly be a worse: not if England & we stay the summer.

To-morrow I go to Pusey House. On *Christianity & Civilization.* By myself—at 5, & dine there afterwards with the clergy. I am not keen on this clergy speaking, and I don't know that I'm very good at it. It's long since I wrote any verse except the poem in the letter to you. A strange woman in Stockport has written praising the *Dove* & asking if I have written anything else. Ha!

I think of you every morning. I usually wake about 6, & then half-wake, & half-sleep with an eye on the clock, till 7.30 when I wake M. He is a little more agreeable in the last couple of days. Yesterday I went to Magdalen; to-night I shall compose my to-morrow's address. On Sunday I had better do something to Ruth's play[31]—bother it! It's exactly where it was ten weeks ago,

It would be a good deal of very serious use to me, beloved, if you would consider reading for the Criticism book,[32] as you suggested. I know you can't at the moment (a) because you have no books (b) because of the environment (c) because of how you are feeling. But a preliminary selection by your Highness would help enormously—presently. And I must do those poems . . . for your book.[33] Perhaps if [page missing]

11 March/41

Dearest,

Yesterday's was a bad letter, I fear, & then your charming note made me ashamed of it. But you will be kind and forgive it. I suppose it is the spring which makes one so done; I really have never felt so worn. Not worn-out exactly, but generally done in. I have had the honour to remark before that there is no relaxation in Oxford: whatever one is doing, one can't *flop*. However, I won't repeat myself.

I think I will come to Lutterworth on Saturday. I know it is only a short time but we can talk better (at all risks!) than writing or phoning. Besides—.

I was a little sad to-day to hear that a bomb destroyed a shelter in the Essex Rd. near the Angel at the top of Pentonville Hill. It is absurd that one should remember one's childhood's wanderings there, but that is more part of me than (except for you) St. Albans, & much more than Oxford. I used to walk over to Leyton along there. This is perhaps sentimentality, but you will understand.

No acknowledgement from Miss Lee.[34] I hope she approved my note; I don't see what more I could have said intelligently, do you? Nor no other letters of concern. M. & I went to see *Mrs. Warren's Profession*[35] last night; Peter[36] being unexpectedly away, I was offered the possibility & thought it would be sound. All went well, though I walked & talked like agog on eggs.

And of course a fellow to whom I referred in *Witchcraft* as "the late" turns out to be alive. I *hope* Fabers' have corrected, but . . . Curse all hack books! But bless you.

Serge

Oxford
12 March/41

Dearest,

I thought your letter this morning was one of the wisest you have ever written. It had all your qualities in—wit, loving-kindness, sympathy (is that the same thing?), lucidity, intellect, & I could add more! But that should be enough to show you how I read. It makes me realize more than ever what a noble and princely-hearted creature you are, and also how we *have* stood together & been together & nothing can alter that: not even war. Though I admit that the past seems hardly enough; I should like the present & the future too!

I loved your description of the rector's visit; no wonder it went well when they had you to arrange it all. Without you it would have been a poor business. But you are a glory; as I began telling the world thirty four years ago & have been telling it ever since. And shall continue.

I still think I *will* come on Saturday,[37] if it doesn't upset Michael. He knows I am thinking of it. He is going to the dentist this week, & has just rung me up here. I haven't been out to lunch to-day; it's too horrid weather & too expensive. So I am writing to you. I wish M. could have a day or two with you on his own, but he's being very good. I am learning (yes, indeed!) to take the criticisms placably, & to fall in with them; presently I shall be so docile that you will be surprised at the difference in me. If I come we will talk about London. I have been asking Miss Peacock about Easter: she, & I, think probably Friday to Sunday. But M., I suppose, may or may not get Saturday. Let us talk.

Miss Lee has written thanking me for the note—I enclose hers. A completely unknown woman has written rather touchingly thanking me for the *N.C. Year*;[38] she is looking after her mother "who is failing mentally, & I don't love . . ." or words to that effect, & the book has cheered her. I have replied encouragingly. I have an idea for a book (of my own kind) on the Saints[39]—particular Saints—to follow up the *Dove* & be called the *Gates of the City:* they needn't all be Saints, at least canonized. Let us discuss it.

Foreigners continue to appear at S.P.Rd.; just let out of internment camps & looking hopelessly for jobs. It is a dreadful world. Anne feels she doesn't do the proper thing by her aunt—doesn't in fact love her enough, & has been consulting me on what to do.

O your letter was good and beautiful and cheered me up—being you, and all Your Lordliness's self. It is wonderful how I repose on you—whether you are here or not. I think it would be lovely if you could come, but I lean on you anyhow. Who else? Where else? Echo answers—I suppose Echo would have to answer "Who" & "Where" at once—which might defeat Echo!

All love, & thank you. God bless you.

Serge

Oxford
19 March/41

Well, well . . . at 12 last night, as I was about to go to sleep, the alert went. So up I sprang, & into my clothes I got, & downstairs I went; and Anne & I kept our dutiful watch. Beatrice was the third and she remained in her room,

dressed & awake, but aloof. Gerry was Home-Guarding, but if anything happens on Friday it will be his go. We heard planes & an occasional distant crunch,
but no more; & at 4.30 we thought we might (against our strict duty!) go to
bed. The All Clear, however, came soon after. I now feel a little flat & stale,
but not too done. I have arranged with Page that he shall take my Friday duty
here, and I shall take his on Tuesday, all rather patriotic.

I also went with Michael to the dentist this morning: he looked a little white
afterwards but was quite pleasant. Then I went for a bus to get here, but of
course they were all full, & I had to walk down. And that is my tale of valor-
ous woe.

I am sending this to London to welcome you. I will not now repeat what I
have said before so often about your being there at all or being there without
me. But I shall (as it sounds silly even to say) think of you all the time until I
arrive.[40] I had thought of going down to St. Albans early on the Sunday, &
staying Sunday night in London—returning early Monday. Then I could see
my mother, leave M. to have a few hours with you, and spend Sunday night
with you. Of course I should come back early Sunday afternoon. I have no doubt
this would be the best plan, if it could be managed.

Miss Peacock is going (I know not why) to Rugby this week-end. She tells
me there is an evening train from Oxford at 8.8., getting in about 9.30. I don't
know if that would be too late. M & I, if we came by it, might taxi out; & go
back by our usual route on Easter Monday—with you? There is a good deal
to be said for getting him to L. then if we can! Let us discuss!

And now love & blessings. And take care!!

Serge

Oxford
24 June/41

I could wish HSM had been moved to go away on Friday instead of to-day; I
would have been in town by now. But he wasn't, and as both he & Cumberlege are away I suppose it must be this eternal paper problem which has carried them off. I seem to have less & less work of any value to do, which is tiresome, because it means stuffing up with imbecilities of one sort or another.
This afternoon indeed I tried to copy out a poem about Centaurs,[41] but it failed
to find an end, so I left off to write to you.

Everyone seems to think that the invasion is off for a couple of months,
say, unless the Russians are got under in a week or two. I have read that the
Germans expect to take two weeks, for as much conquest as they need to do.[42]
But it will take two or three more for them to switch back again; so I hope at
least that you & I will get our Lincoln week over first!

I cannot bring myself to write of what the flat looks like to you, and I think
the only thing is not to wait for M. but to send you the Pleshey pound here-

with. I should like it to be waiting for you; it shows willing, at any rate; and—despairing of persuading you of more—I shall continue to attempt to show willing until death (as they said years ago) parts us. The pounds may become shillings, but they will continue to arrive—kissed unless you forbid, but I think kissing them is an agreeable habit of devotion.

I have looked up the trains & I shall catch the 5.55 up—& probably have to stand! and serve me right for being in Oxford at all. Lord! how angry I was last week at coming back.

Lord David[43] was very agreeable last night; sorry he missed you; looks forward to meeting you; has ordered the *Dove;* didn't know of the novels. To-night we fire-watch: on Friday Trevor[44] will have to do it.

God bless you.

Serge

Oxford
26 June/41

As it were, a dove before me—fluting its wings. You will be, I suppose, with Michael now; I hope not too worn with ashes. And now I have nothing to say, but the dove-wings shall do my business. I have asked for my rations, & I wait for to-morrow; meanwhile (as is most suitable) correcting the proofs of my *Romantic Theology.*[45] Till when, blessings—peace!

Serge

Oxford
11 July/41

If I didn't keep on losing things life would be a little more comfortable. I have mislaid my long-sight glasses . . . not that I used them a great deal, but they were a change & an ease. I dare say they will turn up; also I daresay they won't!! My pen has been away for a couple of months having a new plunger put in—& is there any prospect of getting it back? No. So I have to sit at a desk when I want to write & try & manage my unreliable hands there. O madonna, the INCONVENIENCE of life is detestable.

M's glasses have come—(I wish you guessed how delirious my handwriting makes me; in a few months I shall be illegible! I am fretted morning, noon, & night.) —he has written the enclosed note to say so. I am sending—no; I have sent the cheques: £2.16.0. That's that. I am in much more of a nervous state than he seems to be over his registration[46] to-morrow, I shall go round if he likes, & hang about not far off. Meanwhile I tried to telephone you yesterday, & failed, & have put through a call to-day. But telephoning is like my writing & my seeing—a tiresome half-efficient business.

I have the honour to enclose *it,* my love. And if you say that I think, when I have sent *it,* I've done everything, you will be so wrong that—even the animal creation would be shocked: even the inorganic, meaning stones & things. Pound notes are but a symbolism—but I always thought it a very sound symbolism. The rich may send it without loving, but not the poor like us: O no. The passion with which I try & follow up with one is but a sign of the heart's preoccupation. That is why I demur to your saying "generous." Generous, quotha! am I generous to my eyes if I bathe them or my leg if I rub it? "So much the more," as Milton said; and "how much the more"[47] as our [page missing]

Oxford

14 July/41

It is probably the relaxation of my insides that makes me feel so sorry for myself to-day. No-one loves me, & there are no worms[48] in the garden. The immense & awful boredom of this "Covey" is too much. I have had to do up the parcel of laundry 3 times through a sheer break-down of intelligence: the very hairs of my head are weary. And my bowels are incontinent.

You will say this is little enough. And you will describe my boredom as pleasure and my endurance as enjoyment. You will be more wrong than ever you can imagine. If it were not that I fear you would not approve it I should ask you plaintively whether you won't save me at least. Quicksands, as the Psalmist[49] might have said, surround me on every side. Michael annoyed me by occupying all the time yesterday morning; I was waiting in the middle distance to be called back to the telephone. But no—& did you then think that I didn't want to speak? I will not believe you did: the thought harrasses me, all the same—

At this point I was called away by Sir Humphrey—to tell me two things. The first was that our poor old Mr. Leonard is dead at last. He died yesterday morning & is to be cremated at Golder's Green to-morrow. I am writing to Mrs. Leonard on both our behalfs. It may be very desirable that we should be in London for the week-end; because the idea is that I may take over editing the *Periodical*,[50] & there's some stuff at 27 The Pryors which I ought to get hold of. It is therefore officially & personally that I hope we may be able to be at the flat. I must be up "on business," & so therefore must you—yes! We could then both go.

The other piece of news is that Hubert[51] has been trying to commit suicide, & has been stopped by the police & is now in Brixton. I must not write or even telephone details, [page missing]

15 July/41

Dearest,

Your Saturday & Sunday letters only reached me this morning. I am as torn with desire to get you away from there[52] as I was with anxiety to get you away from danger. It is heart-aching that you should be tormented so; & that's not exaggeration or violence or anything but truth: & it was a shame that I couldn't get through to you in all those hours. Miss Peacock tells me the trunk calls are terrible; but the evening has generally been better—however that too failed last week.

I am sending another pound with this—which seems the simplest way. It puts it into your hands & you can do what you think best. I shall try & ring you up to-morrow—as & how it proves possible—to converse about the week-end. I have written to Mrs. L.,[53] & I will see H. again. But if I have to go up any way to get some stuff from the Ls, I shall stop a night or two: at the week-end, & you wouldn't like me to be alone?

My stomach—no, my bowels—go on being avid & I had cramp in the night two or three times; & altogether this morning I am feeling a wreck. But I suppose it will be past soon. Miss Lee has written asking if I can help them to get rid of the remainder books, & I can only think of Basil B. I will talk to him about them: no word about the legacy.

You do not altogether believe that the only place where I have ever found rest is lying against you, but it is so; always so, and now that I don't find that primeval and original peace, I begin to feel myself losing hold. No doubt a Christian should not, but no doubt your husband does. These things are so much facts that they can hardly be expressed, even by me, in words. You are the absolute Fact of my life; consider if I miss *that*—flesh, mind, & soul. I always needed—& now always. There is not even a choice; it is merely *so*. Set that as a mere beginning of letters; they grow passionate in years.

Serge

Oxford
29 July/41

I have been rather dallying the morning away at Magdalen, where Lewis & Tolkien & others unexpectedly collogued. And arrived here to find your letter—which indeed I had thought of several times. Myself, I had thought I had a past which completely consisted of the *emphasis* of the importance of "marriage & a wife." Now St. Paul did a little under-rate it,[54] but I, my love, have corrected St. Paul. Or shall do by death-time. Does not the *New States-man* review of Auden's new poem[55] say: "He acknowledges debts now, not only to Marx & Freud, but also to Pascal, Kierkegaard, & Charles Williams"? But I will no longer press my principles, but your face—though indeed they are the same thing: my latest poems labour with the problem of expressing it— no small problem. And now the *Times Literary Supplement* devotes a leading article to my introduction to Milton,[56] we certainly are some-one in the world. Laying it at your feet as ever, and assuring you that Our labour to convince you is more than we ever have taken or could or would take over anyone else for anything at all. Tell Alicia that I divide the world into (i) my wife (ii) other people, and refer her to my early & late poems for proof.

But that is irrelevant: like Alicia and—other people. Irrelevant: do you see? You & I will spend years together yet in peace when all our jobs are done; and the kingdom of heaven shall be joyous through you. And now you will think I am babbling, & indeed I had better have written of Mrs. H. But as for Your being "stupidly sensitive"—O come! Come, in fact! . . . however, I will say that. If I had another note, you should have it: I would rob all pigeon-cotes for you. Why? because a wife & marriage are—after God—the most important things in a man's life? "A man's"? Say mine, love, say mine.

Serge

Oxford

1 August/41

Dearest,

It is quite unbearable,[57] and you must not bear anything that we can prevent. I know exactly what you mean about Win; I know her advantages &—my God!—do I know her disadvantages! From the very first Sunday I spent at L. I knew it, & I don't approve & never have approved of—approve, quotha!—I have intensely disliked & hated . . . however, never mind that now!

I shall see you to-morrow. We will not bring the case, & I have written to Lincoln saying that I can't come for the week. If they really must have me now I will go for a couple of nights—at least I have offered to do that. But if anyone in Lincoln, Lutterworth, London, or Oxford thinks I'm going to spend that week away from you, they are quite astonishingly wrong. And if you think so, so are you. I will be at Lutterworth or we will go to London*—as you can & like, & as the specialist fits in. We will settle that.

This is not unselfishness; it is pure selfishness. It is what I want to do—not what I think I ought. I had looked forward to Lincoln with you, but Lincoln without you would be a pain in my heart. And everywhere.

Till tomorrow. Blessings.

Serge

*Not Oxford, because I do want to get away from it for as long as is possible.

The more I think of London—if it could be—the more I like the idea. It shall be wholly as you feel. All my love.

Southfield House

5 Aug/41

Not being able to do anything more useful or indeed more happy, I said my prayers for you in the car. Since indeed from our first acquaintance—odd to think we ever did not know each other!—I have always kept in mind the knowing you in God: there being no other way seriously to know. And *therefore* all other knowings being conditional on that; and also dependent on fidelity to all original knowings: that is, on the continued affirmation of our loves. But by the end of our lives, dearest pet, you will no doubt have understood my use of words; *or,* more likely, I shall have used words as you approve. For I am in passionate agreement with Leonardo da Vinci, who said "do not lie about the past"; only I go farther even than the divine Leonardo, for I say that the affirmation of the past in God is the gift that our Lord whom we received on Sunday gave us; and without that, in him, all human relationships are vain. And it is this which causes all other people besides (I do not say except) your sublime Excellency to regard me as one with you—because many a fool can make all sorts of professions, but only those who are not fools can keep their doctrine homogenous and consistent: and that I have always done; and there is no part of it anywhere, spoken or written, which does not depend on this. So, I repeat, I said my prayers for you—for that I can do more easily than to pray personally; and I think no day goes by that I do not think so of you—& I hope you can say as much, lordly-eyed that you are; for if not, I shall maintain that I am the more faithful of the two! as I said yesterday that I am the more needy of the two. For you have sometimes offered to do without me, but that I should live so has never entered my mind nor can.

But all that is but an outbreak after the week-end—any intercourse with you always excites my powers: otherwise they do but turn in on themselves, unless indeed they are caught by the Church militant upon earth; to whom I dismiss my students, most fortunately. Talking of which reminds me that Lincoln is very beautiful, warm, & sympathetic. It says "Our chief thought is for you & Mrs. Williams, & our hope is strong that all may be well with her. Clearly we can't ask you to come even for the shorter time." They hope "for this great privilege & happiness later on," & they send "both of you our love and sympathy & good wishes"; & they are "yours ever." Very proper, charming, & Christian. I am sending them half-a-dozen of the Dante pamphlets[58] with a note of thankoffering; & I have no doubt they will study it with the orthodox interpretation which even you, blessed one, deigned to give it.

I am madly transferring corrections in *Forgiveness,* and improving it here & there. But as for yesterday, we did very well with the journey; though our Mr. B.[59] is firm against picking up the Army which I wished to do. But he said he was afraid of the car breaking down because of the bad petrol or the "mag." or something, & indeed it did make curious noises: so we rushed on. We reached Oxford about eight, and went in to S.P.Rd., where there were only Gerry & Archie. So we considered what to do; and M. said we were both very flat & would be bad-tempered—which was true enough—& he wanted to tell Margaret about the coat. So we went round—rather (can you imagine, dearest?) against my will; and he told Margaret who was thrilled, but as he had not taken it—saying it would be better to speak first—she is still disappointed of seeing it. But I will forgive her some things because when I said once that I longed to save you pain she said that she thought I was so much one with you that it was a union that suffered together and I was too much a part of you and you of me to be anything but ourselves. Which was not perhaps lucid but as I agreed with it I forgave that. It being (a) true (b) what I say (c) what you—yes, you do—say.

But I went to sleep at twelve—M's toilet kept me till then; or I should have been off by eleven—& woke at one, & was awake till three, and then went off again till after six. And I brooded unhappily over Alicia, & unhappily (but blessedly) over you: and how you were the grand Fact, & how every week does but show it the more. Though for a mingling of your goodness & the world's disease at the present Lutterworth is a crystallization.

Sir Humphrey asked after you this morning, I having explained last week that I was *not* going to Lincoln; so I told him the facts—or the most important as regards us. He did not, I regret to say, produce a cheque. But I shall spend the next few evenings on Ruth's play,[60] thus making up for my extravagance on fares! no; it was your extravagance really, was it not? for you not only urged me to do it—which another wife might have done to another husband—but continued to urge and approve, which only your Glory does. And when I have got the fee I shall send you another pound for love.

You will let me know as soon as anything is fixed? I am your "beder man" for times & places. It was a beautiful time, & had we been alone in London would have been perfect. Meanwhile I adore you. Also I love you. Also I need your Blessings.

Serge

I think, having no money after all has been paid—rent, telephone, fares—I *must* send you 10/- at once; from Me for You.

Give my regards to Miss Kinselle.

Oxford

6 August/41

Well, we have sent *Forgiveness* off. The main doctrine is that it is a Mutual Act: and is a great exchange of hearts. And as you & I have exchanged hearts for so long, *if* there is any forgiveness anywhere, and *if* we are mixed up in it, we might not be its worst practitioners, and our union might be the lovelier. This as you choose, but any mode of more intense union is fortunate as between us: it is, with you, a question of foundations.

I allow that does not help you to rest nor give you good nights: the union of pain & religion is the darkest of all. I have always wondered at your practise of it. It is the labour of writing the book that has concentrated me on that side of love—for some explanation, I mean. But the explanation is in life: so tell *Alicia*. God send I am less troubled when my time comes; it frankly terrifies me. But I—

—now the telephone interrupted. It was ("believe it or believe it not") Norman Collins.[61] He is in Oxford & leaving by the 6.25. Could I meet him at 5.45 for a few minutes? I have said yes. Why? You know N. bores me as much as most people. I suffer slow death with them; yes, but I do: you do not allow for it, & then I break down: 'tis the cause.

Sir Humphrey spent half an hour yesterday talking about his retirement when the war ends. I said I should leave soon after—as soon as I had my pension & while I could still make money by writing. It does begin to draw nearer! and then you will have me at home all day, and you will find that a new experience. But then we will have bus rides and wanderings at night and tea as we choose. And no-one near.

Last night I tried to work on Ruth's play[62] and shall to-night. To-morrow I understand Sir H. will be away and I am thinking of offering to go to the pictures with M.; it would be kind, do you not think? He consulted me this morning about what he should say to B.B. concerning his rise—very charmingly. Certainly the last two months have been an easing of the strain.

Why have I not more cash to send you? Well, I have not—at the moment; so you must love me without it, as I.

Serge

S.H.

7 August/41

I am going off this afternoon with M., so I am writing earlier than usual that I may post before I do. But—Alicia! Though I am not in the least surprised; my only wonder is that she hasn't done it before, & my only doubt about her doing it was whether she could. I wouldn't stay for a week if I were her—having the money I would see I had the comfort too. Of course, she will be an awful strain wherever she goes:—the doctor, as well as Win, will miss the cash. If you run a Nursing Home, you have to *run* it. Good God, darling, if I had written books in that way, my name, as they say, would be mud among all the publishers. But you know that.

Personally I feel relieved: you will be at liberty—& it has been your heart's goodness to A. which has chained you mostly (you must remember I have seen you with her!), and *I* shall not have the thought of your being "on a savage farm"[63] all the 24 hours. I take it you haven't heard about the specialist yet? I sit here, as it were booted & spurred, waiting: now if A. can be got off, we may at last be able to act. If A. will go and the Russians will hold and I can decide on my next book for a reasonable amount, our future shall be happier.

You know I realize, as I write, that I am much more pleased than (for A's sake & Win's) I ought to be. I am very, I am impossibly, delighted. Push her off, & come. "My heart leaps up when I behold Alicia going off," as Wordsworth[64] didn't write! I have sent Lincoln 6 Dante pamphlets for them to study. They study marriage and we renovate it: cheers!

I saw Norman[65] yesterday & Sarah & the daughter Anne with him: they had all come to Oxford from Newbury for the day on business. Sarah is much older looking; she loathes the Newbury cottage—outside sanitation, difficult help, no hot water, & so on. She takes the child in to Newbury to some school every morning, & then has to hang about Newbury till midday waiting to take her back. Norman is still at the B.B.C. & says he is now Manager of the Empire Service—whatever that is. He is also writing another novel of about 200,000 words—about the war of 1870. I *didn't* ask him if Victor[66] would publish it!

Nothing more of interest. As soon as we know about your specialist, & A. has gone, we *might* manage London? I want to discuss possibilities with Nancy Pearn, with whom I correspond vaguely because I can't make up my own mind. I *want* to spend a year on poetry but I don't see how I can. Yet unless I do I shall never get down to the second *Taliessin* book. However this morning (while thinking of you—yes!) I realized what exactly the gentleman in the burning tomb whom Galahad freed symbolized!—and I hope I remember. (Nothing, I may hastily add, to do with you directly—and don't go remote on that remark. I mean it was an abstract & geometrical, & not a personal, realization: and if you think ANY human creature in Oxford—except perhaps C.S.L.—would understand me there, you are *wrong*.)

But I worry about your never-resting; only I am pleased about the end-in-sight. (I might call my next novel that—End-in-Sight; only it sounds rather like Cold Comfort Farm.)

Vaguely wave these pages in front of Miss Kinselle, so as to show how I write daily. I feel it would be good for her.

Blessings.

Serge

[The following sonnet and note were found in the file immediately after the preceding letter. It might well have been an enclosure as the closing lines of that letter could suggest. Its dating would certainly fall within this time frame.]

The consciousness that nothing loses, all
    the present's gloom or transitory jest
    playing before that background, the long quest
of life for its last meaning making call
on that for perseverance; nay, the ball

of Earth itself rolling—it has been professed
so many a time!—along that road; the Best
being known in your beginnings; and the tall
tower having for entrance and for stairway you—
so much do I choose or merely find is true?
Nay; if I choose I already find it so,
and if I find it, yet I choose to choose.
Necessity and Free-will these I know
their names being yours, your face of theirs the news.

Tell Alicia that all theology is clear to anyone who studies you—no, do not;
the poor dear will not understand. But her holding your noble and admired
hand touches me; I have done it too often not to know how she does, and I
will lend it to her; but it is a treasure; restore it. God gave you admirable hands;
I shall understand their power when I have analyzed them in more verse. They
are cells of my reclusion; the night calls me to them and the day reminds me
of them; they are sun and darkness in one.

I have spent a morning on the sonnet, making it a prelude to myself, coming as I wished; if you do not like it, I shall not like it myself; but I do at the
moment. It is all "metaphysical"—well, I cannot help that; it is mine &
therefore so. But it means as much as any light comedy, & for the burden of
meaning—you will carry *that* like a flower. Most women would be crushed
by it. "Have I tried?" have I?—my dear, do but look at them: who could? It
is pouring with rain; I shall stay in; if I were to have a drink with you I would
go out—hardly otherwise except for a legacy or the Laureateship. Permit
them only for rivals; they should but be yours. Till Friday.

Serge

Oxford

11 August/41

When I think we might have been wandering together this week, contemplating—at least I should have been contemplating—your movements with
that serene satisfaction with which I always have regarded your movements:
at least, I am not sure that serene is the right word, for there is an activity about
it; I am made one with you in that great study. Say, Joy; and even then do not
say enough. There was in the Middle Ages a phrase—*amor intellectualis*, intellectual love, and for that matter there still is; the philosophers use it; but
that is the way in which I look at you. For, as I have always said and shall always say, the speed of your motion is a thing to be studied carefully. In the
period between my early verse and—all that I have not yet been able to do—
I ought to be doing now—I have continuously brooded on that movement &
that speed; indeed, I think any speed in the present verse is due to your own

physical. *Amor intellectualis*—I love you with vision, but though the vision is mine the spectacle is yours; that is, you provide it.

But this has taken me away from thinking of us in Lincoln. I am enclosing a letter from Fr. Mascall,[67] whom I think you have not met; it will show you that Lincoln at least, like all the rest, unites you with Dante in their study of me. I am in an odd way pleased to know that they are praying for you; it is very proper and profitable. But you cannot say that they do not regard you as Important. Taught, if the least of your servants may say so, by me.

Michael sends his love & is going to write to you. I leave him to discuss the coat. Margaret was very thrilled; I darkly suspect she yearns after more clothes than she gets, but I don't know. I gather that she felt that in these days she ought not to accept so much without wishing to pay something, but she was anxious to accept it anyhow, as it were! However Michael will write about that; it was his errand!

I have returned the Insurance claim all filled up; they suggested we should re-insure but I have said that I doubt if I can arrange that. In ordinary times I should probably have done it for another ten years, but I wish the cash to be at our disposal in these days.

I woke many times during the night; you live so much in my mind that that is inevitable. The hour back is pleasant to me only because it is agreeable to you. O I babble—take the first page of this letter for truth and the rest for chit-chat of no value. The *universe* applauds the *Dante*—"an original, profound, & brilliant study of the Way of Love, both humanly sensual & divine." No more reviews of that yet.

I must to work again. I love you & infinitely miss you.

Serge

Oxford

12 August/41

There was nothing on Sunday, my heart, except my thought of you. I am aware of you so much these days; and the cruel situation[68] in which you are. I have been thinking of coming over next Friday night; how does that strike you? On Thursday I am probably going to Amen House at the firm's expense to clear my room of the books that still remain in it. We are, I understand, making efforts to get the rates reduced (which must be terrific) and are emptying as many offices as possible. A year ago I should have been a little sad, but now I don't seem to mind. So many more dreadful things have happened that I don't mind at all about getting rid of such books of my own as are still there. I shall go up by a day return and I shan't let anyone in London know I am up—there won't be time to see Eliot or my agent, & I can't think of anyone else I want to see. So I shall have a quiet little—slightly destructive—day.

Did I tell you that I hear from Eliot that Belgion[69] is a prisoner in Germany? I suppose he must have been caught in Greece or Crete, poor fellow. How one writes to prisoners I don't know, but I shall find out. Last night I had a long conversation with John Spalding about Life; he was—he is—very unhappy about being caught up into the Army kind of life—"the toughs"—and that in an Oriental town for years—years because he will be one of the last (being in an hospital) to get free at peace. (O—peace!). So it was one before I reached my room.

Belgion (to return to him) was never an intimate but it all adds to the general gloom. I have heard, incidentally, nothing of Hubert[70] lately. Sir H. is away for a few days, & said nothing before he went.

This only to tell you, beloved, what there is.

[Unsigned]

Oxford

13 August/41

What a day! (and do not think I forget the flat!! I don't. I cry—almost—over it.) Oxford is now improved by having its bus service cut down by a half—at least on my route. Busses seem now to run every quarter of an hour—& aren't worth waiting for. This may be temporary, but I must say the Cowley Rd in the rain doesn't seem enjoyable: especially as I can say modestly that last night I *did* rival you, because there was a long alert. Nothing happened, but we were up for hours. If you say I wasn't lugging an old woman up & down, O madonna, I shall agree!

I have seen nothing & no-one to give me any cause for saying, thinking, or writing anything. Ashley Sampson[71] who asked for the Forgiveness book says it is "original & provocative." But he has added chapter headings which I left out deliberately, & annoys me; & he wants another 5000 words.[72] I was afraid he would. It was supposed to be 40,000 and I could only give him 33,000; at least, I have only given him that. My mind gave out then. You see now that what I say about Oxford is true—to be 7000 words short on a contract is really shocking.

The Central Ordnance Headquarters—somewhere in Middlesex—have asked me to go there on Wednesday in November "to open a debate among officers, other ranks, & civilians." They say "with a friend," I suppose to answer my opening . . . I have asked Gerry to come. No-one else occurs to me. But I feel, if I am asked, I ought to do these things. . . . It is, oddly, the best I can do for my country, except in trying not to grumble.

To-morrow I go to Amen House. It seems we are paying about £1600 rates on it, and are hoping to save some £400 by clearing the smaller offices. I was compelled to admit it seemed worth while. But I shall return in the afternoon, & not try & do anything else. I still look forward to something different in

London, but if we were up I don't want to spend hours messing about with O. Press books.

It is sweet of you to write. You make me feel sorry for poor old Alicia. As soon as I can raise a cheque I will send you a pound so that you can get off at a moment's notice—well, you know what I mean. I am wholly at your disposal, waiting (I repeat) "booted & spurred." But after I had written yesterday it occurred to me that with Miss K. there you might prefer I left coming at least till the next week-end. If A. is still alive. I take it she is really sinking.

This, dearest love, is a dull letter. I have a headache & am cold & glum: and I don't want to walk back up the Cowley Rd. Absurd resentment! My heart beats to you, by night and day. Preserve yours for me.

Serge

Blast Ashley Sampson! and much the same to W——.[73]

Oxford

17 Aug/41

This is but a note to confirm the idea that I should come on Friday?[74] & to send you the enclosed thing about Henry. We have just had a rather dull Russian priest in to tea—not that that has any relation either to what I was saying (*or* to this illegible writing!). The rest of the day I have spent chiefly on a book on St. Leo the Great[75] for *T & T*. Theodora has just written a charming note about my last review thanking me for it, though *I* didn't think it was very good; & saying that Eliot says it is time I was written about, & he will do something sometime on me in *T & T*—

This only for amusement. It is "all I, I, I," with less justification than you have. I was relieved to hear you had even one better night—rather better. But I am sorry it is taking so long.

All my love. This is a poor note, but I have been thinking myself dull over St. Leo & my hand tired with scribbling. God bless!

Serge

Oxford

19 Aug/41

Another stolen day, as one might say! I haven't been out, & I've spent the afternoon till now writing my extra chapter[76] for *Forgiveness*. It would be nice to have cleared it off before the week-end; if I can finish one or two other trifles it will be still nicer. But what to turn to next I don't quite know. I should like (i) poetry (ii) Dante (iii) a novel—or perhaps a thing on Blake thrown in. But we will talk.

A secret in your ear—Gerry told me that there is a possibility he may go to another job.[77] This is *so* secret that I breathe it to no-one & nowhere but here; but I couldn't resist telling you; besides (as one always says) I don't suppose he meant you. He has been restless here, & of course the future outlook is not extremely encouraging. I think he is right; if I were he, & could, I should do the same thing. Nothing is settled; I will tell you any details I know when I see you. If he does go, he will leave Oxford, except perhaps for an occasional weekend. I suppose someone will have to take his job, but I don't know & can't think who. Advertisements & publicity are very dull: thank God they aren't my pigeon.

"The old order changeth, giving place to new"[78] with a vengeance. Miss Peacock, at this rate, will be the only one left—except me—with Hubert[79] in a home. And I am more than ever only a half-and-half. But I do not press that view on Sir H. & Jock.

I hope you think that serves for to-day's news! For me—I thought about you obscurely as I wrote my MS., but not as regards *Forgiveness* as with reference to Immortal Love and the saints, who come in from time to time. I had your letter this morning & it was sweet.

Till Friday then & blessings.

Serge

I do not forget Alicia nor you holding her hand that I did not refer to it to-day. Do I? Could I?

Oxford

27 Augt/41

We are going to ring you up to-night, & when you get this, you will have heard all. I thought of doing so myself at lunch time to-day from here, but M. had said he would ring me up if he heard from or saw Basil this morning; so I waited—& then it got too late. But, as I have to remind myself, I shall have talked to you soon.

Your letter to S.P.Rd this morning for some reason touched me sweetly—not that you don't ever & again but I like to tell you so particularly sometimes, with a point & a point & then a point. And I meant to kiss your hand as sweetly over finding (permit, Excellency) *Taliessin* in Alicia's room. I think it must have been that which sent me to the new efforts during the week-end. What I need, with you & like you, is a little lounging before taking anything up now.

I have had a nice letter from Welch[80] saying he shall not try anything of the kind this year but is anxious for a Radio Play on the Three Temptations[81] for Ash Wednesday & hopes I may do something for All Saints next year. Sweet of him.

And there, looking forward to conversation, I end for to-day. I hope you have the cheque. My heart palpitates over M., but I hope for the best. I'm thankful he has had some kind of job with some men anyhow. It isn't his death but his army life[82] that weighs on my heart—poor wretch! But he will very likely do better than anyone could expect. He has, in fact, at Blackwell's.

God bless you. Till to-night.

Serge

4 Septr./41

(Written with your pen!)

And have I dropped in for it! Sir H. was on me three minutes after I arrived; it seems Robin also made some sort of effort at suicide[83]—fundamentally arranged (we think) not to succeed. Sir H. obviously expected me to produce a priest out of my pocket, but I appeased him by writing to Pusey House. And I shall have to go & see Fr. Parker—& so on & so on.

At the last sentence *Time & Tide* rang up.[84] Will I write the Notes by the Way for next week—200 words by Tuesday morning? I will. What on? God knows, but I shall soon. . . .

God bless you, angel. It was a perfect time. And now *Time & Tide* are going to pay for it by this little extra work: is not that lovely? You shall have the cheque when I get it—in October.

I love you very much. Blessings.

Serge

I am now signing letters about Robin.

[Undated]

Herewith are two pounds, my angel! will that be all right till next week? If it isn't, tell me; God forbid that you should feel I'm doling out money—but you know what these things are.

I feel I haven't written enough about your pain—be sure it is not because I haven't thought about it and been worried by it. But—as you have said about me sometimes—I don't always like to speak of it. I wish I could find a way of giving you peace and—plenty. I was going to say, and so I do! But I think of you always!

I saw Robin Milford on Saturday; he is staying down here till he is pushed out of the army by the doctors. He looks pretty bad. It is a very odd thing—all these young geniuses seem to be even more distressed than we were when we were young. I feel sometimes it's a good thing I have always had to work or I should have done less—& less good—stuff than I have!

O and I have been meaning to send you the note on your book: here it is. And so God bless you—

You are lovelier than "the evening sky
Clad in the beauty of a thousand stars."[85]

Incidentally, & before I forget, I found out by accident from Gerry yesterday that he is now paying £1.10 at S.P.Rd. for himself. He referred to it as if we both were, & I hope I didn't give away that I wasn't. And of course he has, I suppose, his laundry in for this. But I wasn't sorry to know. No-one has said a word to me on the subject—I mean there has been no kind of suggestion that I shall pay more. "I should think not," you will say, & I too! But still—I am glad there hasn't.

I look forward to your coming back with M. next week.[86] We could then go up together to London on the Wednesday after, & come back together on the Friday. Somehow this week I feel very tired; if you ask me, I think it's the reaction of having a room to myself. The sensation that no-one is coming in is luxurious; this is no insult to Michael; it is bound to be true—for me—of any one but you. And also I have slept only on & off for a few nights.

I thought Churchill—*for* Churchill—was comparatively cheerful. Anyhow he said nothing about invasion; it does begin to look as if that would have to be postponed.

I am clearing off my odd articles one by one. I finished the revision of the broadcast talk last night, and I shall, I hope, clear off Paracelsus[87] to-night. Then the Shakespeare for *Everybody,* & the glancing over *Forgiveness* will finish me except for Ruth's play. I shall do that next & then be clear for what I may find best next.

Bless you; thank you. My thoughts return to you.

Serge

No insurance man to-day: to-morrow? I have a 2d stamp ready for the receipt!

Oxford

1 Oct/41

I have just remembered that you said you would like to see Anne's[88] pamphlet; so I have raked it out, & enclose it. No doubt, sooner or later, HSM will do another volume containing them. I send also TSE's new poem[89] which he has sent me. Michael has been looking at it at Blackwell's & tells me he thinks there is a lovely piece on the second page. If—without perjury—you could say something to that effect, I think it might be profitable & encourage him to read more on & off.

We composed last night—he & I—a letter to his admired Mrs. Hughes for her birthday. I mention it because by the time he had finished I was quite astonished at the realism. He explained about his being here, & said that the change had made him "as intolerant of everything old as he was enthusiastic for everything new," & was very critical of his behaviour. He also said that his registration[90] & medical had suddenly shown him the advantages of the Blackwell job. But I think myself that he has had one of those jerks of advance which we have always noticed in him at times; certainly there is a change. He is very nice to the aunt, & he has said nothing offensive about anyone or even Oxford! He hasn't even been to the pictures this week yet, and he even said last night that of course he *might* one day lose his interest, though he didn't think so. As for Gerry & he, they get on like twin stars. I do hope he won't be called up yet; if he goes on like this, another three months may establish him. I find he has even heard of Dekker, Middleton, & John Ford!! Dare we, madonna, think that our son may flower late but strong? Bless you for it, if it is so, and it will be worth an occasional trip (by him) to London. I have written at length because I have written gloomily before; and because my heart [page missing]

Oxford

2 Oct/41

I do dislike sleeping on things that positively *smell*. What they smell of I cannot think; I should say "stink" if I did not wish to be careful of my words. And having arrived here at 8.45 I recopied verse till 2.30, slept on & off till 6, & returned to a bath & breakfast.

To-day I have had an unexpected cheque for a little over a pound from royalties on the *English Poetic Mind*.[91] This is the second cheque for royalties in a month. If this goes on—on old books—we really shall have a little money coming in when we are "old & grey & full of sleep."[92] Enough, anyhow, to pay for cinemas, to which I hope we shall often go!

But also to-day I have had a long conversation with Milford about HJF.[93] I had a note from him saying could we meet when I was up, but M. gave me a twelve page letter from Peterkin[94] to read which was all about him. In a sense there was nothing very new, but Peterkin was very fed up, and no-one knows what is the right thing to do. Sir H. is going to see the doctors to-morrow, & hear their report. He promises to let me know what is said. The difficulty is that he doesn't think (I can see) that F. is reliable in a business sense—nor is he overmuch; on the other hand, even if M. would discharge him, it would (he says) do us a lot of damage in the musical world, where F. has many unreliable but talkative friends—& some sound people like Vaughan Williams.[95] So it's all very difficult.

Robin[96] is understood to be worse & to have tried to throw himself out of a window. They are now talking of some new electrical treatment discovered in Austria. HSM is afraid of a madhouse (to be quite frank) which he thinks would be horrid from every point of view. I really am rather sorry for him at the moment. He has his faults, as I very well know, but I do think that to have both Robin & Hubert more or less on your hands is a little hard! I feel I may find myself in London any day interviewing one or the other!

O I yawn! I am very sleepy & shall try to go to bed to-night early. The voices of the women in uniform which float up to me merely make me sleepier. Did I tell you that a fellow from a house in the Bridge of Allan has written thanking me for my books—& for the doctrine of co-inherence & exchange? Well, he has; and I desire there may be no more of this suggestion that it is something between me &—never mind. S. Athanasius & the Bridge of Allan—those are *my* stand-bys.

I am now about to send the rent—10/19/2.
that is what
my thumb suddenly
does[97]

I shall send you a pound from the *E.P.M.* when I change the cheque. Thus (if I may) contributing more to your frock. Don't forget to send me the doctors' bill!

O I love you, though my eyes are too dull to see you. They look towards you steadily all the same.

Serge

[Undated][98]

No letter from you & an indecipherable scrawl from Robin! I do not think that is a very good post—though I hope it means nothing too bad on your part—no pains. And if it does not, I am almost moved to think it a good thing that there should be a morning sometimes without a letter, for it does make me pull myself up, & though (in the beautiful sense) I am mad about you, yet I do not wish to be as "looney" over you as Robin[99] over God. For then one does not even love, nor can; one is a dancing wet rag. There is a greatness in one's relations with one's wife which is wholly unique; for all intimacies, as fair ceremony—inches in advance of social ceremony: the courtesy of archangels, it should be, and if you say that I am not noticeably archangelic, why, I can but kiss you & hope for the best. Damn the war!

My thumb & hand are not, you will observe, too good to-day. I hate your being where you are; I hate being where I am. I could almost break down on your heart, but there are always things to *do*. O this everlasting *doing!* I will abandon it all when we get together—& only write an occasional poem—for fun.

No news, & no discussions yet. I am always a day or so late, now they have altered the posts. But that can't be helped. I can only send what I can,* with a prayer that the significance of it may seem to you worth while.

Serge

*(it is Time & Tide this month!)

It was beautiful to hear you this morning, though I was so sorry about the biliousness. The only trouble about writing to you on Sunday is that almost nothing has happened. I have all but finished my article,[100] though indeed I ought to write it out again, but I think I shan't. We are at the moment listening to this afternoon's Brain Trust on the wireless—Professor Joad's answer[101] about superstition has reduced me to a state of gloom: he says it was an article of belief in the Middle Ages that so many angels could dance on the point of a needle. It wasn't. It was a question raised, as an academic point, among the intellectuals. If this is the Brain Trust, heaven help us all.

When I say "we" I mean the Aunt, Anne, & me. Michael has just retired after tea. He has the most admirable public moments: at lunch he unexpectedly displayed a knowledge of the novels of Mrs. Henry Wood.[102] The Aunt, also unexpectedly, agreed with him. He still remains good-tempered—or at least not irritable, and it has been one of the quietest weeks (on that side) I have had. Just as well—considering the darker possibilities at the office!

I loved the frock, and I visualized you in it, and thus caused two loves to co-incide. And I was also gratified that you liked Eliot's poem,[103] because so did I, and it is always agreeable to agree with you—as indeed I so often do! and thus loving you doubly, I am always yours.

Serge

Oxford
13 Oct/41

I have been spending a hideous day cutting up and sticking up proofs in order to try & finally produce the *Periodical*.[104] The grand difficulty of that in a place like this is that everyone sends bits of things, & as then the Clarendon Press offices demur and delay, the net result is a hotchpotch of what seems jerky bits. And then they all have to be fitted into so many pages with scissors & paste. And one never gets the last corrected bits, & authors & so on write up grumblingly. Still I would rather do that than be in Poltava or Kharkov or even Moscow. I have a headache & I have missed the 4.30 post, but I shall go round to the G.P.O. to get this off.

Michael & I are going fearfully highbrow to-night. We are going together to see Chekhov's *Cherry Orchard*. It is weeks & weeks & weeks since I have been anywhere—except for you & me going. And I never thought I cared for Chekhov. But M. read in the *Theatre World* that no-one could be supposed to know anything about the theatre who didn't know Chekhov, so he felt he ought to go; and *I* thought he ought to be encouraged in this more intellectual amusement, so behold the result. We shall, I darkly suspect, both be bored. But we shall have been slightly out-of-date intellectuals. And anyhow, while he goes on treating Blackwells with comparative good-nature—& me too—I would do more than sit by him in a theatre. I keep on wondering if he will suddenly become irritable, but so far there has been no more than mild criticism. An astonishing breathing-space!

And I am now going to clear up odds & ends. Till Friday! and all my love.

Serge

Oxford
All Saints.[105]

I had meant to send some money to-day, but the bank was so full that I abandoned the effort. To-morrow, I hope. All being well, I mean to be with you as soon after five as possible—I have the appointment at 7.30 at the club in *Pall Mall*.

Evelyn Underhill is to review the *Dove* in *Time & Tide:* she will be applauding, but vague. I had rather something more incisive, but it cannot be helped. G.H. has done it for the *S. Times;* it would be agreeable if it were in on Sunday. I should dislike seeing my first Sunday review without you to find it: it is so old, beautiful, & happy a custom. I remember us reading the *Observer War in Heaven* review together, & at Canterbury. . . . O certainly a score of blessings!

Leave it at that to-day, dearest! they run about me like Doves, which, of course, they are. Yours & the Holy Spirit's.

Serge

1942

1/Feb/42

Dearest,

It's all very odd, don't you think? However, I suppose we must be glad that things, with Michael,[1] I mean, are as good-seeming as they are. There seems to be no difficulty about the job, & after he has got on to June & finished his second year, we must try for something better.

It was a curious night! I woke at four again & was up for a little; then I dozed off. This morning I went & had my hair cut & a shampoo—not before time, but I didn't dare stop yesterday. To-night Mr. Zernov the Russian is coming for the night. I am suffering from a severe re-action, & feel a good deal shaken. Me for my bed as soon as I can make it. Gerry is in London, so it will be a sedate four-cornered dinner. No sprats, I fear!!

I have sent Welch the first part of the play;[2] he may as well see if he likes that, & it will show I am trying. No payment for *Samson*[3] yet; you shall have it when it comes. I was delighted they had finished the boiler so soon; at least it does give a chance of a bath. To-day is hideous here—a cold miserable thaw with the prospect of more frost to-night. To-morrow I shall drop in at Magdalen in the morning.

Well—all my love & all my thoughts. I rest in you in spite of separation. (But my hunger has disappeared!)

Love—& then love.

Serge

9 Feb./42

I have written to the Key Flat[4] on the lines we agreed—adding that perhaps they will take it as the formal notice, though I will repeat it at the beginning of April. Also mentioning the £20, & the difficulty of maintaining two establishments. And vaguely thanking them, but saying that it would be unfair to let them do the decorations.

I shall send you some more money when I change a cheque to-morrow. I expect the gas bill & the boiler bill any day, but I shall still be cuddling the £20 odd when all that is paid, & there is all to come in. So we can look forward to June in comfort.

My clergyman on Saturday was dull; he suggested I might like to go to him for a week end. I have forgotten where he ministers, but I shouldn't like to. His chief concern was for me to suggest a book he could write—introducing psycho-analysis & theology. I shall have to give him a bash lunch—but Fuller's won't break me. Mr. Auberon Herbert was very deferential yesterday; however, he still keeps some bearable sherry. He had been reading & admiring *Descent into Hell*.

I gave your message to Margaret, & she & her mother asked us—& they said us—to accept a small present of £5 towards the boiler cost. Which, after proper protests & rather highly, I did. Shall the Children of Israel refuse the spoils of the Egyptians?[5] To-day I have bought scrambled egg sandwiches—but I do not think I like scrambled eggs so much as sausage rolls. I shall look for sausage rolls to-morrow. But I am infinitely grateful to you for showing me M.&S.; it solves a problem.

Michael has written telling you how he had dinner in Exeter last night. For Michael he took it fairly calmly, though he was nervous; & I don't wonder. I'm always nervous about such things the first time. They went to the picture[s], afterwards, & he was in an agony about his trousers. However, all went well. I was in bed reading when he came home. But I then made us some tea upstairs for the first time for weeks; fortunately I had a little in our tin; and that seemed to be a good idea. He thanked me for saying the right things; but I assure you it was nothing to the fervency with which I thanked God for the same thing.

No other news. It's odd that I haven't heard from Welch. I never expected that they'd use the play,[6] but I thought it a good thing to keep warm with him. To-morrow I must try & settle my next week's operation.

I slept badly last night, & I'm sleepy now. Excuse. I kiss you steadily. God bless.

Serge

8 April/42

It has just burst—the weather, I mean—into frozen hail, but it has now ceased and the sun has come out. Like what your voice might be on the telephone—to compare sight with hearing. Remind me to write you a poem on that similar to the one on you singing the Gloria:[7] one of my better earlier efforts!

I have heard from the hotel[8]—all is well; they have booked a double-bedded room for those two nights; now for Milford and the police—better make sure! It's very proper that the We who is you-and-me-in-God should assist at the Enthronement. If I could write a poem on *that* I would send it to the Archbishop with *Forgiveness*. It is charming of the universe, after what you said about the Archbishop, to send us both there!

Nothing else—at all. I will ring up to-morrow as near one as possible and you might tell me what Michael is doing at the week-end. I did ask but he was not communicative.

O it was sweet to hear you, and you are a DEAR.

Serge

Canterbury.

[24/25 April]

It seems the natural thing to come straight back & send you a line to thank you, once more, but never too often, for everything you have done in these days. It depended so much on you, as indeed everything does, & I lay at your feet the admiration you ought to believe. It has all been a very odd & very lovely business, & from the first Saturday it was suggested you have been everything the most rigid "artistic temperamentalist" could desire, & done more "than ever I desire or deserve"—well, not more than I desire, because I desire infinitely, but more than I deserve. But these three days could so easily have been spoiled—& spoiled, in a way, for ever; & now they have not been & cannot be. They are perfect, after their kind, for infinity: "so singular in each particular, that all their acts are queens."[9]

So there, Madame, & thank you. And be a little beautifully pleased with yourself for me.

S

3 May/42

Dearest,

I sent off a parcel this morning with my own 2 shirts, &c, & also the various shirts which are, I think, Michael's. Also a night-robe of yours. Other oddments shall follow as & how.

What I mean to do at present is to come up by the 5.50 on Saturday. At 3 in the afternoon I have to go to Robin's[10] house, but that can't last more than about an hour or so. Thank God, one can get to London later than 7.30 in the morning! That was one of the things that made Lutterworth so hideous. The next Saturday I have to speak somewhere for the Fellowship of Reconciliation[11]—I forget why, but it's all very solemn & Bible-studying.

If, by any chance, TSE should write proposing some week-day for dinner I would come up then & spend the next day instead of the Sunday. But I don't much expect him to.

The enclosed card arrived this morning in a letter from Patrick McLaughlin. Owing to Robin's hours, I can't get up in time for 12.30. If it wouldn't bore you too much, and if you felt up to it, it would be very kind of you to go for both of us. I should like to encourage the re-shaping of St. Anne's[12]—only because you & I liked it; and as P.M. says they are going to ask me to do something presently it would be only courteous. I have told him I am sending the invitation to you to see if your engagements permit. But (if the least of your servants may say so), besides all the other goodnesses of your being in London, it's lovely to feel that I have, as you may say, some one who is myself there. It's been very disconcerting all this time to feel I had no-one who could speak for me and be me. This (I may add hastily) does *not* take away from your own person, life, & function. It is as a great Ally & Consort that I entreat You to deign to assist Us. We have done pretty well in going for each other in different places. And what more lovely?

I send the other pound. More to follow.

All my love.

Serge

P.M. said he hoped Michael would go too if he cared to, but he (a) probably won't & (b) will be at work.

Oxford

23 July/42[13]

Beautiful of you to write so soon![14] M. here a little fed-up; he says he needs a tonic and he needs his holidays, & had a little vituperative excursion on Oxford, Blackwell's, &c. No one (you will be astonished to hear!) understands him. But be at ease; there was no row—which I attribute to your so recent influence on *me*. And if you had seen him smiling at the aunt you would not—no, you would not have believed it was your son!

Anne & the aunt went out & I sat down to forgiveness[15]—& was interrupted by a visitor who had been once before—a young man from the Foreign Office who is now to be attaché at the Embassy in Chile. He was the man who when introduced to me first said: "I have been reading you all the way down in the train." So we talked of the war & Kierkegaard till 9.45, & that was the end of Forgiveness.

To-night I return here; M. having expressed his intention of walking down with me—sweet of him. The fruit cake, which I have just eaten, was very good; so is the ginger. This also I believe to be not the Cakery but you. The rest of the ginger is to last me to-morrow & Friday! so let us hope I don't get hungry in the middle of the night!

Thank you for asking Alicia! You tell me what is right & she shows what's wrong . . . ! But, feeling Alicia is my Rival, I'm not fair to her.

The week-end is a rosy—mist? never! say, diagram:[16] a pattern (setting your pain aside) of delights. But O Madonna, *was* I gloomy yesterday. I woke at 5.30 & stayed awake recollecting you: I might certainly have got up & worked!

Serge

Dearest,

I'm alarmed about you. I thought of you continuously yesterday (the more I'm with you, and more I dislike your being away), and it was a shocking day here, & I feared things might be going badly, back & other ways. Here M. & I (naturally!) get on very well,[17] though he was enough on edge to show that we did quite the right thing. If he hadn't had this break[18] we should have lived in a continuous storm! I gather from him that B.B. quite expects him back sometime, &—he himself said he thought he must go back for a little. But God send another job offer.

A letter from Ursula saying let him come next Sunday & stop for as long as he likes. Subject to you, I suggest a fortnight. It will take up part of his time and perhaps then another week at Lutterworth.——

I was interrupted there by a call from Lady Henderson. About fire-watching. Beatrice & I went to the lecture last night, and now we all are re-organizing everything. I have suggested that unoccupied rooms shall be un-blacked out but locked. Also we must have more water-containers. Sand is now out-of-date. And so on.

John T.,[19] I understand, goes away on Thursday. He is being very "helpful"—thus annoying Gerry—but I gave him *Forgiveness* as a recognition of his changing the Ration books, which he urged that we should do on his little [?]. Also he fetched the meat & so on. Everyone is out this afternoon, including M. & me who go to the pictures.

If only you were here next week!—I am finishing off the BBC play[20] & getting it away to-morrow. Then a couple of articles and I am free for E.U. whose money I still await. You shall have another £5 as soon as it comes.

I wish you were asking me to tea. My hand is a little aching, but not to speak of. I will perhaps, if you are up to it, ring you up Wednesday morning early. Always & eternally yours,

Serge

The D's go to London on Tuesday for a couple of days; I shall not be sorry!!

7 Sept/42

Well, by now I hope M's with you. We got him off very nicely, though the case seemed to me very heavy. But he would have everything, and he carried it so well to the bus that I realized it would be all right at the other end. I have posted the parcel of three shirts to him this morning, and also paid the radio bill. I went back & tidied the room up—and that, one may say, was that.[21]

It is cold here to-day, & I am colder with wondering about you and a slight depression over M. I'm sure we did the right thing, and he needs the rest & everything. Still—I wish I had never had him down; it was a mistake. But I console myself with the thought that he has now at least *had* a job. Leave it; there is no use, as you would say, in champing things over. I was reading Von Hügel's[22] letters this morning, for Underhill purposes, and I came across some interesting chat about the "hysterics" observed in the lives of some saints. I toyed with the idea that, all in due time, M. may become one. His mother (I will swear) has given him great examples—without the hysterics.

I would write like Shakespeare to woo you again—lighting a verse for each step. One of these days—but you must wait a little till my public work is done— I will write you another group of poems; to end with, shall it be? after the next ten years is done, and we away somewhere. How many were there in the *Stair?*[23] I have just looked—84. O I shall never make as many of my new compressed style; a dozen of those early sweetnesses would go into one line of my greatness; but you shall have 30 or so—a new high kind of sonnet, new to English. Say yes and be lordly-kind; are you not? Your eyes look to me from my bathroom door and from Sir Humphrey's chair. 'Tis a cold day, all the same, and if things are tiresome and your back troublesome, you will not care for more promises of more poems. They never kept a woman warm yet, a body or heart; but leave it now—

And so I must. I must read through the Welsh play,[24] & get that off. It is comforting to think M. will be at peace to-day, and not be on my nerves. But every activity here ceases; I shall be driven to reading E.U. I will ring you up on Wednesday morning early—about 8 if I wake. I woke at 5 this morning; praise me!

I love you.

Serge

14 Sept/42[25]

Your letter of this morning quite cheered me up for a little. I had been feeling very down about everything, but even a flicker of temporary brightness is something to be thankful for. I had a note from M. saying he wished he could stay for more than a fortnight, "but that we must see."

Phyllis has written, hoping to come later & offering you, me, or M. "a haven." I did wonder whether you'd care to go there for two or three days of change & rest. But that we can see. I'll bring her letter at the week-end.

I was thinking of coming on Saturday & stopping till Tuesday; and what about us both going to Leicester on the Monday? This is only a suggestion—if you felt like it. I've been [what appears to be a "g" and then an illegible scratch]. Now I had to go down & fill my fountain pen there & do you imagine I can remember what I was meaning to say? Some immortal thought has escaped me forever. I seem very sleepy, but it's a dull heavy to-day which partly accounts for it. Sir Humphrey has been talking about a ms., & I remarked that when he retired we should cease to publish any intelligent books at all. So he said he knew *that*, &

that Jock[26] would never publish what we, on the whole, have meant by a good book. What a prospect! A gloom looms over our—over my—official last years.

'Tis the only gossip! No money yet, but I don't look for it till Thursday or so. This is a poor note; excuse. My eyes, my love, are heavy! Be ever blessed. I was thinking yesterday how good you had been to me! I love you.

Serge

22 Sept./42

I do not know whether I feel most blessed or most torn, most happy or unhappy. I felt very queer coming back,[27] though I ate the sandwiches with gusto, but I was pricked to the heart and hated Oxford when I reached it. It is a bitter business, and only now bearable in the strength of the prospect of getting a place that is ours.[28] But the unity of our resolve is a blessing; did we say it at the same moment? I almost think so. There is a note from Welsh here saying that he has passed the play on to a John Burrak [?] who will produce it; it is down for Sunday,[29] I hope. The point about mentioning this is not merely to tell you (though it *is* that) but to say that this means that the BBC will thus pay the I. Tax, & leave the next £50 of Underhill clear for us. In fact we needn't wait for that; we can use the BBC first. So that there will—praise God!—be no difficulty there!

Gerry hasn't been at the office since Friday; his rash, I suppose, is worse. Miss Peacock says she has heard of several cases of the sort which the doctors cannot diagnose, but attribute to malnutrition.

Nothing else here except business. I have some notion of trying to put a few readings from Dante over on to Welsh;[30] it would do no harm if it didn't come off, & might be useful—in every sense—if it did. I shall turn it over in my mind.

But I shan't be at ease with anything or anywhere until you are—let me say until *we* are established and you are there. I still think we did quite right to clear out when we did, but now it is time to do the opposite. I would rather, almost, come to our own place more rarely, but I do not think it would be so. One can always find reasons for going to London besides weekends.

Thank you for your loving-kindness as well as your love. It was a beautiful birthday.

Serge

There was something else—have E.U. letters[31] & a long letter from Lucy Menzies!!

It will be a lonely un-homed room to-night!

23 Sept./42

First—the points on which I have to report. No parcel has yet come with the frock. I asked Beatrice, & she said no. She, by the way, is another victim of the prevailing skin trouble. Anne says she has a kind of eczema which keeps her awake at night; & that Ellen has something of the same kind. (I did wonder if M's rash was increased by it.) My barber tells me that they notice the great increase in scurvy, which is from (he says) the lack of cooking-fats.

Well, then I remembered to ask Anne about the shoes; & she said yes, of course. And would you like your [?]³² to have thinner or thicker, for the ceremony³³ or for after; and will you pick & choose when you come. She is going to London to-day to stay with the aunt till next Monday. I ran into her as soon as I got to S.P.Rd. last night, and told her how worried I was about the situation—the situation? you, but also Win. Also that you would be here on Saturday week.

Michael rang up this morning, to wish me a happy birthday; very nice of him, even if he did get the date wrong. He says he feels better, but a little "mizzy" still; he has sent in the form and written to Blackwell. While he was on the phone, he had a letter from Theodora saying she was going to see Viola Garvin, & if he were not employed by the BBC should she speak to her, since she (Viola) often had ideas? I suggested he should drop in on T.B. this morning, & he was struck by the idea & said he would. He thinks her very nice, and he has obviously made a hit or she would not take so much trouble. Oddly enough, Lewis had rung me up yesterday about my Dante pamphlet,³⁴ which *T&T* asked him to review. But he thinks that he & I had better not review each other's books any more, & he suggested Anne Ridler (having liked her poems). I approved & have written to Theodora, saying that they might perhaps use her on & off. If they do, everyone will be indebted to me. You will see that it came rather apropos, because it looks well for me to be recommending youth to Theodora while she is engaged with our own youth.

I woke this morning saying aloud—"I must have everything—scissors—adhesive tape—no, no—the . . . my wife!" This is literally true. I can't think why the scissors & adhesive tape came in; perhaps I was dreaming. But the last two words were so strong that I sat up and looked at your bed before I realized where I was. Is not that a pretty story? and is it true? I repeat, literally.

Incidentally, Michael seemed highly to approve of the London return. He even said that he would not so much mind being in Oxford if there were a place in London—which I can believe—and that he was looking round. A note, by the way, from Ursula said they would be delighted to have him for another week—"he is really no trouble at all & is being quite charming." But the point of the letter is to demur to the cheque, which she asks if she shall pass on to M. However, I think she had better keep it; her mother, she says, thought we might be "offended" if it were refused, but Ursula had told her we were not given to "taking offense," it would be much nicer for us if we knew he was reasonably happy in London, and would we accept £10 towards his extra cost there, because we should be doing them a favour by letting them. So I said I was clearly of opinion that he had better be there, & passionately of opinion that you & I ought to have a peaceful time; & that I would not at the moment take it, but I would promise to ask for it if I was short. They could hardly be persuaded to this, but in fact I would as soon it was held in reserve; and at the moment Fabers £9, & the offered £10, and the odd £5 Mrs. Harari will sometime pay & the BBC £35, & the other Underhill £45 spread before me like a golden river: from which even the Income Tax £36 seem to draw only a little off!

I've made out a cheque for Anne covering up to next Saturday; & to cover the balance waiting Bourman's & Insurance. The manager of the University Arms at Cambridge has booked us a double room from 22–26 October.

O now this is all finance; but as it is a mildly more agreeable finance than we have sometimes had, I hope you'll forgive it. You will appreciate my feeling that it's wise to keep in with Faber's.

Your dream was charming—well, no, it wasn't! But I see dreams go by contraries, for here am I toying with the notion of always having a small balance.— I shall ring you up to-morrow. God bless!

Serge

29 Sept/42

Is it only a week since we parted? I admit that, in the pouring rain this morning, I did think that to travel last Tuesday was better than to travel this. But it still seemed a longer time than any normal measurement of time allowed for.

If I had a pound in my pocket I would send it at once; as it is, I must give it you. Why thus? because Fabers have sent another cheque for royalties on *Witchcraft* & on *Shadows of Ecstasy*. *Shadows* has sold 170 copies ("spinal sales"—I think that means remaindered, still, never mind!) *Witchcraft* 90 in six months; *Descent into Hell* 19, & 132 "special." Anyhow the net result is a check for £9, which is completely unexpected. I begin to think my royalties really may go on. *Witchcraft* has done not at all badly. Be pleased; you shall have your share with more love that *it* shows!

I've been trying to ring up Ursula to make further arrangements about M. I am quite sure he had better stop up there a little while longer. B.B's letter was quite nice, & if he can see a few people & try things, it will be more to the point than anything else. . . . Anne says that Barrett Friedman[35] (the painter whom you liked) asked after him, & said that he might be able to do something; she is going to send him the address. The more buttons the better. I rang up Ursula at Paddington yesterday afternoon, but she was said to be "on leave."

Just after that Margaret rang me up & said they wanted to see me & could I go to dinner last night. So I did, & it turned out that they thought, if you were coming over, [page missing]

All Souls.

Well, and as I walked to the P.O. last night, I said to myself, or indeed almost aloud: "I want my wife." Now was not that natural, but yet beautiful? it was so immediate & sharp a cry. It was interrupted by two soldiers who wanted to be directed to Lloyd's Bank, which seemed curious at 10.30 on a Sunday evening. But I found it for them, at Carfax, & went on my way still saying, "I want my wife." Please the Holy Spirit, before the BBC do another play, I shall have her. *If* they ever do, which after last night's[36] rush & hugger-mugger I should think unlikely. "But I was very sad, dear Friend."

Basil has just rung up to read me a note from J.G.W.[37] saying he'll be pleased to see M., & that he owes me a letter. As mine was only about M., I take this as faintly hopeful, but dare not allow myself more. I am lunching again with B.B. on Wednesday to keep everything simmering.

I have the blanket here & the mittens, & put them on and round me for a little while this morning. After the bread, which was very nice. It's a little warmer this afternoon here—but I think I was a little cheered by this morning's head-lines; for the first time the Americans & the Russians AND the English are all attacking. I said the war would begin, as a level thing, this autumn, & so it has. All my earthly hopes are summed up in: "Victory for our country, a job for M., peace for you & me, and perhaps (but I don't press this) a little more power to write still!"

I do not forget you have no money. But I have postponed drawing a cheque this month as long as possible. I shall do it in a day or two & will send. O and I have now written to Budneau's—something ought to be happening there, or they must tell me why it isn't.

I think of you and the——state of things all the while. I've said so often "How lovely *when*—" that I'm ashamed to write it again. But I shall, all the same.

God bless you. I love you. I adore you, and shall.

Serge

1943

It's been blowing very hard all the morning, and each time I've thought & wondered about you. I begin by being thankful you are coming out . . . well, out of the Dale, & then spin round to thinking of how & what things will be like. But you *did* say this morning that I'd done so much for you . . . all sudden, you did; and if you will say the same when I die, at least *something* will have been won out of chaos.

I've written to Bowman's, to Wallis[1] (about the sweep), & to . . . now, who else? Someone . . . I don't know.

This morning Anne S. asked me something about one of my books just at the end of breakfast when only she & G.H. are there. So I broke the news to them—about the degree,[2] I mean. I'd spoken about the flat[3] (or they'd asked) earlier. G.H. said not to be persuaded to buy a gown because I could always borrow one . . . but I don't know. I could borrow while I was here, of course, but afterwards . . . . He thinks the cost of gown, hood (so there is a hood), & cap was in usual times about £5 or £6, & the fees about £20. Which is what I dimly thought. This morning Ursula rang up to congratulate me, having heard from Michael. She says M. is *very* pleased . . . so I owe him my thanks. I do like him to show well. She wants to come, "if it's convenient." (I thought she would!) G.H. thinks anyone can go, but are supposed to be under the convoy of "a member of this University," but he has put himself at your disposal, & anyone you bring. I haven't seen Sir Humphrey yet & have said nothing here.

I have eaten the rest of the cake, some of your cheese, & a tiny piece of chocolate for lunch. I now feel I had better make my notes for to-morrow's paper on "Is there a Christian literature?"[4] So I have written this first. And all my love. God bless you. It was a lovely two days—yes?

Serge

Dearest,

Let me say first—no, let me say first that I love you; but secondly, that I have provisionally finished Evelyn.[5] The Introduction has finally to be typed & read, and no doubt there will be all manner of questions & minor discussions, and proofs, & so on. But the great main work is done. I hope to send off the Introduction to Hampstead on Tuesday. You will let me add that it was very nice that we both went up when I got rid of the *Letters*[6] on Thursday.

I saw HSM on Saturday—or rather he stopped me as I went in to Southfield House. Had I, he asked, heard any rumours? "About me?" said I. "About you," said he. I said I had had an official letter. So we talked on the lawn, & of course he was very pleasant. I asked him if he knew what the fees, if any, would be. He said he hadn't the slightest idea, but (whatever they were) they would be paid by him. So I said, "O well, but . . ." and he said "goodness gracious, yes!" Which was all very agreeable, though I foresee a slight snag, because I want him to pay for a book, & in the end I daresay the fees will come out of that . . . but at any rate there will be no serious immediate call on us. Margaret is saying that they would like to pay for the gown & things; that we shall see—no doubt I shall, rather pontifically, let them. Somehow I always manage unintentionally to let the favours seem on my side. But the main thing is that we can now play with the pleasure without dark thoughts in our hearts, & still look forward to having my teeth done, if you wish, in the near future. It is universally agreed,[7] as indeed I have always heard, that a honorary M.A. is the only M.A. worth having.

Barbara[8] turned up for the week end, & has asked me to do an article on Eliot's last poems for the *Dublin*. Which will bring in £5 in May. Very proper & convenient. Pusey House[9] went off all right—half a dozen clergy & twenty undergraduates. Fr. Parker (you remember him?) made a speech & agreed with me all through.

It is—for all dangers & difficulties we foresee—an untold relief to me to feel we are doing something. It is like the first movement of something new; & I hope the conclusion of Underhill & the coming of the degree are favourable omens. I give it—or gave it this morning in church—to the Holy Spirit; we will be in him & for him all through. Be blessed, & take all my thanks for all. I will ring you up one morning—Wednesday? let it be that. I missed your voice today, but I thought it wiser not; let us float over another two days, & then—? Into our own pavilion, with whatever temporary faults. "A wife & no wife?" no—"You are my true & honourable wife."[10] Do but sustain Your Glory's nobility for yet a little. I am Master of Arts? O no; it is you who are mistress of all the best.

Serge

16 Feb/43

Dearest,

The Vice-Chancellor—Sir David Ross—invites us to lunch on the 27th . . . "you & Mrs. Williams." So everyone else can go in a bunch; presumably the Vice-Chancellor's minions will see *you* safely to the Convocation House. I have been sent a paper of Instructions to Honorary Graduates. "The honorary G. should wear a dark suit. A white tie is not required. The robes will be supplied for the occasion by the University & will be arranged for by the Vice-Chancellor's Secretary." And so on. So I can get my own—which I must & will have—at leisure: much better. No word about fees.

It would be very agreeable if Michael would & could come, though he'll have to have the whole morning, because he'd have to catch the 9.45 down. I'm inclined to think that if the D's. would give him & Gerry lunch, the four of them could come on together under G's gown-cover, if it's true the public have to go under the escort of "a Member of this University." I will see about Thursday evening—though I've a faint suspicion they are going to a Philharmonic concert that evening. (Without me!!) I'm fire-watching Wednesday night down here, so (for once) I'm glad you're not coming on Wednesday. A quiet day on Friday—& you & I might go to an early Communion on Saturday.

The provisional last of Evelyn[11] goes off to-day. Also a review to *T&T*—with a letter telling Theodora. If I could find an excuse for writing to T.S.E. I would tell him.

I was very glad to hear about M.; perhaps the new prospects cheer him. He's a nice creature when all's said. I'm so grateful that all coincides—you leaving, he better, me degree'd. The warmth of the flat worries me a trifle—perhaps more than a trifle. But anyhow the summer is before us now.

God bless you.

Serge

17 Feb/43

Darling,

It was a shame to disturb you this morning, & I was distressed about you & worried about Win & the phone. But the telephone had gone wrong, and I had promised to speak, so I hopped out of S.P.Rd., & went round to the Randolph where I tipped the porter to put the call through. I couldn't think of any other place, and I couldn't think of your *possibly* waiting. It'll all be simpler when we have our own.

I hear at Magdalen that Chapman[12] has been very active in our matter—which in a way is a pity; because in my worst moments I do not wish to owe the Press a pin's head, & I most certainly do not wish to be patronized by Chapman & Milford. But it's difficult to find out exactly how much was done by whom; and of course, as far as outsiders go in the future, or indeed as far as most people know at present, it's an honour . . . well, so it is, of course . . . but I mean . . . O I don't know what I mean. I think I am suffering from re-action; this exhaustion catches me every now & then. And I want to be nice & good & I'm not feeling so a bit. You will have to keep me faced in the right direction, as you have done so often. There are wells of hate[13] in one which are terrifying, & wells of suspicion and even malice.

This is nice talk, isn't it? and a fine start for new things! Don't let the fire-watching prevent you coming on Wednesday; I didn't mean it that way—only that (for once) I could bear not to come to Banbury the Thursday morning . . . no; I know. I really am babbling; forgive all. I shall leave off for to-day, being always your devoted

Serge

19 Feb/43

I shall ring you up *once* more—on Sunday.

Darling

Herewith

(1) £2 for journeys. The Oxford train (you'll remember) is 4.45, & I will meet it on Wednesday. I shall have to tear myself away for the night,[14] but I shall be back early in the morning. I'll see what can be done about dinner.

(2) A cutting from the *Oxford Mail.* You will see that the Secretary of State for India is to have a doctorate, which will add to the grand official tone. Scholer I have met; he is a tiresome man, but very learned. These two are M.A.s already. Of the other three—I dimly seem to have heard of the first as a big voice in education; Captain Lord Romilly I once met at Christ Church—a pleasant fellow. And the third is your servant. On the whole I am quite pleased with the assortment. A Secretary of State gives tone; & there is no-one to rival me in my own line.

(3) Merely for amusement—a cutting from this week's *Oxford Magazine* quoting me. It could hardly have come more apropos. I think I shall slip off to it on Tuesday quietly by myself. It's hardly ever done & I can hardly do less.

I suppose we shall all be at the Vice-Chancellor's lunch—I mean all us five & our Ladies. It's quite the correct thing—though I wish it had been the late V.C.—G. S. Gordon. Sir David Ross is a philosopher. However he'll have to have Mrs. Avery [?] & I suppose Lady Ross will have the Secretary & either Scholer or Lord Romilly.

I think I shall make arrangements for tea at S.P.Rd. afterwards. I did think of taking a room for tea at the Mitre, but it isn't worth the expense. The others will go back, & you will wait for me, & we will arrive together. The Ds are very anxious for us to dine there Saturday night, & tea at S.P.Rd would fit every-thing. They are giving Gerry lunch who will look after them, and Michael if he comes, & Raymond if *he* comes—after Cambridge[15] we feel anything may happen. But you & I will be away from all these arrangements, loftily lunching with Cabinet Ministers and V.Cs. The Chancellor, of course, is Lord Halifax[16] who is ambassador to the United States, & out there.

This is all about the first Episode; but at the moment there's nothing more to be said about the Second. But your leaving L——at this moment makes all the difference to me, I can tell you! I really think I couldn't have borne it otherwise.

All love.

Serge

Southfield House
2 March/43[17]

Dearest,

I've been so long anxious about your surroundings that it's not easy to think you may find them at least half-pleasant; but I find myself thinking of the flat with such content—temporary content, anyhow—that I could all out relax. Let me hear that you still approve, & I shall be confirmed in my view that it was one of the most delicious weeks[18] ever we have spent. (But I hope the electric people have come.)

A few notes here of congratulations—Hugh MacDonald, Schuler, Foss, Sisam. Sisam says he knows "the Vice-Chancellor was very active in moving it," which is gratifying, if true, because it lifts it still more on to a non-Press level. H.M. says it should have happened long since; he'd better hurry up & make Cambridge do the same, but I can't tell him so. I shall find out to-night if there are any pictures in the *O Mail.*

Clara Smith thanks me again for the Introduction—which is very agreeable; I mean, to think I've pleased them all without lessening my Own Vision.

And now I must work. God bless you; thank you for everything, & it was a lovely time.

Serge

3 March/43

I have to go off this afternoon to talk to the Christian Students about Drama, so I send a line now. I have got Lutterworth so much on my mind that I cannot yet easily believe you may be—and O blessed, do I hope you are—at more ease. Miss Atkinson oppresses my working, and I have twice thought I saw Mrs. Green in the street, and I dream of you there—& then wake to find you aren't. But I hope things are going well. I thought of you all alone last night, & did I wish I could have stayed! But I will be up Saturday week.

I enclose the *Mail* picture, which just misses me! and one of the [illegible] from the *Times* in which Anne declares that she & Michael can be imagined to be seen. No other writings have come in; these are from Margaret & Gerry.

Meanwhile a don at Lady Margaret Hall has written to C.S.L. (approaching the Throne by a roundabout method) asking if it would be possible for me to lecture next term on Wordsworth.[19] It is, she says, greatly desired, both by her colleagues & the undergraduates. I had thought of Shakespeare, but in view of this petition, which CSL forwarded, I have augustly consented. Certainly I never thought once of being entreated by Oxford to "come & help them!"[20] I will do Shakespeare next year. But I really must see about a gown soon.

More important, I shall see if HSM or the C.P. will publish the lectures turned into a book.[21] If one of them will, it would be an admirable arrangement; then I could perhaps do a novel next. I have the cash particularly in mind for (i) something at your back (ii) Michael's 21st (iii) my incidentals—such as fares (iv) my insurance (v) next year's Inc. Tax and gas & things. I've paid Anne— I only saw her at breakfast, so no chance of seeing how she is now. (A dreadful business!)

I reported to the Ds last night; we a little mingled anxieties about the great Berlin raid. Then to Magdalen, & CSL told me he had heard I was the only Graduate who seemed to understand what a Ceremony[22] was, & what it was about.

All my love. I hope the E.L. has come. The gas, I fear, may not yet. All blessings.

Serge

16 March/43

It's as well I have the mirror of Your Excellency in Her (for so they say in State Documents, & not merely Your, as you & I would) own apartments[23]—that is, Your apartments mirrored in Your Excellency's eyes: which when they smile, as they are most apt to do—Your Excellency having such a way, trick, and very inmost catch of smiling as no woman save Helen, or perhaps Mother Eve herself ever went beyond—all good things are shown in them, and therefore a drawing-room or so were nothing out-of-the-way to see there. For lesser poets see castles or angels or I know not what, but I (being, as Your Highness very well knows, as much beyond such gay-flies & gad-flies as below Your own most royal glory, satisfaction, & celestial image of beauty) see there the things in which You mostly take delight; and the more I think of Your drawing room with You in it, or You with it in Your eyes, the more it is in my conceit the best room in London, or indeed in the yet unGermanized world; & I take it as a very good omen that the world shall be as free as You in it. Not that I don't pledge myself that, if You come to mislike it, I will mislike it too; and my chief concern is to build up behind You a certain sum of money that You may shift anywhere. Only at the moment I would be as well pleased if You did not too much dislike it for a few months: since now I have seen You in it, I am drawn hourly to some such contemplation.

And, as I was about to say, it is as well, for nothing else happens to give me any substance or subject for writing: no proofs or letters or money. Except a note from Phyllis M.P., hoping we are established & asking when You will be free to receive visitors; so I have told her to let you know when she is in town. Thus you can show yourself just as little as you should be able to, very much yourself and the consort of ourself; as in the poem you heard the Lord Bors[24] said, or words to that effect about his own wife, who in the poem is a visible apparition of the Princess of the Grail Castle; for as for Taliessin himself wife he had none nor mistress nor love, except (as the old books teach) a mystical knowledge of an image of the Grail who was a nun,[25] and anyhow Taliessin was only a voice and hardly human; but Bors a father and a husband and a quester of the Grail. But why I wander in this again, God He knows.

There is another Canadian officer in S.P.Rd., & the Aunt is expected before next week-end. Gerry is back here to-day. If I do not write to-morrow, Your Sweetness will remember I am at Reading.[26]

And so I rest, always your servant,

Serge

25 March/43

(Quarter Day[27]—but no special bills for us . . . how nice!)

My poor, poor sweet, how maddening for you! I can't help, even so, being a little pleased that it was *our* place & not some-one else's where it happened: you & I have always done nobly by each other in such things. But it was shattering & infuriating for you, and you who would have been so kind to anyone else to whom it happened will hardly be kind to yourself. My poor dearest love!

But you seem to be working wonders with Michael, & the letter he sent about the book was very pleasant. In spite of the tiresomeness, there seems to be a kind of peace emanating from 23[28] which is affecting all of us. Only your back interferes with it for you, lamb! well, and for me too because of you. But even I even here feel some effect of the change. For last night I was copying out a very long poem called *The Prayers of the Pope*[29]—working on it, I mean—and in the middle I thought of you and felt almost again—what I haven't felt for so long (except indeed on a few evenings when you were at Oxford & I was doing something of the kind; but *not* E.U.,[30] which is accidental & not essential of me)—a kind of calm and repose in your being. Which I never could while you were at Lutterworth—not at all because of anything you said but because of what, & all, I knew. So if that goes on, as I deeply hope, with prayers to the Holy Spirit, perhaps even my verse will improve. If it does, when we come to the third Taliessin volume, you shall have the dedication of a work not unworthy of you.

I have given your message to the Aunt,[31] who has now got your address. I have had a long letter from my uncle which, so far, I have not faced up to reading. And it is pouring with rain, & (in view of our past) I can't help wondering if it is Coming Through anywhere. But I hope not: O I do hope not.

All thanks, & blessings. I am so glad about M.

Serge

30 March/43

I am asked to speak at Pusey House next Monday evening to a group of people of whom Eliot is to be one. If this comes off—though my first impulse was to refuse—I may have a chance of talking to him about future books. I had rather hear his views before tackling Sir H.—though I have almost decided that the next shall be on Wordsworth & be called *The Figure of Power*.[32] . . . O but I think I told you! Sometimes I fear I repeat myself to you too much; you must, Darling, forgive it. Tis the fault of this way of communication; speaking, I hope I should not.

Apart from the Monday invitation, the last 24 hours have produced nothing new. I worked at verse for a couple of hours last night—only to know it must all be done over again, & yet again. My last style[33] is my best, no doubt, but is it the most deceitful! & (unless one is careful) the most monotonous. I grow more & more inclined to think that all lies (as you said) in the Holy Spirit—the roseal light[34] in *Taliessin* & the soil of the rose-gardens. There are no poems in English, so far as I know, about the Trinity like these!

O you will be bored—no, you will not. I hope to catch the 5.50 on Friday; it gets up by a quarter to 8 & I shall be home by 8.30 or so. Till when, & always, I kiss you.

Serge

6 April/43

Dearest,

I've been at the same Conference all the morning & have just dictated a report for Sir H. & Harrington. Eliot was very agreeable, but isn't going to be in London till after Easter, when I am to dine with him one evening. I talked about the question of a novel which he raised, and said I was willing to write one *if* finance can be arranged. He is to try Fabers out—but of course he won't until after Easter. Then I made my speech, & what with one thing & another was too fussed to get to sleep till 3.

The nuisance about TSE is that it reduces my reasons for coming up—not that I should worry much over that! We will see how money & everything goes & I will let you know. It will be but postponement at worst, for I shall have to come up some time to settle. I find that the evening for my reading or whatever is Wednesday 5 May.[35] I should much wish you to come to that if you would: bear it in mind. If I am really going to read *Taliessin*—I suppose for about ½ an hour, the other hour being taken up by other "turns"—you ought to be there. And you come for the lecture on 18 May.

To-night I am thinking of making a (probably false) start with the Wordsworth book.[36] It is long since I have done that without having fixed up publication *first*. But you see I am getting reckless—no; *not* reckless. What I mean is, that some-one will certainly take it. How having a reputation helps one!

It has turned cold & windy. My mind is fuddled with religion & education & my eyes are tired. I subscribe only & always, madonna, your most devoted

Serge

8 April 43

It's very quiet in Oxford on a Thursday afternoon! I found myself thinking of Michael on his Thursdays with a good deal of sympathy—about Yourself I do not use the word *sympathy*, no, indeed; something more vital.

Last night I reported myself, so to speak, at the R., & murmured about chairs. They are certain they will have to get rid of some. Margaret thinks we should do better if we wait till they find (as she is sure they will) that they must get rid of more than they at present mean to, but that we can all see. There is a tendency to discuss (separately) Isabel's death; Margaret is in a "state" about it, poor dear, and very aware that she is not of importance to anyone. She gets these spasms of terror from time to time; I say & do what I can, & tell her that you & I will always . . . & so on. But, of course, nothing sounds convincing; she occasionally believes she will hardly remain sensible. I shall (under God) soothe this, & so you presently. But it *is* a great fear in her.

After which I went back & copied a poem, taking the very devil of a time to re-organize into significance Taliessin's magical changes in the cauldron of Ceridwen.[37] I could write a book in less time than it takes to revise a dozen lines of verse; but I must admit that I am more capable of writing than I have been for two years or more, though not more inclined to write. In fact, I positively loathe the writing. The Index to Dante[38] looms, but I shall get down to that at the week-end.

Anything else? nothing else. No letters this morning except an old gentleman sending me a pamphlet on "Britain Invincible." Which I would rather read about in the newspapers. It does begin rather to look like it!

All my love & kisses. My regards to Edith.[39]

Serge

It is you who must be tired after St. Albans, but I hope you got your things. I doubt, when it comes to the point, if my mother will ever get up to you. It must have pleased her to be asked. I suppose I ought to go both there & to Leyton[40] at Easter? . . . m'm.

I am toying with the idea of spending next Tuesday night with you; coming up as I did last Friday, going to see Nancy Pearn & Theodora on Wednesday & catching the 4.45 down. If I can manage that, you might perhaps toddle round with me on the Wednesday, lunch, & so on? It will be a more comfortable way than coming up one morning & going down the next, give us as much time, & take less from the office. But I will let you know if it can be done. There's really no excuse for it!!

Herewith another £, with love. As to *Taliessin*,[41] it will do exactly what I want—& that is, get these present poems out in a reasonably cheap form, & leave me free to get on which I can't while they're hanging round. There are not enough to make a book, but there are just enough for this. If the Lord puts in my way exactly the convenience I want, I should be unwise to refuse it. Let us on, my sweet! there is not *all* that time to do what must be done. Trust me not to let you or the poems down, & to know what I am doing and why, [page missing]

Darling,

Many happy returns![42] I hope so; to me? I am sure. It was, perhaps, the only *certainly* wise thing I have ever done; marrying you. The whole effect of You on me will only be known on the Day of Judgement. I have said a good deal about it, but—

Here I was interrupted by Sir Humphrey telephoning to say that Anne's[43] second baby has arrived. It is a girl; its name is to be Alison; & mother & child are doing well. So I pass on the news.——

I was about to remark that when you say "Love can endure separation" you say more directly what I mean by

The light must become the granite
and the granite the light.[44]

But we do say the thing we both mean. There is a term for the union of granite & light which I have not yet found, but I shall. And better than either.

I'm spending time on the Index to Dante[45]—a very dull job, especially as I want to keep it short. But it has to be done. I shall, I hope, do up the laundry to-day, remembering your petticoat & a few cigarettes; because I don't want to bother over a parcel if I come up on Tuesday. I'll write to-morrow if I'm not coming.

All my love.

Serge

16 April/43

I had meant to do several things to-day & perhaps write to M. But the Bishop[46] of Chichester has just sent me a long Report about "family life & marriage" & romantic love (not by him); which is to go to a "Council of the Churches"— saying that he knows it is all wrong, & will I write him a letter he can send on to the Chairman putting it right? I have therefore embarked on a re-statement of all that Your Sublimity's eyes & forehead first taught me & have continued to teach. I have laboured over those principles for 35 years, & now for some few I have been enabled to teach them publicly.[47] It seemed to me in the beginning that something should be done about them, but I had not envisaged the way in which it would happen. That, however, is the business of this Omnipotence; not mine. Ascribed to Him & to You be the Glory.

So I am scribbling this now, before lunch, & I shall get down to my revision of the Report afterwards. Here a little & there a little.

Bless, divine lady, the work, & pray for it. It is little enough, but part of Our job. And I would have it done as well as possible for your sake by whom it began & the Lord's who showed it in you.

Serge

27 April/43

Well . . . I have, more or less, retired into my usual opaqueness . . . an automatic opaqueness, under which no-one but you ever gets. That is why I shall reserve for you the dedication of what I hope will be my, till then, best & greatest poems—the third Taliessin volume; only Taliessin will have vanished by then, & we shall have only the loftier & more remote image of Percivale. I was very touched with your liking the *Pope* poem.[48]

But indeed you are infinitely wrong when you say I need—or wish—to see people. I neither wish, nor, but for a certain necessary check on my own intellect, do I need. Now less than ever. And I look forward, sooner or later, to *not*.

It was a comfortable journey. I read the *Prelude* half-way down . . . resenting even the divine Wordsworth, & thinking that I could write you a letter about O—& beside which even M's would pale. And then I ran into McKinnon to whom I heard myself being polite. He is torn & dissatisfied with *his* book—whatever it is; something about the Christian & war. . . . No, sweet, it is not anything in me but the wish to do my final job that eats me, & the general lack of that Nourishment I suppose; not certainly here. Living, I am already a Myth; that has its advantages in occasional amusements such as reading one's poems or dining or what not. But within? truly, madonna, I think I live less every day there. "All my fresh springs,"[49] quotha! The "well" image[50] is the better; if circumstances cover it, is it to be wondered at if the well's owner grows ghostly? So I do, faith! thinner in flesh as a symbol of it.

I scribble nothing, yet something! The poems were read to some twenty people . . . all very strange and young and deferential. One or two questions from one or two who (to my surprise) had obviously read *T through L*. "What was the meaning of Broceliande?"—and they gave the "c" the soft sound; so Your Judgement's decision has spread properly. "A right"—did you sometime say?—"to your opinion"? Ask the East and the West, the North and the South, how often that opinion (like its mistress) "walks in beauty, like the night."[51] Children yet unborn teach their tongues a pronunciation which you decreed. At least, they do in Oxford and wherever the Oxford young disperse to every three years.

Sleep, and then sleep. I could now; shall I to-night? It is almost tea-time; I have spent these forty-five minutes on so small a note. It is the writing that is the business, but to-day, by slow care, I am reasonably legible. I brood over your light-filled hand[52] at Paddington. [page or signature missing]

4 May/43

O but I wish I could remember what I wrote that pleased you. If I thought it out carefully, of course, I should; it is because I write from the heart straight on that I don't! But then when I succeed, it is the more joyous—yes?

I have just arrived from my first Wordsworth lecture. Lewis is full of pupils, so I strolled alone (carrying my panoply) to the Taylorian, and found that having put me in a room the authorities had been compelled by a shocked senior "member of this University" to take me out & put me in a Lecture Hall. A good number of people turned up, & it seemed to go reasonably well, though one can never quite tell; we shall see how many come next week. What is more important is that I have at last begun to put the business side of the book[53] in hand. I told Sir H. yesterday that I should get Miss Pearn to write to Miss Peacock, & I have told *her* to ask what she normally would. Thank God for a literary agent! It will save embarrassment. I am, I admit, a little worried about the book—don't seem to have got enough stuff for it. . . . But we will hope!

I am very sorry about the back & very glad about the coal. It's a great relief. But how noble of you to go to Leyton—you will let me think so! Love and all blessings.

Serge

There is still seven pounds to come to you for this month, & I think the best thing will be to send another two at once, thus reducing the main amount to five. Do you not agree? So herewith, & blessings.

I have to send you kind regards and remembrances from Uncle Kenneth Spalding whom I met in the street. He has got rid of his house at Hazlemere & says he is feeling a little lost. So we communed on our separate derelictions and he asked me to send you all kind messages.

Also from Havard[54] who turned up all in a naval lieutenant's uniform yesterday; when he & Tolkien & the brothers Lewis & I had dinner at the George. He is rather gloomy over his practice; he had made arrangements for another man to take it over, & then the other man suddenly took another job. So, as far as I can gather, Havard had simply to go off & leave everything, & goodness knows if he will ever get his patients together again, when he comes back. There is something to be said for having a job under all inconveniences.

To-night I have to perform at the Literary Diversions.[55] As you aren't here I have changed my mind about reading my own poems—or at least I shall only read two (*Mount Badon* & *Lancelot's Mass*), & for the rest of the time Malory and Tennyson. I think sooner or later I shall be definitely asked to give a reading, but I will make it later rather than sooner, and hope you will be here for it. I am told that more people were at my lecture yesterday than have ever been known in a Third Term course; this I do not believe. But it is perhaps related to the truth. If David Cecil[56] is made Professor of Poetry, I shall give lectures also and knock his audiences sideways.

The Ds. may come tonight, but do I go with them? No, madonna; I go, awfully alone, from S.P.Rd., and am to be met at the door, like Royalty, by a Mr. Ian Davie who has arranged it. He is an undergraduate and has sent me a book of verse which he has just published: all fearfully deferential. Very young; & it makes me feel very old and established. Which otherwise one might not altogether think.

No word from T.S.E., so it looks as if I should be up on Saturday. I am sorry it will be so late, but what will you? Better after Robin M., than not at all. You shall bless me for my second lecture.

Lewis made some generalizations about women (probably false) last night. I said that, whenever he talked like that, I always felt it was true of every woman except my wife. To which they all said they had never heard the truth about marriage better put. I'm not sure what they meant, but as they all obviously thought that you & I were absolutely unique and superb, I thought you might like to know. And if you demur, I shall say only that I do at least know my male friends well enough to judge their tones and meanings. So there! Blessings & love.

Serge

Strictly, since I shall be up to-morrow, why write? Besides, I am sleepy. I have had two bad nights, because the images in the *Prelude*, and in my own verse kept me awake. Wordsworth, the more you look at him, grows greater; he is universal; we have read too many short poems. One cannot know poetry by reading or writing lyrics. I find I have written in my copy of the *Prelude* a note: "Compare marriage" against these lines—

> Along his . . . veins are interfused
> The gravitation and the filial bond
> Of nature that connect him with the world.[57]

How do you like being called "The gravitation," &c.? Besides, you cannot say that note was made consciously for you, for indeed I have only just found it.

I am trying to write a poem on Taliessin taking Camelot; but everything interferes. It is absolutely necessary for me to get rid of these odd poems somehow; they clog me, & I must get on to the Dolorous Blow and the Conception of Galahad. It is not yet too late for me to best all the rest of my generation at their own game. It is really a very good thing to wake at night—one does not write, but the myths shift and change. . . . Now this is all unimportant— no, it is very important, but I was going to sympathize & condole about your poor back and Michael. So I do—and yet this is a greater tribute.

Serge

How charming of you to write so sweetly! "Did I?" said she; and I, "But if I think so?" Not but what I am sorry for poor Mrs O & delighted about Mrs J. In my time I have heard of a number of these people who go about saying that one should simply refuse to pay—about rent, about income-tax, about jobs. In the end they nearly always lose. My own line is to watch one's step, pay when one must, and safeguard one's future. . . . Do you remember our long-past Mrs. Donnally telling me (more or less) that I ought to throw over the Press and be a journalist? Or words to that effect. We should have been even less certain of our footing all these years!

I might as well write about the war for all the news there is. I have been talking to a young undergraduate poet who got up the affair last week[58] & whose name is Ian Davies. He was most respectful, & doesn't write bad stuff. I congratulated him on not being afraid to introduce Artemis & Galahad & so on into his stuff; & he said rather charmingly "You have done all the pioneer work." Too sweet—the young poets! To feel indeed that one was just their pioneer—no; there is more for them than that. Do you remember Kipling—?

> After me cometh a builder; tell him
> I too have known.[59]

... and if my genius is clouded, I hope my talents may remain. My genius[60] wants to get on with poetry now, and is sulking[61] in its tent. Though there again—there are no *characters* in Taliessin; there are only functions and offices.[62] All my work is, in a way, abstract; that is its difficulty, but perhaps its beauty (what it has!). Theodora, in a short note, says that *Beatrice* is "the most exciting and delightful book I've been near for a long time." I send you the *S.T.* review. Bumpus are out of stock; Blackwells are out of stock—I hope this means cheques later on, & honestly I think it may! It obviously is, for that sort of book, a real success!

It was lovely with you. God bless. All my love.

Serge

14 May/43

I was supposed to lunch at the R. to-day, to hear of the London visit, so I went around with your letter—to find (most unexpectedly!) they have already taken a flat. It is at Rodney Court, in Maida Vale—on the 6th floor (with a self-working lift)—at £200. They don't actually take it till the June quarter. On the main road, & buses stop outside the door. You'll probably know it. Isabel is a little shaken, & a little brooding. They are very grateful for your thought and message; indeed, I thought Isabel played rather wistfully with the idea. But now they are committed.

You'll probably know the place. The idea is that we should collect the chairs—no; I mean they should have them delivered as soon as we have chosen them. It was a charming gesture of yours to send the news, and both of them were very grateful.

To-morrow I speak for the Fellowship of Reconciliation[63] (whatever that is) at Ferry Hindsey. I shall give them a short abstract of what I send to the Franciscans at Cambridge. The index to Dante has gone back, & now we only await the book; though it's a nuisance it won't be out this term.

Bruce Montgomery (whom you may remember) has had a play accepted by the Arts Theatre. It is, he tells me, probably to be produced in June; so I have said that, if possible, you & I will go. He is so perfervid an admirer that I can hardly do less. It is odd how some of the young read me. Ian Davies (whom I think I mentioned) alludes, casually as it were, to "the epic tradition of *Taliessin*." They are very high & haughty about Auden and Spender and so on. One young man told me that every public-house in Oxford has heard bits of my "geometrical verse" spoken!

Gracious. Everything happens so differently from anything one imagined. Kiss me; you and I. I have kissed the note I send herewith.

Serge

What horrid ideas your sympathy puts forward—a positively loathsome fantasy! in fact, I had to read the letter some four or five times before I could really grasp it as being sympathetic! Never mention Lutterworth[64] to me again, my dearest! And here had I, all the week-end, been reposing on you and recollecting how marvelous you were at the time of the first draft of *Descent into Hell* . . . and that has been our only other hold-up. When you have had as much experience of rejecting Mss. as I . . . but give up our own place . . . good heavens, my blessing! And now here am I trying to correct and condole with you. Heart of my heart, come, come! . . .

I have just got back from seeing Eliot who was anxious to talk to me about a novel. This would be a great change, & I have also chatted to him about the book on Arthur.[65] He goes back to London to-morrow & will discuss everything with his firm; but he himself is willing to take everything. So do not let us be gloomy—not that we were, though your letter was in a sense the consolation of despair—to which (thank you!) I decline yet to retreat. Be tender, most sweet lady!

It is settling in for a storm. Bless you, and bless you again. To-morrow I shall change a cheque & send something. I love you.

Serge

It's very hot and thundery; the day lies on Oxford like . . . like one of those blankets I used to tuck in too far and too tight. I would take off my elastic stockings, but some-one might come in in the middle. "Why did I put them on?" Because they have been very useful and good, and I do think they have kept my veins down, so that I do not care to leave them off for more than a day or so.

Michael's American has just rung me up. He is to be in Oxford on Friday & I have arranged to meet him at 12. He was extremely polite. I shall do what I can. All the same, I feel more & more as if a kind of shell of me went on operating in the world, and being as adequate as possible, and even (let us hope!) agreeable, but without any connection with me. It's a very odd sensation, but I suppose inevitable when one has lived for years, most of the time, in a town where no-one is of any serious importance to one, where no-one touches one's heart, or makes the slightest difference to one's feelings. Some things here are more convenient than others—that is really all. It's convenient to lecture because I have something to say, & thus I get it out of my system; it's convenient to let all the machinery run as easily as possible. I always have preferred a certain efficiency and (I hope) always shall; let me be almost automatically efficient. But where is the real I? In your heart, [page missing]

I seem to remember that yesterday I was meeting you on the hill;[66] at least when the future denounces the Press as you say—well, and at that it may! it will if it knows of us, and it is likely to know of us—it shall have you to turn to for admiration. I will not be content that you shall be held as Mrs. Wordsworth or Lady Tennyson; no, no, my sweet; I will restore adult marriage yet. But you are a dear half to laugh, and I love your smile much more even than your proper vengeance. It is one of your greatest properties; I cannot describe its brilliance.

—bright as a sudden irrepressible smile,
sweeps across the golden-fleeced landscape.[67]

. . . Only you will think I have forgotten your pain; it is never so. And my mother . . . still less (no, not less) . . . I will go or write to *her*.

I have asked Anne (he said, going off the great glory of the smile) for soap-flakes, etc. And am promised them. Last night everyone was out, and I read *Descent into Hell* and *Witchcraft* on the veranda, to make preparations for the novel.[68] TSE was rather more than receptive; he was even eager for that. And he wants the Arthur[69] some time. But I wish the novel to be *very* good, if I do it; no . . . I have forgotten what you call it, but I know what you mean. You are right—yes; yes. If I ever demurred, it was not at the fact but, might I say so, at your slightly surgical knife-way of putting it. You have an adult mind but a blasting style. One screams slightly, however true. But we *will* try and make this adult; no back-chat, no facetiousness (O my jumping mind!), no . . . no anything.[70] Never mind now; only let your courtesies be as tender as they are true.

Crockery, like everything else, breaks down around us. It is the little normal renewals that are so hard to miss, all the conveniences of life. Had it not been for this accursed war, we should have been doing now better than ever before. And will yet, please God. I cannot help a certain satisfaction that the English & American armies are now demanding the surrender of our enemies' own real territory. This is the real beginning. It would be delightful if the first island fell while we were together in London.

O God bless you; you become dearer every day. Be still my own most gracious lady. Even Oxford has the loveliest memories—Magdalen Bridge when I told you of the Degree, for example; and the afternoon when we bought the Hat. These are the treasures. One day, in my last and greatest power, I will write a poem of them. Dante once composed a poem with the names of 63 (was it?) beautiful Florentines; I will make one of 63 beautiful Michals. There is for you—"an oath, an oath, I have an oath in heaven."[71]

Blessings. Till to-morrow. Be ever glorious.

Serge

To it again, as one may say. But a depressing "it." I must repeat what I said recently, that I operate here more like an automaton than a man, and I am in the period when I find everyone's face repulsive;[72] and their voices unendurable. However, I must endure the one and not repel the other. Excuse the faint—faint? call it faint—sense of gloom.

It was a nice time. Though it will be nicer when I can come up with a pound or two in my pocket. There is a certain freedom then . . . felt by both of us, though you never show it; unless when the pound is there, when you manage to *be* what you have never not been. If you follow that. But my letters are becoming as complex & almost as long as my novels. I now lie at night (if you will excuse the remark!) with a kind of ghostly skeleton of a novel,[73] and wake scared and unrefreshed. I ate the buns & cakes at 2, after tossing & turning with my ghost. It is to be remembered that on the previous night I had, in your arms, slept well.

The train-inspector was awfully firm about 3rd class tickets & would not even allow them in the corridor. So we had a peaceful journey—& did I go into the corridor to smoke? No, madonna. At Oxford (tell M.) the first form I saw was an American officer & the first voice I heard an American voice. Perhaps better *not* tell him that Isabel means to set to work on a pair of socks for him—I having mentioned your message. I also said you had meant to write, but they said it was we who had done them the favour.

Business letters here, but nothing personal, or of interest. I was given coffee at St. Hilda's[74] this morning before the lecture; some fifty there—very good, when you think that I am (in every sense) outside their courses. But I suppose I am, as you may say, a change.

Say a few prayers for my imagination. It languishes in a kind of fever. All my illnesses are mental, but my body pines sometimes under their stress. And so no more at present from your

devoted

husband

20 June/43

Dearest,

It was so much of a relief to hear this morning that I am almost knocked over. I had been imagining the very worst things, and though I don't over-rate the moment, still M. did sound moderately at peace. As for me, I had tried to make a real start.[75] Nothing much occurs to me for a plot, but we begin with Light—in a picture, but still Light; & there was a good deal about that in *Descent into H.*, so perhaps I am on the right line. Anyhow I can't waste any more time before beginning; even if we re-write, we shall have something to re-write.

It is true I very nearly wrote a poem about you instead, beginning

As first the Unbegotten Light
    flashed on me in your smile,
so lift now to its farthest flight
    my new-advancéd style.

Let others in attention learn
    from it their great affairs:
see, when its fleeting pinions turn,
    'tis you their swiftness wears.

My noblest verse, my aptest prose
    can tell no tidings new;
vast is their scope, yet they disclose
    all where, the heavenly you.

If I, by conjurations, find
    the epigrams of truth—
did they not show when you were kind
    in our outrageous youth?

Without you, nothing would have been;
    without you, nothing could.
Now though I speak strange tongues, my queen,
    I speak but as I should.

I speak but of that very light
    in you and in the skies;
daughter of Glory, turn your sight
    and hail me as I rise.

There you are, after all! Blessings.

                                        Serge

21 June/43

Herewith some instalment. You are wonderful in these things, but it shall never be my place to insist on your being *too* wonderful. The appearance of Your Beatitude, "as of the sun shining in his strength,"[76] is no doubt a kind of miracle. But our Lord has warned us against expecting miracles[77] continuously. So, as an Archangel said to me in the night, "Do you not lay violent hands on the Ark[78] of the Covenant, when you expect Madonna your wife to make bricks without straw[79] and meals without money?" And *I* said: "But I never do!" And he said: "Ho!" "So I awoke, & behold, it was a dream."

But you must discourage me from relaxing; that's the last thing I must do. Now, more than most times, I must compel my Imagination, which is slow and dull. Wordsworth—as I have proclaimed to all Oxford—said it was power.[80] But mine has gone into a rock-cell and will not come out. There is something to be said for writing books on subjects to be found elsewhere than in the mind of oneself; not relaxation, but a double portion of power, is the need. Spurred by a sense of Your achievement—no; I am serious; do but consider how you have brought off this last week. I have prayed & worried, but you *did* it—I am determined to do all I can. Bless me to it, most blessed!

Serge

25 July/43

Dearest,

I will send you another pound to-morrow. I've been disappointed not to have done better this month. It must have been a dreadful time for you—all these weeks; *and* with your poor, poor back!

I send you herewith the *T.L.S.* review of *Beatrice*.[81] I haven't yet had the usual cuttings of any; the Press Agencies now send only in larger batches. But I searched Oxford for a copy of this; not only because it's quite as good, & certainly a long, review, but also because it's the best short statement, by anyone but me—& of course he takes it from me—of the whole business. If you substitute "Michal" for "Beatrice," you get the whole thing, so far as I can see it, that I have been saying since I met you on that January day in 1907. And the minute I saw, in the office copy of the *T.L.S.*, this statement, that minute I decided to get a copy to send you if I could, before other people saw it. Which (not having yet a copy for myself!) I now do.

How astonishing it seems to me that Your Sublime Serenity should ever have doubted that unceasing cry![82] What is the intellect (admirable as yours & mine is!), what is this or that, what is happiness itself, compared to that intuitive knowledge? That—which is never clouded by disputes or by the years; that—which is apt to gleam as brightly from your smile or your wit, your head or your hand, as ever it did; that—to which I have never, never, been false—not though the whole great creation had, & has, to be its balance and compeer; that—to which you and (one must certainly add) Beatrice are the only public witnesses in 600 years. . . . O I could add "that" to "that" & never stop! Why, to send you money (poor as it is) is not, & never has been, merely to send money to one's wife; it is to maintain in action that translucent thing, it is to serve a demi-goddess ("she seemed to him the daughter of a god"),[83] to bear witness to a Fact as fixed as breath itself. Live up to it?—can you? can I?—but lose it ever? never you, never I. An infinite charity is demanded by it; this is its seal in heaven, its certificate on earth. Still wear that royalty, darling!

I am often a fool, but never the kind of fool that is blind to that. You need not fear—it is not only unnecessary, it is impossible, for that Virtue to fail.

My ink runs out. Believe.

Serge

I have just said aloud: "How pleasant to be able to send my wife two columns of study of her from the *T.L.S.*" Excuse; it was but a small brag!

15 Augt./43

Your letter was one of the beautifulest you ever wrote, & I loved it. But you mustn't bother yourself to send things, though I also love your food. I'm so glad about M., & I only hope it's lasted.

This morning Ruth (who arrived last night) & Anne & I went to church at 8: and no-one turned up to take the service for ten minutes or so, and then a lay gentleman walked up to the front & said that the priest who was supposed to come had gone away, & nothing could be done about it. So we all went home. Since then I have been involved in a long conversation with Ruth about the principles of her productions. And Miss Webb-Paploe has rung up to ask if she can call. (I think there *must* be something more than Fear in my religion, do you know? But I meant to tell you how much I liked your discussion of it, and how full of insight I thought you were.)

I am labouring on with Chapter 3,[84] though other oddments are interfering—odd books, I mean. But I hope, faintly, for the best. It may be that my whole style is so changed since I wrote my last novel that I'm practically trying out a new technique. After all, even *D. into Hell* is six years old, & in six years one's prose does alter. Fortunately. The "back-chat" doesn't have to be kept out; it doesn't occur to me to put in. How nice you were and how right I am!

God bless you. Tell M. I remember last Sunday with much pleasure. And for yourself—I loved it all, & you.

Serge

20 Aug/43

I hadn't realized you too were having a visitor! it's very kind of you . . . yes, but it is; kindness, in the sense of a natural outbreak of love, is your Name. But thank you for liking the poem;[85] it was one of my most truthful outbursts. I shall have it typed and put among my Miscellaneous Poems—along with the others admiring you or retreating[86] to you. Now if you had to choose one of those two, which should it be? the retreat, I think. No woman is as mental in reaction as any man, and are not you more true woman than most? 'Tis a fact that other women[87] are not, to me, women at all; they are merely feminine shapes of men. This is a profound remark and explains much in my public career. "My soul is like a star and dwells apart"[88] *except* in a London flat. The proof (as you know too well!) is that only you can get under my skin. . . .

However . . . I have soothed & composed Raymond.[89] The children have had measles, also whooping-cough, but are well now. He is doing (he says simply) five men's work. And in a most uncomfortable office. We both dined at the R., & then he & I had a long private talk. He is—you will suspect this—now that he knows where I was born—in touch with the Office of Works about preserving the house:[90] he has been to look at it—all quite safe and not even modernized without, no, not to a very old knocker, unlike those on either side. Carefully avoiding, most exalted lady, saying "Good God!" (how right you are!) I will merely say "Well, well!" But I can't think the Office of Works will.

Some Society connected with the University of Birmingham invites me to Speak to them in November. As a "Christian scholar" on some aspect of my own subject on which the Christian faith throws light. This is a sound subject, if I hadn't exhausted Milton, Dante, & Romantic Love. However, as they offer five guineas plus expenses, I shall certainly have lectured at Birmingham. Remains to think of my subject. I shall have to stop the night, which is tiresome. But I'm not going to throw five guineas away. November (if they pay at once) will be the easier. But O for a draught of the blushful Hippocrene,[91] to suggest a subject!

No further news. It's a dull day, and was only at once brightened & darkened by thinking of you all through breakfast: now take "darkened" rightly; you know what it means. But I loved your Little Mother Oliver: Barbara[92] is expected for the week-end, which means I had better switch off the novel on to my Dublin . . . article,[93] which she may be wanting. Ever—and thank *you* for the poem—

Serge

Forgiveness of Sins has suddenly produced £2. I send you one at once. Really, my sales are looking up: we shall yet find my royalties useful in our retired days.

Also I have sent off 2 shirts & an old pair of trousers of M's. He won't thank you for them, but it helps to clear up here, as you said.

3 Septr./43

Dearest,

And here I am again. I meant to write to you from Staines yesterday, so that you should have a letter this morning, but somehow I didn't. And now it is (to-morrow) four years since you and Michael saw me into my taxi for Oxford, and one of my most vivid pictures of you is of your smiling good-bye. What a noble creature you are! the greater the crisis the more sublime your power and lightness. And I do think that you and I are nearer and more closely knit even for the separation. And they tell me that on the 8 news, it was announced that the English landed in Italy! All blessings to them and to us.

I was very much struck by your remarks yesterday on my novels. You have still a little . . . devastation (let us say) in your language, but I realize that there is something profoundly true—an insight of the most accurate—in your comments on the wives, &c. (Mind you, they weren't *meant* like that, and I doubt if they strike men quite in the same way.) It's a weakness in the books, but that (I admit) only means that I can't do women—and never could. You were terribly[94] right. I've almost decided not to have any human beings in this novel; no, that would be absurd, but you know what I mean. Three quarters of my mind is delighted that we are so at one about my discarded chapters;[95] the other quarter is sad about the wasted work. Two months almost thrown away! But perhaps something better may come.

Nothing particular here. A delicate diplomatic business awaits me about what I do with the Underhill typescripts. Both of the High Disputing Parties want it back; and I—well, I have now finally to placate and arrange. If the London party insist, it will have to go back to them, but then Lucy M. will be very cut up. However, it must wait for page proofs.

M. very nice last night and on the verge of real honesty about himself. His mind has an astonishing accuracy at times, and though I have to walk very carefully about these books, because they are not in my "style," the real thing is not to despise them but to proceed slowly on. We have decided to try and go out together next time I'm up. I am as acutely aware as anyone that this is due to a lot of things, and that the two years of agony here show . . . they show a lot. But I labour in my vocation, as I may.

The Theological Literature Association[96] has thoughtfully arranged its next meeting for Monday 4 Oct., in the afternoon. So as, if I'm up on the 11th, I shall be up on that week-end next, I shall be able to spend the Monday morning playing about with you.

Meanwhile I'm a little anxious now about the Flecker book.[97] But something must be arranged, & if God sends this . . . I doubt if she's got the material, and I doubt if I can satisfy her Evangelical zeal for "God's Glory"; she takes a simpler view of it than I. However, it may please the Omnipotence to condescend [page missing]

6 Sept./43

Dearest,

. . . and then a complete blank took me. Do you know the curious feeling? One has been on the point of a remark, and everything disappears. Rallying my scattered thoughts, I still cannot remember what I was going to say. I know I was thinking of how you must be looking forward to Thursday—but that wasn't it. Or I might quote Shakespeare, & say: "Madam, you & I have loved, but that's not it."[98] Though of course in a manner of speaking it must always be it, or the important it. And indeed, branching off for a moment, I may say that one of the reasons I was glad about the notices of *Beatrice* is that I have at last publicized indirectly the early Vision.[99] I send you Dyson's notice in the *Spectator*.[100] There is a terrific two column thing in the *Tablet*[101] which I don't send because I must send a line to Christopher Hollis, the writer. It gets rid of me in the first paragraph and gets down to the idea, having remarked that the book is one "to be read and re-read until it becomes a part of the furniture of the mind."

Also a letter from an unknown clergyman about the *Dove*. Also from the Lady Lesonfield about the *New Christian Year*—but *she* only wants to know about Kierkegaard.

And at the beginning of another sheet I am still no nearer my earliest thoughts. I have written a thousand words of the new beginning of the novel,[102] but I am not much happier. It's all so *dull*. The fact is that my style is becoming more difficult to write . . . but I have lamented this to you before: let us think of something else. It gave me quite a thrill to see in this morning's paper a picture of the English flag, the White Ensign, floating over an Italian town; this does look like victory and the end.

I shall write to Mrs. Flecker[103] to-morrow; my typist is over-rushed to-day. Meanwhile I need books, but for once I can't say I've got them in London; I haven't got them at all! . . .

O darling, what a dead dull uninteresting letter. It can't be helped. You know my anxieties and worries, and I Know yours. And if nothing happens—why, how can I imagine excitement? Forgive all and bless me.

Serge

23 Sept./43

Herewith; at least I hope so. It's true that I haven't yet changed a cheque, but I shall do so when I've finished this letter.

It's the time of year when everything here seems to begin to be worst. I think of you in the cold mornings, and I think of you when I am toddling up this lane. And I think how you must be feeling, & I wonder how you are. And I wonder if—at any one moment—you are as BORED. It's a shocking thing that I should be, because that won't get books written. Nor shoes mended, and I keep on putting that off; it will never do. Why do I feel a little as if I could cry? "O Solitude, where are thy charms?"[104] Not in Oxford! "Forlorn," you wrote the other day; you have a genius, madonna; forlorn is the right way. It's astonishing how the thought of *doing* anything weighs one down. . . .

Well, but need I let myself write so direly? No, to be sure. What is there to report? Little. Mrs. Flecker has sent me the *Life* of her son by Geraldine

Hodgson; a silly book as far as I have gone; of course, he died young, & one should not blame him, but he must have been tiresome in many ways. The book—mine,[105] I mean—shall, I think, be a discourse on the theme of Responsibility—its necessity, the late Victorian version of it, the perversion of it, the serious and lofty passion of it, & it in Dr. Flecker. Now there is the first synopsis for you! do approve. More encouragement, therefore more power, lies in you than you wot of; you do not know how much your praise of me for abandoning those other chapters pleased me.[106] You are the most austere of creatures as regards my style—praise to the Holiest! I shall hope my last book, my very last, shall be fleckless from your point of view; I promise you if you were content, I would be.

O lud, we are on my work again! Tut! But then what else happens here? Nothing, except in my mind; and the creative energies of my mind (as they once were!) I do not otherwise discuss—O well, with C.S.L. a little. But outside that—The aunt is coming to-day till Sunday; can one, I ask you, call that a happening? *Time & Tide* have sent me a book on Petrarch,[107] of whom I know nothing, except that I vaguely feel that his Laura comes a good way after Beatrice & you. A young woman in the WAAF writes to me from Brechin, Scotland, to say she heard me lecture on Wordsworth & can I tell her now anything about publishing, because she would like to get in it after the war. Poor wretch! a lot of chance she stands. And of course she wants "the administrative & more literary side"—she would. If there is one word a publisher—believe you me!—shies away from, it's the word *literary*. I shall have the honour to make *that* clear to her.

H.S.M. has just sent up a MS. on Wordsworth. I don't feel that I'm likely to like it, & I am absolutely certain that he is not going to do it—I will say that for him. But even so, it's necessary to look at it. Pray, pray, for the ships to bring grass—a particular kind of grass—from Spain; they make paper of it.

I will try & get Michael's figures out of Blackwell to-morrow, & send them. Reassure him I have not forgotten.

I am, lady-wife,
>   your respectful and adoring husband,
>>   with all that can be said in a kiss,
>>>   a real kiss

>>>>>   Serge

>>>>   5 Oct./43

I have never, I think, loathed Oxford more than last night, and I have never—even I—disliked parting with you more—never; and I said so, on and off, for what remained of the day. It was perfectly abominable. Besides, I kept on thinking of your shoulder and of M., & feeling I was abandoning you to it all, & yet God He knows I wouldn't if I could help it. It's a cold unpleasant morning to-day, and it exactly expresses my present feelings. Even a cheque for 1.13.0 from the Press for royalties on the *E.P.M.* hardly cheers me. It's about time *Reason & Beauty* hurried up; I'm still pounds down on that.

Waking at one ("my custom always when away from you") I got on with the novel,[108] & wrote about a thousand words, going to sleep again about four. I hope to do some more this evening. I've promised Anne S. to go with her at 6 to the induction of the new vicar. Why any vicar should come to Oxford—!

Meanwhile I have brought your cheese—but it was too sweet of you to give it me—down here with some sandwiches. The other Gift survived the journey very well, and I have kept that at S.P.Rd. It's useful if I work late or in the night. Which is still really my best time—only now unencouraged by your appearances with all kinds of sustenance. And O for tea this morning!

Still we added another lunch to our Rosary of lunches. What a gleaming necklace they will make for you in heaven!

No other correspondence of interest. A review of *F. of B.* (I do *adore* your saying you hardly dare look at it) in *Theology,* a little dubious of the main thesis, but ending "it exhibits more profound moral and spiritual insights than have so far been brought to bear." After 6 centuries of Dante comment, this is pretty good!

O I love you, & you are my breath of life.

Serge

7 Oct./43[109]

I have just sent off a small parcel for Michael, containing two or three periodicals he asked for; tell him I will write in two or three days. Also I will send you some more cash this week, as soon as I have been to the bank—I've paid the rent, the electric light, & Anne; & there's still something *in* the bank. What a wonderful invention royalties are!

Last night I pushed ahead, writing another 1500 words.[110] Worry about you & M. took me so much that I couldn't get comfortably on;—but I won't repeat that now. Oxford is now a kind of pale shadow in my mind—it floats like an unreal pageant. The proofs of the new poems[111] have at last arrived, but I don't much suppose I shall like them. It's extraordinary how dull my own work seems to me. No; they are not dedicated to anyone or anything: they exist only, but it fidgets me to have them about unprinted, and prevents one at rare intervals getting on with something else of the kind. What with the proofs & the Falstaff review[112] & the novel & next week's lecture this week is pretty full, and yet you have no conception how your little finger is more real than all. I am your love, but without you I could not even love: O wonder! But I wish I were not so troubled and you not so tormented. I worked from eleven to one last night & ate some of your sandwiches "& so to bed" where I slept from 1.43 to 7.45, and woke by you—yes. And so to-night & to-morrow.

God bless. I pray for it night & morning—for you.

Serge

7 Oct./43

These poor little letters of mine almost make me weep. They have so little new to say, and they can so rarely tell you or bring you anything unexpected; and they talk interminably about myself. They do occasionally say something true and beautiful about you, it is true; though I don't mind telling you that I at moments realize that I may, all along, have treated even you rather too much like a man's image of a woman! This is a very shattering thought, and arises entirely out of your criticism of the women[113] in the novels; which I shall always bless Waterloo & the Staines train for. I don't mind about the novels; that can't be helped. And I'm quite content to treat all other women as being rather inadequate images of men: as far as I'm concerned, they are. But you are neither inadequate nor an image of the male, and long meditation on your remarks, & how it explains everything that is wrong with those books, arouses in me a deep suspicion of my capacity . . . never mind, but it fidgets me a little.

I'm so nerve-ridden over Michael and his goings-on, and also about the need for him to have some better opportunities, that I can't get on with writing. Also your poor precious back. So that I begin sentences and leave off in the middle and fidget; and the nearest thing to the present situation is writing *Henry VII* against my will and against time when you had pneumonia. (Goodness, what a bad book that is! and, of course, they would have copies second-hand in Black-wells!) And I think of us both all lonely—though I don't seem to be! But I am. The room, once you are away, goes on being a boarding house room—

I'm putting a couple of pounds in with this. Like these letters, it seems so pitiful. And it comes this Friday instead of me. . . . Anyone but you would say this was a depressing letter, but I've been depressed ever since 5.30 on Monday at Paddington. I am the heir to all M's feelings against Oxford.

Win has sent me a pair of socks—sweet of her. To-day nothing else: except your blessings. How ungrateful I am for all our good times; and it was a nice lunch. And I don't treat you like a man's image,[114] do I now? (But you were inspired!) And perhaps better days are nearer. And you'd be more unhappy elsewhere, wouldn't you?—O I'm babbling. But you're very, very dear and very, very good.

Serge

10 Oct./43

Nothing—*nothing*—makes me more miserable than not to speak to you on the telephone. I guessed before M. rang up how bad you were, and then I rang off before the time was up, & I hope it didn't annoy him, because the thought of it all breaks my heart. At least it makes me feel very sick. And now we have to cope with these two American girls. . . .

Certainly it's a very different week-end from last! I've been sitting in the dining room alone; Anne away. G.H. on duty, the other two removed somewhere, and looking at the paper and thinking of you. We shall go on fighting through to the end, but we both of us depend so wholly on each other that these years have hurt us both, and we both have to go on. But you have the worse time physically—don't I know it! The bitterness of the whole thing is beyond description. And you have to keep M. & I have to keep novels—O love! and again O love!

I'm writing early because I can see I shan't have more time. It's a gloomy prospect & being bright! . . . you have nobody & I have too many nuisances; let us—believe you me!—share a loneliness, & so I do. I have promised to ring M. up to-morrow, & will try & do it about 8. But I should like to ring you up on Tuesday—perhaps about 10 to 10.30, if I can get through, just before my first lecture, to encourage me. If I can't get through then, I'll do it from the office in the afternoon.

O sweetest! I do feel so with you & for you. Words—for all I use them—are so silly, and you must forgive all this. Even you don't know how *not* hearing you goes through me. But you wouldn't have it otherwise, would you?

Serge

Anne J. has told John she can't understand the Spalding passion for black *stonecold* coffee at Sunday breakfast. Thank God someone has!

12 Oct/43

Dearest,

An odd day! one that, if I were not well aware of my failures and of bad luck, might set me up a little. After telephoning to you, I went off, & arriving at the Taylorian found the hall practically full—which startled me, & of course people will fall off, still, I don't deny it was pleasant. It was only a preliminary lecture, & not one of my best, but it seemed to go all right. Towards the end I had a faint sense that they were restless—or almost—but I found out from Tolkien afterwards that the Queen was in Oxford, & no doubt this explains it. We shall see next week how many will stay the course.

Then I ran into C.S.L. by chance, & he told me that one of his new pupils had said to him that it was a very exciting term; so CSL asked how & why, & he said that C—W—was lecturing; & he added (according to C.S.L.) in awestruck terms: "His *poetry!*" After which I came on here and found the essay by the son of the Bishop of Chelmsford, which he wanted to write, & has done. He, distinguishing between TSE & me, says that Eliot's poetry is "at the foot of the mountain . . ." whereas mine represents "the creature of joy & miracles led to the summit of the mountain by Beatrice." I begin to feel that Christopher Fry was right when he said that it was the young disillusioned generation who found in us the true Romanticism.

Let be. I tell you because I think you will be pleased—pleased for it and for me and for you. It does not break either of our lonelinesses but it does perhaps make them fruitful to others. I would rather have comfort, but if I can't have that . . . I think sometimes that if I were offered the throne of Shakespeare, I should like to be offered it, merely to prefer a happy year with you— I know, I know; who wouldn't? but it's nice to say so; yes?

Mrs. Flecker hopes you'll go & see *her* one day after 18 Oct.; yes—& so do I, if it's at all possible. Anyhow, she is looking forward to seeing her [you?]— she feels you & I are like her & her husband. Ha!

And have *one* pound after all that!

Serge

13 Oct./43

Well, well . . . it is 4 & I have just returned from conveying M's young woman round Oxford. Anything to please him *and* our great Allies. I so far agree that it's one of the more important things in the world to get the common people of us & them together—you giving them food & me showing them "this university." I will write to M. to-morrow about her. She thinks he is "sweet" and "wonderful." She thinks there never was anyone who knew more about books. "Why, Mr. Williams, M. sure does know everything." She was a nice creature & much disposed to be impressed by England, where she has been exactly 3 weeks. And by Rupert Brooke, for whom she has a devotion of the first kind.

Apart from that, & from having at last succeeded in taking my shoes in to be heeled, nothing has happened. I spent yesterday evening on the novel, & have now written almost a quarter of the first draft.[115] But I am worried about the "consolation" you required & I promised; perhaps it will appear. At present it seems rather sinister. However, there are ¾ of it to go, but I am so anxious to please you with it that I fuss a little. It will amuse you to know, after being so much accused of "obscurity" that the Bp. of Chelmsford's son says that I have "unlike Eliot, a terrifying simplicity." Wasn't it Wordsworth who said that every great poet had to spend nearly all his life teaching people how to read him, and then they were surprised to find him so simple? It looks like happening!

This is a poor note; imagine it kisses; and return them. I wish it were this week-end! But with any luck we will break the next 3 weeks with a night before I go to Birmingham. I can't get over the fact that they pay!!

Serge

Dearest,

But you must not think you ought to write, though indeed I love it. I won't have you worried about one thing which is at least in my control. I've told Mrs. Leonard you will probably ring her up if possible; and I've told Mrs. Flecker I will give you her message when I am up. I think, if it were possible . . . if you felt like it and up to it, but I know all about appointments . . . it would be useful if you could see her. You remember your great success with the Bishop of Chelmsford, in regard to the Evangelical idea? Mrs. F. in her last letter said that her husband was a great Evangelical. "(I don't fancy you are)." She showed no hesitation in being grateful that I was doing the book, but I should like her to feel that all was well—poor old soul!—and I fancy you could put that over, as a wife. Also she is clearly fussed by the notion that she didn't quite do him justice, and as a woman whose husband can testify that you did him even more than justice you might console her there also. She is becoming aware that he died 2 years ago "and people forget." I'll say they do, & I doubt if the book will ever be published.[116] But, *if* there is an opportunity (I know the doubtful chances—but there's no hurry) I think you could add another old lady to your diadem of souls, while I toil at the diadem of Letters. There's something very agreeable in working together like that . . . our Lord dividing his activity, & so on.

I have written to M. an account of yesterday, as full as I could remember, in order to please him. I gave her[117] a quick lunch at the R., for partly the same reason, but as she doesn't drink or smoke to speak of, it wasn't expensive. Also I like occasionally to appear detached at the R.; the last was Hugh MacDonald and that was months ago.

The Queen of the Netherlands and Mr. Bruce Montgomery are taking their degrees to-day. B.M. is proposing to write an essay on me in a book of essays[118] on Jonson, Wyndham Lewis, Peacock, & two or three other classics. The Miss Sinclair[119] has written to say that she will be at Eaton Gate near Sloane Square certainly on Monday 25th. I have suggested calling there between 2 & 3. If she agrees, will you have lunch with me again on the Monday, all being well? Then I can go & see her, & see what the situation is, and we can meet again for the train. I might try & catch the 4.45, as I have a lecture the next day. But the lunch would be a good idea.

To-night Renée Haynes[120] has asked me to go round and meet A. L. Rowse,[121] who is something at All Souls, & writes sometimes in the *Observer* & wants to meet me. I didn't know R.H. was in Oxford—nor is she, it seems, except for the night. Rowse, I suspect, is a tiresome man; I reviewed his poems—not too enthusiastically—& I have quite forgotten them. However, no doubt we shall get through, but I'm not keen on it.

It would be rather agreeable, don't you think? if I made another shot at ringing you up next Tuesday morning. It just occurs to me that if I'm in London the next Monday I shan't see the office between Friday afternoon & Tuesday afternoon; & if all goes as I suspect, in the week after I shall come up on Wednesday & go to Birmingham on Thursday. And S.H. will just have to get along.

Now if yours was a dull letter,—*if!*—what, madonna, is this? don't let's inquire. It is well-intentioned, say love-intentioned—but how much does that cover? I profoundly condoled with you on yesterday, & M & the Ds. I was much affected by you this morning even more than usual. Also this morning I drifted into the Depot to make them take the 3 *Plays* out of the window & put in the *Poetic Mind;* if I am lecturing, people may as well see the better stuff, *and* what may bring us in a penny or two. There are 2 or 3 of my books it bores me to see, & no-one else read. The *E.P.M.* has some value still, I hope.

All my devotion & love.

Serge

15 Oct/43

I'm sometimes inclined to think that the reason why I don't write well here is because of the very dark temper I am in all the time; & that this explains why our mood is either sinister or dull. You can't imagine how I dislike people's *faces.*[122] Only the conventions of years of social behaviour stop me, I sometimes feel, shouting at them. It isn't, I allow, their fault, but that makes no difference. There are moments when I am tempted to make sudden unpleasant remarks. You can think I mean whom you please, & you will not be wrong: in fact, you will be entirely right. About *everyone*—I repeat, everyone. It is worse with the women than with the men, because every woman actively repels me, whereas the men are only passively unbearable. I am coming to a point where you will be my only link with humanity. Have we a reputation? are we known? O madonna, madonna, do I pay for it, as much, believe me, as you!

This outburst is no doubt due to so much return. Anne S. is back, & the Ds. are, I suppose, back. They all seem, in a sense, to close the door upon me. A little masculine chat sometimes—yes; a little incense & admiration from the young—yes; let me indulge myself so far: it is the only way one feels one's work at all useful. But else—no. I discuss nothing about my books; no-one knows what is happening in the novel; I keep profoundly "myself to myself." I heard some time ago that one undergraduate had referred to me as "a legendary and secluded figure." That was proper: so I will be. I break out of my clouds to lecture and return again to my clouds.

Forgive. I wish M. could (bless him!) find an alternative place, & you & I could find somewhere nice, & live—O a long time, with no-one. Breaking out into visibility just occasionally. Perhaps, some time . . .

Renée Haynes looks . . . I was about to say 60, and then remembered that we are getting on . . . say 80 then. It is very extraordinary how much younger you look than any woman of 50—pain, pressure, poverty, & all. Like (perhaps) me and Gerry. Her husband is in Africa, & she [R.H.] has had another baby. Rowse was very polite, a know-all and a great talker. There was another woman, the wife of Geoffrey Warder the M.P., who told me how much De la Mare admired my work. I knew that anyhow.

To-night Gervase Mathew is to take me to meet a clergyman called Austin Farrer,[123] a philosopher & theologian—whose books are far too learned for me. But *Beatrice* has allured him, I am told. I got back in good time last night and wrote some more. I have pushed on to 102 of my slips; if I can manage as many more without breaking down (I mean the back, not me), it will be pretty secure. I must break off soon to do something about Flecker; Mrs. F. is obviously yearning. Underhill ought to be out soon; I have returned the poems for page proofs. As things have turned out, after *Beatrice*, I think they may have a chance of more sales.

This is all no doubt due to the second week end—when I always feel lowest. And you? But we will have a nice time, & (if you can bear it) another lovely lunch. And no old Pearn in the morning.

God bless you. One herewith.

Serge

18 Oct/43

If I could know how you are before I write each day, it would be convenient, would it not? because then I should be able to know better how or what to write. "The soul,"[124] wrote Wordsworth, "Remembering *how* she felt but what she felt Remembering not . . ." and a good deal depends on the *how*. For indeed, as you know, there is not much *what* to write about, in a general way. And would I bore you if I could help it?—never. And anything more revolting, if you are feeling bad, than continuous chat about reviews & things I can't imagine.

Reviews? My mind flitted to them because the *Listener* has just done me very well; two columns of serious chat, bringing in the *Dove,* and talking about its "brilliant pages," & saying that "It is possible that modern criticism will prove to have no finer pages than . . ." the *Figure*. I don't recognize the style, and it's unsigned. I'll send you a cutting as soon as I get it. Hugh MacDonald met me in the street and said that he'd recently seen Robert Nichols who was lonely and neglected and tiresome. Do you remember the old years when he was everyone and I used sometimes to go very dark and you had to console me? And now—! H.M. said that it was an astonishing thing how my reputation continually increased & how I had stayed the course. Blunden[125] (he says) giving up his job at Merton in order to write little books—which (said

H.M.) nobody much wants, and he (H.M.) doubts if Blunden can keep it going.

All very odd. All the same, I might have gone under if you hadn't been there to ease me. They were dark days[126] in that way. I know money isn't much, and pain is, & . . . O well, don't let's compare. It was largely you.

Love, and thanks & blessings.

Serge XXX

20 Oct/43

Herewith the *Listener;* also *Theology.* It is clear that, as soon as possible, I must do a succeeding book—*Essays in Romantic Theology,* I think. For I do think that the weight, length, & seriousness of the reviews show a certain need for the doctrine. Meanwhile, among all the other things, I labour, as St. Paul said, "to confirm the Churches."[127] My priest at Rochester has been reading *Descent Into Hell* which "throws a quite new light on the Atonement"; and my Methodist minister at Blackpool says that the *Dove* is "the greatest blessing God has given me for a long time." He is buying all my books by degrees, & he adds: "The new light is glinting through what I am privileged to write and say in Methodism. God bless you for all of it."

Be tender & excuse; it isn't, I think, mere bragging. I do not quite sit easily to this; my fresh springs are in you, but if villages are built on the banks of the river it is always because of the wealth of the springs. And I come and drink of the springs before I confirm the Churches.

I have now to draw up a note on F.P.'s work—but not for Oxford. Sir Humphrey read me a letter yesterday from Collier Abbot, who is at Durham and edits Gerard Hopkins's letters, saying that, if Sir H. thought F.P. would like it, he thought he could get him a Durham M.A.; F.P. has done a lot of work on G.H.'s prose. Sir H. & Sisam leapt at the idea; I have suspected for some time that they were in a fix about Oxford. *I* need hardly tell *you* that I cannot help being—rather unkindly—pleased too. Durham is a reputable place, & next to the two great Universities, & it will leave . . . well, it will leave . . . you know what I mean. Oddments like chief cashiers at the C.P. are quite another business. So I am to write something (most secretly) about him. (I fear that our Mrs. Page may murmur, & even suggest his turning it down. Would you, in like circumstances? Let us be honest; both you & I might. I indeed should probably be furious. But of course the official game—Sir H's & Sisam's—is to play it up: which Sir H. in his own inimitable way was busy doing to me yesterday. Everything he said was right & true—& yet . . . Durham? Hush!)

I have accumulated the marmalade & will bring it. I devote the waking period of every day to thinking of you and praying for you. When the public work is done I will write my final poems for you. God bless.

Serge

Your letter was sweet, and thank you for it. Except that I was sad to hear of your bilious attack!

CSL takes quite your view of the present novel—it's marvelous how his opinion runs after yours, considering your view of his writings! He has fallen heavily for what he's heard; saying it's much the best thing I've done & that I have more power in my little finger than all of them in all their bodies. I hope he's right, but I don't seem to be getting on very fast; Betty[128] is still leaving King's Cross—O we hadn't got to Betty, I forgot! never mind.

Mrs. Flecker is a little bewildered by the technical phrases in the agreement, & also (very nicely!) wants me to have a royalty. It won't make any difference on that book! But N. Pearn is writing to sooth & explain—& take what she offers.

I'm rather glad about Edith, & very sorry about my Aunt.[129] I must go over in two weeks' time! It's a sad business, & I only hope won't knock her out first.

Otherwise, nothing. Things seem to have gone as dull here as for you . . . or almost. I'd better do my lecture to-night—how nice when our routines can be intermingled again! And really the end does seem to be coming slowly. Thank God we're not Germans.

I adore you. Also love. Also long for. Also—all other proper verbs.

Serge

B'ham to
Leamington
4 Nov./43

I don't know if I can write in the train, but I might try—so as to end the day as it began. I've not done badly, thanks to you; tho' there was an awful moment before [illegible word][130] when I thought I was in for one of my old bad wind-attacks. I never quite got rid of the fear of operations then—like you with your pneumonia pains. And I thought it would be awkward to be unable to lecture! However, it eased off; & apart from bruising my knee—*not* in the black-out but round some damned corner, I've got thro' all right, though I wish I wasn't getting out at Oxford. They paid a pound for expenses, so it literally cost me only the taxi-fare this morning! A Cadbury in the chair; about 208 people; silent and attentive audience; much applause. O our old John o' London meetings![131]—yet in a way they were more fun.

(First stop—Leamington Spa, I suppose. Then Banbury; then somewhere; then Oxford. If I were not so unhappy about you & M., I should be reasonably content: a job done, money earned, a proper instruction given. But I *am* too miserable about both to be able to read; though now I have closed the day with you, I must try & think about the novel.[132] I *must* discover what to do next.)

Cadbury had obviously never heard of me, but he had been given (obviously by someone else) a few lines about criticisms, novels, & plays which he read. The head of the English department however knew the proper things & was about to read *Beatrice*. Others had heard of the Oxford lectures. We were 20 minutes late starting, so it was 2 before we reached Birmingham. I ate some chocolate & drank my dose [?] on the way. But I want to be coming home, to a quite peaceful flat & you. I can do as much as—I probably do better than—ever, but it takes it out of me more, & there's nowhere to relax afterwards. I could cry with pity for myself; you will say I should do better to pray for you, & so I will! Did you not save my stomach this very morning? And my back is a little aching, & my legs are very much aching, & I want to be taken care of! And please, if I do not write that often (but I expect I do!), it is because I do not wish to seem to burden you. But at 9, in a train, may I not release myself? Given you do not guess how I play my part everywhere, & can never, never, unlock! Turn you the key in the wards, and unseal "the hushed casket of my soul."[133] Shall I write you a counter-sonnet to Keats? shall I? why not? that & what money I can make is all I can give. Does a place in English literature move you? not much? alas, one cannot enjoy.

//after which, all the lights went out & we rode on in darkness. So I thought about the novel, willy-nilly!

Miss Sinclair[134] writes to say that her Committee are enthusiastic and accept my terms, though some are shy of "launching out": so they very well may be. But that's for them to decide. They (she says) will write officially. And I shall transfer the negotiations about royalties on performances to Miss Pearn, & indulge myself with the prospect of the money. And of you & me going— yes, really!—after the war to see a New Play of mine.

God! the *Observer*—not having reviewed *Beatrice*—now writes to ask if I will review Binyon's *Paradiso*[135] for them. Only 500 words, but worth doing. It's nice, I will say, now, in your & my last period, always to be approached and never to have to run round. (Except, of course, [page missing]

it now; no, still there it is. Let's try—we are now on our way to Banbury.

> Unseal the changing casket of my soul!
>   turn the key there! The Image I present
> everywhere is as fixed as Caesar's pole—
>   the star remote that shines on each event
> changelessly—for all lightness changelessly.
>   But if it crimsons sometimes, and (above
> the worlds) vibrates, and someone says: "O see,
>   what colour takes it suddenly? what love?"
> then the Chaldean angels of my heart

shall answer: "Potent are the myths; but this
comes of no myth, lives from no sacred art.
This is her presence whom the married kiss
so steadily renews in fame and flame,
whom men call Michal, God some lordlier name."

—Done, & before Banbury. One of these days you shall copy it out for me to have a copy! Good night.

8 Novr./43

Madonna,

Well, about not hearing you when M. rings up, we have talked! . . . but hope I shall to-morrow. Miss Gardner has asked me to lunch to meet the young man who wrote the *Listener* review. He is asserted to have been "knocked over" by my books, & to have taken 3 months over the review.

The young rise continually—could I be of any use! B. Montgomery (as I meant to tell you) produced a young Lieutenant who has just been "stupefied" by *Descent into Hell*, & was speechless—merrily goggling; sweet of him! "Male & female created he them." But I should hate an overplus of females; not that I have them. I have sent the letter about the play on to N.P., to write to Miss Sinclair. All I have to do is to *write* the stuff. These—— lectures take up time. I have to re-read the plays.

M. sounded tolerable, but that (I well know) is nothing to go by. He asked (hide this letter!) so enthusiastically after my back, on your behalf, that I thought there must be a catch. (I'm sorry about Sunday, but I saw no way to get out of it.) Actually it is better, though still a touch tiresome.

Binyon's *Paradiso*[136] has now reached me from the *Observer* & from *Britain To-day*, an uninteresting monthly! I have headed off *T&T*. Obviously, I am soon going to be *the* Dante man. *Blackfriars*—that is, the Dominicans,—is most polite, though (yes, you won't believe it, but it's true!) deprecating my too-insistent morality. I always told you I was more moral than the Church itself, & the Dominicans seem to think so. But then that is largely due to the shape of your face, & to your way of moving. Largely; I do not say God has not had something to do with it.

The details of great glory strike
on bone and flesh and soul alike,
Compelling me (through you) to be
a preacher of morality;
For how should one who saw your cheek
at all in other language speak?

Well, how should he? But I shall not be moral if I do not get down to my work.

I see—O do I! —you had a horrid time last night. You don't guess how the things fidget me,—though the back & M's tempers are worse. But all ways I am afraid. Cowardice?—well, after all, it's for you largely.

God bless you, all love.

Serge

23 Novr/43

Only a note—since I shall see you to-night. I have had a letter from a female Don asking if I will take four of her people in pairs for private work on "Shakespeare and contemporary dramatists" next term. C.S.L. & Tolkien tell me this will be paid for, roughly, at a guinea a time; which would mean £12–£16 for the term. So I think I do; it will mean reading up on a few contemporary dramatists & modern critics, but it seems a pity (a) to throw money away (b) not to put Ourself over Oxford while We can (c) not to save them from Blunden or Ridley or what not. Monday & Tuesday evenings, I think, for an hour a time.

Nothing else. It was so sweet of you to ask about the eyes that I all but lost my head! but they don't hurt me in the least; they only get a little blurred. But I do feel that we may have a touch more money this next year—if I do well— that I can't bother about that. I should like to buy you a hat (or the equivalent) every month!!

Till to-morrow.

Serge

9 Decr/43

Well, it is true I slept, but one feels stale the next day . . . though as seventenths of England is doing it, one ought not to complain. But the getting-down and getting-back are a nuisance. I wrote a little novel, but I've got to a point where the dead young woman has just met Antichrist, and what they say to each other I simply cannot begin to think. I suppose I have by now very nearly done half, which is encouraging, but needs tightening up, as you would tell me had you heard it! (But then no-one else . . . O well, yes, CSL has heard a little more, but only a bit; so there!) However, so far as I can see, there isn't a "bright" remark from beginning to end. No jokes, no cleverness, very little conversation; just ghosts and the horrors and beauties of my undoubted style.

It would, I suppose, look well to go round to the R. to-night; one can hardly eat there on Sunday for one's own convenience without taking some notice, and to-morrow I am supposed to be open for questions on my lectures at St. Hilda's—

I have just remembered the rent—*and* sent it. Also I have just now paid the Club money, so I send a pound along. I'll send the Xmas box money presently. This is for you with love & kisses.

Serge

9[10] Decr./43

Better yesterday than to-day. I think—and to-day I haven't been out at all since I got here this morning. Cheese sandwiches & your cake—of which I ate a good deal last night. To-night I find we are fire-watching here; which reminds me to say that Gerry who came back last night, but not by my train, & says he begins his job on the Monday after Christmas. It's odd how I didn't want him to—O not because I want him here; simply because I know I don't want him to be able to do anything. Which, as we said on the telephone, about the faces,[137] is very shocking, & shows what evil is in our natures, or rather mine. I want him to go on being rather a failure and translating French novels, while I get long reviews and lecture in Oxford, and am generally more successful. If you hadn't been so very anti-persecution minded yourself, & always discouraged it—on my word, madonna, I don't know but I mightn't have fallen . . . I have had some dark times of general envy and jealousy, and that is one reason why I never dared *begin* thinking anything unfair. On that subject at least I had to "under-exaggerate" or I might have been like Herbert Palmer or Lady Watson. So God bless G.H. & let him get on.

It was nice ringing you up . . . and going back to the last paragraph Mrs. Flecker says "I am perfectly satisfied with your work and its tone." She is, is she! She has also sent it on to her son & daughter for them to see . . . this almost annoyed me, but (for the reasons above given) I thought it had better not. So it isn't. But . . .

Tell Michael the Jane Austen book has reached me. I will post it on in a day or two. Otherwise nothing of interest. No money & no poems.

But it was a lovely time. And the telephone was a good idea. And thank you for everything.

Serge

30 Dec./43

How sweet of you to send my aunt[138] the pound! I hope to put an extra one in here to make it up. It's wonderful, so it is, how we agree with each other on things—and especially in disposing of cash. I'm delighted about the coal, because now it's paid for there's a chance it'll come before the other runs out.

"I too have not been idle."[139] I've sent the rent (with the letter) *and* the electric light. I've also made out a cheque for Anne & another to change at the bank on Saturday, when I'll send some more.

This morning I was rung up by Harrington from the C.P.,[140] who said he had travelled from London last night with a man named Venables who belonged to some group of masters for teaching English, to whom M. had been kind in Bumpus's. He and his group are meeting here for a day or two, & want to get in touch with me. The usual thing, no doubt; but it amused me to have the awful majestitude of the C. Press invoked. In another ten years the King'll be used as go-between.

O I'm so *sleepy*. This night-at-S. House—business always leaves me stale, sleepy, & fretful. Like M. But this morning's paper was one of the better kind—victories on the sea; in Berlin, & in the east. I think it'll be some time before the Gr. start another war.

O sleep, my lovely! That's my idea. And you with a cup of tea at four. Bless you! And then bless you.

Serge

1944

Well, dearest, here are the two pounds. Let's say a happy New Year again with them.

M.'s review arrived safely. I think it's good. But he hasn't chosen his pen-name,[1] & perhaps I'd better ring up & find out. I was thinking of ringing you up on Wednesday afternoon from here—yes?

I have written to Birmingham saying I'd rather go next term. The same to the Warden of Radley.[2] I have told a group of students of the *Dove & Forgiveness* & the rest that I will come to see them the Sunday after next. I have promised to see a conscientious objector next Tuesday and a priest sometime later. This is what we call public life! I have also two letters of inquiry to answer by post. Let's hope it can be said that—"the Eternal Master found

His single talent well employed"![3]

Somehow I thought I was farther on with the novel,[4] though now I think, of course I see I couldn't have been. But 50,000 words does leave about 40,000 to do. However, we both ought to be grateful I've got as far, and I shall try & get on during the next few nights. The poor Mrs. Flecker will be writing again soon!!

O love, this is a catalogue! Excuse—I seem to be pressed to-day. But the sun is shining, & it's the third of January. Perhaps the last winter here (as I insist on believing) is going to be warm! Next week I shall just have left you and my tutorials will be beginning.

All love & blessings.

Serge

I sent a small parcel of washing off this morning!

I send herewith a copy of M's review,[5] which has gone off to *T&T*. I think it's very clear and well-put and has quite the right balance. It's very agreeable to find him blossoming into this flower.

But for him to ask you to get a tie & for you to do it, is a pattern of courtesy all round. It's a better start to the year than last was . . . & I send a pound towards the tie & as a kind of thank-offering. If we can keep up those books from time to time, it may help now, and might be useful in the future. I hadn't begun reviewing at 21!!

The Oxford Society for Social Studies has asked me to speak on "The Artist's Attitude towards the Community"; it depends on their arranging dates. I don't know what the phrase really means; and I shall say so. At least, that's not quite true—I know what they mean, but I doubt if it's valid. I doubt if I, as writer, have any attitude towards Society except, of course, to do something about it. But—however, I needn't feed my sweet on this slightly dry subject. I will save it for the day when I toddle to the restaurant beside you—Club, indeed! Did I tell you, however, that Basil is putting me up for the Union here? All I know is that the Oxford Union is a well-known thing: one can get lunch there, if not too crowded; and it has a library, and reading room; and it might be convenient some day in the future. If they let in Non-University Ladies, I'll give you lunch there one day. I understand that the subscription is quite moderate.

You poor dear with Mrs. Oliver! It's a great tribute how, from me downward, everyone relies on you—though trying to you! But your description made me smile. So I shall ring you up on Thursday instead: mind you have any instructions ready.

O God bless!

Serge

12 Jan./44

Less & less happens. It will become necessary soon to write about the novel.[6] Now I do not mind doing that in order to tell you, or to relieve my mind, but I do not wish to do it because there is nothing else. Still, since we are on it . . . I have pushed slowly on, and written another 3000 words or so. O if next week, & the week after, & then another six, were not here! I have read some of it to CSL & Tolkien (you will forgive that; and excuse its technical usefulness) who admire & approve; if I saw the way to end, I might be appeased. Magdalen[7] thinks it "tender & gay" among all the melodramatic horrors—let's hope so. But then (which shows their judgement!) Magdalen thinks you the most admirable woman of all—who do not leave rations till noon, nor have every room upset all the morning, nor go in for spring-cleanings. I told them this morning the story of *Michal & the Sweep*, when you called him from across the road and all was done in 20 minutes . . . "Yes, Charles, but then you are very fortunate." Need they say so?

O darling, I write all like this, & lament it. But how can I do? can I translate into words an ache in my heart & genitals? no. You will say these are letters to "a man's idea of woman"[8]—what an illumination that remark was! but you must be kind & let them pass. They are but daily messages: be pleased to forgive. I do not like always to write about anxieties—M. & your back & your cold & the flat & the coal & so on; it isn't because I don't think of them—every hour, & then some.

Let me kiss you on it. I love you.

Serge

15 Jan./44

This to-day (i) because I wish you to have the enclosed by Monday (ii) because to-morrow is going to be full. All the 6 tutorials are calling in a mass at 10 to have their times arranged, and their various readings mapped out. I can't think what to give them for essays, but I must decide for them. When I shrink alarmed, I say to myself: "Come, come, £20! And probably more easily earned than most!" Then I must get back to Flecker; our W.-Paploe is coming to tea—alas!; and I shall wind up with 2 conversations at the R. I have made up my mind that if Margaret is hoping to come to any of the lectures, she must read Shakespeare properly. I simply will not stand for being merely me—so to put it. The Divine Shakespeare is the thing, & she must get to it. I am infinitely bored and exacerbated with "patronage" of the dead great; usefulness to the living is another matter. But all this hooey about whether X was a better Falstaff than Y, when they don't begin to understand what Falstaff *is*; this borrowing of a hundred clichés and lapping up the dregs of culture; this unintelligent swallowing of our great tradition of august & awful verse—no. You will think, madonna, I am in a bad temper! It is not quite so, but the English upper classes sitting cosily round the divine poets agonizing over their task always has and always will rile me. It's all over and around us. I would rather the b.b.c. Four programmes; *that*, at least, is not pseudo-culture, not a polished incapacity for understanding anything, a mock and muck of intellect.

Ouf! I feel a trifle better now. It's only occasionally I allow my irritations an airing; but this flatulence is all round one here; and it maddens me. I except Magdalen. And I don't know how it's to be cured; but I know very well that I will never encourage it. I am none of your jackals[9] of literature to be clad in lions' skins. And lions themselves can only be attracted by lions' food. Of which none is offered—for the poor boobs do not even know what lions eat. They offer us pap and think we-*we*-We—like it. Good God!

Yes—well. Kiss me and appease me. Let us now rake out this pound-note & kiss that. O most blessed lady, from what infinite dolours your own natural greatness has saved me! If you had been pseudo-cultural . . . "It cannot be; it is impossible." Yes, I know; but permit the hideous impossibility to loom. It does but increase my gratitude and admiration. Be ever, ever so.

> Each your doing,
> So singular in each particular,
> Crowns what you are doing in the present deed,
> That all your acts are queens.[10]

I will say so of you all where—and, if I can, I will ring you up on Tuesday before my lecture—just for once!

Au re-voir, ever noble! Star and scintillation of perfectness!

Serge

27 Jan./44

O my darling, your poor poor back! . . . it is such a shame, & I hate being away almost more then than at other times. Just as if I ever feel ill, I want you more then than even at other times. (I'm always thankful that I've never had to lie up here when you weren't about . . . well, I never did anyhow but you know what I mean! I should physically loathe other people: it's odd how that dislike of others' bodies,[11] which was always marked in me, grows stronger with the years; even the mere sight of them revolts me. It's what I suffer most when I come back here—always from the station; the dislike of seeing their faces. I admit I feel it most in the women; they must, I think, seem to be profane mockeries of you. At least, I can find no other reason for the intensity of my dislike.)

Alas, I began about you and got off on to me! You will say that is like me!! But it was about you at bottom. When I heard that you had spent the 10/- on my suit, I thought it was too sweet of you, but I looked madly round for another 10/. Not finding one I'm sending a pound; we can pretend one half belongs to next month.

I shall, I fear, catch the 5.50. I've heard nothing yet from the lawyers. If I don't hear, I shan't go. God send they don't write. And you & I will have a cosy morning . . . like we did last time, even though you were suffering then. My work provides surcease.

God bless you. Till to-morrow.

Serge

2 Feb./44

Dearest,

How wonderful of you to do it! and how lovely of you to write! This also is rather in haste, as to-day is sprinkled with tutorials. . . .

and there one of them interrupted me; and I Take up My Pen again much later, to resume thanking you. I'm delighted to know about M., & I only hope he continues to like the things. About the £4 due—I won't forget it, especially Win's. It's borne in upon me with some gloom that I shall have to manage a pair of shoes . . . but I want to try for you to have something first! You oughtn't to spend all your time getting things for others.

I have had two letters that rather pleased me. One from the Vicar of Little Malvern, who has been reading me on the *Cross*,[12] and thanks me for saying that the creation needs justifying in view of all its horror. He says I am the one and only writer he has come across who has said this, & he feels it deeply.

The second is from W. H. Auden,[13] in America, to whom, as a politeness, I sent the *Stars*.[14] He is very polite—"You are the only writer since Dante who has found out how to make poetry of theology & history." "There is already in this country a little band (little but enthusiastic) of C.-W.-ites." And so on. Rather charming! But now I must read his books!!

I am not writing very well today! I shall ring you up some time on Monday afternoon. And I am in your debt for everything, but then I love being in your debt, and don't mean to try & pay it off!! Continue, most indulgent lady, to be a creditor . . . of love . . . and a debtor too!

Serge

5 Feb./44

You do write the nicest letters . . . a lucidity, Majesty, which I cannot too much admire; my mind relaxes in it, as my flesh in your bed. I mean, for example, what you said of Mrs. O's fantastic imagination, and about going to the cinema with M., & your sudden and just remark about "quidi." Very odd, that. I never noticed it before. I will send more next week. Nancy Pearn replies, thanking me and you warmly, saying that Oxford is the idea, and adding that she expects the cheque and contract any day. So long as it comes by the end of the month, it's all right by me.

I found myself this morning thinking how admirable it would be if I could get a Readership[15] here when I retire. I know it may be only a dream; on the other hand, CSL & Tolkien are only human, and are likely to take more trouble over a project which would enable them to see a good deal more of me than over anything which didn't. And I think, in the future, they *may* take steps. Let me know your reaction;[16] you shall not live anywhere you do not wish. But it would be very odd indeed if these years of trial and stress and separation eventually produced a much easier time later on, and bore fruit in more steady money just when we could do with it. O I know; a thousand things may go wrong. Still . . . we have not altogether failed to put ourselves over Oxford. And Oxford might . . . it just might . . . want me.

Dreams. But I thought, last night, as my young Scot took me to the Indian restaurant for curry, how amusing it would be for you & me to dally in the streets on a fine day, and go to the pictures, and sometimes go up to London for a night or two at a *good* hotel, and a dress, and a theatre or so. Or Bath for a week. Dreams. But if I can make those dreams actual by anything, by God, will I do it! I am thinking of my next prose books with that in mind. I shall hope to be free for the next in October, and I think *The Figure of Arthur*[17] would be a nice pendant to *Beatrice,* and the kind of thing that would help.

We had an alert on Thursday during the tutorial, but it wasn't my evening, so I thought of you and continued to converse on Blake. I asked Lewis's brother[18] how much CSL talked during his tutorials, & he said "From 88 to 99 per cent." Now I should not put my own monologues at more than 65 per cent; so I think I do better!

O God bless you. I almost feel the hint of all restoration in the air.

Serge

22 Feb/44

Dearest,

Last night I switched on the midnight news, while trying to think of something to say about *Antony*—& I may say I failed, so it was *not* a good lecture, & I was (for almost the first time) rather glad you weren't there, because I hate not being at my best in front of you: for others, it's their look-out, though just too bad!—well, I switched it on, & thought I heard the London *All Clear* Coming through from London, and concluded you must have had another raid. I cannot find anything in this morning's papers, so perhaps it was only an alert. But it made it even more difficult to think of *Antony*—I'm no good as a critic: my personal intuitions disturb me too easily!!

It's colder than ever to-day; there was some snow this morning just before the lecture—which (I hope it was that!) reduced my audience. But we've done fairly well for six weeks, & I can't be surprised if there's a drop in the last two.

I have accepted the Dante Society, leaving the dinner to God! I have written to the B.B.C. man,[19] saying that I should like to chat with him about a possible subject. I don't at all mind whether I do it or not (except for the money), and I'm not anxious to seem too eager. However, it is worth exploring possibilities.

Bruce Montgomery has sent me his first detective story, which I'll bring when I come. He adds to his letter—I'd forgotten I had told him—"I saw Michael's review; Very good, I thought."

I ate some of your cake & cheese, & a tiny bit of the chocolate at 1 A.M., & very good it was! One day, I shall get all that—as disguised as necessary or as flagrant as possible—into my poems, either the Myth poems or more personally. It's very important that someone should, & there's no one but I to do it.

Do you remember that odd girl Frances Murrey at the Stepney vicarage? She is a friend of Anne's—& she has just sent me a brief note; from Brentwood where I gather she's a nurse now: all it says is that she "feels so overpoweringly that I must thank you for the *Figure of B*. It makes such a difference." How? Where? Madonna, do I know? But if she's ever near me, she had better come & see me. "For this among the rest was I ordained."[20] Shadows, as I had the honour to say to you in the bus, but shadows of their own. I gather from Anne that she's generally unhappy. Not that I personally shall be any use; impersonally, perhaps.

This morning at 6.45 I woke with violent cramp, and told you aloud. But you weren't awake, & I told you again. Then I found I couldn't find my way about the room, and I realized you weren't there, & couldn't make out what had happened. It might have been a scene in one of my novels. After hopping dementedly about for what seemed an age, I realized slowly where I was. (This is *not* invented; it is cold fact.) I couldn't get you to hear. The immediate leap of my instincts to you is almost the best substitute for you . . . though to substitute me in any way for you is not very exhilarating.

All blessings. All thanks. All love.

Serge

10 March/44

I shall put a call through soon, & meanwhile I shall write. Having just eaten four—but smaller—sandwiches. Egg. I am becoming a positive connoisseur in sandwiches of the Marks & Spenser kind. Woolworths seems to have given them up; at least they never have them when I pass in the mornings. Now one could maintain that there is something almost Pathetic about me buying sandwiches of a morning—and have I done it all this week? No; because Monday you had fed me on cake. But otherwise—

Robin M. has just been I—at least, I mean he was this morning; and I maintain firmly that you can hardly call him either famous or well-off or . . . whatever the other thing was. But he seems better. He asked me if I knew what it was to feel your brain never stopped & couldn't relax, & I said, more or less: "What do you think!" He is over till to-morrow for some music somewhere here: fortunately *not* for the weekend.

Our F.P. has been written to by the University of Durham at long last. A man named Collier Abbot there suggested it; F.P. having done a lot of editorial work for him. He is asked to go there—in June, I think, for the degree-giving. All very fortunate. I could not decently have resented his being "done," but all my lower self would have preferred he wasn't! Leave me alone here, & let him be crowned elsewhere. But otherwise I am glad; the poor dear deserves it all.

Meanwhile, I have written to the B.B.C. man proposing next Thursday—either morning or afternoon, but not between 12 & 2. Then I will bring up the cash for the Hat or/and whatever, and either we will get one or you shall hang on to it; as [page missing]

13 March/44

It was marvellous to hear you yesterday. Unexpected like. But very unique, besides a delight. Except for meals I worked steadily ALL yesterday: Flecker in the morning; on novel in the afternoon & evening. F. has one advantage— one is not tempted to vanity. One is a little tempted to carelessness (if it isn't one temptation, it's another!), but I fight it. I've done most of another chapter, but the Old Boys bore me.

However, in virtue of the Old Boys, why not let us exchange 10/- for love? Why not indeed! If this too is drudgery, how sweet, most excellent lady, is drudgery! Which reminds me to ask if by any chance you saw a review of contemporary young poets in the *Sunday Times;* because Gerry got the *S. Express* in mistake, & I'm told that this review began by saying that, "after being expected to admire *The Waste Land,* we were now expected to admire Taliessin's Logres." Very odd if it did! because it must mean me, and it must mean that T. is regarded as equally influential with T.S.E.'s *Wasteland,* which I should *not* have thought. But these things are so unexpected.

Pass it. I write as & how, chatting to you about what there is. No-one's more conscious than I of the occasional dullness . . . but what will you? yesterday held no news, nor to-day so far. I hope to get an extra cheque from Fabers this month for *Beatrice;* I do rather want to know how it's sold. "This letter is all I-I-I"; well, but the last was U-U-U. Now wasn't it? Kiss me and say so. There's a piece of Fine Writing in the novel about a husband bringing his wife a glass of water[21] which reminds me of many things.

God bless.

Serge

I sent a small parcel off on Saturday.

14 March/44

It's a gloomy day, and I am gloomy. It is extraordinary how I dislike people.[22] You know, darling, either I shall have to believe in God seriously or it'll get the better of me. In a way they don't even impinge on me, but when they do I hate it. This is, no doubt, the result of being separated from my Center— meaning you—and living on the circumference of an ever-twirling circle. Robin Milford asked me if I ever felt as if I couldn't relax to which I said peevishly: "Ever feel! I never can."—Twenty-three planes have just flown over with a loud noise. I hope they're going to kill Germans, because until we have killed enough Germans I shall—we shall—have no peace. I want to eat sultanas in a cake at home. I want . . . well, never mind. I will tell you to-morrow. I have written a long article on Virgil[23] & almost finished copying another chapter of the novel. To-night I shall go back to Mrs. F.

Between that point and this a cheque has arrived for £16. This does not cheer me up, but it's useful: and I have the honour to send you a pound immediately—in accordance with our usual custom. The £16 is all (you won't believe it) royalties on books already published. It's composed of £10 more on *Beatrice*, £5 on *Witchcraft*, & £2 on *Forgiveness*—less various charges. I'm a little surprised; though I was reckoning on a little more from *B.* It's sold another 800 copies. *Witchcraft* goes on steadily at about 100 a year . . . quite reasonably good for a 3 year old book. I think the man I like best in this world is Mr. Geoffrey Faber. We *must* finish the novel and get on to the prose book—the King—meaning *the* King, Arthur.

As for rain-coat, nothing doing. I should hate wearing it here. I don't in the [page missing]

17 March/44

I have put a call through to you on the chance to say that I have been in and fixed up Tuesday, between 1.30 & 2. It seems that the Proprietor—or whatever he is—is out between about 12 & 1, which will suit us. But I only saw a boy, & will check it on Monday.

Yesterday *was* nice, wasn't it? especially from the time I got back onwards—it is always nice when we have time to dally. I send you another pound h/w for the fare, & I will have the cash ready for the glasses, & for more hours sleeping. I've sent off the electric light bill—now that *is* cheap.

A letter from my Aunt[24] to say that Probate has been granted & she's got the money in the bank. I shall have to go over—at least—on Sunday week. There are just two or three books for King Arthur[25] I may want, which aren't easily getable—but be at ease. Most shall go to Foyle's. But not (I think) the only valuable one! And I have an address to write to about the MSS. When *I* die, there won't be more than the MS. of any poem I happen to be working on: not, I hope, the "Colophon to Dante: In a Letter to Michal," which will have been, let's believe, published. I should like (a) to finish *Taliessin* (b) to be made Laureate (c) to publish the *Colophon:* would not that be sweet? (after all, when one hears the word "spectacular" one has to remember the *Figure of Beatrice:* no other wife has been inside such a pageant, & influenced the true Romantics. But pass—kiss me and let be!)

Kiss me anyhow.

Serge

[The following letter in verse exists in two versions, this and another that is heavily revised. This one seems, therefore, to be a final version. In the script only one correction occurs. Line 4 in stanza 2 reads: "(lording my verse) your still prophetic fire,"]

18 March/1944

Of old, when Emperors or Ladies died,
they were (historians tell us) deified;
their private beauties or their public wars
incontinently raised among the stars;
they, putting that conclusive glory on,
within the lower heavens for ever shone.

Perchance, as men count immortality,
even on this earth you shall remembered be,
and future generations shall admire
your still (lording my verse) prophetic fire,
and at St. Albans or in London say:
"Here once that Lady walked who taught our day
(by her first apparition, and by all
her carriage, through each fate that did befall)
what our too-clouded culture has forgot—
what the great Vision is and what it's not."
Thus while your high and planetary sphere
revolves, a smaller star shall hover near,
attendant on, ascendant from, your head,
an emanation from which rays are shed—
the opening of this morning's note, which shall
be a fair moon [or "noon"] in some short interval
of your—O more than solar plentitude!
in your own writing, as in this verse, viewed;
your strong "Serge darling." This within the sky
of Oxford, and of England, hung, and I
looked and beheld it, in the cloud-brimmed arch
of heaven, translucent, this eighteenth of March,
of our Redemption nineteen forty four;
let time and place so seal what is much more
than they can be, and yet in them subsisting
rules by its golden light their bitter twisting.

Take this, O sign, O striver in the good,
so seen, so read, so shown, so understood,
and know your strength so travels in my blood.

Serge

22 March/44

Dearest,

Going off at a tangent, I wish to say that I wish you to open an account for yourself at some bank, and I will start it with £50. The Post Office, if you like. Or as you like. Then you will have something you can get at—occasionally, he added hastily.

Why thus? Madam, the "Councils of the Four Women's Colleges and the Delegates of St. Anne's Society" have just sent it me—asking me to accept it as a personal gift, and "as a tangible expression of their gratitude." Why the Women? For two reasons—(i) they think of money quicker than men (ii) there are very few undergraduate males reading Literature at present. It came through a Don at Lady Margaret whom I don't remember ever to have seen. But if I may lay it complete at Your Most Serene and Adorable Excellency's feet—assuring Your Excellency that this is the most exquisite moment of all lecturing, and that I would do twice & three times as much with joy to be able to cast it before you—why: if Your Altogether Glorious and Beautiful Sacredness permits—? Do permit.

And now you will think that I am making too much of a Fuss about an ordinary thing. But I have so long wished to have even a small extra to offer, being even more aware than you of the maddening limitation of cash, that I am too much delighted. By Friday I shall be recovered, and less pleased about "this University," though not about your permission. And that's enough about it, but do take what Omnipotence allows.

Oxford is buzzing with rumours about trains; I hope none of them are true. I cannot believe that the day after to-morrow will be difficult—only if by chance I don't turn up—but I shall.

It was a great shame yesterday—though it was cold & blowy & rainy here, and I tried to persuade myself that it was as well for your sake that you hadn't come. But it was a poor effort. And we will fix something. And I do, do hope you're not in much pain!

I gather last night was hideous. We had the alert at 1, just as I was thinking of going to bed, & were on duty till 2.30. But no attacks. This morning's papers suggest a perfectly awful time in London! O miserable me to be away from you then.

Kisses and love.

Serge

I sent off two shirts this morning—service!

11 April/44

Well . . . many happy returns to both of us.[26] It's been a blessed companionship to me; without you I should have been a fool and lost—lost in this world and most probably in the next. It was you who first turned me from a versifier to something like a poet; it was you who "preserved me still," always have and always will (I hope!). Now, as everything here & in general changes, it pleases me a little to think I never for a moment thought anything else, nor could.

I shall ring you up to-night. Meanwhile I send on letters from *T & T* for M. . . . No; it'll look better if I send it separately, & please him more. It's about his pseudonym, but all quite friendly, & they say his review is "excellent."

Nothing of interest here. I have made out a cheque to be changed to-morrow. It's true we should have had the loose covers anyhow, but might they be considered our small present to ourselves?

Mrs. Flecker is in bed! She mustn't die or where will your birthday present be?

All gratitude & love

Serge

18 April/44

If I had any sense, I should be ringing you up again; you may say: "But why, Illustrious, wait for an excuse?" and then I should be stalled for an answer, since indeed your face, though more valuable & profitable than all the money in the world, is yet out of all proportion to money, & cash can hardly be offered as a reason for not invoking it. Face or voice—imagination does not separate them; the profile[27] is the assent. Now here I am breaking into metaphysics, and you see how impossible it is that any except Dante and perhaps Patmore and any [of] my own creatures—creations; nothing less—& you should follow it. The assent is the profile; the profile is the spirit; the spirit is the Way. So the profile is the Way. This is a great saying, and full of profundities, but only I define it & only you—ought to—believe it. But generations shall.

But I did not mean to write so . . . what you call smarmy and I call doctrinal; it was but an accident; forgive it. I gave Chichester[28] your message—taking advantage of his asking after you & after M. We sat in Sir Richard Livingston's drawing-room, and talked of high ecclesiastical affairs in low voices—the statements of the new Catholic Archbishop[29] of Westminster, & such things. (He thinks of me as a "pillar"—so let him!) He seems to bear up pretty well, but he told me to thank you for your understanding. Which I do.

I have had a letter from Phyllis Potter asking me to go to Pleshey to give two addresses in October, & have provisionally agreed. She says she is to be in London at the week-end, & is asking herself . . . no, asking you if she can come to tea. I do NOT want her particularly—anyhow I must be at M's disposal on Saturday & away on Sunday. What *I* want is two secluded days with you: and that is all. Expect three (which I shan't get), or four, or to infinity . . . after a century or two we should come out of our seclusion & entertain.

Which reminds me that our Miss Gardner asked me the other day if it would be worth my while to consider a provincial Chair for a few years. I ran into her & said something polite about the Women's Colleges; and she told me that a few of the Council were afraid that I should be offended by the offer of money—good God! She also said that one or two of the Birmingham people had raised the question of offering me presently a Chair there. "And smiling put the question by"[30]—meaning me—meaning I did. It is *Beatrice*[31]—id est, you—that has helped to do this. As a prelude to Oxford. But, as you said about the flat, "Don't let's worry yet." But I do continually about the flat; it is gnawing at my centre. I am not, I assure you, wasting time—only things take so *long* here. Nothing gets finished, & nothing that is seems valuable.

I shall catch the 5.50 up tomorrow. Till when, most adored lady, all love & blessings.

Serge

24 April/44

Well . . . well . . . and am I here again? I undoubtedly am, if human things are to be trusted. This morning I woke at 6, which was not too bad after having worked till 1; & so possessed was I by the memory of the last four mornings that I felt I should be really ill if I didn't have a cup of Tea . . . hoping you were, about the same time. If you ask me, I believe it's your provision of that cup at home that is the sole reason for my genius; without it, I never really start the day at all! Anyhow, this morning I couldn't bear to go from 6 till 8.45, and at last, about 6.15, I went down & got a teapot . . . but no milk; I wasn't up to bothering about milk; and coming upstairs I nearly fell over the banisters—what excitements one lives through! —but didn't drop the teapot, though I bruised myself all down one side . . . too, too pathetic! . . . however I got back, & made tea, & went back to bed, & read Marlowe's *Tamburlaine*. It's true, to be quite honest, that I dozed again over it, but still I was getting on with my job while you were with yours, only less efficiently, for I still cannot think of any real illumination on Marlowe. I wonder sometimes if sleeping from 11 to 5 wouldn't be a good idea; of course, all the great Medievals worked very early in the morning without tea, but then they probably had ale—hideous thought!

I will admit that, as I lay in bed at 6 & looked at the room, it struck me with some pride that there was no Tidying Up to be done before you came. There are perhaps rather more books & papers on the occasional table than a chaste taste would approve, but very few more; and the chest of drawers is clear except for the one row, and there were no odd clothes or other things lying about. "Really," said I to myself, "if Madonna came in *now*, I should not be ashamed!"

I have announced our intentions. Anne sends her love and hopes you will come for longer. She is likely to be here after all, because she doubts if Ellen will be back and she can't anyhow leave the rest of the staff if Ellen isn't . . . that, I hastily add, is said to be true infinitely, & not to have any relation to Your Excellency's coming, as they are said to go all to pieces, & Anne thinks that bad even if she & they were alone in the house. But I could have borne her to go away this time! The D's. send their love & hope you will dine or lunch or dine & lunch or whatever you choose: I said that we would lunch after you had come & had a drink with CSL., re: thus (you will observe) distinguishing between people who meet the Great casually in rooms & pubs & those who only meet them by formal arrangements occasionally. If then.

A disappointing accumulation here. An application for a testimonial from a last year's pupil; a long letter from V.H.C.[32] (if you remember him) about commas in invoices (yes? yes; never mind; it was very dull); a cutting from an Australian paper saying that I have "a cobweb-spinning subtlety"—ass!; a new translation of Augustine's *Confessions*[33] from *T&T*, with a note sympathizing with Michael, about which I will tell him when I write. And forms & things of the most complex kind from the Embassy, all referring to Statutes & Regulations—about which I will also tell him, & you needn't bother; I don't begin to understand them myself at present.

It's a cold & horrid day. I have two cheese sandwiches & a large section of your cake. And "where am I? and why am I where I am?" . . . I feel better for the three days—& anyone who underrated their loveliness would be . . . he would be like Evelyn in my novel.[34] They were very, very good, & so are you. And I love you and always shall.

And thank you for everything

Serge

29 April/44

It would be nice if you got this before you left; if I post it this morning perhaps you will. I wish the sun would come out again to greet you; perhaps by Monday *it* will.

I've just had a letter from Patrick McLaughlin to which I shall have to give some attention. All about the Ministry of Agriculture and an Archbishop's Committee; "Farm Sunday" and Rogation. The Committee are inviting TSE., Dorothy S., & me to get together and (if I understand aright) prepare a year's cycle of services for the Church in country parts. The proper side of this is that for this sort of thing, they are at least beginning to turn to someone who can write. The dubious is that Eliot's style is one thing & mine another; D.S. has dramatic capacity but little style.

However there it is. I have always been a Bishop's man, and if an Archbishop's Committee wants anything . . . of course there won't be a penny in it for anyone. But they are prepared to let us take two years over it! Anyhow (i) it will mean London visits at first, and (ii) how fortunate my teeth will be done.

Till Monday, most blessed. I will meet you outside the station at 3.25.

Serge

4 May/44

If, at any time of life, anyone were to ask me if I would rather have a poem or £2, I know which I should say. When I was very young, the grand bluff of art did rather take me in; the "spend a penny and buy a lily" idea. But now—no. I should be a much less good poet—& I am rather a good poet—if I failed in Johnson's immortal phrase "to keep my eyes on the guineas." But you may well argue, most accurate Lady, that these pounds are not for you, but for the accomodation of Our house, which we so continually choose to maintain; & so they are, & You ought to have as much for Yourself, & if I can get the money for the novel[35] out of Faber before your birthday, so you shall. But I doubt that, though I am about to make a maniacal effort to get it finished this week-end; if only I could see what to do with everyone in the last 12 pages. But it *would* be nice to get it off on Monday. Hush! don't let us provoke the gods.

I'll make a note of 10 June & discuss with M. when I'm up. I really will try & write to him to-morrow; did you tell him to ask *T&T* for the book he spoke of? be so kind. I've been improperly fiddling about with fiction to-day, & there's only time to write to you. Which somehow is always found!

(A large bang somewhere; practice? practice.) It was lovely of you to write about the lecture. Continue to see me so—if at all possible.

All love

Serge

5 May/44

Good that Win doesn't have to go in—though it'll be a fearful bore for her to go over. Still, she'll be on the spot at home. As for Fielden,[36] it's very interesting. I rather feel that our people are not going to begin until they feel they can really smash; when they do, there will be absolute hell over there for a few months, and no doubt lots of set-backs & so on, but the great climax won't be far off. I said to my barber this morning: "My last May here!"—and he agreed. So, you see, he Probably Knows Something. (As our poor dear I.D. would say about any little goose she knows—"He's IN—" O la, la! I must not be unkind.)

I have been approached by the man[37] who, years ago, did *Heroes & Kings*: a nice fellow. His firm, which does a good deal of printing for the Press, is thinking of launching out into publishing again, & are asking if I see my way to being a kind of literary adviser . . . consistent with my Duty to the Press. With the Press in its present state of (i) no paper, (ii) Sir H. losing interest (iii) GFJC having quite different tastes, I see my way very well. I may go & see Strong on Saturday morning; his office is in Shaftsbury Avenue, and find out what his views are. He's sent me a MS. to look out already, & I now await his financial suggestions. As my retiring age draws nearer, I become keener on watching for proposals of this kind. But be at ease; I have never yet let myself in for anything doo-dah & never shall. Hubert[38] is the typographical director, & has been for twenty years, but that, if anything, is slightly to the good. Anyhow, I should like to see him on Saturday.

And I've just realized that I have only three more lectures. In a way, I'm glad you were something of a climax. I couldn't have borne for it not to happen. Next time we won't even lecture; we'll have coffee, & wander, & play.

There was something else . . . I know there was . . . but what? Nothing important. I am mad set on finishing the novel,[39] if only I can think of an end. And then Flecker & the play. And perhaps the prose *Arthur*[40] in the autumn. God bless you for all.

Serge

15 May/44

St. Augustine,[41] coming on top of You, almost reduced me to tears. For he keeps talking about his exile from God in language which I understand enough to be disturbed by, but when this comes in a time of real (well, the other is, of course, even more real, but you know what I mean) separation, the total effect is overwhelming. Especially when you add the sense of Your separation from me! And so altogether I wept interiorly and now I am in no state to listen to essays on the Elizabethan Drama; which seems to have little to do with either God or You. In spite of that great line: "There where I have garnered up my heart"[42] . . . and it was only this morning that I understood how right Shakespeare was to say "garner"—meaning all the harvest of all the ears of corn, all the years.

I wish it was a better novel;[43] I am bitterly disappointed in it. And yet a little perverse imp in me dances with glee, and says: "I told you that without Her you could not be good," & it adds: "and I told Her too, and She did not believe me though you did. Which was a tribute to Her modesty but less to Her divine accuracy." However, we shall not quarrel over that. I am in a quandary because I wish you to admire it immensely, and yet I wish you to realize that, lacking You, my genius stumbles. And I do not see how even You are to do both at once.

I think I hate the flat because you have been in it so much without me, & it is full of both our loss . . . O this will never do; I shall weep myself into an [page missing]

17 May/44

In spite of my "thrasonical brag"[44] to you of my business capacity, I have made one slip. I thought Fabers were to pay the other £20 for the novel on receipt of the MS., but on looking up the agreement I find it isn't till publication. Tiresome, but not *very* tiresome; only I hope our Mr. Winstanley won't finish the teeth before I've finished Flecker. Apart from that lump sum everything is all right. And I only tell you because I have always chatted about such things. This morning my barber sold me some razor blades which I hope M. may find useful. I shall bring them when I come.

Merely to continue gossip, darling, I hear that our poor Cumberlege, having to turn out with his whole family from the Harrington house, has now to split up in all directions. He himself is going into rooms in his old college, Worcester, at the end of Beaumont St. His wife and small daughter have gone to some other friend in Oxford, and when his two sons come back from school they will have to be found beds elsewhere. Meanwhile he has borrowed a trunk or two from Sir H., so that he can pack away his books in the Harrington garage. It was through running into him & Sir H. with these trunks that I heard the sad sweet tale. Sad, no doubt, in itself, but sweet to me. I adore hearing of these people's difficulties;[45] Miss Peacock says the warmth of affection between the Harringtons & the Cumberleges has noticeably dropped.

It's still markedly cold, though a pale sun is shining on the barn. I've had no letters at all—let alone money or admiration; but I have dictated one to Nancy Pearn, reporting the delivery of the novel (Grr . . !) and discussing where I shall send the four religious plays.[46] I doubt if Fabers will want them in addition to the novel and the Arthur book, but they may. Anyhow we shall see.

Perhaps it would be a good idea to send my Love a pound at once, and the other pound on Saturday. I think it would, and I think I will go and change a cheque. Do you know I have a vague sense of having written that to you before? Thank God for the University, say I; these tutorials with their agreeable source of a cheque in June are a man's salvation. And I can see that Mr. Strong[47] is going, with any luck, to be useful!

I could do with one of your cups of tea; very much I could. The shoulder pain seems to have gone away; I wish I could think that your new pain hadn't come back. It was a lovely lunch on Monday: let us often do it! What *was* that marvelous dish we had here at the Mitre after riding back from Marston? I was trying to remember while I was breakfasting by myself this morning; at least these days I'm generally three-quarters through my breakfast before any one else appears. Except when G.H. is down here.

This is half a dull letter: pardon always. I looked up the poem on you this morning to read at Friday's tutorial. What an Invaluable Addition to Literature Your Highness has been—to criticism as to poetry. And must the intellects of the young be nourished by Our past? They must; they are. All love.

Serge

Dearest,

I really was shocked about the coal people. When all is said about difficulties, while after all it's we who suffer from more than they, it's quite improper and scandalous that they should go on like that. No-one knows better than I do—because I've seen it, year in & year out—how nice you are to these people. Good heavens, part of the pleasure of going shopping with you is to hear your voice when you're talking to them! It's what makes it a delight to go with you anywhere & if they can't do as well, they might try. But you have been so sweet in that way.

It's hard on Mrs. L., & I'll write—if I remember . . . ! And we will try & call. She must feel it very much now with R.M.L.[48] gone & all! I suppose Julian must be clean on 50 now? Or am I merely silly, as I so often am about dates?

And I have lectured for the last time this year—a little woolly here & there, I thought; and I felt curiously as if it were my last lecture in Oxford. If there ever are any more, you must come to the first, & start me off properly. But I don't think there will be, somehow. I daresay that's nonsense, but it's how I feel: plus the pleasantness that you have heard me—in Cambridge, in Paris, in Oxford. *And* thank you.

"Hovel," madonna? You've—we've—done too much of that. I've no use for it. I know you've always been wonderful about my own work—I may say so *today;* you only, have stood by it in fair and foul . . . believed, helped, nourished.[49] But I can't be bothered any more. If time allows—yes; there are a few things I'd like to do; but I assure you I've no sense of regret. I'd rather turn an honest penny by reading a MS than write *Taliessin* for nothing. Perhaps, with you at hand, I might feel differently; because you always have that kind of sub-driving effect on my genius and (so to speak) wake it up. If I could ever be persuaded that genius was related to sex, I should think that helped to prove it. But all I want now is enough work to make some cash. I really am oddly uninterested in anything else. Though of course I speak & so forth when I'm asked.

All the same, it's lovely of you to say what you did. But I *should* like to live in some decent place—I mean, apart from your making every one Home.

All love,

Serge

It was, I suppose, to be expected that after my exhibition (between ourselves) at Paddington, I should spend a rotten night; which I found myself gloomily regarding as an only too proper penance. If one allows one's temper to get twisted, it's hardly surprising that one's body should follow suit and one should have cramp and wakefulness. I pushed through the tutorials, and read half a *Strong*

MS.,[50] and I am feverishly taking up the others to-day. No; feverish is quite the wrong word . . . forgive it & me, & for yesterday. But I was very embittered, & I do hate people's faces[51] . . . & I am unworthy your love. Still . . . continue.

Nothing very exciting was waiting here. Another MS. A letter from Patrick MacLaughlin saying he will be here on the June 10 weekend & can we meet to discuss Rogation rituals, &c. I suppose we can, except on Sunday evening when I am speaking at Somerville on Symbolism. A letter from Miss Morison, whom you now know, asking if I can take four lots next term. The idea of making £30 in a term seems really not a bad one: it ought to be possible to put that complete towards moving . . . besides anything else. (And of course it's nice to feel the tutorials have been accepted wholly by the authorities . . . or would be if I were in a more blessed state of mind.)

Another young poet has sent me his book. I'm beginning to acquire a positive library of them, though so far none of them particularly thrill me. Miss Webb-Paploe, emerging from several months' absence, wants to come over on Sunday; why do these people derive so much more pleasure from seeing me than ever I possibly can from them? I operate all impersonal like; it's a kind of ritual which goes on till it's over. O as I said to you: "Is this, madonna, fame? is this monotony of labour & dullness reputation?" And You very rightly said one would miss it if it hadn't been; yes, Sophia (Sophia? Greek for Divine Wisdom; the Church of, at Byzantium, &c.), how right you are!

Well . . . it was a lovely time; yes, it was. And it was a jewel. And M. was charming. And praise God that abortion of intelligence[52] which is supposed to be a novel is left behind. And thank you for making me invent a Home Secretary for the next; you've no idea how right you are, and how unwise recurrences of dead bodies would be. We have had sad examples—Defoe and Scott; it is never satisfactory. I send you £2 herewith; I will send more on Saturday.

You are always very sweet, and my petulancies are unworthy even your rebuke. But it is partly on your account. Bless you. I love you.

Serge

2 June/44

There is, apart from the satisfaction of it, one thing to be said for a daily letter; it recalls one, like prayer, to the steady channel of life. There may be eddies or even waves in it—as they say in the Bible: "Come, thou North wind, and blow, O South"[53]—but there it is, "without o'erflowing, full."[54] But to-day it is full only of itself; nothing else has happened. I have conversed with Miss M. on the telephone, & promised to see her people next Wednesday at 8 to fix up next term, if I'm here. The University has sent me a formal note to say it proposes presently to pay me £22 for tutorials this term. I have sent Strong[55] a bill for £5.5.0. which he will pay when we have our next meeting. Which I shall suggest should be next time I'm up: & that will be a fortnight to-day.

Another book of verse from the young. If this goes on, I shan't be able to read them all. I must bring them up next time I come—or as soon as I *have* read them. This is what we did once—only not much. But perhaps they are not doing it much . . . I babble; it is because I am still irritable and sick at heart. I mustn't go all over it again. You encircle me like the air, and I feel for you and then you aren't there; you are wasting your sweetness[56] on . . . well, not on me.

O encourage me, beloved! I shall make this play[57] as bitter as I know how. I'll show them what I think of men.

But I do love you.

Serge

6 June/44

Having talked to you this morning—and nothing, except your letter (sweet!) and a letter from Winstanley appointing 12.30 on Sunday, 18 June, having happened since . . . except indeed that, all owing to you, I heard the 9.0 Forces News Flash, & so was in on the first moving.[58] I understand that our people have issued a statement since then, but I haven't heard it. I find it makes one feel a little serious, even solemn; this is what we have waited for; this is the serious opening of the end, however far. We might even be, I suppose, driven off, but we shall return. It's begun: with terror and pain and death inconceivable, but it has begun. And the English & Americans, as never before in history, have taken Rome.

Oxford begins to look transient; the end has begun. . . . O I am glad that unknowing I rang you up this morning. As it happens, it was even better than getting through to you yesterday. I shall always remember how you & Freedom came together. But then your second name has always been Liberty. I'm glad we've got a foothold in London; the rush may begin soon.

O & Sir H. has to be out of his house by 24 July. And Vivian[59] is home on leave. Sir H. told me both these things yesterday. I must be allowed to repeat that the first faintly amuses me.[60] I should think, in the circumstances, he'd be sure to go to New College: I don't see what else he can do. There are, even so, his things to store. Well, well . . . the ungodly do not always flourish.[61] But I didn't say that to him.

All blessings. I've changed M's cheque & sent him his pound—let him have it as soon as possible. And let us pray for victory soon. All love.

Serge

7 June/44

Dearest,

How fortunate it was that I didn't get through on Monday! For now—all owing to your having heard the 8 news—you are for ever tangled in my mind with the invasion and the return to Europe. And that—for me—is as it should be; it's almost a symbol of the private & public sides of my (call it so!) thought—say, Beatrice & the City. I a little wish that I could add the third thing, & spend my own days working on Taliessin; I should feel I was doing something more to the point of these great things—of you & Europe—than Flecker and tutorials make me feel I can. Tutorials are no doubt useful to the young, & certainly to me, but . . . And my small volume of poems[62] does not appear; and the poem called *The Prayers of the Pope* is not inapplicable to these days. However, each to his job; "they also serve"[63] who only write about nonentities, if they try & write well and charmingly.

I hope all will be well in the train on Friday week, but I felt yesterday when the Thing[64] had begun that I should at least understand if they suddenly cut everything off. It's odd what a difference the happening makes. I could imagine myself surrendering to that situation with resignation, but to no other. Like what I've always said that all my activities—from verse to instruction—are hard on the condition of You. You are, as it were, the necessity in me by which all else exists. As I said once, when someone—I've forgotten who—was talking about G.H. & his wife: if that[65] had (unthinkably?) happened to me, I should cease all other relations and withdraw wholly. That is fundamental to everything. Success? I do not think, you know, if someone said that to me, I should feel that I had been anything but a success; say rather—that the Thing itself had been of the nature of success. O madonna, that you & I can write of it so is itself a small glory. Yes?

And now I have written myself on to a new page and have nothing new to fill it with. I have a long letter from my budding doctor at St. Albans, begging me to go again, & saying that all were interested & some "much more than interested." So I suppose I shall; it's more of a labour than it used to be, but perhaps that's proper.

God bless you, and bring us sweetly and strongly together again, and all things into himself.

Ever

Serge

Did you hear the King? I thought it was magnificent & quite unexpected—all that about the Queen's "waiting upon God." It must be generations since an English King has spoken so to the People.

9 June/44

My little Saturday note . . . while you, I suppose, are at the Library, issuing. People like Mrs O.[66] do more towards creating a serious and bloody Revolution than many worse people: that's a quite serious remark. Deep, deep, in their hearts there lies that denial of spiritual equality which is (however unrecognized) the active element in all neighbourliness & friendship. They will be kind, they will give, they will pay—but it's always They who do it. It is They who decree & decide. Now you & I, in our separate ways, are proud enough, God knows! but we are not, I think & hope, "stuck-up." Mrs. O., like all her kind, sticks herself up . . . her Self as judge, bestower, and almost the small God of her environment. It only sometimes crops up—but when it does . . . ! It is, I think, one of the things I believe to be most dangerous. "Be not high-minded,"[67] said St. Paul, & meant that sort of thing. You are probably the only person who can put up with her and defeat her; but then you have a spiritual instinct exactly the opposite of hers; you have more generosity in your finger-nails than I in my arm or she in her whole body. I *don't* mean merely giving things; I mean an innate swiftness of . . . of something very much like love—real outgoing love. Continue, most dear lady, that most noble mode of glory; I certainly have always adored and certified to it. It's our only balance & hope—in the State, in the Church, in the Gospel. It's what the Mrs. Os don't realize; they sit back in their They-ness and are bountiful (if possible) to a sub-ordinate & subservient world. But if it isn't subordinate—Ho! And it won't be—always.

Excuse this essay . . . but I do feel her to be very dangerous indeed, the more so that she hasn't the slightest idea of it! I've been trying to think of something to say about Symbolism for to-morrow night; not, so far, with much success. But I suppose I shall get through. I am also passionately waiting for the University's cheque. It's been sweet of you—all these years—to talk as you do about the cash. You can't *possibly* do more than you do . . . "all your acts are queens,"[68] including your finance.

Sir Humphrey has just been in to tell me that Vivian R. has reached Berkhampstead at last on leave; then I suppose he may be sent to France. (How wonderful at last to write "France.")

All blessings & all love. The shirt & cake are perfect.

Serge

And anyhow I *like* domestic letters; it's *our* domesticity. And it's as much part of even my poetry as the Nature of the Blessed Trinity—see all my Works. And anyhow I like them.

15 June/44

Last night on this fire-watching I fell into temptation, and read Churchill's life of the Duke of Marlborough, instead of working. I was very touched to see that he always wrote to the Duchess as "my dearest soul," and while he was winning smashing victories in the middle of Europe was always saying how he was looking forward to spending his future years with her. "You will have," he wrote just before Blenheim, "to take care of me." Directly after Blenheim,[69] he sends her a tiny note, asking her to tell the Queen, and saying he will write to the Queen in a day or two. This so much reminded me of my ringing you up to tell you about Faber's. Obviously the Duke sat down in his uniform to write just as I picked up the receiver: the desired, the inevitable, action! Choice *and* necessity. The Duchess was obviously a much greater woman than I had supposed. One does not act so unless one's wife is really "closer to me than breathing, nearer than hands or feet."[70]

I shall be up by the usual train to-morrow; I fear no earlier. They have cut out the 4.30 up. On Saturday I have an appointment with Strong's Hungarian at 10.30; on Sunday with Winstanley at 12.30; on Monday with Miss Sinclair at 11. This is all a—nuisance, but can't be helped: except indeed that it gives me a reason for lunching. I do so prefer the 1.45 to the 9.45. On the Tuesday I go to Radley.[71]

The University goes on being most proper. It has sent its tutorial cheque; and it writes (through another female don!) to say it is privileged & proud to have me lecture next term. All is now in solemn order; though Tolkien says it has all been a great fuss about nothing, because the Board of the English School had been responsible all along, & this was perfectly in order. But we have now pleased everyone. As a result, I feel compelled to go to a presentation of *Measure for Measure* this afternoon: everyone seems to be going at odd times . . . and when I say everyone I mean only the Univ. (and not what you *don't* think I do). I shall buzz along by my august self. Several of my pupils are in it. But I feel as if I should go to sleep; my eyes are that heavy. (I wish they'd go on doing things at the Scala.) Claudio is sure to be hysterical and probably Isabella unbearable.

The *Cambridge Review,* suddenly reviewing *Beatrice,* calls it "a serious & original contribution." It also says that it shows Dante "from the inside, as if the author had tried to live the poet's speculative and moral experience." Wiser than they know, my Beatrice!

What else has made you still "the sister's [by the B.V.M.] yet the role."[72]

Till to-morrow.

Serge

22 June/44

Dearest,

I suppose, on the whole, it isn't worth doing . . . and if you say "What?" I shall say sending in an application for the Birmingham Chair. I saw that the B. University were advertising that applications were invited—in the *Times Educational Sup.,* and I rather remembered what they said when I was over. Then last night at this "simple supper," Helen Gardner[73] asked me if I were going to take action, because if I did she was almost certain I should get it. That's as it may be, but there would clearly be a party for me. Applications don't have to be in till 31 July, so there's time enough to talk. To inform you, & to clear my own mind, let me put down the various considerations:

1. The "stipend" is £1000 (less I.T.)
2. I could no doubt do the lectures all right.
3. *If* I got it, I should start with some *éclat.*

I can't think of any more for it. Against:

1. We don't particularly want to go to B'ham.
2. I should lose the (low) pension from this place, & couldn't save enough to make up for it.
3. When I'd done five years there I should be too near the age-limit for these things to take up another post, here or there.
4. Though, no doubt, I'm marvelous on my own lines, I don't carry quite enough real ancient scholarship for a Chair of that kind.

I have a feeling that the pension is what counts. Mine will be disgusting, but it will be there. It's no use getting a thousand for five or even seven years, & then being left without a sou. It'd be marvelous to have enough to live on in some decency and for you & me to be able to play a bit; and of course a job like that means about a third of the year free from work—except reading up. But I should hate our last state. . . .

Of course, I know I mightn't get it. But they were rather pointedly nice over there[.] Still . . . no; I see I am rather slowly deciding against. Ten years ago . . . but then it isn't. No. I've put all this very badly, & you may think I've been merely flattered & lost my head; but I do not think I have, or I should not be thinking it out. Of course, I would rather get the money for the one post without writing these ridiculous books for it. On the other hand, I do not particularly wish to dwindle from my independence into an official Birmingham professor; I would rather go on being C.W., who is merely Ourself, & to whom Universities are grateful.

No; I think I am against. But, my dearest partner, I tell you all (and add—for no reason; none at all—that I have said nothing except in this note my love is reading now!). I shall perhaps ring you up on Saturday—no; you will be going off to the Library; Monday then . . . or sometime; we'll see.

McLaughlin has fixed up his theological meetings for 10 & 11 July—Monday & Tuesday; this is not Rogationtide, but the Theological Pergium. They are to be at St. Anne's House from 11 to 5 each day: if M. isn't coming to Oxford, and I suppose he isn't, I shall come up on the Friday as usual & stop till Tuesday evening. If M. likes, I will go out with him Monday evening. But I hope to see you next Wednesday. I play with the idea of coming up by the 2. & going down next day by the 1.45. If TSE asks me, so much the better.—O this is a dull letter. Excuse. All my love.

Serge

Eliot asks me to dine next Wednesday at 6.30, so that is that. I'm rather glad because I wish to talk to him about the Arthur book;[74] we should do all the better if that could be fixed up soon. I should have come anyhow; but it's officially convenient to have a reason. On Thursday morning I shall go & see Nancy Pearn, & catch the 1.45. I'll probably try & ring you up on Monday morning to confirm everything.

Robert Graves[75] has now taken to writing about Taliessin: or so he tells me in a letter. He has been brooding over our last year's correspondence, and he is sending me a MS. for submission to the Press. I hope we may do it; he is a sound man, if perverse. But I could faintly wish he had not happened on the same Celtic poet!!

Beatrice is going for her Labour interview to-day; it is felt she will disappear soon. My two young doctors from Barts write to say they will be in Oxford during the week-end and can they see me? Very agreeable in one way; as you said, one would grumble if it didn't happen. I can see myself going to St. Albans again soon.

Meanwhile I feel rather as if I had a cold coming on—one of my small sicknesses-after-breakfast days. But I expect it to disappear. I've bought some sausage sandwiches for lunch, & here I shall sit. Sir Humphrey is in bed with a sore throat, so when I've finished this to you & scribbled a line to M., I shall get along with Flecker.

Your letter was sweet, & thank you. I'm still brooding over Birmingham, but I won't discuss it again here. All my love.

Serge

Michael has told me that he made trouble last night. I don't know what damage happened to the place, but after the workmen this must have been a nice thing to happen! The worst curse of your life has been that he takes so after me: to have a husband and a son both spasmodically—well, I am sorry enough; and he says he keeps on trying and seems to fail.

Of course, it's all been due to the money at bottom; though that's more of an excuse for—or say an explanation of—him than me. But I'm very sorry. And I was going to tell you that Dyson last night asked after you and said that you "were as courageous as you were charming"; he always asks after "my lady your wife." O and Tollers[76] said that he thought he ought to send you some small present, "a kind of exchange between royalties" in return for the comb you gave him. It seems his wife has it; she said she'd been looking for one like that for years. So Tollers handed it over, but he thinks that your kindness ought to be recognized.

Nothing of interest is here. I begin to look at the place (at Oxford) with new eyes now that we've made our decision,[77] and I shall do anything in the way of making my intentions clear that I can. As I said, it's the one thing to which I look forward with felicity.

It's odd, madonna, the effect you have on me! No-one but you could in a day cause me to begin to feel impatient of my adored London. And now I begin to! O I do want the next few years to be got through!

But you must be ill enough now. I wish you could get away anywhere for a few days: you have no let-up, while I do.

I shall send some money to-morrow.

Serge

6 July/44

Dearest,

You'll never, never know how sweet it is to hear you say: "Hello, love," on the telephone: if you feel half as much about me, I'm more fortunate, even in this kind of life, than I ever thought I should be at nearly 60. "O it came o'er my ear like the sweet south"[78] . . . I always want to fling everything madly at your feet when I hear you; especially when you say it out of the heroism & tribulation of this week. Perhaps I shall be able to relieve you a little on Saturday and Sunday.

I send another pound herewith. I do apologize for this method, and I'm still very angry with myself for making that silly mistake[79] about Faber's. It's upset my calculations. Of course, it's "as broad as it's long": but the length comes first!

Last night I took a book round to CSL who is having a minor operation in a nursing home in the Banbury Rd, & I went down Keble Rd. The last time I was in it was on the day you came down for your glasses, & we went into the Park and wrestled with suspenders. About all of which I thought, and prayed (clinging madly to faith!) that we might still walk there in peace.

It's rather nice that *T&T* should be "very pleased" with M's work,[80] don't you think? It gives him, in a small way, so much more of a background, because now he and we can fairly say "he is on the reviewing staff," and not only a counter-jumper . . . not that I think that's a proper word for it. If he ever does get to America,[81] he might be able to send them articles from there, which would all help.

Otherwise, this is an empty week. I wait anxiously to hear from Mrs. F. about the final bits, and from TSE about Arthur. It's a little tiresome to have to switch one's mind on to these literary things when you're in imminent danger. And yet if I don't think hard about them all, we shall be in serious discomfort!

I have had (excuse this allusion!) a word with Miss Peacock about what will, if anything did happen to me, come to you from the Press; so that they shall go on paying something regularly till then. There's no sense in *not* making arrangements as far as possible. . . .

The enclosed letter has just been brought to me, and I forward it.

All love.

Serge

11 July/44

I've begun two letters, but each was as heavy—no, not gloomy; heavy—as the millstone we are not to hang round people's necks. And now I sit wondering what has happened to my style—whether I dropped it accidentally while disputing with you or what. I should not be as gloomily light as that had I not spoken to you just now. I hope your letter reaches me to-morrow. . . .

The fact is I am marvelous where my feelings are not engaged! and my touch is certain. Engage my feeling and my effect disappears. Like what the old laws of magic laid down—if a magician fell in love, he was (anyhow, there) no longer a magician. This meditation arises from Mrs. F., who says she thinks God has raised me up to be a friend to her. Compare her with . . . no, don't; no comparisons! Still, you are what I mean! My nerves all run from my heart—leave my heart alone and my nerves are calm. But when the inhabitant of that heart moves or looks awry . . . !

O language, language! language has ruined me and hurt you. I would give up all my poetry to make you happy—yes; I would. Only (a) it would not (b) the idea's silly. . . .

O I'm being stupid. Attribute it to anything but lack of feeling—no; you're not likely to do that. There's never an hour, of any kind, that doesn't bind us tighter. . . .

I'm being stupid still, & I shall cry, and that won't do here, will it? But to cry is not to yield this thing between us to life . . . to give it up, I mean. I hope yet to die clutching it—and I mean you to. More fully, much deeper . . . but one certain fidelity . . . yes; I shall hold it till death. Love? call it so; it is deeper than most think love is. But not was.

[Unsigned]

14 July/44

Whether you hung up or we were cut off I could not tell; you will not think I did. I can think of all the things that brought the back on, but it's most shocking and disappointing that it should have come on. You'll believe that I feel myself something to blame, but then I always do feel responsible for you. It was sweet of you to write so much!

I send £2 herewith. The —— cheque doesn't come, & I'm frightened that Mrs. F. may have been hurt. Nor has TSE written. Not the least inconvenience of the present time is that one's income may be knocked sideways at any moment by offices or houses being destroyed. I do not say it's comparable to the French women in the church, or to your own imminent danger, but it *is* fidgeting. However, we have hung on like this before . . . indeed, come to think of it, there's been less of it of that than there used to be. It was all my fault for making that silly mistake;[82] you must try & forgive me.

By the way, I find I've made another—but this time much pleasanter & not about money. I have miscalculated the Bank Holiday date, thinking it was a week sooner than it was. So when I said "next Friday to the Thursday week following"—and now I write it down, I see it was all but a fortnight; what *did* we dispute about?—I thought that took in the B.H.[83] But it doesn't, of course. And am I likely to come down here on the Thursday & come up again on the Friday? No. So, after all our to-do, here is the Friday to the Monday fortnight in our hands. I admit there's Shrewsbury, . . . & Mrs. F., but that's all.

Milford is moving in here on Monday week; the Spalding parents[84] write to say that they hope to be back before John's birthday on 14 September. Anne rather expects them to take to their beds here immediately after the journey. Unless Mr. Spalding wishes to have long intellectual conversations—but I know nothing of his subjects nor he of mine—it won't make any difference much to me for the comparatively few weeks. Anne says she thinks her father will be a little scandalized at my way of writing. With him "Writing a Book" has always been a very Solemn Thing; writing rooms and privacy and a great air of something going on—like poor dear Wilfrid Gibson, only much more so. How Dante, Shakespeare, and I manage differently!

Which reminds me I must tell you of a small absurdity. Renée Haynes has sent me a cutting from a Madrid paper, all in Spanish, about *Beatrice*. It alludes to me as the "ilustre autor de *Descent into Hell*." which is to say the "illustrious author of *D. into H*," and says that my new "essay"[85] is worthy to be read by all lovers of great "literature." Madrid is a new one on me, but I'm glad that Senor Gonzalez—I know nothing of him—considers me "illustrious."

I go on babbling like this. But between that and work—I cannot even read murder stories while you are in danger; no, indeed I can't. I can't be happy or comfortable anywhere—well, I always was restless down here; but now I can't do a thing. I think of you waking & dream of you sleeping. I do pray. And I have just finished your cake; it supplied me with three lunches in succession—Wednesday, Thursday, & to-day; besides little nibbles at night. So you see how you feed me literally as well as every other way.

Cash h/w. I do *hope* your finger's itched a little bit.[86]

All my love.

Serge

As against yesterday's unexpected guineas, to-day my office telephone bill turns up—15/9, which leaves me, as you will see, 5/3 to the good. I think I will pay it at once, and get it done with. How nice of the Fish[87] to have managed so. It would be, I suppose, impious to suggest to the Fish that he might have made it Two? Probably; these divine Powers, I understand, are a little touchy, and I wish Him to swim in frequently to land.

A nice letter from TSE saying that he is "a wee bit vexed" that Wilfrid[88] has asked me to do the selections because I am always doing too many things anyway & he wanted rather I devoted myself "in a leisurely way" to Arthur. But the real joke is, of course, that WG told me Eliot had suggested me. Now, if it were—who shall we say? O Wallis & the under-porter, I should think one of them was lying. One cannot suspect the Great of lying; but one of them must have got mixed. I suspect W.G. and neither mentions the fee—I bet it'll be £5, but it won't really be a long job.

Also a letter from Veronica,[89] grovelling for having forgotten about me & detective novels. *Time & Tide* positively embarrasses me with its goodwill: I only mentioned it as a half-joke. However, on and off we may get some. Veronica has had a fearful row with Raymond Postgate [Portgate?] who used to do them. I pant to know why, but she doesn't say. And down here one knows nothing of the grand literary Racket.

After a hasty dinner at the R. to report how we all were, to thank M.[90] for doing the review for Michael so quickly & to give her my Spectator one,[91] I went to S.P.Rd, and sat down—there being no one in,—to the play[92] for a couple of hours. I think perhaps I have now organized, though not written, the first act. It's rather too like all my other stuff & almost [boringly?] uninteresting. However, the writing may liven it up. . . .

I *have* paid the 15/9. It's rather close & I am reading a dull MS on the critics of Pope. Last week I *think* I was dozing at home? Your arms are the proper place . . . but in the afternoon? Alas!

All love.

Serge

The first 48 hours of a kind of unreal dream being over, I find myself sinking into the old gloom which my fortnight ridded from me.[93] Yesterday I did feel every way much better for the holiday. I got on with my work, & so on & so on. I re-wrote the first speech of the play[94] & so on. But this morning I woke draggingly, and now I dislike everything as much as ever. . . . However, it would be a poor show for your husband to lose all intelligence when he's away from you. You may be "lost" but I am more of a sheep—yes, indeed.

It was very tiresome of M. to come home. I had been pleasing myself that morning with the thought of you and me together if separate: and here were you rushed and . . . not fussed because you never are but the single morning spoiled as far as that goes. I do think a great deal of your labours!

No sign of the agreement with Faber's yet. But I think I will send you a pound at once, and another on Saturday. We are not run out yet, & it eases me to send it.

What else to report? Did you know that "the Bishop of Gibraltar has a tremendous opinion of my judgement"—no? Nor did I. It seems his sister has written the life of another brother, a G. R. Bunton, whose name I remember from my youth; he was one of those poor dear Liberal Idealists, & an authority on the Bauhaus;[95] and she & the Bishop are anxious that I shall read the part about his religious views and give my opinion & criticism. Odd! They approach through Widderington,—you remember him?—who sends on his sister's letter. She murmurs about "business arrangement," so I take it she will pay— not much, but enough to justify the time. I have replied agreeably. She knows I "shall disagree with his views" so in a way it's a pleasant compliment. Everything points to there being a number of these oddments when we get our Oxford house.[96] (I begin to live in the future here already!)

The cake is lovely. I ate the bun the first evening; some of the cake & some biscuits & cheese yesterday; more to-day. All my lunches this week are in S. House. I shall go round to Magdalen to-night probably.

I really think that without that time with you I should have broken down— in the sense of becoming incapable of doing a thing. As it is, I rest in and work from that renewal . . . not of love, which goes on, but of the signs, intimacies, and food of love. Which I so badly need.

In which always I remain your most devoted lord & husband.

Serge

I keep thinking of your rich eyes at the bus-stop. Why? I don't know; it was just one of those things. . . .

11 Augt./44

I have written a longish letter to M. about the article. I hope it may be some use. A young poet[97]—a Mr. John Heath-Stubbs—is coming to see me in a few minutes: why? Do I know? to pay his respects. (Or, of course, to see if the Press can give him a job. But as, months ago, he sent me his first book, I hope it's admiration and not need.)

The shirt-parcel has arrived; thank you, my sweet, for sending it. The Ms. parcel not yet; no doubt it will. The teeth go on being reasonably comfortable. I found I had taken them out in the night, all unconscious; but that was the first time. I am almost reluctantly driven to believe that they do make a difference to my appearance, though only very sharp-eyed people will notice it.

The news gets better and better, doesn't it? I couldn't help wondering if we shall read that there has been fighting down the Rue de Rivoli or in the Tuileries Gardens: there is almost bound to be. They say all the bridges across the Seine are down, but I suppose that doesn't apply to those in Paris itself. Do you remember the thunderstorm in the Loire? I should like to add a lecture in Rome to my collection, with you and me there—but not very much . . . not to hanker after . . . it would be nice to go to Paris again.

My young poet has come. Till to-morrow. All love.

Serge

12 Augst./44

Dearest,

Two letters from you this morning—very sweet and very amusing. You know I rather adore the fancy of your being just a little "lost" without me. (Not that anyone else who knows you would suppose it! What I mean is that I bet Mrs. O doesn't see you as "lost" . . . but to feel you are . . .)

I send the £2 h/w. The cursed agreement[98] hasn't turned up yet; I hope it will soon, because it'll take Fabers another ten days to get the cheque through. However, it's not absolutely necessary yet! Nor are there any signs of the proofs of the novel[99] or the copies of the poems.[100] In fact, there's nowt: except a letter from my aunt[101] saying she has a chance of selling the books to a local fellow who is interested, & do I think it would be a good idea. I certainly do; he's talking of £40 or £50, & I doubt if Blackwell would & I'm sure Foyle's wouldn't pay more. Also it'll save me doing anything & avoid the slight legal difficulty. So I'm replying warmly, & promising to go & see her next time.

I spent last evening on the Play;[102] having now a serious first draft of a quarter of the first act, which makes about a twelfth of the whole. There's very little of . . . well, of *me* in it so far; you might invoke the Blessed Trinity, to whom I profess I have (like the Black Prince[103]) a Devotion, to encourage it. And quickly. Also, if you had a couple of shillings or so, you might some time buy me two or three more of those little blue exercise books; now I've begun it in them, I should like to keep it all in the same kind and one can keep the acts conveniently separate so. But give yourself no extra trouble, though I'd much rather write in something you'd bought than in anything I got myself.

My young poet[104] came & went; we talked of his work & the Victorians. I am always a little surprised & touched to find myself "an Elder Statesman"— as in "I know, Sir, you think . . ." "You have said, Sir . . ." all that sort of thing. In that sense I suppose you & I have not lived in vain; we have affected Thought, though we see little enough of the result.

And I am ringing you up on Monday afternoon—yes? between three & four or so? or later, if I can't get through then. But on the whole I've been fortunate.

God bless you, my own. You are very, very sweet, & I cry when I think of it.

Serge

The other parcel arrived safely.

15 Augt/44

It's beginning, what with all these evacuees, I suppose, to be difficult to buy sandwiches; this indeed, is a mild blow. But there are growing queues in the morning, even before sandwiches have appeared. Certainly it doesn't very much matter, because if one eats a breakfast at 9 one can very well wait till the finger of cake at 4. Still, though I don't say the sandwiches were appetizing, they were useful!

On the other hand, you would hardly, after these years, believe how I seem to have half-drifted into something like a habit of shaving myself—at least neither yesterday (when it opened again) nor to-day have I gone back to any barber's. I shall, of course, because I do not wish to lose touch, & anyhow they are better at it. But I've been surprised at my own success. It's odd when in general my steadiness is less reliable that it seems to work there. But "praise God and keep one's shaving tube"![105]

Last night I spent sweetly on my own—too, too wonderful! The mere knowledge that there isn't anyone there is exhilarating. I admit I didn't seem to get much done, but I did feel that if this could only go on I might be able to do better. (Do you remember my sending you a Canterbury Pilgrims card from Canterbury? how long ago? I wonder if the shop is standing! And why have I not looked for it when we were there? O the answer is too easy! Because you-in-the-present dominates entirely over you-in-the-past. As Dante & other great ones found with their ladies—permit the comparison! And if you don't see the connection between 9 S.P.Rd. today & that early Canterbury, I do. There are two elements in common—solitude & you.) These are the best days Oxford has produced for me since the war began. Unfortunately they end to-morrow, but to-night is still—let me say, ours.

Edith Sitwell[106] has sent me another book with another inscription. How that woman does produce them! And she is rather good; yes, undoubtedly. I sigh an acknowledgement. I will bring it on Friday, more for presentation than anything else. Yes, I know what you think, my sweet! and I'm flattered. I should be much better—if I produced anything.

God bless you. This is all about me, but in a devotion, as you see, I hope & trust.

Serge

Why am I so sad to-day? your pain? your danger? Mostly, I think; but indeed I am selfish at heart—the rest is the need of you. Many husbands, I believe, think wholly of their wives; but I have never lost a sense of my own lack. Also, you will say I write of nothing else. But what else is there to write of? except you, either you or the closeness of you must be my song.

Meanwhile I send a pound herewith; it is all the immediate cash I have, but I will bring more. I keep on thinking of the X-ray; we will speak. The N.Y.B.[107] have replied not unfriendlily to Jock's letter about M. I shall bring a copy for him to see, and then we must take up his getting on the list—the quota—at once. As much as I expected & more than I feared!

Bless you! My mind is empty. Separation bears me down, but after all I have you. To-morrow!

All love.

Serge

Well, after all, I didn't. For when it comes to the point, its only by work that I can, as it were, catch up with your danger; not that I confuse the two. There is something indecent about my lounging and munching chocolate and reading while you are where you are. It's the same thing that makes it impossible for me to go to a theatre down here under these conditions. So, after all, when I got in, I sat down to the play,[109] everyone else going to bed very soon except Anne who was doing something in the back drawing room. And then she went, & I listened to the midnight news, & then I went and ate the buns and did read; and at one I put out my light, and prayed a little, and presently slept.

To-night everyone is going to the theatre, so I shall have supper by myself. I offered to go out, though as the Ds are also going to the theatre, I should have had to pay for myself!! But no need. You will be alone too; so we shall exchange a separate solitary meal: being exchanged, not so solitary. And then I shall try to get on. I have found one of the *T & T* books very good—almost a great book. It's Mme. Maritain's[110] (I'll tell you about *him*) reminiscences of her conversion. Mostly, I don't care for such books, but this is very moving & dignified. I'll bring it up in case you care to look at it.

Do not be too distressed, dearest, about my work—or my gloom about it. You have to consider that I am at an almost impossible thing . . . the need for a style which is as much beyond my more recent style as that beyond my earlier. I can be content with nothing but a manner of writing which is almost the thing itself happening: purity, clarity, pain, joy. All the "back-chat"—& much else—has slid away; there remains but the facts of existence . . . as I see them. If I had all the money and all the time, it would still be sickness and heart; ill-ease to be able to find it. The little extra rush makes it perhaps a little more difficult, but not very much. . . .

I was interrupted there, and am too self conscious to go back. All I mean is that, fail I or not, it's an effort imposed on me by my . . . genius? let's say so . . . and then I was interrupted again by our poor dear Budgen who finds Sir H's continual presence here very trying, as indeed if I had to take any notice of it I should myself; not meaning that I see him, but that one knows he's about. However, we drift along on our separate paths—so long as I am get-at-able if he does want me.

You remember Doris Dalgleish? She is now trying to get a grant from the Payne Literary Fund. Her arthritis is very bad; she is living with—& on—an aged aunt in the very north of Scotland; she is very unhappy & even more embittered. I have promised to write a letter if it will do any good, as she seems to think it may. Poor soul! She asks after you and M.

The *Spectator*[111] has forked up its small cheque; quick work.

All love. This is a dull egotistical letter . . . but it means well! Dull phrase! say—it aimed at your eyes, & (dazzled) fell.

Serge

23[24] Augt./44[112]

Miss Peacock, coming in to my office just as I was about to write, tells me that Paris is free. I'm really more and more astonished with the brilliance of our High Command; they must be the best generals in the world. For it isn't only the victories; it's the whole astonishing freeing of most of France without devastation. I thought the Germans would be bound to fight for and in Paris, but they've simply been out-manoeuvred & out-generalled. Eisenhower & Montgomery & Churchill must be marvelous! "Praised to the Holiest . . ."

It's delightful about the raincoat; I'm very much relieved. I shall do my best to send you the extra three pounds. In a way, it's absurd—the pleasure I derive from knowing about it . . . just as I do—only more—from your being able to get anything. I mean what's for one is for all. I will say that about us.

Your Monday letter reached me this morning. But so it was "original"! Statements about fundamental things always are; they start from "the origin." It's all but impossible, even for you and me, to *fathom* each other's heart; for—don't you see?—the heart is always growing deeper. But something of those depths we do see—in weekends, in such exchanges as your letter. These, my beloved, are the things that *are*. There is in each of us for the other an eternal fact, a lasting promise: an epigram of it is in the word "loves."

Blessed, and ever-blessed, all love and thanks!

Serge

Well . . . well . . . and do you remember the Rue de Rivoli, where "the Germans had some light guns," and the Ile de France by Notre Dame which we crossed several mornings and which the French police seized? I very nearly rang you up this morning, but I *must* check this beautiful habit . . . and only to say: "Paris est libre—Paris is free." Madam wife, we do see strange things.

Not but what your sweet little 10/= . . . no, 12/=. O well, I can't fling money away like this; no, I can't, and unless I rush out & buy stamps, how can I send 2/=? indeed, I haven't even got a separate 10/= at the moment. So what? But I have two pounds in my pocket, & I shall need just one, so far as I can judge. Then . . . ? yes, certainly. But this, if you please, is for the vests and knickers, and the rest is 6/= for you and 2/= for Michael: there!

A long long letter from Dorothy Sayers—rather sweet; she has, under the compulsion of *Beatrice,* been reading Dante & Milton, & feels she must write to someone, and to whom but me? Quite a sincere letter; I begin to admire Dorothy seriously as a human being, which I never did before. She was a fantasy, but hardly a man and a brother, or at least a woman and a sister. But she matures well. I must bring the letter up.

The night has been incredibly noisy—not only with planes but with practice guns or bombs or something. And the day is like it. The planes never seem to stop. Combining the danger at your end with the noise and number at mine, I begin to understand what one of our smaller days on the Western front must be like for the retreating German armies. "So perish the King's enemies!"[113] I should rather like to have written a poem about the King and the Day of Prayer, & had it in the *Sunday Times.* But I cannot write verse, and so I assure myself they wouldn't put it in!

What else? nothing. O lud, darling, the unending planes! One fades away into the next and several at a time. I'm almost scared at our own power.

Your letter was the sweetest thing. I have always a slight tendency to kiss the envelope at the breakfast table before I open it; after all, it was my habit for all the years since you first wrote—& why break it because of publicity? Ought not Poets to create fashions, rituals, and decorum? They ought. Besides your letters these days are full of goodness and brooding love, & should be kissed before being read.

Be ever your adorable self: you are nobler and lovelier than ever.

Serge

25 Augt./44

Presently I shall cause you to be rung up. There is, as a change, something pleasant in having people . . . not "rush" exactly: no; and an office-boy is hardly to be regarded as "people" . . . but it will do, it will do. A thousand black slaves could hardly be more efficient. I should like to have slaves; I do not wish to be a *litterateur* any more. I should like you to be the queen of Goberide [illegible] . . .

On the other hand you should buy yourself, & for yourself, this week's *Time & Tide*. I doubt if a husband's article, followed by a son's article,[114] has ever happened before in that amiable periodical. There are both your men together, & both quite good. Absurd, but gratifying, incident!

M. has sent me a line about his raincoat & a new American. But he put the raincoat first—charming of him! And I have decided again that the reason I do not write so well is the lack (as well as of you) of your ministrations. At 12.15 last night, I was hungry; fortunately I finished your cake then. But it might have been dripping toast; & it might—O it might have been tea! Come to think of it, I could have made tea; but then I did not think of it. One doesn't—in a pleasant boarding house.

. . . Clearly, my letters[115] will have to be cut before being published! Or shall I add another codicil forbidding them to be published—for 50 years? . . . The fact is, it is 2.30; I have eaten 3 sausage sandwiches, & I am sleepy. . . . O but sleepy! God bless you. I said "about the same time" & so it shall be: about 4.30. I am astonishingly "a man of my word," My love & all.

Serge

31 August/44

Chance has produced this paper this afternoon, which, I hope, is an omen! It seems odd that it should have lasted five years, & come to my hand now. And it is the kind of paper I wrote on for 31 years before the 5—well, well! I suppose after the oldest group of people go, as I suppose they will next year with Sir Humphrey, I shall be one of—if not *the* oldest Inhabitant. It'll be 37 years—since the Press broke on my life. And even so it's younger than you there! you beat it by five months. It's almost unbelievable that you who are still so new and fresh and different should also be the oldest experience of my personal life. Even my verse—good verse anyhow—came after you. Blessed, ever blessed!

I had a nice letter from M, who wrote pleasantly about Lutterworth & said you were thinking of going back on Friday. (I do hope the weather's not been too bad.) And so not to miss two days—I send this note as well as yesterday's to meet you.

The only item of less than interest is that Christopher Fry has turned up again—having been discharged from the Forces. I forget if you met him, & you won't remember him. I mention it because *nothing* else of any kind has happened. I push slowly—O slowly—on with the Second Act.[116] Otherwise I've seen no-one & done nothing. Except observe, with growing peace, that the Victories continue!

Well, & so . . . O just this greeting with love. God bless. Thank M. for his letter, please.

Serge

1 Sept./44

Exactly five years! I was telephoning to you about this time, & trying (with what ill-success!) to be effective. On Monday afternoon I shall ring you up to remind myself of that other Monday—now looking to the Return as then to the Exile. —I had written so far when I had to have a young poet for an interview . . . and just as he sat down you rang up. It was most sweet & kind of you, & so it was of M., & I was thrilled beyond measure to hear you (and to hear him sound agreeable). Next week I shall be coming up!

The Teeth Bill has come and is 16/16/-. It shall be paid as soon as the Play's[117] done: this play will always mean Teeth to me . . . otherwise nothing . . . O except Raymond. I took him to Magdalen last night, & CSL read a long paper on Kipling & I read my essay on Kipling from *P. at Present*, so he had a Cultural Evening. This morning I had him at the Press, & to-night I shall give him a couple of private hours in my Bedroom. I wish I enjoyed the poor darling more.

But I am so thrilled at hearing you, & by your delightful thinking of it you wouldn't believe. If I had any money to-day I'd send it, but I haven't. I hope to manage £1 to-morrow.

Bless you!

Serge

5 Sept./44

Certainly our intellectual level is going down. GFJG & I have just been having a chat about the Papacy & the war. It's hard to explain exactly what I mean, because it isn't that he said anything definitely wrong; only that *all* he said was wrong. It was like someone talking about Shakespeare and not realizing that he wrote in verse; or about cooking without thinking of an oven. He talked about the Papacy in a perfectly natural way. But he never seemed to see that the whole claim of the Papacy is to be supernatural—to be different & to judge differently. I have remarked the same thing with Sir H. & Goffin.

There is always, in everything, that odd—what shall I say? understanding the *kind* of thing one is talking about. It's apt to be maddening. Now I offer no judgements on—say, painting. I know there's a way of looking at pictures which those who do look at pictures have & I haven't. They see the colour-relation perhaps. But about theology & poetry I know something, & what provokes me about all those cultured is that they don't even know their own culture. . . .

Excuse. I hadn't any particular idea of breaking out like that. It's the fault of the lack of anything happening here. . . . Talking about happening reminds me we must add Brussels to the things of which you've told me. I nearly rang you up just after midnight and said: "Well, and we've taken Antwerp too!" But it's 3 months to-morrow since the invasion, & what a 3 months! and now we are all but *in* Germany. God send they don't try & give in too soon; and that the armies go through *their* land.

This is a dull letter: you must forgive it. My meat sandwiches were round but dull . . . suppose they excuse it? Kiss me. I love you.

Serge

7 Sept./44

I break off in the middle of trying to reply to Dorothy L.S. After all, when she's written me 36 pages, I ought to take some notice; besides, she's been very polite to me all through. And as she's very good and intelligent about our Dante, I think it would be a good "idea" if she published it all in an *Open Letter* to me. Or, of course, in any other way. Which I am saying to her.

And last night was perhaps—probably—almost certainly—my last fire-watch here! Or I hope anywhere, but I suppose if there *were* a warning in S.P.Rd., I should still leap for my tin hat. But O how wonderful the last month has been! if I had a hundred pounds I could enjoy it more, & I don't know that enjoy is the word. It's the almost complete *certainty* that's so exquisite; there the Enemy is & what can the Enemy do? Suffer.[118]

Surveying Oxford for glamour, it occurs to me that, outside S.P.Rd., I don't know a single girl; and outside or inside S.P.Rd., I don't know a single glamour. In fact, now I come to think of it, after five years here, I know—

4 at Magdalen (whom I knew before)
David Cecil.
Eugene Lampert (Anne's Orthodox friend who's just written a book I must
   review)
Lionel Ovenden (at St. Edmund School)
Gervase Mathew
Miss Morrison; Miss Gardner.

There must be one or two more? Well, perhaps; I can't think of them. However, I've asked Anne S., as being the nearest both to girl and glamour (yes; all right!), about the sugar.

It's odd though. I'm a pattern, a voice, a name; not a person.[119] I am Bach's *Ninth Symphony,* Shakespeare's *Tempest,* and Da Vinci's *Madonna of the Rocks;* one artistic vision, not a human being, so good, [page missing, or unsigned]

Well, in Oxford the lights have begun to go up; it's disgusting that they won't in London yet. Coming out into the High by Magdalen last night, I couldn't at first make out what had happened. It wasn't really dark. And then I saw over me, very high & dimmed, but real, the electric lights. Only the chief streets, I suppose. But there. My first impulse was of disappointment that you weren't there; I would—O but I would have wished us to see it together. However, it was a good omen & I took it so.

I meant to have sent you the enclosed pound yesterday; you must forgive me. Also I meant to have sent off a small parcel this morning, but when I had done it up the paper looked too doubtful; so I determined to buy some more to-day, & post it to-morrow. A small distraction pre-occupied me, because my bedroom basin pipe has got stopped up; not, I may, I think, honestly say, through anything I've done. There's been no tea-leaves or anything, so my conscience & heart are free. Of course, I only found it out when I had washed, so I thought it best to bale out the dirty water, & leave a clean basin. Which I secretly did. And reported it; so something will be done. A good thing it happened before the Aunt arrived, or she would have had dark suspicions of Something—I can't imagine what.

The missionary Miss Sinclair will be at hand on Wednesday morning. I shall call on her about 10.30, thus leaving myself plenty of time for meeting you for lunch. With any luck I shall just finish it in time, though when they have read it and made any comments about the South Seas, I do think it had better be copied out again. It's in the copying out that improvements lie. Encourage me to it, dearest; you've always insisted on the Best, & it wouldn't take *too* long.

Hubert writes commissioning an Introduction to the *Duchess of Malfi*,[120] which I must now read. I should like to do that really well; after poetry, criticism is my real work. Nothing else of interest—well, nothing else *at all*.

I love you. I also love you. There is something in you which is more than love. If that could be.

Serge

I think of not going back on Wednesday till the 7.40. Yes?

And here I am back here, aren't I? Well, well, it was a lovely time, and by Your next birthday we shall have been together again so long as to have remembered this but what I ought not, in view of my reputation to call a dream. There was a note here from my mother & E—and that, I may add, was all.

I got a seat & avoided G.H., whom, far off, like a chieftain in Homer, I saw loom on the platform. It was pleasant to find the roads from the station dimly lit, & to walk safely! O soon that London may be so!

No cheque from anyone this morning. What has happened to the world? Am I no-one? "Is the throne empty? is the sword unswayed?"[121] But as a pendant to cheques, I shall now copy an extract from a letter from Dorothy,[122] our Dorothy. She has been at a conference somewhere equivalent to the Pleshy one, & apparently TSE was there—and after a general wail about the 3rd rate artists she says,

"at this point Maufe, the architect of Guildford Cathedral, asked a question which would have made Beatrice look at him without a smile not as a 'delirious child' but as a hopeless victim of delirium tremens. With the utmost gravity I replied that if he wanted to study the subject of the Image from *inside*, he had better read *The Figure of Beatrice*, Mr. Williams being about the only person who had seriously applied himself to the disentangling of this very difficult matter—did not Mr. Eliot agree with me? Mr. Eliot, with unfaltering countenance, replied that he did. Mr. Maufe solemnly entered the title of the work in a little note-book—& if he ever reads it he will be 'filled with a bewilderment at the thought of which I grin like a dog and run about the City.'"[123]

Rather sweet? She says that she "pilfered shamelessly" from me in her address, & I admit to a pleasure in thinking of affecting these popularities and through them the world. And let us hope Mr. Maufe's 1/10? in royalties will come into our pockets. It would be a shame if my small capacities gave way now—but just like the Omnipotence!

. . . Nevertheless, it was like the sublime loveliness of your Incelestitude—meaning something or someone involved with heaven—to speak as you did about the Roman Church. I see no more likelihood of that now than ever.[124] But that does not diminish my adoration. I should like you sometime to see my point, all the same, about my wrangle[125] with Jock & the rest. It is not that I am more Roman; it is only that I know what a supernatural claim is. It would be as true about Apollo or Buddha. But we will talk of that one evening when I am tending your toes.

It's tea-time; the cake at lunch was lovely. Thank you for yesterday—& for the Claret. We'll do it again next time—Monday fortnight, yes?

All love

Serge

3 Oct./44

The real fact about this life down here is that it leaves me without any initiative. I used to be tired, but I used to have some imaginative "go"—and now I have none, right deep in me. And I can honestly see no reason at all for that except the separation from you. One is older—but not so old; one ought to be doing one's best work . . . but this living without relaxation anywhere, without (in one sense, & that the most serious) any *ease*, is what gets me down.

None of our difficulties, none of our conflicts, alter the solid fact that I live closed within myself here, and do not with you.

All this arises from a mere chance that the Mother Superior of the Convent of the Sacred Heart, of whom I told you, has written to say she is being sent away from Oxford, and would like to see me before she goes. She fell, you may remember, heavily for *Beatrice*. And I ought to call, and so I will, and I have just telephoned. But O lud, madam wife, how I postponed the effort, how reluctant . . . and staring at the telephone I said to myself, as I have said so often: "Alas, without Her, I cannot do my job; I cannot properly talk to other people or deal with other things." Love, however concerned with greatness & labours, has in it a kind of lightness, almost gaiety. It has in it something of "perfect freedom"; I see that more and more. Of course, I know you are unique in that . . . no, I mean it; in that your glory is—not to "set me free"— that would be silly, but to be in yourself the very freedom which one needs. So that the very word "wife" comes to mean one who enlarges, who restores, who instructs. But I am not clear that many men feel it so. I have been very blessed and fortunate. And that, dearest lady, is why I've never felt any burden in the hack stuff I've done for our joined life. O I don't always *want* to . . . the Fleckers & the rest; but it never *weighs* on me—you agree? I curse a good deal, but it's meant amiable. Given these things have a lightness in them—and that must be from you; it can have no other source. Bed and board, board and bed . . .

Say this is a prelude to my coming. M. asks me if I would come to see *Hamlet* with him, and I will probably ring him up to-night. I never thought it would happen! Besides, he has a more fruitful mind than . . . but hush!

I send off a very small parcel to save me stuffing up my case. All love.

Serge

11 Oct./44

Date (so they say) of Our publication. It is pouring with rain, and the Allies are presumably reducing Aachen[126] "to rubble." Three odd facts, & the fourth— that I am now writing to you—hardly unites them. Or does it? I am not sure that it does not. I am bothered about Aachen; the civilians, as the *Daily Mail* says, in the shelters & the Bishop praying. Not that I disagree with the destruction, but that some other effort[127] ought also to be made: something (you will shrug? no, because (i) you do not shrug (ii) it is no shrugging matter) more in accord with my writing to you. This last is a fact, when all is said, of love; and how to unite Aachen with love? No; the Germans "deserve all they get." Yes, but do *I* deserve your love and my home and such things? Hardly: what then? Here am I approving of blasting German women & children— & men too—and yet all that "your face made visible"—which is love and charity—must be true. Or everything is nonsense. So it may be, but I have decided not to believe that. Love needs, we agree, that decision. And the Prayers of the Pope labour towards a union. It was sweet of you to like that poem; if any are good, that is the best. But if I give it to the world, what do I do about it? Is it enough to write verse? no, no, no. Bless God, my sweet, that I have not been left to verse; the needs of our life have saved me from worse, from the separation of verse from intelligence and life. But there is more to do, if I can. I could cry in your arms for very fear of Judgement—not mine now, but the world's. Your arms, so, would be a token of Mercy & Grace. — O well, winds? bring your arms. They are there, and everything else fades; Everything else? work and knowledge and one's self-importance. The other— always the other; & for me the other—you.

Now this is but an outbreak. Still, I send—how should I not? I am oppressed by everything to-day; which is more serious than being depressed—only easier to ignore. I play with the idea of coming up Saturday week . . . by an early train if I do but wake. Then 10 days after for the B.B.C. . . . which I am trying to satisfy with *Caesar.* But it's hard to think.

Be generous & forgive this babble. I aim at I don't know what. But you are always good. It counteracts all horror. So be content; do I forget that you too suffer? that is serious—I don't.

Bless you. I love you. Kiss me.

Serge

13 Oct./44

To-morrow week then, and wish me well to wake in the morning. This will be but a scrappy note, for I am spending all Sir Humphrey's time to-day reading the proofs of my novel.[128] They are all in and I wish to get them back to-day or to-morrow. As soon as our Dorothy[129] is gone, I shall have to do many things; but she does so like conversation . . . and we sit till 1.30 which makes me very sleepy.

I send another pound herewith, & will (I hope) forward one to-morrow. You must *not* forgo your frock. Good heavens, I have to run after you seeing that you get anything. What with M. & my sister . . . & if you give a pound as from me, may not I send you one as from me? However, this is only housekeeping; so it doesn't count. If I send you another £5 could you manage the frock? If not, tell me what. (You're as bad as one of the most holy and august ladies in my novels—only, fortunately for me, not quite so unearthly. There isn't—alas!—a single physical page in them. Well, in a literary sense—"alas!")

The poems[130] are supposed to be out, but there seem no copies yet in Oxford; anyhow Blackwells have none. I think it's sweet of you to talk of celebrating. I hope *not* to go down on Sunday this time, though it may have to be the 9.45 on Monday. There seems a long & horrid pause in the war, & it's all very long. My room here at S.H. is almost like your flat . . . no-one comes into it. Undoubtedly I am in danger of out-staying my usefulness at the Press: however, I hope to linger my time out!—O now, & Miss K. I think I had better ring you up early on Monday; about 8.30 or so? —I was wrong. Sir H. has just been in for almost an hour . . . about nothing in particular, but very pleasant.

All my love.

Serge

14 Oct./44

I've just caused to be dispatched to you half a dozen of the broadsheets;[131] if they reach you on Monday give Miss K. one. I do like to do a little flaunting of you before the outside world. It is hardly a sufficient return for cake, cheese, chocolate, shirt, handkerchiefs, socks, & pyjamas: and neither Dante nor Shakespeare nor I would think it was. The greater the poet, the more he realizes the true tributes of love. Still, as I have said before, we can only do what we can; and if words are a poor return for cakes and chocolate, why, still it is my *métier*, and that is all one can say. You shall at once pardon and like—or so I hope.

M. Denis Saurat, who presided over that meeting when you & I met Sir Francis Younghusband, and whose book on Milton[132] I recently reviewed, sends me now a poem—in print—of his own. In French: With an inscription: "à C—W—, vrai poete, grand poete, avec admiration" . . . "true poet, great poet" . . . the French do these things very well. Only I do not read French poetry easily; however, I must make a shot.

In the course of Sir H's general babble he said he had heard a rumour that something was to be offered me here, and that the new Vice-Chancellor (who is Sir Richard Livingstone, and brother in law to Chichester, and president of . . . Corpus, is it? no; never mind . . .) was more likely to encourage paying for Readerships than the retiring Vice-Chancellor. I do not myself think that this can mean anything *until* they re-organize after the war. But it shows that things have been spoken of—because Sir H. does not know the Tolkien-Lewis group, so he must have heard whatever he did hear independently which all goes to show that the academic side has really taken me seriously. Sir H. says that if he can at all avoid it, he shall not return to London with the Press—and we discussed its future.

I still think, as I told him, the Chair of Poetry[133] is the real thing; I could run that from London while I finished at the Press. And it lasts five years (and owing to the Retiring age, nothing here could last longer). After which, and in the glow of what I hope might be a successful Chair, we could settle here. But this is Dreams!

I send £2 herewith: and I will try & get through early Monday morning. The pyjamas came this morning; all the rest yesterday. I ate cakes at once; they were lovely. How we do try & feed each other, bless you! All love.

Serge

It seems to me to get colder & colder, and the rain comes in great bursts. There are certain lovely skies between—which seem to have a mysterious relevance to you: just as, so many years ago, the line of the downs used to mean your arms. It is, in a way, a little sad that my verse has grown so high & complex; though indeed one can observe that this happens with all the Great; and the need for poetic relevancies introduces an impersonality; much like the lord Taliessin's with his household—see *The Departure of Dindrane*[134] . . . but I speak now only of technicalities. If I live and do well—in verse—I shall pick up the earlier style into the later; as Dante does. But it's a long and hard way . . . though I cannot tell you how much your liking these poems[135] eases it: and I was very happy that we agreed about the Pope poem. . . . however, I didn't mean to go back to these likes.

The second two arrived last night; I thought they were all 18th century but these were Shakespeare, & I had to re-arrange my ideas hastily. Before they left they made a short speech saying it was good of me to spare them the time. I deduce that it has been explained to them that they should be grateful.

And now I think I had better start sending some cash—for next week. One can't (do you think?) ever be too soon.

All love and blessings.

Serge

How fantasies possess one! Do you know I could, at this moment, almost swear I did not write to you yesterday? I know I must have done, because I have a pound less . . . and yet my mind starts suggesting that I did not send the pound but spent it. All my reason assures me that I wrote; all my emotions, with a strong sense of guilt, tell me I missed. Is not that very absurd? And if one can feel like that about something one knows absolutely isn't true, why, how easily one can feel it about others when it's equally false . . . I ought always to be grateful to you—& indeed I am—for saving me[136] from persecution manias, false fancies, & all the rest. Consider, dearest, that any obstinate accuracy of mine is very largely due to you, who never allowed me to get into the grip of grim shadows. It is, no doubt, your eyes, which (as I had the honour to say) are as bright as ever, & which illuminate the mind and soul as well as the flesh. . . . Anyhow, I send another pound hastily, lest I am bemused again to-morrow.

By an unearthly devotion to duty I have now got 3 tutorials & one lecture done; written the *Julius Caesar* script for the B.B.C.; re-read the *Duchess of Malfi* for Hubert's introduction; & am trying to clear up a few oddments. My pupils this term have even read me; at least, some of them; they allude to *Reason & Beauty* etc. and each pair makes a little speech about my generosity in sparing time; though when you think I'm doing it for cash . . . well, it's all very odd. It's true I don't think *one* lot of tea between 7.30 and 12.30 is really enough; but then I've been spoilt. I can't think why other people don't produce coffee as easily . . . coffee and some agreeable lightness of food (say, a small cake or two) at 12 would encourage me wonderfully. However, one must be thankful for small mercies . . . and when I think I might have been born a German . . . I do find myself a little awed by the present prospects; it's terrible to see a nation finally go down, however passionately one wants it. And the executions of collaborators in the freed countries are rather awe-inspiring too.

However . . . this is no love-letter; or is it? after all, you said you liked this chat sometimes. Till Saturday . . . & I *will* wake. All my love.

Serge

(over)

I'll go out with M. on Saturday evening if he likes . . . I've told him as much.

20 Oct/44

O I am so sleepy! And when one's sleepy reading a MS hardly wakes one up. I think tutorials make one sleepy; however, to-night is my night out & I shall go round to Magdalen. I have promised to dine at the R. first, but I shall leave just after 8 & walk down. It's comforting to think the streets will be lighted.

But except for my intellectual efforts there is less than ever to tell you. My days are a regular routine, as you'll know. . . . O this is a schedule, not a letter; letters to you should carry just a hint at least of

> from his lips
> Not words alone pleased her—[137]

which some people think Milton ought not to have put in, but I sympathize with the Lady Eve. . . .

A good audience at the SCM;[138] & some discussion—very properly earnest, but then so was I. It must be that that is creeping into this letter; also the consciousness that I ought to have got some money out this morning to you. I will do it to-morrow, but I'm afraid you may be short, and I can't think why it slipped me: stupid! Do forgive me.

HSM says he means to retire on 31 March next; how odd it will seem. "The woods decay; the woods decay and fall . . and after many a summer dies the swan."[139] . . . not that I'd call him a swan. But all drops away—you only still (as always,) the central strong pillar. How much I have depended on you—how now! and how fortunate. Be always blessed.

I love you. Kisses.

Serge

Southfield House
23 Oct/44

Dearest,

Rather sadly I am, it seems, now driven back on writing. It's always a depressing time—these Mondays; and in a way worse for you than for me, because I have to rush round in my mind. And you too, but (I hope at this end of the day) not so feverishly. We got down all right, I having grabbed a corner seat . . . owing to a noble lot of 3rd class people who decided to walk down inside! So I merely went in after them & bagged the seat. And I hope you got home as simply.

The SCM[140] want to know if I will lead prayers on Wednesday; I certainly will not. A young poet wishes to call on me; I'd better see him.

TSE tells me that Belgion has been repatriated & can be reached at the Athenaeum. O lor', darling, I'm glad he's free, but I do *not* want him; and owing to my having hardly ever written—well, not often—it's going to be very awkward. Still, it's nice to know he's free. TSE has sent me his book with an inscription which I cannot forbear copying out for you:

"To

C—W—

(who, if any, will understand what
the author attempted & how far
he fell short of it)
from T-S-E-."

Nice of him! And now I must kiss you a thousand times and rush to the *Allegory of Love*,[141] &c., &c., And then another thousand.

Serge

4 Nov/44

After having told you everything, there's nothing more! I send you the pound . . . hoping that you weren't too rushed. A letter from DLS[142] . . . sending me a cutting about someone who is attacking me and C.S.L. on Milton. I may reckon to my credit that I have helped—indeed, it was I who began—to make Milton a live subject. I shall lecture on him next term here, even if I have to come down specially to do it. (It will be exactly five years then since I first, at CSL's invitation, first shyly lectured in Oxford. O well . . . on that side I have not failed, however in others . . . pass.)

The *T.L.S.* reviews the *Stars*[143] longish & respectful—at least I haven't read it yet, but it looked like it. It's odd how now one no longer rushes at reviews. So long as they are *there*—so as to show one counts—one doesn't much mind what they say. About most of them one feels only what Pope said about those of his day—

> And some made coxcombs nature meant
> but fools . . .[144]

no; that's unfair. You see I am still in a bad temper. But it was sweet to see you again in the train. I owe you very much; but among it all I reckon these sudden apparitions very high. Do you remember once buying me the *Times* AND the *Telegraph* at Paddington? Of course, one allows the value of the work in the years . . . I mean you running the flat and I making the money . . . but the vivid moments remain too—you buying two papers for me or I ringing you up this morning. As Patmore remarked:

> What seems to say her rosy mouth?
> "I'm not convinced by proofs but signs."[145]

Something to it!

Otherwise—not much here. Another note from Belgion; I'm hastily sending him the *Stars*. Two more books from *T&T*. An announcement of a new edition of the *Duchess of Malfi* "with a critical introduction by Mr. C—W—." Which I must try & do this week. One or two business notes: that's all.

Thank you for everything. By this time next week I ought to be home. I hope by the time after that to come up on the Friday evening, but I simply cannot fit next Friday's tutorial in anywhere else. But all those things you so greatly understand, pearl[146] among women and ruby[147] among wives that you are! All love.

Serge

13 Novr./.44

I have decided that the only thing I ought to do when I am away from you is great poetry—in which I should in some obscure way return to you. And it's extremely annoying that I can't: and yet perhaps I could do more; perhaps you ought to make me spend at least ten minutes on it every day. But anyhow that's what I thought as the train moved out of Paddington: and now I am more irritable than ever with everything else, and as uncharitable as I can be.

The BBC want to have the quotations from Milton read by one of their people, and only to pay £12.12.0. I suppose in the end they'll have their way, because I'm not prepared to get in wrong with them at the moment, nor am I prepared to lose £12.12.0. But it's tiresome, because I have views about reading Milton, and they'll make him an organ-voice[148] when he oughtn't to be.

HSM. is in London to-day. Which of course means that I shall have to rush up . . . no, I will *not*. I will bring up some of your cake at 12.30, and if Robin is here, very well. If the University cannot over-rule HSM—

You will gather that I am in a towering rage and you will be right. I am gnashing my teeth at everything and LOATHING the world. But LOVING you. But God help anyone else who [wrongs?] me.

I adore you.

Serge

16 Nov./44

My priest from Rochester has just waited on me—a nice fellow and intelligent, knowing what Religion is and wonderfully free from "clericality" while remaining a priest. He is married, devoted to his wife, has 5 children, & would like to meet you as "so much the source of my ideas." His pet among the ideas is the *Dove,* and he has been telling me of people to whom he has lent it and who have profited. Rather sweet and very touching!

As for pride . . . I was very much struck by your distinction between it and the assumption of it; let us discuss it. But not at all, noblest of women, by your other distinction. Your great gifts, which are rare and beautiful, are as much given as mine, and mine as yours. Yours are Beauty, Intelligence, Speed, Charity, and Delight. (I include Wit under Intelligence) Mine are Speech, Doctrine, Poetry, and a certain Lucidity. And we have Labour in common. Yours are of value to things done; mine to things known. We are the world's infinite complements; we are necessary to each other. I study in you the Thing happening (well, and so I do!); you observe in me the Thing declared . . . O I babble, but indeed we do but grow to one Thing in two modes; and indeed three— you, I, and we. The we being how much more the root of you and I than the other way round. Which is why we carry ourselves with high courtesy towards each other . . . or as high as our fallen natures allow.

This is a tractate? no; it is a kiss, all my tractates are your kisses. However, to seal all I send £3 out of the five; the rest to-morrow.

All love and blessings. The letter was *sweet.*

Serge

21 Nov/44

It's perhaps as well, though tiresome, that I shouldn't send another cheque to-day. But I wish I did. Few things—not even lecturing to a large & clamorous audience, which is hardly how I should describe my present—give me as much joy. This is as beautiful as it is proper; and I cannot be sufficiently grateful. It is one of the more exquisite results of love. You will say I talk too much of it; no, indeed; I do but soliloquize to you, and to whom but one's wife should one soliloquize?

I've lectured on the Disintegrity and Vulgarization of the Intellect as shown in the *Dunciad*—not that I ever read the *Dunciad* till a week or so ago. (When my letters[149] to Your Sublimity are discovered by an American professor in years to be, they will be a great give-away of my literary reputation. It will be the only surprise in them!) The audience dwindles slightly, but not more than is inevitable. On the whole it hasn't been too bad . . . considering the Eighteenth Century.

Otherwise Nothing has happened. The last Event was your voice yesterday. I'm very sorry about the fall, & I do hope you're not in pain. I find myself brooding over how many tutorials I can fit in next term, but I wait for our Miss M's Letter to see what she wants. No letters to-day from anyone; that's not unusual. But I want to hear from Sackville-West about Monday.

This is a poor note: forgive. I will deal with the gas, as & when. Meanwhile all love and thoughts.

Serge

23 Nov/44

Herewith £2: I hope not too tiresomely late. But at the moment I feel the world is a little tiresome—no, not in this case seriously: only (to be truthful) a wish that I had some Taliessin poems written. Nicholson & Watson have written to say they have sold 800 copies of the *Stars*[150] in a month out of a first printing of 1000, and will bring out a new edition next year. (This would be very good going for any book of verse, and is a very different business from what it used to be. Besides, it will mean more cash without my doing a thing!) But they also clamour for more; they'd "like to follow it up with a further selection from your Taliessin poems. Would this be possible in the near future?" Well, of course, it wouldn't—because there are no more than 20 or 30 lines written; and I fear, if I did nothing else, it would take me a year to do the next lot: well, no . . . but a good time. They also want to know if they can take over the original *T. in Logres,* if the O.U.P. are not re-publishing.

This selling of & passion for my verse is something altogether new, and I want to cry a little—if you were here I should. I don't say it's much . . . but we have waited so long since the *Silver Stair*[151] for something of the kind: and to be asked for (i) a new edition in a month (ii) more poems (iii) re-publication of old—is all a little shaking. I would ring you up, but in 3 minutes I could hardly explain, tho' I know you'd understand. Besides, I can cry on Saturday. But I do wish I had the great narrative poems which are to follow *done.* Kiss me; you were the first to believe, and you always have.

I'll leave it at that to-day. Kiss me again. We will certainly lunch on Monday.

Serge

29 Nov/44

I've been vaguely expecting a small *T&T* cheque, but it doesn't come . . . of course I may have got muddled and thought it was in last month when it wasn't. But I won't wait any longer, so I send £2 h/w: the remainder of what I borrowed from B.,[152] and I'll settle him out of my salary cheque. At the moment we're a little low, but we shall soon rise again. I hope to send off the *Duchess*[153] to-morrow; last night I revised it and began on the Milton script.[154] Tutorials are becoming a MENACE; Miss Morison rang up last night about next term's—to say that two of her pupils whom she meant to send somewhere for Chaucer had pleaded to come to me for Wordsworth, and she feared I mightn't be here for the summer. So I said I hoped I shouldn't, and I now wait to find out what the number suggested is. I think, if wanted, I could work in ten by abstracting a little time from the office, but I fear no more. However, obviously everyone is satisfied.

Yours is the only letter of any sort or kind this morning—business or (as one may say) public. Obviously everything has come to an end and no-one wants me any more. "Life like a dome of many-coloured glass"[155] is cracking every where. I am thinking of inserting a passage in one of the Bors-Elayne poems beginning

> Shall I fall in love with you all over again?
> Twice—with you then as with you now,
> either co-inherent in either, that brow
> in this and this in that, but both now
> known in the one, and a double glory so . . .

all this through looking at your photograph in the small room. Bors in the poems is a sound fellow, and I hope I am not too unlike him; the divine Taliessin himself is too great for me,[156] and is indeed not so much a man at all as the very Nature of Poetry. Now there is something for you to tell the later inquirers when they come. But I am still very cross at not being able to send more poems at once—or to write them at least.

(Sir H. & Goffin are going off in the car. Which means Sir H. is lunching out. I am going to lunch on Sausage Snacks—I did think of bringing up some of the Cake, but decided to reserve it for the nights.)

I'm very glad about 31, and it's sweet of you to be pleased. You'll observe that in old age I'm getting far more quick at what you might call "Taking Notice." Like Bors again, who (I feel) would be absolutely efficient; which was why he was let in on the Grail. Taliessin would have written a long metaphysical poem about it! no—don't let's be unfair; but he was hardly of human birth[157] (see the *Stars*) and could hardly enter into domesticity; anyhow he never did. But a great being, all the same. It'll be odd to meet him, if I do, in heaven . . .

I mean the original Taliessin. "At that time" says Nennius of the Early Britons, "Talhaern and Neirin and Taliessin and Blwchfardd and Cian were all famous in poetry." But I don't know how authentic the fragments that we have of his verse are supposed to be.

I'll write, if I remember, to 31. Tell M, if you will, I've sent off the *Stars* to Coralie, & will deal with the rest & write to him reporting to-morrow.

How's four pages and two pounds—is not that a letter now? God bless & all love.

Serge

[The following sonnet was found in the file of letters now in the Marion E. Wade Center at Wheaton College between letters dated November 29 and December 1. There is no more specific information about the date of its composition than suggested by the title.]

Oxford, 1944

Out of your breast a planetary fire
    shot, and (as Halley's, riding round the sun)
circled a little while both tower and spire,
    till retrograde it soon began to run
to that unmapped immensity of heart
    wherein (beyond astronomy's figures) first
it was enlivened into motion—art
    having genesis so, and verse; it (after) burst
into this tempered air: men said "Wherer [?] came,
    and by whose word commingled thus live,
and from what beauty's brow lit, this new flame?"
    O if it spoke, what answer could it give
but: "Nay, heaven's space is ever visible; see,
    Verulam and London bore me—and both she."

I'll ring you up on Monday. It may be a little later because CSL & I are formally lunching with Miss Morrison & the Principal of St. Anne's. Perhaps after four.

1 Dec/44

The *T & T* cheque having arrived, I hastily send you another pound. Tell Mrs O. some time that Lord David Cecil and I are now on Christian name terms! He came in to Magdalen last night and in the course of conversation addressed me as Charles and then kind of half-not-apologized, rather sweetly; so I made a suitable answer & proceeded in a few minutes to say "David"— very odd! but he feels I am a husband & a father where the Lewises are not,

& we talk of the difficulties of Babies. But he also told the others that his pupils now, when he lays down the law, look up at him and say "I'm not sure that Mr. Williams would agree with that," & he has to say: "O well if Mr. W. thinks differently . . ." and get out of it as best he can.

Excuse; excuse. This is but a small effort to tell you anything amusing, & I do not wish to bore you with our reputation. I may say *our*, for every reason! and honestly nothing else happens. CSL was shocked when I told him of my barber's shop, and of the Primrose Hill affair, & said very earnestly that I had been preserved "for divine ends." which is no doubt true, but as it applies to several million others . . .

Theodora must have dropped a word at *T & T.* Veronica writes this morning apologizing for not putting me in—in a charming way—and sending me a pre-pull of the review of the *Stars.* Which after saying it's very difficult proceeds to make full amends by saying that it surely "carries an immortal cadence" and that "it is as much astonishment of poetry as we can bear." Quite handsome!

O this is very stupid & no love-letter, which I wish all mine to be. And now I must write to M.! I think I'd better send another pound to make up! With kisses.

Serge

6 Decr/44

Sweet of you to write, Sweet. The Press club affair—or whatever they call it; the thing that takes 4/2 from me every week—having paid out its yearly result, I hastily send you another pound. I have also sent M. one for the *Hamlet* seats. I will send you another to-morrow.

It would make tutorials easier, I feel, if I could ever remember most of my pupils from week to week. I had the very devil of a time when writing my reports, because I simply could not remember a thing about them—neither faces nor essays nor anything, except a general blur. So I had to go very very carefully and write the same four sentences in different words each time. These are the real hardships of the Academic Life. I shall hurl myself into London, the flat, & You with a greater sense of coming to my own than ever—were that possible. Of all men, I was never meant to be away from my wife. But I suppose most of the Armies . . . especially in Burma . . . feel like that. Yes, but that does not alter or lessen *my* feelings. How I do resent the revolting Germans[158] . . . but see the *Dove;* only then I did it in the abstract; now I do it from my own heart.

And I never specially thanked you for the cake; which I hereby do. It had a marvelous top . . . all—sugar? exquisite!

God bless you. I do my best to show him how.

All love

Serge

I will say that "this University" pays in good time; my cheque has come, tho' I have two more "tutes" to do. One this afternoon at 2, & one to-morrow at 10: owing to going to Magdalen to-night and speaking somewhere to-morrow. A Young Gentleman waited on me yesterday to ask me to address the Congregational Society on the first Sunday of next term. Last evening, owing to my pupils singing carols, & then postponing themselves till 2 to-day, I had free and devoted it to getting on with the Milton script.[159] I am catching up slowly, & hope to be more or less clear by Xmas & ready to begin on the King & on next term.

No doubt I shall draw a little on the £30 till Sir Humphrey (as is much to be hoped) comes across for Xmas. But these are due or in sight—

   (i) *The Duchess*—say   £5
  (ii) Milton—   "   £10
 (iii) *All Hallows' Eve*— £20
  (iv) Gibson—   "   £10
   (v) Anything from
       Faber in
       March—   "   £10
  (vi) the new edn.
       of the Poems— £10
               ———
               £65

This, except for Milton & Gibson, without any more work, and all in the next 3 months. Leading up to the tutorials for next term—another £50. And throwing in the present £30—that makes a total of £145. So we can cuddle £50 for moving; buy your coat & M's things almost as soon, I hope, as coupons arrive, and live on the rest. And I needn't bother about arranging for a new book until I have really got on with the King.[160] Praise God.

Excuse; I do so like to tell you. With the warm feeling that if it were the other way you'd be divine. As always—even with your poor cold! and now to S.P.Rd and my tutorial. All love

                              Serge

This year's last letter . . . by the next I shan't be writing, I'm convinced. Whatever happens in the rest of the winter, the spring campaigns ought to be final. I will try & set myself in better heart to the last lap.

Your charming & beautiful letter left me slightly agape. What I make of it is that you are more charitable (to use the word) at heart than I. I think perhaps I'm less quickly moved, but when I am I'm much more resentful—or perhaps sullen. Some weeks ago I was vaguely thinking of taking to my thicker coat—or at least looking at it to see if I could. Unfortunately that Sunday I.D.[161] permitted herself to ask me if I wasn't going to—& that, of course, settled it. I do not allow people to tell me what to do—or no-one not You. I admit I cannot go so far as to say: "If you mention it, you fool, you must know I shan't do it," but that's what it comes to. I never knew anyone who so immediately causes me to do the opposite as that unfortunately old lady—never.

However . . . The local paper says that the County of Oxford has had 5000 bombs on it, which is more than I thought. It's odd they've so missed the City.

This afternoon I wish to finish W.G.,[162] & get him off on Monday; then I can tell you so when I ring up. Sunday I'd better read up for the Prose Arthur[163] (the *prose*) . . . indeed, I've just got up & put 2 books to take back. Term seems to be drawing very near.

I'll send some cash on Monday. All love.

Serge

1945

2 Jan/45

Herewith £2. It was sweet of you to tell me you could manage till to-day . . . till to-morrow, of course! I'll send another £ then.

It's a little less cold to-day, I think—at least, here; but all the papers say London is the coldest spot, & if London I'm sure Hampstead, & if Hampstead I fear our flat. The puddles seem unfrozen, and the sun is faintly present.

I'm madly reading in the History of the Doctrine of the Eucharist, in order to push in to my book something about the grail in history.[1] Rather tiresomely, Sisam can't send me proofs of the new edition of Malory, which will be from the original text, hitherto unpublished. To-morrow evening I've promised to dine with a man who is on the scientific side, but whose wife is asserted to be an expert in the Old French Arthurian cycle. I hope to get something useful there. (And will you tell me why every book seems more difficult than the one before? Absurd, do you think? I cannot but believe it.)

You remember the Introduction to *Malfi?*[2] George Rylands, who was to write on the production, has sent in, instead, a long essay on the play as poetry. And Hubert has sent his & mine to me, pleading with me to adjust and arrange. I did think that was done with! However, I must play with it somehow. But Term approaches, like Blake's Tyger . . . ![3]

Excuse, dearest pet. It will be nice to run up on Saturday; would it were longer, but it'll break the infinite period, & I shall be up the next Friday. The train's supposed to get in at 3.40, so I ought (even if it's late) to be home by 5.

I love you; bless me.

Serge

9 Jan./45

The 9th Jan. is getting on—that is all one can say. It's horribly cold, even here, and what it must be in the kitchen . . . and the lumbago? I do not forget you are going out to-night, and I wish you and I were spending a cosy evening alone. . . . You know I sometimes think there must be a kind of monotony, a sort of repetition, about my letters; they seem to say that so often, and very little else! "Fool, said my Muse to me, look in thy heart and write." I don't know if Sir Philip Sidney repeated himself in the same way; because I don't know the Sonnets to Stella (was it Stella?) well enough. And we haven't his private correspondence, and anyhow he died young; he never managed the greater style. At which I gaze on at your maturer face, in which all the beauty of the younger exists with something other. But this too I have said before.

Well . . . and our Captain Belgion? O well, it all went very well. It was a little expensive, but, by the peculiar Mercy, when I went back to S.P.Rd. from the office, I found a small cheque for £1.6 from Powell Kylie in Sheffield—royalties on the *House by the Stable*, which (it seems) has had 4 performances there, with the Bishop of Sheffield in the chair, or at least being there. And it was quoted in "the Christmas Eve Sermon." So I was able to do my duty by M.B. on the religious profit, so to speak, without feeling I was robbing—say, St. Mary to pay . . . Timothy.

We met at 7—I feeling a little awkward—but we parted at 11, having dined & sat in the Randolph lounge. He was very sensible about the captivity, & made very little of it. Ten thousand of them were taken on the Greek beaches, & taken through the Balkans into Germany. (Looking up, I see it's begun to snow! my dear, and you to-night! . . .) He is now waiting on the War Office. He was particular to inquire after you and Michael; you might tell M. that he expressed his intention of looking in at Bumpus's: apologize—but I can't help it. Implore M. to regard it as an exchange for one of the Americans. He gave some lectures in the prison camp which he has now got taken as a Penguin. He was much the same M.B., planning possible futures which I should think were most unlikely to come off. He is (if one may say so) the typical example of the drawback of thinking in grandiose terms, yet he's not a bad fellow. But if I had thought in that way, we should have had more promises of to-morrow and less assurance of to-day (if possible) even than we have had.

Apart from that—and I now feel easy about him, at least as far as I am concerned—there's nothing here. No letters from friend or foe. The calm before the storm?—I mean, before the term?

I still live in your marvelous *au revoir*. Thank you, he said blushing.

Serge

10 Jan/45

It was very agreeable to hear you this morning, and to hear you laugh. Your laugh down the telephone is one of the richest things I know; and for some years I didn't, among all our troubles, have an opportunity of hearing it very often. But now it seems to me to be much more lying ready at the other end "on and off," if I may repeat my small joke. Which my telephone account is enough to correct!

I'm sorry about the back though. But I was Terrified last night—snow, frost, & you having to go out; and I did think of ringing up late. But then I thought you might be asleep or M. perhaps upset. So altogether I left it. The telephone—especially when . . . O well, never mind. (I was going to say "when M. was at Weston.")[4]

The Parents[5] have "postponed their passage," and ask for letters to be sent on. They sent a cable, and are writing. So that's all that is known. I was quite prepared for them and should have taken them in my stride, but it makes the tutorials easier: in the sense that if dinner's a little late, we can hurry, and they could hardly be asked to. I begin to think now that I shall get away without seeing them.

O and Anne says it's tremendously kind of you, and she'd love to come to lunch if that'll be all right—next Tuesday.

To-night I have agreed to let myself be taken to the theatre. There are no week-day evenings at the Randolph now—nor have been for months! But this is to see a thing called *Winterset*[6] which M. will know about.

The sun's been about a bit. Take care of yourself. At 7 this morning I yearned for (i) a cup of tea (ii) another hot water bottle (iii) being Settled Off—did you ever hear of anything of the kind? Ho, well, I never.

All love.

Serge

18 Jan./45

I had meant to begin to-day by writing to you. But the Vicar of Headington called, and has spent some time with me, asking me to be on their Moral Welfare Council. He—or they—feel that it's desirable to have someone like me—not to bother me to make speeches but to give the Council itself a new light. It meets half a dozen times a year. I've explained that by the time it does meet, I shall be back in London. But till then I shall be glad to do . . . & so forth. A M.W. Council is the last body I ever thought to find myself on!

The second piece of news is not of me. I've had a letter from Belgion saying that he's engaged to be married. How little men know of their friends' affairs! I had no notion of anything of the kind. The lady is named Helen Mattock; he has known her "for 25 years" and she is "the Headmistress of a flourishing school at Peterborough." At present no public announcement is being made, but I am to tell my family circle. So now I do, and now you know.

Birmingham was quite agreeable. It seems I am President of their Society, & the Chairman opened by saying that he felt the Society was practically "a collection of Charles Williams fans." Afterwards he asked for questions, & there were none, until a young woman suddenly gave tongue and said: "This silence is not incompetence but we are breathless with admiration." I talked to them on *Personification in English Verse*—not one of my best efforts, but passable.

I send another pound herewith—in fact I send £2. Contributing perhaps one towards beginning your £5 again. Which leads me to my having had a letter from Fabers saying that *All Hallows' Eve* is to be published tomorrow. (I've seen no copies yet, so if you don't get yours, it will be for that reason only. How many a time now, it seems, I have opened a parcel of copies of "my new book" and each time and all times put the first copy aside to bring or send to you. We won't look for reviews; to tell you the truth, I'm a little afraid of them . . . generally nowadays I don't mind. But this is all wrong somehow, & I don't wish to be told so. It ought to be advertised on Sunday.

This is what they call a newsy letter! But it tells you everything there is to tell. We'll consider next week-end I'm up—Saturday week—about clothes. There will be £20 from Faber's on the one side, & telephone & gas on the other. But February is a short month!

I love you. I love you. And I wished I was coming Home last night on my way from Birmingham! I did.

Kisses

Serge

20 Jan./45

It's just as well I'm going to ring you up on Monday; I need to hear your voice—in general and in particular. The co-incidence of the novel (which still isn't here) with the beginning of term has almost got me down. I've just been making out my list of pupils with their subjects, and this ranging from Malory to Keats almost frightens me. But the novel[7] really gnaws me. I feel as if everyone would sneer at it. This is silly, because you liked a lot of it, and TSE liked it, but there it is! You must forgive me and be kind.

GFJC came in yesterday & said that our N.Y. manager[8] was arriving (he seems to have got a passage) and GFJC thought he ought to see me & perhaps Michael (if it could be arranged in the time). Nice of our Jock to think of it, & makes me repent of the times I have thought ill of him. I shall see what happens, & I'll call M. tomorrow.—O & he will tell you, so this won't be new. Never mind! But it makes me feel that the possibility of America is still hovering. Though he & M, of course, may not hit it off—if they do see each other. However, M. (thanks to you) is in a far better & more reliable state, & has much more real sense than ever before. If it *did* come off, & if he *were* happy and efficient, how you and I might rest! (I think I'd better give GFJC a copy of the novel! he won't much care for it, but he won't see it as I do, and it'll look well!)

Meanwhile, the Russians are getting on, & the whole thing is closing in, don't you think? The Germans must be wishing they'd still got the men & machines they threw away in the West in December. Soon—soon! . . . well, comparatively soon.

I do love you. I also badly need you. Till Monday.

Serge

30 Jan/45

This, I suppose, is a thaw? If it freezes to-night, it will be awfully jolly to-morrow, but perhaps it won't freeze tonight! Anyhow the roads are mostly slush—though slippery slush. But when I went round to the Taylorian this morning, they were half a foot in snow.

Colin Hardie,[9] a don at Magdalen and Sec. to the Dante Society, startled me by coming to the lecture (numbers as last week; Mr. Williams in his now famous advocacy of Chastity as defined in *Comus,* and his Instruction in Miltonic Virtues, "as given before crowned heads"). So I spoke to him afterward about a Dante dinner next term, and he mentioned that it cost generally about £9—which is better than I hoped, & I'm relieved. I was beginning to wish I'd not joined, but I ought to arrange that, and it would be nice to do it. C.H. said something about my being asked to join in special circumstances, but I said that I should hate finance to be one: all most agreeable. It seems that Magdalen is being shy about handing out its remaining wine to the D.S., & it may even come to our drinking beer or cider—sad but (perhaps) convenient!

Nothing else, I think. Sir H. thinks *A.H.E.*[10] the best of my novels; he said he wondered if I had him in mind for Evelyn[11]—which, though I hadn't, gave me a higher notion of his intelligence.

All sweet love. I do hope the bedroom's warmer? and I hope the world may be. Till to-morrow.

Serge

3 Feb./45

Dearest,

I send you the *Herald Review,* which has just reached me. I admit that, except for one sentence (and I don't defend the style!), it could hardly be better. The idea of selling in a hundred years' time leaves me—though, of course, it's what I always intended—a little cold when I think that royalties will stop for M. fifty years after I'm dead. Unless they alter the copyright law.

Bruce Montgomery, who turned up for an hour unexpectedly, told me there was a very good one in the *Birmingham Post,* but I've not seen it. The *Daily Mail* this morning you will have seen. The interesting thing is that it's given pride of place. But the other interesting thing—& a comment on our age—is that Mr. Quennell[12] says nothing about the heavenly side of the book: he goes on about the black magician. Heaven is rooted in Hampstead, and Redemption walks in the City and Westminster. No; like the critics of Milton[13] and Dante, P.Q. prefers to look at hell. (I say nothing about his getting his details wrong; it was Highgate anyhow. But I allow a reviewer may make a slip of that kind.)

They tell me my telephone bill here has come in, and they say rather anxiously to me "It's rather a lot; it's over a pound." To which I replied, among the lesser creatures of the Press: "and very little for the pleasure of hearing my wife speaking." We'll begin another on Monday—say, round about 4 or a little before.

I've done a little more to *Arthur:* feeling a little doubtful if that book will be "an event." But we progress.

All my love, & thank you for supporting *A.H.E.* By now next Saturday I shall be with you.

Serge

6 Feb/45

Dearest,

I hope to enclose another pound—but I must first get B. to change a cheque. I didn't get any brown paper yesterday, but I have to-day, so I shall post off a parcel to-morrow morning—to save myself the trouble of bringing it!

I had sealed my yesterday's letter down, before I telephoned, so I couldn't add the little ripple of sweetness afterwards which I like to do. A vicarious sweetness—yours and not mine—but returned to you it was!

A minor blow has fallen—Belgion has been told by the War Office to report to Oxford! He "looks forward to some nightly sessions with me." The devil he does! I didn't suppose he would return for this. But I can see I shall have to manage something, & that with apparent cheerfulness. O lud!

The attendance maintains itself pretty well. I should think there must be getting on for—200, which isn't bad: say, 150. This morning We delivered Ourself on *Lycidas*—"proving absurd all written hitherto."[14] I shall spend the rest of this term on *Paradise Lost* & conclude next term—if I'm here. But the Germans have now so little hope—indeed, no hope except of things getting worse—that I momentarily expect a débâcle. The Lord has wrought us a great deliverance[15] . . . London is bad, but it might have been Berlin, and Oxford distant, but I might have been lost in the Russian snows. It's a wonder to feel the enemy is saying, in his towns and villages:

"The Russians are coming!" "The Americans are nearer!" "The English are here!"—so perish the Lord's enemies![16]

Nothing else. I labour against time, but I do my best. Take care of yourself for me on Saturday—now do'ee now!

Serge

7 Feb./45

My dearest,

I don't say that I've not been sometimes slightly taken aback by your wit, but I never denied its devastating effectiveness. "Honoured synthetically" is more than wit about one person; it's a whole comment on a whole class of society. It puts in two words what I've been trying to say about all upper middle-class culture: that which no more belongs to my world of ideas than to yours. What Arnold called the Philistines—& yet not quite either, for they too often think of themselves as the true people. But it's something lacking in them which springs from "good honest dung." I have met it a hundred times, & groaned under it. I'd rather be a film star than that, & I'm immensely indebted to you for the phrases. When you are right, are you right!

What I should like beyond anything—though I fear I can't dispose of M. for six months—would be to have that time alone with you. It's 22 years since we did . . . & could I do with it! And that, between you & me, is going to be the chief angle. However, we shall manage it. You & I alone would be a comforting circle: "the still point of the turning world."[17]

But you've done a great deal more than make him comfortable; you've given him the very chance he needed to grow a bit. And if he & I get on better now, we both owe it to you. (And God.) I'll do anything I can; but now the turn is coming, all I want in this world is you, a bearable place to live, some money & enough distant publicity to bring in the money and be amusing. Nothing more.

Till Saturday. I hope to bring an orange or two. And I hope to send another pound to-morrow. Bless you for everything. I love you.

Serge

I sent some things off this morning!

8 Feb/45

Dearest,

Herewith another. If I seem to "dole it out" you'll forgive. I have a faint feeling I may be a little tight for three or four weeks, till the tutorials are paid up. But we've done fairly well in getting what we have. Only I'm fussed about you & about the F.W. offering. But next week is half through the term, & the University generally sends its cheque in the last—the eighteen—weeks.

We continue to run round in Our sedate circle: office, tutorials, *Arthur* or review, sleep. You mustn't think I'm over-bothered with work. I do wish I knew more about the Arthurian stuff, because I can *not* remember all about Pseudo-Wauchier,[18] & c. . . . Talking about "Pseudo" makes me add that it's very odd to hear one's own critical vocabulary coming back from the young. John Spalding told me he heard one of two young women in the street say to the other: "My dear, you must have the feeling intellect"[19]—which is a phrase of Wordsworth's you will recognize from its tendency (like Aquinas & Dante) to recur in my own conversation. They, of course, got it from lectures. But it's odd to think of whoever they were using it.

It's raining steadily here. I appear to be speaking to-night . . . yes, I am. A young man has just rung me up to remind me. On *Poetry in Wartime.* At Balliol.

At 8. The tutorial having been pushed in at 5! Well, let them do it while they have me. Very soon they won't . . . to feel the arms of my true love

Round me once again,

Serge

12 Feb./45

"In vino veritas"[20]—but I was thinking that no *vinum* makes any difference to the *veritas* . . . how sweet!

We got down in time to-day—I clinging to the seat you found me; full but possible. The poor old dear you helped in was turned out two minutes afterwards, but I was respectfully approved by the inspector & left. I deposited my case at the station and came on.

Nothing very much here—2 or 3 small reviews of *A.H.E.*, all reasonably good but unimportant (one agrees with your view in the taxi—"Mr. W's writing gets better & better the farther he gets from earth"!) The B. of Chichester's friend's query (about Childhood and Original Sin—which the Bishop ought to know as well as I). And forgiveness.

And soon I propose to leave for the station (5.30–6.30—meaning to get there), the R. (6.45–7.40), a tutorial (8–10), tea (10–10.30), drafting lecture (10.30–12), midnight news, MS. from Strong (12.15–1). And, remembering you, I will try & do as you say in the lectures & give them all I can!

It was a sweet time. Love & blessings.

Serge

13 Feb./45

Before I get down to reading a MS. on the Lord's Prayer, I will write to you. The attendance at the lectures continues satisfactory:—a few down, but not many. In the fourth week this is quite satisfactory. But I had an unusual visitor—or hearer—this morning; one of M.'s Americans. I had reached the R. last night at about 20 to 7, when he appeared (he was the last one I saw—Charles ?Y. Williams—) & I could do nothing then because of tutorials; but I said I was tied up with a lecture the next morning, so he said he'd like to come, & I met him & took him along. I told him to slip out if he was bored, but he didn't; so afterwards I took him to lunch at the D's expense, & then said goodbye & came on here. (The letter you posted on Monday was to him.)

Which reminds me—would you tell M. that I have a copy of the Renaissance book if he wants it?

I remembered to ask Margaret about her dressmaker, who "is still" in action. I said something about the frock, vaguely, and that you would write. Margaret said something about gratitude & Coupons. But I detach myself there, and merely report. It's a little pathetic to see poor Isabel getting always left behind by the conversation, & saying (so to speak) the wrong things. Indeed, culture avenges itself at last; you must serve it with more than your class-emotions if it is to serve you. There are a million women like her—dangers to the great arts. O I do well always to mock (privately—well, & publicly) at them: they have done more harm than they can ever know!!

Theodora—in a note—thinks *AHE* "a really triumphant success." I still don't believe it; but we'll hope the next one will be better. Otherwise, nothing to-day. The Declaration of the Three[21] in this morning's paper almost scares me; it's so near and so final and so deadly. But, of course, I approve!

O all my love: this does but report. Till again

Serge

14 Feb./45

"Will you be my Valentine?" I would have sent you a telegram if I had thought of it in time. However, as I didn't . . . you may remark that it's also Ash Wednesday . . . and choose.

I have just met our Mr. Walsh from New York. Only for a few minutes, and we haven't yet touched on what we may call business.[22] He goes back, he thinks, next Wednesday; so there's time. I have also had a little chat with Sir H., and he is inclined to think with me that we shall be here till June or July. *If* there was a sudden German crash, things might alter, but he doubts it. So I shall go cautiously on those lines, & arrange tutorials, &c., for next term. Financially, it would on the whole be convenient that way. It would give time for that Fish which ought to be thinking of arriving soon.

(Sir H. more or less asked me if I thought Mrs Page had been a limiting influence on F.P.'s life. It's odd the feeling there is that he's more or less thrown it away; &, of course, heavenly speaking, quite unjustified. But it's there, all the same.)

Except for a longish, & very intelligent, letter from an admirer who compares me with Spenser rather to Spenser's disadvantage,—nothing more. I now settle back & wait for Mr. W.

All love

Serge

15 Feb/45.

AHE[23] seems to have struck a number of people, from what you say, that the *Figure of B.* left cold. I suppose fiction reviews catch their eyes more. Well, we will try & do a better one some day . . . always under your protection & God's; & provided I do not, as you seem to suggest, ascend to heaven in a chariot of fire.[24] Or become, like St. John[25] the Divine, a mere voice in the Rose Gardens of Damascus? or perhaps the Lord Taliessin in those of Caerleon?[26] But your lures of this & the other world detain me; from the roses of your arms to the "occasional"—meaning not full-time meals—foods you display. Shall

I, in the end, become a sensuous poet? unlikely! but that my metaphysics are at the root of sensuousness[27] . . . possible.

Well . . . pass. Eliot "does not wish to press me but would like to know when Arthur is likely to be ready." There being only 3000 words done out of 90,000, it doesn't seem as if the answer was *Soon.* The Bishop of Chichester[28] inquires about the relation of Romanticism to children and to the Gospels; I have written him a short essay. The proofs[29] of the play look sadly at me. I must do something in a moment.

M. was very charming last night, and very agreeably welcoming to the news about a possible Return in June or July. It's almost 2 years since his—& my—outburst on the Hill.[30] Let our Lord redeem all; the virtue of the Blood is greater than all . . . yes, indeed, I believe it. And He seems to have taken action. Adored for ever be . . . &c., &c.

It was sweet of you to take M. to the *T.M.*[31]—sweet to wish for me. All crowns at once, I see, in and on you. Blessings.

Serge

16 Feb/45

I have just put through a call, & I've only just got back from a tutorial—so this is no more than to send you a £3. Another to-morrow.

The Fish—some distance off—has put its head up: the British Council invite me to write a short book on Religious Drama[32] for £50. "Will I consider it?" Will I! I have written politely. It would come in very well: once the King[33] is done.

All love.

Serge

17 Feb/45

Dearest

In yesterday's—almost what you might call rush, I didn't kiss you for your letter; and now you add another to the bird-of-paradise-chorus. I'm extremely relieved that you liked *AHE* as much when you read it as when you heard it. As I keep on saying, I'll try & do better next time. Unless anything else crops up, I'm vaguely thinking that next autumn would be about right for trying another—through the home evenings, with us together, and the black-out gone, and (with any luck) M's prospects brighter. One can never tell, but our Mr. Walsh[34] seemed thoroughly well-disposed to the idea, & said (even if M. didn't finally, want to stay there) it would be good experience. By the autumn perhaps Sir H. will be gone from the Press, & M, in it!! But before you get this, he & Walsh will have had their chat. I only hope they get on. I'll probably ring you up on Monday afternoon to get your opinion of his feelings.

As for the rest—I'm a little conscious myself of a certain new detachment. What you might call my "field of operations" has widened, but it's more markedly remote. I mean that I'm even more of a . . . prophet? priest? something—more of a Voice and less of a man everywhere except at home. At least that's what I feel. I always was pretty much of a slightly non-personal figure, and all my "interests" rather in figures than in people. Perhaps the people in my novels grow more real as my consciousness of actual people decreases. I've never been able to express this very well; but somehow, except at home . . . and perhaps at Magdalen or with Eliot . . . I am always aware of a gulf. My voice— or my style—goes across it, but my heart doesn't. The threat of boredom always hangs in the air. I do think that (religiously speaking) it's very important that I should finish my job, find my last style, make my last shapes in verse or prose or public comments. But that is all. My real interest—outside you & M— is only to be what I was designed to be. O I talk portentous-like; but how else? It's not been an easy business—for me or for you—and yet . . . O sweet, to what a labour you committed us both when you first admired the *Silver Stair*. You might . . . you have always been the first and great Influence; Dante was out because of you . . . have discouraged me then; you could, I think, have done it. Sooner or later I always find myself following your directions (as in the novels? yes, I think so; but it takes time. Even Shakespeare had to work out his own verse slowly). However, you didn't; and, so admiring & encouraging, you see what a journey you landed me in. And, under God, we will do together what remains to be done. I lecture on "The Heaven of *Paradise Lost*" on Tuesday. I may be an archangel there—let us hope so. But I shall *not* there be

your Serge

21 Feb/45

Putting Mr. Spalding's evening shoes back in what used to be M.'s room, I was seized with almost a terror of everything that happened there—no, not everything. I remember a few gay conversations with you—but I thought, bad as our present situation is, and lonely though you are, and bothered though I am, still. . . . But I think a good deal of your being alone; only I hope a few more months may see the end. And I looked at the room, but I refrained from cursing, and thought it wiser to try & praise God.

Well . . . and so I have committed myself to the Dante dinner on 29 May next. It will be a convenient thing to do at Magdalen, and look well from me. Also the Society has just elected Tolkien as member, and it will be pleasant to have him here for the first time when I preside. I said that "as I might not be there much longer" . . . & so on, and Hardie, next to whom I was sitting, asked me what I would feel about a Tutorship.[35] I more or less said it depended on the salary, and I do not expect anything to happen. But as you've so often said it's nice to feel I've put it over even to the extent of it being talked of;

especially as Hardie & I knew nothing of each other up to a year or so ago—so it can't be "old acquaintance" in his case. (How different the Magdalen feeling is from anywhere else in Oxford! I mean . . . well, you know what I mean!)

I have a tutorial this afternoon, moved from last night, and another this evening. After which I want to do a review. I must at Easter make a great effort about Arthur.[36] Perhaps, once I'm with you, I shan't feel this labour & dislike of doing those things—all the more maddening because I ought to be able to make good stuff. I look forward to the high summer, and a couple of weeks relaxing with you first; it's now clear—what was always clear to us—that apart from you I can't work properly, and can never relax at all.

A young gentleman has sent me an article with a covering letter saying how much it owes to my work, & that I first showed him the organic connection between Catholicism and Europe. Did I now? I suppose it's all right. But very nice of him.

So far I haven't seen Walsh,[37] but I hope to catch him to-day sometime. And now I'm off to my tutorial. In 3 weeks they will be Paying me £48. *All my love.*

Serge

22 Feb./45

And I wager you gave Wallis[38] almost, if not quite, your last shilling! (He is, for all the "blackmail," a useful man to have about; but then you treat him nicely!) I send a pound with this which may just help—but I'm shocked and depressed at having managed badly. But I will do better, I hope, once we get into next month. Forgive all.

Miss Morison rang up last night about next term's lectures & says she wants all the time I can give her for tutorials. She shall have it. Apart from money, we may as well leave in a blaze of occupation. Mr. John Hampden, of the British Council, is to discuss the book on Religious Drama[39] with me on Tuesday week at the Mitre. Which is very useful—if I can break Arthur[40] in the vac.—

How I do repeat myself! But my eyes are continually on having a sum ready for moving. I don't want, we don't want, *another* winter: it's been too long already. This damp and growths in those flats are too loathsome. And it's sweet of you to have been so sympathetic and handsome. But really . . . !

I found your Tuesday's long letter when I got back yesterday and I'd already posted mine. But I've no patience with husbands who "must" do this or that. And I do so agree with you about the young married. "It's marriage dressed as 1945, but it's just marriage" is most profoundly true. And you're a dear.

[Unsigned]

27 Feb./45

Between activities—the greatest activity. You might not think that to write to you could properly be described as such, but I think it might, & undoubtedly it is. There is about it a punctuality—a kind of "formal" (now don't go off on to our modern misuse of the word; remember "soul is form and doth the body make")[41] assignation which is proper, pious, profitable, and peremptory . . . but you will argue from all this that I have nothing particular to say, and you will be right. The audience this morning kept up fairly well—pretty good for the ninth week; next week, on Adam & Eve, concludes this term. Miss Plumer has written to say she's delighted I'm going to continue next term; so that's all right, and you'll come down one week for the last exhibition.

In a little while I hare off to my Moral Welfare Committee . . . so long as I can find the place. Everyone seems to regard me as a Moral Teacher. Which, having learnt from your eyes, hands, arms, & thighs—see all my work—how not?

Serge

28 Feb/45

Dearest,

The Stratford Memorial Theatre have suggested that I might go to them for a week between April and September to give some talks to English & Allied Forces during the Season. They were put on to me by a minor woman down here. I suppose they won't pay, but they invite me to be their guest. Now I think that this is just what you and I might like—a week in Stratford, a few addresses, a few performances, & a good deal of wandering & laziness. I have replied saying that any time after next term would suit me—after 23 June; that I should like to come with you & make it part of my holiday; that I don't expect them to pay, but perhaps they could fix up a hotel for us. I think it would be delightful . . . and we were saying it was about time something happened, were we not? So be prepared to find us both there sometime after June.

(I quite realize about M., but we can arrange something?!?)

I have sent off this morning the companion to Mythology, & an extra one of M's books I left behind by accident. The Moral Welfare Committee was small, sedate, and . . . moral. Lectured on the Facts & Purpose of Sex—yes, really. I was rather high & C.W.-ish, as I now tend to be with such oddments, but of course most polite.

But I do hope you are taken by the Stratford notion!! I am—so much. We might—given the weather—have a lovely time.

Blessings.

Serge

1 March/45

March has come in blowily enough, but the sun's out this afternoon. I've just had lunch with Basil,[42] who with his co-director was also asking if I were going to stop here by any good chance. It's all very charming, of course, but I still doubt if anything will happen—yet. I go on hinting that the Chair of Poetry[43] is what I should like . . . without, you understand, asking . . . .

A small cheque from *T&T* fits in and explains the enclosed. If M. has another short week, you'll need it. I shall send another on Saturday.

Perhaps next Thursday I'd better go straight to see Higham[44] from the train: what do you say? Shall we lunch somewhere & then either do a film or go home & "relax"? What do you say?

I'm terribly sleepy, but I still think fondly of the Stratford project.[45] I see it was the British Council who asked me, & not the Theatre, but it comes to the same thing: they're arranging the courses. Nothing to-day of any interest.

Till to-morrow, sweet. All love,

Serge

2 March/45

Your Hill letter (as I may call it) only arrived this morning . . . O but that's when it ought to have done. I was highly touched by your consideration for her . . . though I needn't point out that your own "effectual fervent prayers"[46] for her would do more. I am darkly convinced that one ought to live in prayer, and when we re-gather ourselves you & I will try. I will—otherwise: or rather, besides—turn it over in my mind; being a little conscious that I've always shut myself up against her, even more than I generally do—more consciously, I mean. But if you are going to command me. . . .

Well: anything else, is there? The B.B.C. are broadcasting in their Overseas Service "C- W-'s poem called 'The Epiphany.'" Will you tell me why these people ALWAYS pick out my worst poems? The only good poems in my early books are the ones to you, well, practically, & I don't say all those are good. But— especially the Romantic ones—bear "the unimaginable touch of time"[47] better than the rest. However, if the B.B.C. are forking out a guinea, let them.

I was quite scared when I found M's note of the address on the manuscript. I had visions of him turning the whole place upside down for it, not finding it—O I cannot tell what I thought! So I thought I'd better phone him. You & I will chat on Monday afternoon—yes? I'll get some money to-morrow. "This University" has sent me an official note of sums due and promises to pay "as soon as possible" after next Wednesday. Cheers!

I love you. Thank you for your sweetness.

Serge

5 April/45

Dearest,

I think your letter was one of the nicest you've ever written, and very, very kind—and I don't mean kind in the dull modern sense, but in the old, which is more like "warm and loving." Anyone who has lived through two world-wars, been married to an "immortal," never had enough money and never really grumbled, thought her son was going to be (i) blind and (ii) silly, had pneumonia, endured much pain, ...

Now I had got there when Professor Wilson Knight[48] turned up with his new book on Shakespeare. (Which I suppose we shall do.) And interrupted me. But I was about to remark . . . And

And is swift and witty and passionate and lovely now, even much more than when she was young and came through the snow up Hollywell Hill. Zionish? May I call you Zion,[49] or an image of . . . no, Zion is Jewish; let us say Sarras[50] again.

The Stratford people[51] have sent me a booklet which I will bring to show you. The proceedings begin each Monday at 6.30 with a Civic Reception. I seem to have to "talk" on Wednesday, Thursday, & Friday mornings at 10.45. I am down as "Distinguished Poet & Novelist," & Author of the *E.P.M.*[52] I've confirmed 23 July for us, & I look forward to it.

Martin Browne[53] wants to do the *Stable* for the Forces in Belgium. I've told him I can't manage anything about seeing him this week-end; but in a fortnight's time perhaps . . . I can see that I shall have to do one or two things then!

I don't dare think about the tiles [?]!! But I can of you.

Serge

11 April/45

The sleep of Oxford and/or of middle-age is on me. I can hardly keep my eyes open. What is it Tennyson says about "tired eyes"?[54] I've opened my window, though to be sure it's not so *very* warm this afternoon. But it may freshen me up.

I wonder how things are with you? To-day, I feel, was the day promised. I had a reply from Warren—very polite. And I had the insurance receipt. Not an entertaining correspondence, you will allow. But Honest. We pay our way.

I had a gentleman wait on me this morning who is engaged on a Great Work in poetry, & has given up *all* for it. He is a pleasant fellow, by no means a fool, and 34. He writes better stuff than you might think, & he has saved up enough money to live on for a number of years & he has put all thoughts of marrying out of his mind & so on. Each to his own method—I could not have done it so. Nor did Shakespeare.

Why are you not here to give me a cup of tea, & then make me do some work? An infinite distaste of writing is on me—exasperated by my visitor's devotion. At 34 I should have thought it mattered; now I know better. I would rather have a comfortable house for the rest of our lives than write the *Aeneid*.

"Come to me in my dreams!" It's long since Sunday.

Serge

And if bath and seat are in by now, I shall have, for some hours . . . I was going to say no more to wish for than in 1917. But that would be too hasty a tribute unless spoken, because if I spoke it I should be with you, you see, & so . . . O how long & tiresome a sentence!

Hadfield[55] has just been in to see me; he tells me that he is to open the Jewish Department at Amen House on 1 September. It is thought by Miss Peacock that this is the latest date we shall now begin to work to. I do not myself much expect us now to be earlier by many days, but we are certainly making the first shy motions. We intend during the next two or three months to send books and papers up. Oxford now begins to look really beautiful to me; and I please myself with the hope that Whitsun may be lovely for us. Next term I shall make some money, & we will look forward to many possibilities in the future.

And then we will add the finishing touches to 1917.[56] There were no letters at all to-day, so you see I had no distractions from it.

I have got down to King Arthur[57] every evening, & got some done. To-morrow I must think about sending you some money; not that I've forgotten! . . . but I look out now over a barn that will soon disappear from my eyes for ever. Bless you for all the years—before & behind. And kisses on them.

Serge

13 April/45

Was there ever such a heroine as you . . . at a time like the present, to get shoes mended & back to me between Monday morning & Thursday evening! How you manage your man I can't think! I feel I ought to go with you some day and offer him a pound! I'm sure he deserves it more than most do.

But I've taken advantage to send off another pair; a parcel with the shirt & oddments also. Tell Michael it looks as if we were going to have an American lady in the house for a little . . . the wife of the Professor of Modern American History, who has just arrived & been wished on Anne by the parents. *No* glamour, I gather.

I send a pound herewith, & will continue. I do hope that in a few days you'll be able to write to Bath, or will the bedroom interfere?—O and I gave your message about would it be convenient quite for Whitsun, & I am to say that it will be delightful, & any hour at any time.

It's rather a blow about Roosevelt,[58] isn't it? We did need all he & Churchill could do to hold the Great Alliance in the West together. I don't mean it will break—no; but he & C did what, in a way, you do; they held it on the friendly terms that are—*I* think—the most important thing at the present time. It's the most urgent fact that we & the Americans shall work together, & every

cup of tea or cake you give them is of almost as much use as the San Francisco Conference:[59] yes, undoubtedly.

By the way, coffee is as difficult in Oxford as in London. I shall send my
representatives about, but I hear that it's practically non-existent.

I have been tidying my bathroom up as a First Step—throwing away papers & sending books back to stock. Miss Peacock asked me if I wanted all
the books to go to my office or my flat . . . going white, I said: "the office, of
course." Apparently, we shall be rather squeezed at first at Amen House. I hope
I shall get a room to myself . . . but she seemed a little doubtful. Too awful!

I shall ring you up on Monday, shan't I? Thank you for everything. All love
and duty.

Serge

18 April/45

I have just reached here after addressing some 70 men & women of the Forces
& the Allies on *Twelfth Night* which they are to be taken to see at Stratford
this afternoon. I was rather gloomy about it beforehand, but it went very well,
and there was an outburst of applause when I left. I may, if wanted, do it again
next week. I have a faint belief that they pay me a guinea, & if next week comes
off, there, you see, will be our two extra pounds. And you won't think that
I'm "having to do it for that" because, if I'm free, it's the sort of thing one *must*
do anyhow. Patriotism, & so on.

Hugo Dyson[60] is here for some Educational Conference, & wishes to show
me off to two of his pupils at lunch; all his pupils, he says, having been
brought up on me. It's a good thing to have the Milton book[61] coming because
I ought to have something more out on English literature, though of course
I'd rather do more poems. But I expect *Arthur* & *Milton* to bring in continued
royalties. I've reminded Higham & Nancy that I used to review murders, &
with the peace should like to take it up again.

O & what was wrong with the blades? No, my sweet; they *were* Valets &
they fit.

Handwriting a little difficult after lecture. So Will Now Close, with Much
Love.

Till Friday

Serge

24 Apr./45

Dearest,

What an odd thing experience is! And why (you will say) this general
maxim, this platitudinous truth! Well, it was borne in on me by two things.

(i) Last night, when I was writing a review by myself in the drawing room
Mrs. Milford—the Vicar's wife—rang me up. "I know how she had been

moved by *A. H. Eve?*" Having once met her in the Post Office—and what was I doing there? sending a parcel off—I did. She & a friend or two would very much like to talk to me about it; was I free on Friday evening to come to coffee about 8:15? Well, I was. So I shall. A prophet, & all that, I gather. What do they want to know? God knows. But I will play my part. With great presence of mind, I said you had been asking after her and the children; she said I had forestalled her: she was just about to ask after you. But these groups perplex one; what can I define that I have not defined? or propose that I have not proposed? However . . .

(ii) On the other hand, this morning here on what was my own heath—so to speak—I found that a problem had arisen. Whom should we ask to write a book on Shakespeare for the Home University Library? Would you think there could be—*here*—more than one answer? There could; there could, in fact, be any answer but that. We discussed A, B, & C, anyone except . . . Except . . . Of course they may think of me yet, but I think it unlikely. Or—let's be fair—they may want a different kind of book from mine. But it's a little strange to be superfluous where one has been Someone; in all the literary world there is no place where I am as negligible—in the most charming way—as here. This is a rebuke to egotism. I allow that Sir H. was not in on it, but I doubt if Sir H. [page missing]

30 April/45

And now I sit writing to you and wondering if the war is over . . . perhaps by the time I get up on Saturday it will be. It would be rather nice to have a bus ride together on the first Sunday afterwards, & I see that that is why my aunt was sent out last time. Encourage M. to go to Reading; I'll pay the fare.

You'll be, I think, mildly amused by the bills about St. Marys. I am sandwiched between two Dignitaries. Like this:

Sunday after Ascension	The Archbishop of York
Whit-Sunday	Charles Williams
Trinity Sunday	The Bishop of Oxford

. . . so there we are. Anne S. who went to church at 11 yesterday says that they had a strange preacher who alluded to the writings of C.S.L., C.W., &—yes, I fear—Dorothy S. (But that can't be helped!)

O it's freezing here—& with you! I thought of you—no, I felt you—a great deal all over the week-end. But the thing's ending, & soon I shall look out at my barn for the last time. Perhaps one day you & I will drift up this way in peace and joy.

Serge

I think you may dismiss the horror. My recollection is that it's the end of May when the notice goes in. I began to look for the agreement this morning but didn't at once see it, & fancy it may be in your bureau. But I will say you will do me the honour of thinking I'm generally right about these points. So courage, my love! the Rubicon is still in front of us.

It is understood here that we are to infiltrate back during August & September, finishing everything by 30 September. Sir H. is going all reserved & gloomy as the undoubted point of his final disappearance strikes him. Goffin tells me that I am to have my old office—which on the whole I think I should prefer. I shall linger there, a superfluous but kindly treated . . . O well, don't let's be bad-tempered and resentful. We shall see how everything works out.

I send another pound herewith—thinking of your distresses with the most real heart-beats . . . in fact, they out-cried the German news. And yet it's odd— both of those "bad men" are dead & gone to . . . whatever. Hitler didn't really expect, five years ago, to die in his ruined cities. I am very glad the fighting has been so heavy in Berlin; and may it be fifty years before it's built again.

Till Saturday: all love.

Serge

It'd be almost ungracious not to send one line in answer to your sweetness. I feel as if I were ashamed to bring you so old a man; you should have something—no; perhaps not, & I may not really be so old presently. It's all lovely of you; & I must end!

Serge

In a way, not being with you makes the awareness of you, anyhow over this Peace,[62] more acute. I read in a mid-day paper that the U-boats have stopped firing, that the Air Force is surrendering: the Air Force that you & I heard in London on those September nights. It was *so,* then; it is otherwise so now. They've failed; they've been broken. And you—especially—have helped to do it. Victory depended on you.

Not being with you, I'm glad we had the week-end. And I hope M. got home all right. Mine was a crowded train, but it got into time, & I was in bed by 2.30. (This morning Margaret rang up to say Isabel fainted again—at the Playhouse—on Saturday; I must go round to-night before the tutorial. She is to go to the Radcliffe for examination to-morrow. This by the way.)

I cannot quite get over this peace, this morning—or the newness of it. We have missed 6 years, but we might have missed more, & it was nice to have the week-end union *before* the Peace. You were very good to me yesterday; I had cramp again this morning but without a break-down (temporary)!

I ran into Gervase & told him about the *Life of Jesus*.[63] He said that was quite simple: all I had to do was to have the 4th Gospel typed out & sent it in as mine. He added that nothing was a more exact C.W. style than "In the beginning was the Word," & St. John was clearly my disciple as well as Our Lord's. For amusement.

Be ever, ever blessed. (We will have more money soon.) I adore you . . . yes, but also you are very lovely.

Serge

8 May/45

I have missed you a great deal to-day. I should have liked to knock about with you—but there it is! It was nice to kiss you this morning, but I've been bothered since I discovered there wasn't a post to-day. In the hope that there may be one to-morrow, I'm sending £2 herewith.

It's very quiet & silent now. It's also pouring with rain. I'm sitting on the balcony alone in the house. This morning, having nothing particular to do, I went up to S.H. & exchanged a word with Miss Peacock, then I drifted to Magdalen, next with the two Lewises & Colin Hardie & had a drink, lunch at the R. (Isabel is to go to the Radcliffe for examination), came back here, & after slipping out to post this . . . & I hope there is to be a post . . . shall turn to Arthur.

And it's done. I've a dim sense of relief—it *might* have been your mercy; the awful days when I thought the enemy might for ever be between me & you didn't come to the worst. The mourning & the burying are done. And presently. . . . There couldn't have been a better Peace Sunday than last. I wish we were together, but that was very good. And now it is nice to be done.

Say all the right things to M. about Whitsun. It is lovely to feel it possible to be one with you over it, even if. . . . We are, in a way, blessed.

All my love and gratitude.

Serge

[On May 10, 1945, C.W. became ill, and two days later Michal arrived from London to be with him. He was taken to a hospital for an operation for the recurrence of an old problem, the result of a previous operation. He died May 15 without having regained consciousness. He was buried in the churchyard of St. Cross, Holywell, Oxford.]

Appendix

As I Remember Charles Williams

BY MICHAL WILLIAMS

My husband, the late Charles Williams, died in May, 1945, at the age of fifty-eight. His death was untimely and he could not stay to do all that he had proposed.

We who admire his mature poetry cry lament for those final Arthurian poems Charles was going to write. If the poetry of *Taliessin through Logres* and that of *The Region of the Summer Stars* is to many of us a strange, exquisite tapestry woven in colours of rich beauty, what might we not conjecture of the loveliness and revelation of that unborn poetry? Not today and not tomorrow shall we know. Nor shall we know the pattern and scope of that "one more novel" unless in that high town which is eternity our dead are bidden to continue their work of high intention.

It was during one of the last week-ends Charles was ever to spend at home that he spoke to me of his post-war writing, and of his desire to get to work on the final Arthurian poems.

Then he said, "And I shall write one more novel, which my faithful public will not like, I think. This time it will be a straightforward one. There will be no black magic, no dancing figures, and no supernatural beings wandering through its pages."

When I saw him off at Paddington Station, we somewhat facetiously anticipated the publication and reception of this novel. Would even Charles' most avid readers discern any departure from type, we asked each other. Or, contrariwise, would his faithful public murmur that, though they had eaten of the novel, they had not dined? Unfortunately, the Oxford train made its appearance at this moment, and we had to say good-bye.

Do you know Charles' poem "In the Land of Juda," in which he tells of our first meeting?

Where did you meet your love, young man,
 Where did you meet your love?
"I met my love in a noisy room
 With a carven roof above."

What did you say to your love, young man,
 With all your mother wit?
"'Hot it is!'" or 'How do you do?'
 And there was an end of it!"

Who was beside you then, young man,
 Who was beside you then?
"Gaspar, Melchior, Balthazar,
 And a crowd of shepherd-men?"

What did you say to them, young man,
 Silently, through the din?
"Princes, when ye come in to her,
 I pray you, lead me in."

It seems as yesterday, the night so long ago, when Charles and I first met, helping at a parochial children's Christmas party at St. Albans.

For the first five minutes of our meeting I thought him the most silent, withdrawn young man I had ever met. For the next five minutes I thought him the nicest young man I had ever met. For the rest of the evening I thought him the most talkative young man I had ever met, and still the nicest.

It will always be an unsolved mystery as to how we left that noisy room and found ourselves walking in the shadow of the vast benignant Abbey. Myriads of stars looked down on us. The pleasant Abbey meadows tilting gently down to the river seemed to reverse their slope to gaze at us as we passed by. And as we walked, Charles talked. He talked of Browning. I must all to myself have heard his maiden lecture—given at rapid pace, yet lucid and arresting in spite of its length. Whether I would or whether I would not I heard Sordello's story told.

When lass meets lad and each is but twenty-one and the lass has no silver, the lad no gold, and the career of each is in the making, they must be abundantly thankful to see one another occasionally from opposite sides of the road. Little did Charles and I see of one another those early years. But Cherubim and Seraphim saw to it that we sometimes met at the cross-roads. One road led to meadows where, in summer, the red hot poker flowers blazed greeting, and the ripening corn waved and bowed to us. In springtime, the fields were faery with anemones and along the hedges clusters of primroses and celandine and cowslips bloomed anew. We would take Charles' book and boon companions along with us: Shakespeare and Wordsworth and Milton, Donne and Crashaw, St. Athanasius, or rather, his Creed, St. Augustine and the Lady Julian of Norwich. Also came Swinburne and George Meredith and Coventry Patmore, Francis Thompson and Alice Meynell. Nor must I forget G. K. Chesterton and Hilaire Belloc. And those are not the half of them. Lovely those walks and literary conversations but we had never talked of love.

One January night I went to a lecture. On my way home and almost within sight of home, Charles overtook me. He put a parcel into my hands, saying he had written a Sonnet Sequence called *The Silver Stair*. Its theme was Renunciation. Would I read it and tell him my opinion? And he fled. I thought "Oh dear! Is he going to enter a monastery?" and wondered about visiting at such places.

I read *The Silver Stair* by flickering candle-light in my cold attic room. There were eighty-two sonnets and I read them all. So lovely they seemed; I read them again and again. Comprehension dawned and I cried aloud "Why, I believe they are about me!" I read them again to make quite sure.

Next day I wrote my first letter to Charles. It seemed to please him and though *The Silver Stair* had Renunciation for its theme our walks continued. We still took our literary companions with us and Love came too.

I read my first letter to Charles again a few days after he died. It was a very good letter. I burnt it and I burnt all my letters to him in the fireplace of the room in which I am writing. Charles had liked them. Their purpose was fulfilled. I watched them burn. Red and gold the flames from them. Red and gold my love for him.

After our marriage in 1917 we came to live in London. Charles was already working at the Oxford University Press, which had its offices in the City, and I had a teaching post in the Soho quarter. London gave us Hampstead Heath and Ken Wood, which later on our son Michael and I were to explore so happily. It gave us too the river and Westminster Abbey, and high above the City buildings close to where Charles worked, was St. Paul's.

"Wearing lightly then the yoke of union" there were new experiences and new adventures. Charles took me to call on Alice and Wilfrid Meynell, to whose kindness he owed the publication of his first book, *The Silver Stair*. Alice Meynell could only be likened to the Dark Lady of the Sonnets, and she had a lovely, caressing voice. My memory of her has never dimmed.

We lived in a modest flat at the top of an old Victorian house. All our flats have been modest and starkly inconvenient, and usually there were many ill-lit stairs to be climbed to reach us. They did not deter visitors. Once, Eric Gill came to dinner and stayed until 2:00 A.M. We talked of life after death. Contrary to what you might think, it was an extremely happy talk.

The fleeting years saw Charles' work gather greater momentum and attract attention, and people began to discover the manner of man he was. There were many demands on his time and many engagements to take him from home, including lectures he gave so brilliantly. His creative work was thought out in oddments of his time and he moulded it in the evenings and late into the night. He had a habit of waking me at any hour of any night when he was writing a book. I would wake from sleep to hear him saying "What about a cup of tea, darling, then I should like to read you what I have written this evening."

When he wrote the play *Thomas Cranmer of Canterbury* for the Canterbury Festival of 1936, I was awakened at mid-night to go to the death-bed of Henry VIII. Round about midnight too, I was called from my bed to hear of Damaris Tighe's adventure with the pterodactyl in *The Place of the Lion*. I am not brave when I hear a mouse, whether by night or day, and to hear about the pterodactyl at such an hour was indeed alarming. Moreover, our flat had a sky-light that could have been purposefully designed to admit such a creature. When Charles was writing his life of Sir Francis Bacon I was aroused at 1:00 A.M. to hear the details of the great man's passing.

I heard the last two chapters of *The Greater Trumps* at 3:00 A.M. I loved those nocturnal readings and the ritual that went with them. Making tea and cutting wafer-like sandwiches to refresh my tired husband. Then the reading and discussion, and of course more tea making. I spent considerable time in making tea.

Charles read extremely well. He could also chant, not so extremely well, long, swinging poems, like G. K. Chesterton's "Ballad of the White Horse." He would chant as the urge took him, in restaurant or taxi or along the Queen's most populated highway. Not for my meek passivity on these occasions did Charles re-name me Michal, after Saul's daughter.

Charles and I were not together very much during the years of war. We met when and where we could and wrote daily to each other in between.

He was longing intensely to come home again. Death came to him when he was almost on the threshold. When he died grief for him went very deep. I think people loved him not only because he was ineffable and endearing, but also because he was all things to all men, in the sense that all who had to do with him found him adequate.

Charles died at Oxford, the city that loved him and took him to its heart and honoured him. I like to think that he rests there.

Darker to me seemed the shadow of the great Abbey. There were no stars. The meadows averted their gaze as I walked by them alone. As I came to the great cedar tree its branches seemed as arms outstretched to comfort.

I did not go to the cross-roads.

Glossary

Some of the names of persons, places, and things listed below are much too well known to require identification. They are included in the listing, however, primarily to indicate possible ways in which they may have influenced Charles Williams's thinking and writing.

W. H. AUDEN, a British-born poet, became an American citizen in 1946. His early poetry expressed a very liberal, near-Marxist reaction against a perceived social and intellectual climate in Britain. By the late 1930s it became clear, however, that he was returning to his Anglo-Catholic roots, and in October 1940 he became formally a member of the Anglican Communion. C.W. first met Auden in 1938 while he was working on his anthology *The Oxford Book of Light Verse*. Auden described this first meeting: "In a publisher's office, I met an Anglican layman, and for the first time in my life felt myself in the presence of personal sanctity." On October 16, 1940, C.W. wrote to Michal, "He feels that I 'have a Divine gift as a teacher'. . . . He has gone all Christian and is composing verse under your husband's influence." In 1956, Auden dedicated the poem "Memorial of the City" to "the memory of Charles Williams."

"THE AUNT." The lady so addressed throughout the letters is Rebecca Marion Hill, a relative of the Spaldings whom they called "Aunt."

GEORGE KENNETH ALLEN BELL was dean of Canterbury and later bishop of Chichester. He supported the Confessing Churches during their struggle against the Nazi regime and at the same time opposed the indiscriminate bombing of German towns during the war. In the early 1930s he asked C.W. to read and help revise the manuscript of his, *Life of Randall Davidson*. Apparently pleased with C.W.'s work, the bishop called on him again in April 1940 to work on a report for a Council of the Churches for which he was responsible. C.W., always in need of money, responded gladly.

BIRD AND BABY. Popular name for the Eagle and Child, a public house in Giles Street, Oxford, so called because its signboard pictured the infant Ganymede being carried off by an eagle. The Inklings often met there for fellowship and literary talk. A plaque identifies the nook they habitually occupied.

BASIL BLACKWELL. Just out of Oxford, young Blackwell went to Amen Corner in 1911 to gain insight into the publishing business before settling down to a career of operating the famous Blackwell Book Store in Oxford. Intending to stay for a year, he, at the request of the Press, agreed to remain for an additional four months. He later wrote, "The lasting impression made on me at Amen Corner was one of reverence for scholarship and enthusiasm for any book that advanced the cause" (Peter Sutcliffe, *The Oxford University Press* [London: Oxford University Press, 1978], 162–63). C.W. had joined the Press in 1908. During World War II, Blackwell was a good friend to C.W. and a sympathetic employer of young Michael for over a year.

E. MARTIN BROWNE, promoter of religious drama, actor, director. From 1919 Browne was the motivating force behind the organization of the Religious Drama Society centered at Canterbury Cathedral. George Bell, then Canterbury dean, later bishop of Chichester, was president of the group, whose purpose was to stimulate interest in and to produce religious drama throughout the Church. In 1923, Bell called a conference for exploring a plan of action toward that end. C.W. was present, and it may have been there that he first met E. Martin Browne. Three years later, in 1935, the Canterbury Festival presented T. S. Eliot's *Murder in the Cathedral.* The following year the society invited Williams to provide the play for the summer season. The result was *Cranmer.* Browne himself played the part of the Skeleton to Robert Speight's Cranmer. Highly pleased with the production, C.W. wrote a sonnet to Browne, six lines of which Hadfield quotes (*An Exploration of His Life and Work* [New York: Oxford University Press, 1983], 139):

> Must you show me the Skeleton then, not only in art
> by one part played and other parts designed,
> but by the bony fingers probing the heart,
> chilling and determining the pretentious mind?
> Must you show me, I say, the way I hate to go,
> Yet lately drew in a chart, of such neat lines?

When World War II broke out, he organized a company of players to take religious drama to troops in Europe. Its repertoire included *The House by the Stable* in May 1945.

LORD DAVID CECIL (Edward Christian David Gascoyne) was at the time C.W. knew him a fellow of New College, Oxford, and a member of the Inklings. He was later the Goldsmith Professor of English. In 1940 he edited *The Oxford Book of Christian Verse,* including Williams's poem "At the 'Ye who do truly.'"

GEORGE KEITH CHESTERTON, the popular wit and stylist, brilliant conversationalist, poet, novelist, biographer, and essayist. He had some influence on C.W.'s earliest writing, but it is no longer apparent in the later novels and the Taliessin poems.

NORMAN COLLINS worked with C.W. at Amen House in the early years but left to join the old *News-Chronicle* in 1930. From that post he sent C.W. many detective novels to review. Later he joined the Gollancz publishing firm that at the time was publishing C.W.'s novels.

GEOFFREY F. J. CUMBERLEGE. Assistant to Sir Humphrey Milford and his replacement as publisher upon Sir H.'s retirement shortly after C.W.'s death. C.W. was less than an admirer of Cumberlege.

MARGARET DOUGLAS and her mother, Isabel, were friends of C.W. They settled in Oxford during the war, and Charles was recipient of much kindness from them. Margaret typed several of his manuscripts.

HUGO DYSON was a lecturer in English at Reading University during C.W.'s years at Oxford. He met C. S. Lewis in 1931 and became a member of the Inklings group. In 1938 Lewis brought him to London to meet C.W. During the war years C.W. saw him occasionally, generally in company of Lewis or other members of the Inklings. After C.W.'s death, Dyson was elected fellow and tutor in English literature at Merton College.

T. S. ELIOT, perhaps the most influential poet writing in English during the first half of the twentieth century, met C.W. at one of Lady Ottoline Morelle's literary gatherings in the early 1930s. The ensuing friendship was both professional and personal. His name is one of those mentioned most in these letters. Fabers, under the editorial direction of Eliot, published *Descent into Hell, Witchcraft, The Figure of Beatrice*, and *All Hallows' Eve* (including a later edition for which Eliot wrote an introduction). In his second essay on Milton (*On Poetry*, 1957) Eliot writes, "I can give only one example of contemporary criticism of Milton, by a critic of the type to which I belong if I have any critical pretensions at all: that is the Introduction to Milton" *English Poems* in the 'World Classics' series, by the late Charles Williams." On February 17, 1945, C.W. wrote to his wife, "I've never been able to express this very well; but somehow, except at home . . . and perhaps at Magdalen or with Eliot . . . I am always aware of a gulf."

HUBERT J. FOSS was a longtime member of the Oxford University Press whom C.W. knew from early days. A musician of some standing, he was influential in establishing a successful music department. He also wrote music for the several entertainments for which C.W. wrote the texts that were presented largely by and for the staff in the late 1920s. He was also a director of the Henderson and Spalding printing firm, which published *Heroes and Kings*. Later, when he developed psychological problems, C.W. became his sympathetic counselor.

ADAM FOX became a fellow of Magdalen College and dean of divinity in 1929. He was elected professor of poetry in 1938. In 1942, he left Oxford to become a canon at Westminster Abbey in London. C.W. knew him as a member of the Inklings.

CHRISTOPHER FRY. In 1940, when C.W. first mentioned Christopher Fry, he was not yet established as a popular playwright. He had published *The Boy with a Cart* in 1939.

His best work, however, was published after C.W.'s death. In a letter of October 2, 1943 (not included in this collection), C.W. writes, "I begin to feel that Christopher Fry is right when he said it was the young disillusioned generation who found in us the true romanticism."

ROBERT GRAVES saw himself primarily as a poet, but he also wrote many volumes of essays, fiction, biography, and mythology. His works in the latter include *The Greek Myths* and *The Hebrew Myths*. C.W. mentions him especially in relation to Taliessin.

GRAHAM GREENE, poet, dramatist, novelist, and essayist, served during World War II in the Ministry of Information, and it was in that capacity that C.W. knew him.

COLIN HARDIE was a classical tutor at Magdalen College and a member of the Inklings. He was also secretary to the Dante Society and helpful to a very grateful C.W. in securing membership in the prestigious organization.

RENÉE HAYNES was the author of *Pan, Caesar and God*, the third book in the "I Believe: A Series of Personal Statements," published by Heineman. C.W. wrote *He Came Down from Heaven* as the fifth in the same series. He met Haynes at a party for contributors to the series and saw her off and on while he was in Oxford.

DAVID HIGHAM. Curtis Brown was C.W.'s first literary agent. At some point in the early 1930s some of the people left Brown to start a new firm, Pearn, Pollinger, and Higham Associates, and Williams went with them. The firm is now called David Higham Associates and still handles the interests of C.W.'s estate. In late September 1940, Higham entered the army and Nancy Pearn became C.W.'s chief contact at the agency.

HOARE-LAVAL PACT, which was proposed by Pierre Laval of France and accepted by Samuel Hoare, foreign secretary of Great Britain, ceded to Italy certain Abyssinian territory. It was widely considered in England as a betrayal of the League of Nations and the dismembering of Abyssinia for the benefit of an aggressor. The resulting political storm resulted in the resignation of Hoare and the succession to his office by Anthony Eden. The subsequent failure of the League to agree on a course of action permitted Mussolini to continue his aggression against helpless Abyssinia.

GERARD HOPKINS. C.W. knew "Gerry" from his earliest days at the Press. Gerry, the nephew of the poet Gerard Manley Hopkins, was in charge of Press publicity. Like C.W., he spent his entire career with the Press. The two men remained friends throughout, although their relationship became strained in the early 1930s. When the Press moved to Oxford in 1939, however, each, leaving his wife in London, took up residence with the Spaldings. Inevitably they were drawn together. When, on the day following the cessation of hostilities in Europe, C.W. was taken ill, Gerry watched over him until Michal arrived from London. It was he who wrote the obituary: "'The City of God in which he never ceased to dwell, contained Amen House as its noblest human monument, and all who lived and worked in it were citizens with him" (quoted by Charles Hatfield in Brian Horne, *Charles Williams: A Celebration* [Herefordshire: Gracewing, Fowler Wright Books, 1995], 19). Hopkins's literary work was composed largely of translations of the French into English. He also did some reviewing, including the review of *The Descent of the Dove* (*Times Literary Supplement*, Nov. 11, 1939, 652).

RAYMOND HUNT was a member of C.W.'s earliest night classes in London and an ardent admirer of both the man and his work. C.W. always spoke affectionately and appreciatively of him. Hunt faithfully recorded the London lectures in shorthand, and both the original and the transcription are now in the Wade Collection at Wheaton College, Wheaton, Illinois. Hunt projected an ambitious project of collecting and preserving C.W.'s work for posterity. He visited C.W. several times during the Oxford years.

INKLINGS. A group primarily of writers, sharing many common views about literature and religion, who gathered around C. S. Lewis. Members included such names as C. S. Lewis, J. R. R. Tolkien, Charles Williams, Owen Barfield, Lord David Cecil, Hugo Dyson, Adam Fox, Colin Hardie, and John Wain. They met regularly on Thursday evenings in Lewis's quarters and sometimes on Friday mornings at the Bird and Baby (see above). During his years in Oxford, C.W. was frequently in attendance. He often read from whatever work he had under way. The criticism of the group and their encouragement were undoubtedly helpful. They provided him an opportunity he had never before experienced to discuss his thoughts and writing with a comparatively equally talented group of literary men.

THE REVEREND HENRY LEE was coeditor with Daniel Nicholson of *The Oxford Book of Mystical Verse* (1917) under C.W.'s editorial supervision. The two men became lifelong friends. Father Lee became the vicar of St. Martin's in Kensal, and in 1929, C.W. wrote *The Rite of the Passion* for the Ash Wednesday devotional service in his parish. C.W., writing of him when in 1941 he died, said, "I must have met Henry in 1917–18. . . . There are others I could have better spared." The meeting could not have been later than 1917, however, because the anthology was published in that year. Interestingly, two principal characters in *The Greater Trumps* (1932) are named Aaron Lee and Henry Lee, the former the grandfather of the latter. Perhaps these two sometimes misguided but always honest seekers for spiritual reality are a tribute to his old friend.

THE REVEREND PATRICK MCLAUGHLIN, an Anglican priest, was vicar of a parish in Bishop's Stratford. He was active in church affairs and interested in religious drama. He was cast to play the part of Ced in the production of *Judgement at Chelmsford* which was canceled because of the outbreak of war in 1939. He also represented the archbishop on a committee composed also of T. S. Eliot, Dorothy Sayers, and C.W., the purpose of which was to devise liturgies to celebrate seasonal events in the church calendar in rural areas.

ERIC L. MASCALL was a distinguished theologian and writer and a professor of theology at King's College, University of London. C.W. reviewed his book *He Who Is: A*

Study in Traditional Theism, saying, "He defines at what point the discursive reason properly produces an 'apprehension'; and this apprehension, he claims, is objectively certain. I have maintained, on another matter, something too like this to deny it now. But we must know what we are doing. I concede that Fr. Mascall makes hay of many arguments against. It will be useful for his opponents to read him. But his supporters certainly must; we had better know what we are trying to say, and no one of late years has put it better" (*Time and Tide* 24 [Oct. 9, 1943]: 828).

Mascall's essay "Charles Williams as I Knew Him," a helpful insight, is included in Horne, *Charles Williams,* 1–5.

GERVASE MATHEW was a member of the Catholic Order of Dominicans and a priest and lecturer in modern history, theology, and English at Oxford. He was an active member of the Inklings.

HUMPHREY MILFORD became publisher of the Oxford University Press in London in 1913, after having served as assistant secretary in the Oxford office. His high sense of mission as a publisher is suggested by his response to a statement that the *National Dictionary of Biography* was a white elephant: "Very likely; but it is the sort of animal that ought to be in our stable." The major portion of C.W.'s career in the editorial division was spent under his direction. Sir Humphrey recognized C.W.'s gifts as an editor and a writer and very early became his patron, adviser, and friend. In 1917, he accepted C.W.'s second book, *Poems of Conformity,* for publication. This was the first of several that were to bear the Press imprint. During the many years the two men were to work together they developed a relationship of mutual respect and affection that was broken only by Williams's death in 1945. A few months later Sir Humphrey retired. He died in 1952.

THE MITRE is an Oxford hotel with a taproom frequented by Williams and his friends. Following C.W.'s first Milton lecture at Oxford, C. S. Lewis, J. R. R. Tolkien, and Gerry Hopkins took him there to celebrate the occasion. C.W. often entertained his out-of-town guests there. The Mitre bar along with the famous Bird and Baby (see above) were centers of relaxation and literary talk for C.W. while he was in Oxford.

OXFORD PILGRIM PLAYERS. The Oxford Pilgrim Players was organized and directed by Ruth Spalding under the patronage of the archbishop of Canterbury, the archbishop of Birmingham, and The Reverend Scott Lidget. John Gielgud, the distinguished actor, served as president of the organization along with vice presidents including T. S. Eliot, Dorothy Sayers, Dame Sybil Thorndike, Dame Marie Tempest, and the Lord Bishop of Oxford. The group consisted of professional players, five men and three women.

Spalding's productions during the war are described by Fred Eastman in "While Bombs Fell on England," *Motive: A Magazine of the Methodist Student Movement,* Sept. 1941: "religious drama carried on under circumstances that have probably not been equalled since the early Christians defied a Roman dictator's ban and met for worship in the Catacombs. Here is a typical scene. . . . : 'Incendiary bombs were falling on London. The center of the ancient city was ablaze. Cultural landmarks, centuries old, were going up in smoke. Detonations of Hitler's heavier hell-openers shook the earth. But down underneath the ruins of a church, in its crypt, some hundreds of men, women, and children were witnessing a group of actors presenting a religious drama. Should the play stop? the director asked of the motley audience.' 'No, no! Carry on, please!' . . . And the play went on."

The group doubtless contributed to C.W.'s developing dramaturgy art. In the autumn of 1939 he wrote *The Death of Good Fortune* and *The House by the Stable* for Spalding. These plays were produced in the autumn of that year and subsequently in many parts of the country. *Terror of Light* was first presented by the company in May 1940. In August 1941, C.W. wrote *Grab and Grace,* which was given many performances by the Pilgrims in various places. They also performed *Seed of Adam* three times. In early 1941, C.W. wrote especially for the group a play titled *Frontiers of Hell,* which, however, was never produced during C.W.'s life. Its first presentation before an audience came in February 1996, when Spalding directed a reading version of it before a meeting of the Charles Williams Society in London.

The following statement regarding relationships within the company was drawn up by her, with the help, she says, of Charles Williams.

THE CO-OPERATIVE COMPANY.

The Company from its beginning has been run on a democratic and co-operative basis, that is, it attempts to make its *artistic aims* a basis of its common behaviour. It encourages a sense of decent responsibility in its members towards each other, and a reasonable freedom of courteous criticism and a general method of self-government. This necessarily involves a "hierarchy of functions"; that is, that a proper command and obedience rules in all active operation of the company. This hierarchy is not petrified, in other words each person must preside in his own proper place and time. Equality of person and hierarchy of office is the general principle.

Personal Relations are proper to this company as to any. These should be of such a nature as to contribute to the health and good working of the whole company. "Pleasantness" (in Dante's sense) is proper, "distraction" is undesirable. Semi-casual pre-occupations (physical or mental) are apt to bring about a certain disruption and hence—anarchy in individuals and in the community.

FREDERICK PAGE was in the editorial division of the Press. Sometime before 1908, he met C.W. at the Working Men's College, where both were students. Page, employed by the Oxford University Press, needed an assistant and recommended C.W. for the position. On June 9, 1940, C.W. began in a position which he was to hold until his death. The two men remained friends although their relationship was often strained. It was he who informed Michal of C.W.'s relation with Phyllis Jones. Page introduced C.W. to Alice Meynell, the well-known poet, who read the manuscript of *The Silver Stair* and not only recommended it but helped finance the cost of its production. Page was also instrumental in getting *Poems of Conformity* published in 1917. Through most of their time with the Press they shared a joint office.

COVENTRY PATMORE was a late-nineteenth-century poet best known for his sequence of poems celebrating married love, bodily and spiritually, *The Angel in the House* (1854–63). His first wife, Emily, subject of the poems, died in 1864. He later married again. After converting to Roman Catholicism, he became increasingly associated with other Roman Catholic writers, including Gerard Manley Hopkins, Francis Thompson, and Alice Meynell. C.W. was especially attracted by Patmore's sacramental view of marriage. C.W.'s own views on marriage as sacrament involving equally body and soul did not so much derive from Patmore as Patmore's views confirmed his own at a time when theologians in general were hesitant to speak so openly about the sexual relationship.

HELEN PEACOCK is described by Charles Hadfield as follows: "head of Production, tall, plain, honest-looking, blunt of speech, with piled untidy greying hair pulled back in a bun, always dressed in blouse and skirt, the battleaxe of the Press. She was the Press's German expert" (Horne, *Charles Williams*, 9). She was one of the longest tenured members of the staff and, at a time when the personnel was rapidly changing, C.W. had a special fondness for her. They spent many office hours nostalgically recalling the "good old days."

NANCY PEARN was C.W.'s contact with the firm Pearn, Pollinger, and Higham Associates that served as his literary agent.

PLESHY was an Anglican Retreat House in Essex near Chelmsford. Included among guests and speakers were Evelyn Underhill, Charles Williams, T. S. Eliot, and Dorothy Sayers.

PHYLLIS POTTER, director of the Chelmsford Diocesan Drama Guild, wrote to C.W. in early 1936, requesting permission to present cuttings from *The Rite of the Passion*. He graciously assented. Thus began a relationship that was to last as long as C.W. lived. At her request he wrote *Seed of Adam*, which she produced in late 1936. In 1939, also at her request, in celebration of the twenty-fifth anniversary of the Diocese of Chelmsford he wrote *Judgement at Chelmsford*.

EDWARD BOUVERIE PUSEY (1800–1882) was an avid promoter of the Anglo-Catholic Movement in the Anglican Church during the nineteenth century. He sought to restore Catholic theology and to reemphasize the importance of sacramental and ritualistic worships. After his death, friends founded Pusey House on the campus of Oxford University to be an institution for providing theological study and pastoral care for the Oxford University Community. C.W. maintained a continuing relationship with the institution throughout the years that he was in Oxford.

ANNE RIDLER was a distinguished contemporary poet whom C.W. met while lecturing at Downe House School in Somerset. Anne was a senior student at the time and already a fine young poet. She made an impression on C.W. that was to develop into an affectionate relationship and a correspondence that continued through the years. Ridler, as C.W. anticipated, fulfilled her youthful promise and is today widely recognized as a fine poet. She also became a sensitive commentator on C.W.'s thought and art. In 1948, she edited and introduced *Seed of Adam and Other Plays*, followed in 1958 by *The Image of the City and Other Essays* and, in 1961, by *Selected Writings*. *The Image* contains one of the finest summary statements yet written about C.W.'s thought and art.

SARRAS. C.W. no doubt borrowed the term from A. E. Waite's *The Hidden Church of the Holy Grail* ([London: Rebman Limited, 1909], 133, 289, 363, 364) in which it serves an important function. In Waite's use, it is not another term for heaven itself but is called a "spiritual place in sarras on the confines of Egypt, where the Graal, upon its outward journey, dwelt for a period, and whither, after generations and centuries, it also returned for a period. As this was not the point of its origin, so it was not that of its rest; it was a stage in the passage from Salem and a stage in the transit to heaven." There the Grail quest was consummated; there Percival and Galahad were caught up into heaven; and there their bodies were buried. From there Bors was returned to his earthly tasks. C.W. uses the term ambiguously, both as a place out of time (for Percival and Galahad) and as the experience of the timeless within time (for Bors).

DOROTHY L. SAYERS was a novelist, essayist, lecturer, and Christian apologist. Her detective novel *The Seven Tailors* first captured C.W.'s attention. He later recommended that she be asked to write the Canterbury Festival play for 1937. He saw her occasionally and carried on an extensive correspondence with her that continued as long as he lived. She was inspired by *The Figure of Beatrice* to launch a project that occupied her for the rest of her life. She wrote C.W. on August 18, 1944: "I have embarked upon an enterprise for which you are entirely responsible." She had begun the translation and annotation of the *Divine Comedy*. When she died in 1957, there remained thirteen cantos and all the introduction and annotations yet to be done. Her good friend and distinguished scholar and translator Barbara Reynolds completed the work.

KENNETH SISAM became first assistant secretary to the Delegates of the Oxford University Press shortly after World War I. In 1942 he advanced to the rank of secretary, a position he held until his retirement in 1946. In his position with the Clarendon Press, he published three of C.W.'s books of criticism: *Poetry at Present* (1930), *The English Poetic Mind* (1932), and *Reason and Beauty in the Poetic Mind* (1933). He also published the first *Oxford Companion to English Literature*, which was the beginning of an important series of "Companion Books."

J. R. R. TOLKIEN was Merton Professor of English Language and Literature at Oxford from 1945 to 1959. He is known popularly for his mythological novels, particularly *The Hobbit* and *The Lord of the Rings*. He was an intimate friend of C. S. Lewis's and a regular member of the Inklings group. He did not, however, share Lewis's enthusiasm for C.W. Humphrey Carpenter quotes him as saying in 1965: "I was and remain wholly unsympathetic to Williams' mind. I knew Charles Williams only as a friend of C.S.L. whom I met in his company during the period when, owing to the War, he spent much of his time in Oxford. We liked one another and enjoyed talking (mostly in jest) but we had nothing to say to one another at deeper (or higher) levels. I doubt if he had read anything of mine then available; I had read or heard a good deal of his work, but found it wholly alien, and sometimes very distasteful, occasionally ridiculous" (*The Inklings* [Boston: Houghton Mufflin, 1979], 121).

EVELYN UNDERHILL was born into a well-to-do-family, christened in the Anglican Church, and educated at a private school in Folkestone and at King's College for Women, London. Of an inquiring religious temperament, she early joined the Order of the Golden Dawn, a secret mystical society. In 1907, she underwent a religious conversion that pushed her in the direction of the Roman Catholic Church. Her inability to accept the literalness of some of its teachings kept her from making her submission. Nor, at the time, could she wholeheartedly embrace Anglicanism. She began a study of mysticism and in time fell under the influence of Baron Friedrich von Hügel, the liberal Roman Catholic theologian and philosopher. After a struggle, however, she became a practicing Anglican. From the 1920s onward she was much in demand as a spiritual director and conductor of religious retreats. She was often at Pleshy (see above). She also became a member of the Fellowship of St. Alban and Saint Sergius, an Anglican-Orthodox Fellowship. In her latter years she became a passionate passivist and a member of the Anglican Fellowship. She wrote many books of a devotional nature. It is possible that C.W. first met her in connection with A. E. Waite's Christian branch of the Golden Dawn.

OLIVE WILLIS was headmistress of Downe House, a distinguished school for girls in Somerset. An admirer of C.W.'s work, she, in the early 1930s, invited him to lecture at the school. At various times he spoke on Blake and Bacon, and much of that material later found its way into *The English Poetic Mind*. It was at Downe House that he first met Anne Bradley, later Ridler, who became a close friend and sympathetic critic and editor of his work. Ridler is herself a distinguished poet (see above).

Notes

Persons, places, and things that recur repeatedly in the letters are identified in the Glossary and not ordinarily repeated in the notes except to provide a last name.

1939

1. Sir Humphrey Milford.

2. The secretary, Kenneth Sisam.

3. Milford children: Robin Milford, son of Sir Humphrey.

4. Hubert Foss.

5. Professor H. N. Spalding was a distinguished scholar of Oxford University and founder of the Spalding Chair of Eastern Religion and Ethics. He and his wife were in the United States when war was declared, and they remained there for the duration. There were three children— Anne, Ruth, and John. During the war their house became a haven for many who, for various reasons, were displaced. C.W. and Gerry Hopkins, who came along with the Oxford University Press when it was evacuated from London, found quarters there. The general management of the house fell to Anne, whose gracious manner and democratic spirit made the situation as pleasant as war conditions permitted. Ruth, who founded and directed a company known as the Oxford Pilgrim Players (see Glossary), traveled to many parts of England presenting religious plays. She was often away from South Parks Road. The younger brother, John, spent time in military service.

6. "Dislike people"—an unexpected statement but it appears again and again. See Feb. 17, 1943, n. 13.

7. St. John of the Cross, sixteenth-century mystic and joint founder of the Discalced Carmelites. For C.W. on St. John, see *The Descent of the Dove*, chap. 8, 179–81.

8. Adam Fox became a fellow of Magdalen College and dean of divinity in 1929. He was elected professor of poetry in 1938. He was also a member of the Inklings.

9. The Mitre was an Oxford hotel with a taproom frequented by the Inklings. Following C.W.'s first Milton lecture, C. S. Lewis, J. R. R. Tolkien, and Gerry Hopkins took him there to celebrate the occasion. C.W. often entertained out-of-town guests there. The Mitre bar and the famous "Bird and Baby" were centers of relaxation and literary talk for C.W. while he was in Oxford.

10. Edith, his sister, lived with his mother in St. Alban's.

11. Royalties on the American edition of *The Descent of the Dove* from Longmans, Green and Company in New York. See also undated 1939 letter, n. 26; Oct. 13, 1939, n. 47; Oct. 25, 1939, n. 59.

12. Mrs. Oliver, a woman of their London neighborhood whom C.W. refers to as an example of middle-class values.

13. Rudyard Kipling, "The Cat That Walked by Himself": "He walked by himself, and all places were alike to him."

14. *The Descent of the Dove* is often referred to in this abbreviated form.

15. Curtis Brown was C.W.'s first literary agent. At some point in the early 1930s some of the people left Brown to start a new firm, Pearn, Pollinger, and Higham Associates, and Charles went with them. The new firm, now called Higham Associates, still handles the interests of his estate. During the war years C.W.'s primary contact with the firm was Nancy Pearn.

16. The bishop of Chichester, was George Kenneth Allen Bell. He supported the Confessing Churches in the struggle against the Nazi regime and, at the same time, strongly opposed the indiscriminate bombing of German towns during the war. In the early 1930s he asked C.W. to read and help revise the manuscript of his *Life of Randall Davidson*. He called on him again in April 1940 to work on a report for the Council of Churches for which he was responsible.

17. Thomas Cranmer, 1489–1556, became archbishop of Canterbury under King Henry VIII in 1532 and was martyred under Queen Mary in 1556. He is the subject of C.W.'s play *Cranmer* written for the Canterbury Festival in 1936.

18. Ursula Grundy was a close London friend of the Williamses who was especially helpful when Michael was having problems in Oxford.

19. Margaret Douglas (see Glossary).

20. *New Christian Year* (1941) printed devotional readings from Christian writers for each day of the church calendar based on the ordering as it existed at the time in the Anglican Church.

21. *Passion of Christ* (1939) is a small book of Lenten readings described by C.W. as "the gospel and narrative of the Passion with short comments taken from the saints and doctors of the Church."

22. The Keays-Young woman was an Oxford resident from whom the Douglases rented living quarters when they first arrived in Oxford. She was a casual acquaintance of C.W.'s.

23. The reference to the previous evening with Mrs. Keays-Young indicates that the letter was written on October 4.

24. C.W.'s courtship of Florence Conway began in 1908 and continued through World War I. For details see Alice Mary Hadfield, *Charles Williams: An Exploration of His Life and Work* (New York: Oxford University Press, 1983), 15–25.

25. Review of *Map of Love*, by Dylan Thomas, *Life and Letters Today* 23 (Nov. 1939): 237–39.

26. See Sept. 15, 1939, n. 11; Oct. 13, 1939, n. 47; Oct. 25, 1939, n. 60.

27. Olive Willis.

28. City and Dome: reminiscent of "The Two Domes" in *Windows of Night*, 27, where they stand for the spiritual and the temporal, or, as he puts it in another place, nature and grace.

29. Anne Ridler.

30. Thomas Stearns Eliot.

31. Montgomery Belgion, a writer, was a close friend of T. S. Eliot and a prisoner of war for a period of time. C.W. counseled him after his release.

32. Raymond Hunt.

33. Daniel Nicholson, with the Reverend Henry Lee, edited the *Oxford Book of Mystical Verse* (1917). It was at this time that C.W. met the two men and perhaps through them made his first contact with A. E. Waite. Both became lifelong friends. In 1935, referring to Nicholson, C.W. wrote to T. S. Eliot after having spent an evening with him: "I have not known so happy and easy a time since the dearest of my male friends died two years ago" (quoted by Hadfield, *Exploration*, 128).

34. Anne Ridler.

35. Sir Arthur L. P. Norrington at the time was junior secretary to the Cambridge Press and in 1948 became secretary.

36. E. C. A. Parnwell was a longtime staff member of the Oxford University Press.

37. Theology: "Divites Dimisit," an early version of "The Prayers of the Pope," *Theology* 39 (Dec. 1939): 421–24.

38. "Magic" is the short title by which C.W. often refers to *Witchcraft* during the time of its composition.

39. "Chamelon" is the title of a series of small books published by the Oxford University Press.

40. Spaldings.

41. Karberry was a member of the Oxford University Press staff.

42. Review of *Map of Love*, by Dylan Thomas, *Life and Letters Today* 23 (Nov. 1939): 237–39.

43. Review of *A Pacifist in Trouble*, by W. R. Inge, *Time and Tide* 20 (Dec. 16, 1939): 1617.

44. Apparently he refers to reviews of *Men, Women and Places*, by Sigrid Undset, *Sunday Times*, Oct. 29, 1939, 5, and *Man in the Streets*, by V. W. Garratt, *Sunday Times*, Nov. 19, 1939, 5.

45. See n. 37 above.

46. *Time and Tide* article: Is this a slip of the pen? Could he have in mind the article "Sensuality and Substance" published in *Theology* 38 (May 1939)? In it he discusses Dante's concept of romantic love as a means of achieving unity of body and soul (sensuality and substance) in one's approach to God. The essay is reprinted in Anne Ridler, *The Image of the City and Other Essays* (London: Oxford University Press, 1958), 68–75, and in Charles Hefling, ed., *Charles Williams: The Essential Writings in Spirituality and Theology* (Boston: Cowley Publications, 1993), 113–23.

47. See Sept. 15, 1939, n. 11; undated letter 1939, n. 26; Oct. 25, 1939, n. 60.

48. C.W. was right that nothing came of it.

49. On November 16, however, C.W. writes, "Doctor given . . . copy of the *Dove*."

50. This is the period in late 1939 and early 1940 later referred to as the "Phony War." In the beginning the French army was mobilized along the common Franco-German frontier between the Rhine and the Luxembourg border. Following the collapse of Poland, the French withdrew to their Maginot border. In the weeks of October the British army arrived to join the French, but seven months of relative inactivity followed.

51. The St. Pancras Theatre was a professional company where *Cranmer*, following its run in Canterbury, was performed with Miss Kindersby as producer. In March 1940 she produced *The Rite of the Passion*.

52. G. F. J. Cumberlege.

53. German troops, led by Hitler himself, had entered Austria on March 12, 1938, and on March 18 Austria was declared a part of Germany. Those Austrians opposing the takeover were subjected to severe treatment.

54. Henry Lee (see Glossary).

55. Serge is the name C.W. most often signs to his letters to Michal and is the name she calls him. I have found no conclusive explanation of the origin of the name "Serge." C.W.'s son, Michael, says that he has a vague memory of hearing that it goes back to early days—perhaps to the World War I period at the time of C.W.'s close friendship with Harold Eyers and Ernest Nottingham. It is related, he thinks, to some prominent figure in the Russian Revolution. Whatever its origin, C.W. preferred that she so address him.

In turn, he called her Michal, a name borrowed from the Old Testament story about Michal, daughter of King Saul, who chided David for dancing enthusiastically before the maidens to attract their attention. Hadfield suggests that C.W. thought his wife was like Michal in her attempts to curb his lack of restraint when he recited poetry.

56. C.W. had written a favorable review of *The Family Reunion* for *Time and Tide* in May 1939. He may refer here to *The Idea of a Christian Society*.

57. For the *Time and Tide* article, Oct. 13, 1939, n. 46.

58. Unsigned article in *Times Literary Supplement*, Nov. 11, 1939, 652.

59. See Sept. 15, 1939, n. 11; undated, above, n. 26; Oct. 13, 1939, n. 47; Jan. 15, 1940, n. 10.

60. Through Fred Page, C.W. met Alice Meynell, poet, essayist, and friend of poets—

Francis Thompson, George Meredith, Coventry Patmore—in June 1911. She read the manuscript of *The Silver Stair* and not only encouraged publication but also provided funds that made publication possible. C.W. never ceased to acknowledge his gratitude.

61. C.W. had reviewed *The Family Reunion* in May 1939. The book he speaks of here was perhaps *The Idea of a Christian Society.*

62. Anne and Vivian Ridler.

63. T. S. Eliot, review of *Descent of the Dove, New Statesman and Nation* 18 (Dec. 9, 1939): 864–65.

64. Eliot and Belgion.

65. Anne and Vivian Ridler.

66. Henry Lee (see Glossary).

67. Anne Spalding's parents were still in America at the time of C.W.'s death.

68. Drama for St. Mary's: *The House by the Stable* and *The Death of Good Fortune,* plays he wrote for Ruth Spalding and her company.

69. This and the letter following are both dated November 8, 1939. It is apparent from the content of the letters, however, that this one precedes the other.

70. The Germans launched their attack on the Netherlands on May 10, 1940.

71. For the plays, see Oct. 29, 1939, n. 68.

72. The first Milton lecture was delivered January 19, 1940. The famous *Comus* lecture came the following week. See last paragraph of February 9, 1940, letter for C. S. Lewis's comment.

73. The Order is a reference, apparently, to the mystical order of the Golden Dawn to which Henry Lee, Daniel Nicholson, and A. E. Waite belonged. C.W. met Lee and Nicholson in connection with the publication of *The Oxford Book of Mystical Verse* and through them was introduced to A. E. Waite. Trouble arose in the order causing Waite in 1915 to found a new branch known as the Salvator Mundi Temple of the Fellowship of the Rosy Cross. Williams always referred to it, however, as the Golden Dawn. It was into this new order, distinctively Christian in contrast to the older one, that C.W. was received on September 21, 1919. He was an active member until 1927, after which he no longer considered himself a member. Perhaps he asked Lee to refresh his memory about the rites in connection with his work *Witchcraft* that was published in 1941, or, more likely, for the unfinished novel *The Noises That Weren't There.* On June 9, 1940, he wrote to Michal, "I have a kind of yearning towards a novel, but I don't see my way yet. However, if I do think of something, I will promise you that Lord Arglay shall NOT come in." On June 21, 1940, he pled "Think of a subject for a new novel, I beg you, let it be supernatural this time, because I am more certain there." On December 17, 1941, he reported "A charming letter from T.S.E. . . . encouraging the novel." Almost a year later he is still uncertain: "But what next to turn to I don't quite know." It wasn't until 1943 that he settled down to serious work, when on August 5, he writes, "I am labouring on with chapter 3, though oddments are interfering—off books, I mean. But I hope, faintly for the best. It may be that my whole style is so changed since I wrote my last novel Descent into Hell that I am practically trying out a new technique." Perhaps his style had indeed changed but his predilection toward the occult remained. The effort, however, ended in failure and was abandoned. On September 15 he wrote, "Three quarters of my mind is delighted that we are so at one about my discarded chapters; the other three quarters are sad about the wasted work." He is referring to his unfinished novel *The Noises That Weren't There,* the beginning of a strange story of wartime London in which the eerie noises of the city under attack were but a "pressure felt in her body and changed by her body into the noise." For this mystical-magical concept he could find no satisfactory developing action. He did, however, salvage a small portion of the manuscript that described the light in a painting by Jonathan Drayton: "It was everywhere in the painting—concealed in the houses and in their projected shadows, lying in ambush in the cathedral, opening in the rubble, vivid in the vividness of the sky. It would everywhere have burst through, had it not chosen rather to be shaped into forms, and to restrain and change its greatness in the colours of those lesser limits. It was universal, and lived." In this last, his best novel, he succeeds, I think, in transcending while still using elements of the occult as expressive pointers beyond mere magic.

For further information on C.W. and the occult, see: Huw Mordecai, "Charles Williams and the Occult," *Charles Williams: A Celebration*, ed. Bryan Horne (Herefordshire, England: Gracewing, Fowler Wright Books, 1995); Roma A. King, Jr., "The Occult as Rhetoric in the Poetry of Charles Williams," *The Rhetoric of Vision: Essays on Charles Williams*, ed. Charles A. Huttar and Peter J. Schakel (Lewisburg, Pa.: Bucknell University Press, 1996).

74. Jean Smith. See letter of Nov. 14, 1939.

75. Renée Haynes was the author of *Pan, Caesar and God*, the third book in "I Believe: A Series of Personal Statements," published by Heineman. C.W. wrote *He Came Down from Heaven* for the same series and saw Haynes off and on while he was in Oxford.

76. "If nothing happens" is a reference to the "Phony War." See Oct. 13, 1939, n. 50.

77. Gerard Hopkins.

78. Delegates were the ruling council of the Oxford Press.

79. Taunton, county seat of Somersetshire, founded by the Anglo-Saxon king Inc, has played an important part in the history of England—a pretentious name for a young child.

80. Other critics have challenged some of the information in the book, but it is important to keep C.W.'s purpose in mind. His subtitle states it clearly: "A Short History of the Holy Spirit in the Church."

81. There is no way of knowing precisely with what C.W. was agreeing. Relations between Michal and Isabel Douglas were sometimes contentious, Michal fearing and resenting Isabel's perceived efforts to "control" Charles. Hadfield tells of the incident following the first presentation of *Terror of Light* in which the Douglases expressed annoyance with Michal for her criticism of the play (Hadfield, *C.W.: An Exploration of His Life and Work*, 191). C.W., however, took her criticism seriously and made corrections in the text which he considered improvements. He intended to revise the play thoroughly, turning the prose into poetry, but he died before this was done. See especially letters of May 9, 14, 15, and 21, 1940. The thrust—and severity—of Michal's criticism is suggested from this short paragraph written to Phyllis Potter on May 16, 1940: "The Play—TERROR OF LIGHT—as I saw it on Saturday was a very bad play. Too many long cumbersome sentences, too much that was facetious, & too much Charles Williams being more than a little wilful & intellectually superior. There was a dreadful love scene between John and Magdalene, or at least a banal scene."

82. See letter of Nov. 10, 1939.

83. John Topliss was a longtime friend and a member of C.W.'s class in London in the late 1920s. He visited C.W. in Oxford when he was on temporary leave from the army.

84. William Ralph Inge (1860–1954) was dean of St. Paul's Cathedral in London and author of many theological and devotional writings expressing his sympathy with Platonic spirituality.

85. The Reverend A. R. Vidler was the editor of *Theology* magazine, in which some of C.W.'s most important essays appeared, including "Sensuality and Substance." The magazine also published a very favorable review of *The Descent of the Dove* which he greatly appreciated. In a letter to Phyllis Potter (January 12, 1940) he wrote, "He said it had been left to me to write a history of the church 'from the point of view of God.'"

86. Raymond Hunt.

87. The Christian quotation book was *The New Christian Year* (London: Oxford University Press, 1941).

88. Henry Lee.

89. *Doctor's Dilemma* by George Bernard Shaw.

90. George Babington Macaulay, "A Jacobite's Epitaph."

91. In C.W.'s play *The Death of Good Fortune* the following exchange occurs:

> MARY: Live; do not sleep; tell us what he says.
> G.F. [moaning]: O . . . he says: "Good Fortune, you have your fortune
> yours is the only fortune; all luck is good."

THE LOVER: That is it! that is it; All luck is good.
Why did you tell me to be resigned? Fool!
Why did no one tell me? —all luck is good.

92. Pax, a pacifist organization.

93. In January 1938, C.W. lectured on Byron and Byronism at the Sorbonne. This was his only visit to the Continent.

94. *The House by the Stable.* According to Anne Ridler, this was the "most widely performed of his plays."

95. "No-one" is undoubtedly a reference to Phyllis Jones (Celia), who, after the breakup of her marriage, returned from Java and was sporadically in Oxford with the Press. For further details consult Index to Hadfield, *Exploration.*

96. The performance was of *The House of the Octopus.*

97. Hugh McDonald was an old friend from London days.

98. Algernon Blackwood (1869–1951), was a prolific writer in several genres but especially remembered for his stories of the psychic and macabre.

1940

1. Robin Milford was the son of Sir Humphry Milford. C.W. counseled him about his psychological and religious problems. Jan. 6, 1941, n. 3; Feb. 5, 1941, n. 19; Oct. 2, 1941, n. 96; May 3, 1942, n. 10.

2. MacDonald was working in Cambridge during the war.

3. The plays *The House by the Stable* and *The Death of Good Fortune* were written in late 1939 and first produced by Ruth Spalding and her Pilgrim Players.

4. Miss Kindersby produced *Cranmer* at the St. Pancras Theatre, a professional company in London, following the play's run in Canterbury. In March 1944 she also produced *The Rite of the Passion.*

5. C.W. lectured at Pleshy, the Anglican Retreat House, in January 1940.

6. The firm of Victor Gollancz by this date had published *War in Heaven* (1939); *Many Dimensions* (1931); *The Place of the Lion* (1931); *The Greater Trumps* (1932); *Shadows of Ecstasy* (1933); and *The New Book of English Verse* (1935), which C.W. edited and introduced. The reference here is perhaps to some social affair staged by the publisher.

7. Apparently these were letters written to Florence Conway, whom he met in 1908 and to whom he was married in 1917. During the interval he was working at the Oxford University Press in London. It is certain that she destroyed her letters written to him in Oxford, and apparently she destroyed those written earlier.

8. For "my Nativities," see Jan. 11, 1940, n. 4.

9. The pageant *The Judgement of Chelmsford* was commissioned to celebrate the twenty-fifth anniversary of the Diocese of Chelmsford in the county of Essex. It was already in rehearsal under the direction of Phyllis Potter when the production was canceled in early September because of the approaching war.

10. The check was from Longmans, his American publishers; see Sept. 15, 1939, n. 11.

11. For Nancy Pearn (see Glossary).

12. "Ver" is obsolete usage for spring.

13. Review of *The Testament of a Friendship: The Story of Winifred Holtby,* by Vera Britten, *Theology* 40 (Apr. 1940): 319.

14. Review of *Archbishop Laud,* by H. R. Trevor-Roper, *Sunday Times,* Jan. 28, 1940, 6.

15. This was the beginning of a long series of lectures that C.W. was to give to great acclaim at Oxford before his death in 1945.

16. "Down to Milton" is perhaps a reference to his current lectures.

17. Michal planned to visit Phyllis Potter in Essex and C.W. had suggested that she go "the 3rd March week-end."

18. "Magic" is the title by which during composition he often refers to the manuscript that became *Witchcraft*.

19. Review of *The Last Rally: A Study of Charles II*, by Hilaire Belloc, *Time and Tide* 21 (Feb. 24, 1940): 198, review of *The Novel in the Modern World*, by David Daiches, *Time and Tide* 21 (Mar. 9, 1940): 254–55.

20. Probably review of *The March of Literature*, by Ford M. Ford, *Theology* 40 (Apr. 1940): 311–13.

21. Review of *Anthology*, comp. by Edith Sitwell, *Life and Letters Today* 25 (Apr.–June 1940): 211–13.

22. The Salisbury shows were his two plays. See Jan. 11, 1940, n. 4.

23. For Pentecost he wrote *Terror of Light*. A first version was presented in Oxford in May 1940 and revised after the first performance. Written in prose, the play, even in the revised version, failed to please C.W., and he determined to rewrite it in verse, lengthening it perhaps so that its performance time would be approximately two hours. He died before this was done. The first published version—consisting of the revised script with the original text given in footnotes—is that included in John Heath-Stubbs, *Collected Plays by Charles Williams* (London: Oxford University Press, 1963).

24. Father Clare was rector of St. Saviour's Church in London.

25. On February 1, 1940, the Russians attacked the Mannerheim Line, and by March 15 Finland accepted defeat on terms demanded by the Russians.

26. See Feb. 7, 1940, n. 17.

27. "Fish's mouth" is based on Matt. 17:27. For C.W. and Michal it meant a piece of good luck that came unexpectedly as though by miracle.

28. The book *Witchcraft*.

29. Mrs. Henry Wood (1814–1887) was a very popular author of sensational and moralistic novels including *East Lynne*. She is considered a forerunner of modern detective story writers.

30. After the series of lectures he is giving.

31. Annual meeting of the Church Literary Association. He is reported to have given "a wise warning against the propaganda which cannot realize that there is anything to be said on the other side, and against the sacrifice of accuracy and intelligence for the sake of a misleading and often exasperating simplicity. Zeal and sincerity are not enough. There must be understanding of the mind, the misgivings and the atmosphere of the age, with, of course, the conviction that for this age, as for all other ages, there is only one way of salvation" (Report in *Church Times* 123 [Feb. 9, 1940]).

32. There are four letters in the original file numbered 107, 108, 109, and 110, which are all dated February 27, 1940. Their contents make it impossible for them to have been written on the same day. The letter immediately following is dated February 28, 1940, and the date on the one preceding (106) is illegible. The four letters here fall between February 20 and 27. Based on content, it would seem that the placement in the file cannot represent the sequence in which they were written. For example, in Ltr. 109 he writes, "shall ring you up to-morrow." In 108, he writes, "So after ringing you up. . . ." This suggests that the placement of these two letters has been reversed. I have arranged the four, therefore, in the order that their content indicates is most likely and have dated them by placing the original number followed by the more likely one in brackets; for example, 27[24].

33. He preferred that she didn't go down to Essex to visit Phyllis Potter. See Feb. 7, 1940, n. 17; Feb. 12, 1940, n. 26.

34. Basil Blackwell. This and the reference to Edgcumbe a few lines down are in an effort to find a job for Michael, a matter of great concern to C.W. and Michal.

35. See Feb. 27[24], 1940, n. 32.

36. Student Christian Movement was the British branch of a worldwide fellowship whose purpose was understanding and living the Christian faith.

37. Margaret Douglas.

38. Hubert J. Foss.

39. Basil Blackwell.

40. Basil Blackwell.

41. This letter, lacking a beginning page, was marked "undated" and placed in position 11 in the file. Since C.W. writes of having been in Oxford for five months it is reasonable to assume that it might have been written in early or mid-February.

42. Their London flat was on Antrim Road.

43. See. Jan. 29, 1940, n. 16.

44. The "Courage pamphlet" was a proposed wartime pamphlet intended as encouragement to the general public, which, however, was never published. See June 9, 1940, n. 119; June 25, 1940, n. 134; July 4, 1940, n. 136; undated 1940, n. 147; July 18, 1940, n. 160.

45. *New Christian Year.*

46. Sir Walter Scott, "Marmion," 14.

> And dar'st thou then
> To beard the lion in his den,
> The Douglas in his hall?

47. Father Curtis; see Sept. 15, 1940, par. 1.

48. Apparently he planned to write to Blackwell about Michael's position.

49. The Whitsun play was *Terror of Light.*

50. See Feb. 7, 1940, n. 21. The review appeared in *Life and Letters Today* 25 (Apr.–June 1940): 211–13.

51. George Every was a historian, theologian, critic, and poet. In addition to the reference here, he also wrote two articles: "Charles Williams—I: The Accuser," *Theology* 51 (Mar. 1948): 95–100; and "Charles Williams—II: The City and the Substitutions," *Theology* 51 (Apr. 1948): 145–50. He also devotes space to C.W. in chapters 1 and 4 of *Poetry and Responsibility* (London: SCM Press, 1949).

52. *"Faute de mieux":* for want of something better.

53. The proposed book was to be an extensive work that would include a biography and a gathering together of the entire canon of C.W.'s writing.

54. Joseph Priestly was a novelist and popular playwright of the 1930s.

55. "Your back" is a reference to his doctrine of substitution and exchange. See the essay "The Practice of Substituted Love," which appeared first as chapter 6 in *He Came Down from Heaven* and is reprinted in Hefling, ed., *Charles Williams,* 216–30. It is a central theme in the novel *Descent into Hell.*

56. See Feb. 13, 1940, n. 27.

57. Auden left England in 1939 and became an American citizen in 1946 (see Glossary).

58. In light of C.W.'s letter of March 12, 1940, he probably refers to his passionate but platonic "affair" with Phyllis Jones in the late 1920s and early 1930s. The "shock" to Michal came when Frederick Page told her what was going on. For a fuller account see Hadfield, *Exploration,* esp. 81–90, 127–32, and 180. In 1939 Phyllis's marriage to Billy Somerville having failed, she returned from Java, where she had been living, and sought reemployment with the Oxford Press, which had already moved to Oxford. On October 23 C.W. wrote to Hadfield, "I ran into her for five minutes. The image and the loss of the image—yes, I maintain it. O I wish I were free." The word "image" in light of his whole system of thought is, I think, very significant. I agree essentially with Hadfield's statement: "It was not freedom from his marriage he longed for, but from the thirteen-year-old passionate *vision through* [emphasis added] Phyllis." It is true that Phyllis's

shadow continued to hover over both Charles and Michal. He felt compelled to reassert again and again his total devotion to Michal; she, to remain sensitive, cautious. The depth of their relationship, however, can hardly be questioned. His need for and concern for her were genuine; her devotion to him continuing. Michael, their son, says that after C.W.'s death she, on the anniversary of his death and on his birthday, packed a lunch, took the bus, and traveled to Oxford to sit by his grave sometimes for hours. The thankfulness of which he speaks is for the renewal of his original vision of the Michal he celebrated in the early poems. She is unquestionably the subject of all his writing about romantic love during these latter years. See also July 25, 1943, n. 82; Aug. 20, 1943, n. 86; June 4, 1944, n. 65.

59. *Rite of the Passion.*

60. "The Church Looks Forward," *St. Martin's Review* 553 (July 1940): 329–32; reprinted in Hefling, ed., *Charles Williams,* 139–45.

61. Michael's job at Blackwell's.

62. Hubert Foss.

63. This could refer to review of *Passion and Society,* by Denis Rougemont, trans. Montgomery Belgion, *Time and Tide* 21 (Apr. 13, 1940): 394. More likely, however, it refers to review of *Grand Inquisitor,* by Walter Starkie, *Time and Tide* 21 (June 1940): 587–88.

64. Alexander Dru was an editor and translator who in 1935 approached the Oxford University Press with a proposal that the works of the Danish theologian and philosopher Søren Kierkegaard be published in English translation. The project was given to C.W. for editorial supervision. The first of several volumes that followed appeared in 1936. The impact of Kierkegaard's thinking on C.W. was tremendous. See, for example, his statement in *The Descent of the Dove,* 212–20.

65. Ursula Grundy was to be confirmed in the Reverend Henry Lee's parish, London, a ceremony which C.W. and Michal attended.

66. Walter Douglas was an old friend of Anne Spalding's from the Ruskin School of Drawing.

67. In an encounter on April 8 between British and German naval forces north of Bergen–Shetland Islands the British destroyer *Gloworm* and the transport *Rio de Janeiro,* loaded with British troops, had been sunk.

68. Lutterworth in Leicestershire was where Michal had been staying with her sister during the heavy bombing of London.

69. The possibility of Michael's finding a position with the American branch of the Oxford University Press in New York became increasingly attractive to C.W. in the months and years to come. See May 29, 1940, n. 104; Sept. 3, 1940, n. 183; July 6, 1944, n. 80; Aug. 17, 1944, n. 106; Jan. 20, 1945, n. 8; Feb. 21, 1945, n. 37.

70. Anne Ridler

71. Mrs. Wallace, a nurse, was a member of the household in Lutterworth. See Apr. 18, 1940, n. 68.

72. Dwight Moody and Ira David Sankey were popular American evangelists who conducted revival meetings in the United States and England in the late nineteenth century.

73. Tom Burns was a staff member of Longmans, Green and Company, New York, who published the American edition of *The Descent of the Dove.*

74. *Terror of Light.*

75. *The New Christian Year.*

76. Review of *The Testament of Friendship: The Story of Winifred Holtby,* by Vera Britten, *Theology* 40 (Apr. 1940): 319.

77. Review of *The March of Literature,* by F. M. Ford, *Theology* 49 (Apr. 1940): 311–13.

78. Fr. Thomas Parker of Pusey House. See Apr. 29, 1940, n. 81 below.

79. He did write articles for the *Dublin Review,* beginning with "The Image of the City in English Verse," *Dublin Review* (July 1940): 39–51, reprinted in Ridler, *Image of the City,* 92–102. He also did reviews beginning at about the same time.

80. See Apr. 23, 1940, n. 73.

81. Pusey House was an Anglican center in Oxford named for Edward Bouverie Pusey (1800–1882), who was one of the leaders of the Tractarians, a movement that emphasized Catholic theology and ritual in the Anglican church.

82. Adam Fox became a fellow of Magdalen College and dean of divinity in 1929 and was elected professor of poetry in 1938.

83. *Terror of Light.*

84. He was called up for army service in late 1941. See the last (undated) letter for 1941, n. 105.

85. "Simon: . . . if there is cause for gratitude I shall pay in full. / Peter: You can never do that. No one can" (Heath-Stubbs, *Collected Plays*, 358).

86. They were going to St. Mary's to see a performance of *Terror of Light.*

87. "The Church Looks Forward," *St. Martin's Review* 553 (July 1940): 329–32, reprinted in Hefling, ed., *Charles Williams*, 139–45.

88. Bishop George Bell had agreed to pay him £15 to help revise a manuscript the bishop was writing. See May 20, 1940, n. 96.

89. On May 13 the Dutch government and the queen sailed for England, and on May 14 the army surrendered to the Germans.

90. *Terror of Light.*

91. John Trevor was a member of the Pilgrim Players.

92. See May 14, 1940, n. 87.

93. "The Image of the City in English Verse," *Dublin Review* (July 1940): 39–51, reprinted in Ridler, *Image of the City*, 92–102.

94. According to Hadfield (*Explorations*, 23), C.W. was passed unfit for active service in World War I. Instead, he dug trenches in Hyde Park, London, and did civilian war work in St. Albans.

95. The Americans supported the Allies economically and technically from the beginning, but it was not until after the Japanese bombed Pearl Harbor on December 7, 1941, that the United States declared war.

96. For the bishop's manuscript, see May 14, 1940, n. 88.

97. Michael had begun work on April 1.

98. *Terror of Light.*

99. The play had not been rewritten at the time of his death. See Feb. 8, 1940, n. 23.

100. See May 8, 1940, n. 82.

101. In the original letter file this poem is given a separate number. It seems obvious, however, that it is an enclosure to the letter above, dated to coincide with her actual birthday.

102. The words "uncertain, heavy, lost" are reminiscent of Virgil's intercepted falling through space in "Taliessin on the Death of Virgil" and of Wentworth's falling into endless space in *The Descent into Hell.*

103. Psa. 118:23.

104. For the New York branch, see Apr. 18, 1940, n. 69.

105. On May 27, 1940, Belgium capitulated to the Germans. The British Expeditionary Force and other Allied troops, trapped in a narrow strip around Dunkirk, were instructed to evacuate by sea. More than 345,000 men, many of them British, managed to escape the rapidly approaching Germans. Although their equipment was lost, their heroic operation was a tremendous boost to the British morale.

106. Royal Army Medical Corps.

107. Author was unable to locate this article.

108. See May 30, 1940, n. 105.

109. "Pleshy" refers to the long-delayed visit with Phyllis Potter. Feb. 7, 1940, n. 17; Feb. 12, 1940, n. 26; Feb. 27[24?], 1940, n. 33.

110. Student Christian Movement.

111. Apparently this article was never written.

112. On June 22 the French surrendered to the Germans on their terms, and the armistice became effective at 1:35 A.M. on June 25.

113. Beginning on page 230 with the sentence "The Body and Blood of Christendom had been declared to be divine, human, and common; the body and blood of Communism were thought to be human and common; the body and blood of the new myth were merely German. It set itself against the very idea of the City; it raised against the world the fatalistic cry of Race. There was, no doubt, every kind of excuse; Europe had not behaved well to the Germans, nor the City to the barbarians. But whatever the cause, all Christendom in Germany felt the result." He continues to the end of the book—a statement that does not ignore ambiguities and contradictions but, nevertheless, rationally and forcefully states the case against both Communism and Nazism.

114. Sir Samuel Hoare, British foreign secretary, in December 1945 accepted a plan by the French prime minister Pierre Laval that ceded some Abyssinian territory to Italy. The treaty was strongly opposed in England, where it was regarded as a betrayal of the League of Nations and the dismembering of Abyssinia for the benefit of an aggressor. The result was the forced resignation of Sir Samuel, who was succeeded by Anthony Eden.

115. After a gradual erosion of Austrian independence, Hitler and his army entered the country on March 12, 1938, and on the following day proclaimed the union of Austria with Greater Germany. For a fairly comprehensive statement, pro and con, on the suspicion that C.W. harbored a tendency toward "political authoritarianism," see Robert Conquest, "The Art of the Enemy," in *Essays in Criticism* 7 (Jan. 1957): 42–55, and the responses thereto in the following issue.

116. 1 Cor. 9:11: "If we have sown unto you spiritual things, is it a great thing if we shall reap your carnal things?"

117. Dawson was the editor of the *Dublin Review*.

118. "The Image of the City in English Verse," reprinted in Ridler, *Image of the City*, 92–102. See May 15, 1940, n. 93.

119. A proposed wartime pamphlet intended for the general public. See undated letter, n. 44.

120. Graham Greene was a popular novelist who worked in the Ministry of Information during the war.

121. Lord Arglay was a character in *Many Dimensions*. Perhaps she thought he too had a "man's image of a woman."

122. *New Christian Year.*

123. See June 7, 1940, n. 113.

124. After the blitzkrieg across France, the German army crossed the Seine on July 9 and on June 14 entered Paris.

125. Speaking before the graduating class at the University of Virginia, President Franklin D. Roosevelt revealed that he had attempted to mediate between Mussolini and the Allies, but instead of responding favorably "the hand that held the dagger stuck it into the body of its neighbor" (London *Times*, June 10, 1940).

126. *Tenez bon:* "Stick to it."

127. The synopsis of the Courage pamphlet. See June 9, 1940, n. 119; July 6, 1940, n. 139; July 8, 1940, n. 145.

128. *New Christian Year.*

129. This passage appears in *New Christian Year* as follows: "Let us love each other in the way God wishes and let us not be frightened of the love which is the very name of the Holy Ghost, and let us thus courageously await the will of Him Who made us for His glory."

130. See June 11, 1940, n. 125.

131. Precise dating of this letter is impossible. It is placed here on basis of the following internal evidence: (1) Michael arrived on April 1; (2) the first indication of C.W.'s disappointment was expressed in the letter of April 28; (3) reference to progress on *Witchcraft:* on April 9 he sent a portion to Margaret to be typed; by April 29 Eliot had at least a portion of the manuscript; on June 26 he expressed the intention to work on the last chapter of "Magic"; his reference might

coincide with events taking place between Italy and Germany in May and early June. For years, in spite of military unpreparedness, Mussolini had carried on a continuing flirtation with Hitler. In November 1937 he joined the Germany-Japanese Anti-Comintern Pact, withdrew from the League of Nations, and increased Italy's armament program. In 1938 he had passed social laws aimed at Jews. In May 1939 the informal Rome-Berlin Axis became a binding alliance. This letter must have been written when *Witchcraft* was in the late stages of composition and during a period before the alliance was firmly sealed. In light of the statement "peeved with Italy" and in lack of more specific evidence, I have preferred a later rather than an earlier date and so placed the letter. See June 11, 1940, n. 125.

132. *New Christian Year.*

133. Henry Lee.

134. See undated letter (1940) above, n. 44.

135. Haverstock Hill is a steep rise from Chalk Farm Road to Hampstead High Street, a spot C.W. always associated romantically with his early courtship of Michal.

136. See undated letter (1940), above, n. 44.

137. I suggest that this description is less of her the woman than for the sake of her function. He prefaces *Taliessin through Logres* with a statement from Dante's *De Monarchia*, 1.3: "The essence is created for the sake of the function, and not the function for the essence." The figure of the watch tower might well be based on Isa. 62:6–7: "I have set watchmen upon thy walls, O Jerusalem, which shall never hold their peace day nor night; ye that make mention of the Lord, keep not silence. And give him no rest, till he establish, and till he make Jerusalem a praise in the earth."

138. He was thrilled over the prospect of her taking a trip to Canada as sponsor of a group of refugee children. It did not work out. See July 9, 1940, n. 146.

139. Curtis was secretary to Sir Humphrey. Apparently C.W. had approached the Press about publishing his "Courage" pamphlet. See June 11, 1940, n. 127; July 8, 1940, n. 145.

140. Graham Greene. See June 9, 1940, n. 120.

141. *The English Poems of John Milton,* World's Classics (Oxford: Oxford University Press, 1940).

142. Exod. 3:22: "But every woman shall borrow of her neighbour, and of her that sojourneth in her house, jewels of silver, and jewels of gold, and raiment: and ye shall put them upon your sons, and upon your daughters; and ye shall spoil the Egyptians."

143. Robert Browning, *The Ring and the Book,* 1.1391–92: "O lyric Love, half angel and half bird / And all a wonder and a wild desire."

144. See July 6, 1940, n. 141.

145. See undated letter (1940), above, n. 44.

146. He was relieved that the trip to Canada did not materialize. See July 6, 1940, n. 138.

147. Apparently the "Courage" pamphlet which the Ministry of Information had refused. See undated letter (1940), above, n. 44.

148. Perhaps Henderson and Spalding, who used the imprint of the Sylvan Press. They had published *Heroes and Kings* in 1930.

149. Dawson and Ward were staff of the *Dublin Review.*

150. Part of his doctrine of co-inherence. See n. 153 below.

151. In Shakespeare's *Troilus and Cressida* in a witty exchange between Paris, Helen, and Pandarus, the epithet "sweet," "honey sweet" appears over and over. If C.W. had a specific line in mind it would be hard to identify.

152. With time, C.W. altered his view of Oxford. See Feb. 5, 1944, n. 15.

153. *The Way of Exchange,* a pamphlet in the New Foundation Series, 1941; reproduced in Ridler, *Image of the City,* 147–58; Hefling, ed., *Charles Williams,* 204–15.

154. The work was never completed.

155. "And the people gave a shout, saying, 'It is the voice of a god, and not of a man'" (Acts 12:22), said regarding Herod, who "gave not God the glory; and was eaten by worms."

156. Hubert Foss.

157. Hitler hoped, after the collapse of France, that England would agree to a compromise peace and delayed plans for the invasion, a hope that was slow to fade. Finally, in July 1940, he ordered plans for an operation to be called "Sealion" to take place in August, but that date came and went. After several postponements he ordered on October 12 that, although preparations should continue, the actual invasion would be delayed until spring. By then, however, he had decided to invade Russia instead. The prolonged suspense is clearly reflected in the letters.

158. See undated letter (1940), above, n. 44.

159. See July 6, 1940, n. 141.

160. See undated letter (1940), above, n. 44.

161. In connection with preparation of *New Christian Year*.

162. Psa. 137:1: "By the rivers of Babylon, there we sat down, yea, we wept, when we remembered Zion."

163. Shakespeare, *Macbeth*, 1.3.147.

164. Pilgrim Players.

165. *New Christian Year.*

166. Adam Fox (see Glossary).

167. Halifax became foreign secretary February 25, 1938, and served until December 1949, when he was named British ambassador to the United States.

168. Helen Peacock (see Glossary).

169. Thomas B. Macaulay, "The Battle of Naseby":

> Press where you see my white plume shine,
> amidst the ranks of war,
> And be your oriflamme to-day the helmet of Navarre.

The oriflamme, the ancient royal standard of France, split at one end to form flame-shaped streamers, signified courage.

170. See May 14, 1940, n. 88; May 20, 1940, n. 96.

171. *Victoria Regina* was a play by Laurence Housman, published in 1934. When the ban on impersonating royalty on stage was lifted in 1937, it was produced with popular success.

172. Hubert Foss.

173. Jocelyn Harris was an Oxford University Press colleague.

174. W. H. Auden.

175. England experienced some of the heaviest bombing in late July, continuing through August. In early September Michal retreated once again to her sister's home in Lutterworth for an indefinite period.

176. C.W. was scheduled to speak at the Chingford Conference, but on September 10 he informed Phyllis Potter that under the present circumstances he presumed the conference was canceled and that he would find it impossible to be there in any event. But see Sept. 3, 1940, n. 182.

177. *New Christian Year.*

178. Perhaps review of *Boethius*, by Helen M. Barrett, *Dublin Review* 207 (Oct. 1940): 252–53.

179. See Aug. 23, 1940, n. 175.

180. See Feb. 13, 1940, n. 27.

181. Michal and Michael had come down to see C.W. in his new quarters that day the previous year.

182. After the conferring of the Diocesan Youth Conference. But see letter of Aug. 23, 1940. He apparently had a change of mind.

183. See Apr. 18, 1940, n. 69.

184. Largely because of C.W.'s insistence, she was in Lutterworth with her sister.

185. He meant that they would discuss everything about what she should do during the intense bombing. It was decided that for the immediate future she would remain with her sister in Lutterworth. It was not an altogether happy arrangement.

186. His birthday was September 20.

187. She had been in Oxford for a short visit but had returned to Lutterworth.

188. Eph. 4:20.

189. There are two poems: "Bors to Elayne. The Fish of Broceliande" and "Bors to Elayne: On the King's Coins." It could be either, but the latter seems more likely.

190. Perhaps he is responding to her complaint that his female characters represented "a man's image of a woman" and that they are, therefore, unrealistic. See Oct. 7, 1943, first paragraph.

191. Frognal is in Hampstead.

192. His hope was to dispose of the flat in London and for her to come to Oxford for the duration.

193. Robert Browning, *Pippa Passes*, 1:227–28: "God's in his heaven— / All's right with the world!" Out of context, this statement distorts the overall meaning of Browning's drama—as it seems to do here. It should be read in light of C.W.'s statement that "all luck is good luck." See May 15, 1940, n. 91.

194. She had been in Oxford for a few days. For balm in Gilead, see Jer. 8:22.

195. In London.

196. W. H. Auden (see Glossary).

197. He lectured at Lincoln to a group of clergymen. See beginning of letter of Nov. 27, 1940.

198. See letter of Dec. 2, 1940.

199. Hugh Walpole was a popular novelist of the period, satirized by Somerset Maugham in *Cakes and Ale* as a hypocritical literary careerist.

200. L. A. G. Strong was a novelist, poet, and critic known for his fiction that often dealt with the macabre and violent.

201. Frederick Page (see Glossary).

202. See June 25, 1940, n. 135.

203. "Get you yesterday" from London. She was still in Lutterworth.

204. Wallis was the caretaker of the building in London in which their flat was located.

205. "Mansions" is British usage for American apartment house.

206. C.W. at this time was thinking in general terms about writing a new novel. He really never settled down, however, for some time to a topic. See also Nov. 10, 1939, n. 74.

207. Speaking before the British Academy in 1947, Eliot said: "I can give only one example of contemporary criticism of Milton, by a critic of the type to which I belong if I have any critical pretensions at all: that is the Introduction to Milton's *English Poems* in the 'World Classics' series, by the late Charles Williams . . . what distinguishes it throughout (and the same is true of most of Williams's critical writing) is the author's warmth of feeling and his success in communicating it to the reader. In this, so far as I am aware, the essay of Williams's is a solitary example" (*On Poetry and Poets*, 147).

208. He was going to Magdalen to visit C. S. Lewis and probably the Inklings.

209. It is clear that C.W. expected his letters to be published. See also Nov. 21, 1944, n. 149.

210. Felicia Dorothea Hemans, "The Graves of a Household":

> They grew in beauty, side by side,
> They fill'd one home with glee;—

211. Dr. Welch of the BBC.

1. See "Natural Goodness," *Theology* 43 (Oct. 1941): 11–16, reprinted in Hefling, ed., *Charles Williams*, 35–41.

2. Probably a slip of the pen for *Providence and History* by Langmead Casserley, which C.W. reviewed in *Time and Tide*, Jan. 25, 1941.

3. Robin Milford. See Jan. 4, 1940, n. 1.

4. Oldham was with the publication *Christian News-Letter*.

5. His producer was Ruth Spalding. See "Oxford Pilgrim Players" in Glossary.

6. Luke 1:3. Theodora, feminine form.

7. "Dinadan's Song," *Time and Tide* 22 (Mar. 15, 1941): 210.

8. Coleridge, "Christabel," 2.412–13:

> And to be wroth with one we love
> Doth work like madness in the brain.

9. *Antony and Cleopatra*, 4.13,66–68. Of these lines C.W. writes in *Reason and Beauty in the Poetic Mind*, "When he is dead, it is the very means of discovering nobility and the difference between the world and a sty that has vanished. There is no sense of any kind of value left at all" (164).

10. See July 15, 1941, n. 52.

11. He uses this same idea in his description of the Trinity in "The Founding of the Company," *The Region of the Summer Stars*, 36–41.

12. This is probably a reference to the three-act play *Frontiers of Evil* written for Ruth Spalding and her company. It was neither produced nor printed during C.W.'s lifetime. He is strangely silent about it in his letters. It is a bleak, bitter treatment of the powers of evil in a manner that Michal would most likely have discouraged. His only other three-act play, *House of the Octopus*, came later. *Frontiers of Evil* was given a reading performance before the Charles Williams Society in London in February 1996. For an account, see *Charles Williams Society Newsletter*, No. 82 (Autumn 1996): 7–11. See also Jan. 15, 1941, n. 15; Feb. 28, 1941, n. 31; Aug. 5, 1941, n. 60.

13. Robin Milford. See Jan. 4, 1940, n. 1.

14. "Blake and Wordsworth," *Dublin Review* 208 (Apr. 1941): 175–86, reprinted in Ridler, *Image of the City*, 59–67.

15. See Jan. 9, 1941, n. 12.

16. C.W. refers to the index to *Witchcraft*.

17. Basil Blackwood.

18. He had slipped on the ice and fallen.

19. Robin Milford. See Jan. 4, 1940, n. 1.

20. Anne Ridler.

21. Welch was director of religious programming for the BBC.

22. He wrote one play, *The Three Temptations*, for radio, which was produced in November 1942. Not published during C.W.'s lifetime, it was included in Heath-Stubbs, *Collected Plays*, 377–401.

23. Henry Lee (see Glossary).

24. Miss Lee was Henry's sister.

25. Henry Lee (see Glossary).

26. The christening of Anne Ridler's baby.

27. Income tax.

28. Geoffrey F. J. Cumberlege.

29. He wrote an obituary of Henry Lee for the *Diocesan Chronicle*.

30. See Feb. 5, 1941, n. 18.

31. See Jan. 9, 1941, n. 12.

32. He must have in mind *The New Christian Year*.

33. One of the two books of poetry for young readers which she compiled.

34. See Feb. 11, 1941, n. 24.

35. *Mrs. Warren's Profession* is a play by George Bernard Shaw.

36. Peter Jackson was an Oxford friend of Michael's.

37. She was at Lutterworth.

38. *The New Christian Year,* which he often referred to as "my anthology." See Feb. 28, 1941, n. 32.

39. This book never materialized.

40. In anticipation of their weekend there together.

41. "The Departure of Dindrane," in *The Region of the Summer Stars*.

42. As the situation developed, the Germans encountered unexpected resistance that culminated, after many months of bitter fighting, in the surrender of the German army in February 1944.

43. Lord David was Cecil (Lord Edward Christian David Gascoyne), scholar and biographer and vice chancellor of Oxford.

44. John Trevor was a member of Ruth Spalding's Oxford Players.

45. "Religion and Love in Dante: The Theology of Romantic Love," *Dacre Papers,* No. 16.

46. Michael's registration for the army. See undated last letter for 1941, n. 105.

47. *Paradise Lost,* 5.8–10:

> so much the more
> His wonder was to find unawakened Eve
> With tresses discomposed. . . .

48. From the jingle: "Nobody loves me, everybody hates me, / Going out to the garden to eat worms."

49. One suggestive of his mood might be Psa. 69:1–2: "Save me, O God; for the waters are come in unto my soul. / I sink in deep mire, where there is no standing."

50. He did become editor of the *Periodical*. See Oct. 13, 1941, n. 104.

51. Hubert Foss.

52. He wanted to get her away from Lutterworth because of the tension that had developed between members of the household. See also Aug. 1, 1941, n. 57; Aug. 7, 1941, n. 63; Aug. 12, 1941, n. 68.

53. Mrs. Leonard was a neighborhood casual friend to whom C.W. often refers as an example of middle-class values.

54. For St. Paul's views on marriage, see 1 Cor. 7:1–17. His most frequently quoted remark about marriage is from verse 9: "it is better to marry than to burn."

55. Auden's new poem *The Double Man* was published in London under the title *New Year Letter.*

56. *Times Literary Supplement,* July 29, 1941.

57. He found the situation at Lutterworth unbearable. See July 15, 1941, n. 52; Aug. 7, 1941, n. 63.

58. See June 26, 1941, n. 45.

59. A minor staff member of the Oxford University Press.

60. See Jan. 9, 1941, n. 12.

61. Norman Collins worked with C.W. at Amen House in early days. He later joined the Gollancz publishing firm, which at the time was producing C.W.'s early novels. In 1941 he was working for the British Broadcasting Company.

62. See Jan. 9, 1941, n. 12; Jan. 15, 1941, no. 15.

63. See July 15, 1941, n. 52.

64. Wordsworth. "My heart leaps up when I behold / A rainbow in the sky," 1–2.

65. Norman Collins. See Aug. 6, 1941, n. 61.

66. Victor Gollancz, director of the Gollancz publishing firm that published C.W.'s early novels.

67. The Reverend Eric Mascall, late professor of theology at King's College, London, and author of several important theological books. His essay included in *Charles Williams: A Celebration* (Horne, *Charles Williams*, 1–5) gives an explanation of what C.W. meant by "amor intellectualis." C.W. reviewed Fr. Mascall's *He Who Is* for *Time and Tide* (Oct. 9, 1943): concluding, "It will be useful for his opponents to read him. But his supporters certainly must; we had better know what we are saying, and no one of late years has put it better."

68. See July 15, 1941, n. 52.

69. Belgion was a writer and translator and a close friend of T. S. Eliot's. He was for a time a prisoner of war in an enemy prison camp. Williams counseled him after his release.

70. Hubert Foss.

71. Ashley Sampson was an editor at Geoffrey Bles, Publishers, who requested C.W. to write *The Forgiveness of Sins*.

72. The result of the additional five thousand words was a final chapter—"The Present Time."

73. W—— is Win, a member of the household at Lutterworth. See July 15, 1941, n. 52; Aug. 7, 1941, n. 63.

74. He was planning to come to Lutterworth.

75. Review of *The Life and Times of St. Leo the Great*, by T. G. Jallard, *Time and Tide* 22 (Sept. 20, 1941): 802–3.

76. See Aug. 13, 1941, n. 72.

77. Gerard Hopkins was still at the press—at least part-time—at the time of C.W.'s death.

78. Tennyson, *Idylls of the King*, "The Passing of Arthur": "And God fulfils himself in many ways." 409.

79. Hubert Foss.

80. Welch was director of Religious Broadcasting at the BBC.

81. *The Three Temptations*, C.W.'s only radio play, was broadcast in November 1942. It was first printed in Heath-Stubbs, *Collected Plays*, 377–401.

82. See last letter for 1941, undated, n. 105.

83. See Jan. 4, 1940, n. 1.

84. His comment was that the impact of "world history" on "word history" was being radically altered because of the war.

85. Christopher Marlowe, *Faustus*, 1:1335–36: "The evening air / was clad in the beauty of a thousand stars."

86. She would be coming back from Lutterworth.

87. "Paracelsus," *Time and Tide* 22 (Sept. 27, 1941): 820–21.

88. Anne Ridler writes: "The 'pamphlet' CW refers to must have been a publication by Tambimutter for 'Poetry London' of my 'A Dream Observed.' I suppose 1941, though the booklet (21 pages of poems all but one of which I reprinted in 'The Nine Bright Sleepers' with Faber) has no date. It was No. 2 of the Pamphlets" (Letter to author, 1994).

89. Eliot's new poem was *East Coker*, the second of *Four Quartets*.

90. Michael's registration for the army. See July 11, 1941, n. 46; last letter for 1941, undated, n. 105.

91. *English Poetic Mind* was published by the Oxford University Press in 1932.

92. W. B. Yeats, "When you are old . . ." written to Maude Goone.

93. Hubert Foss.

94. In 1923 Sir Humphrey started a special music department and chose Norman Peterkin, a composer of moderate reputation, as sales manager.

95. Ralph Vaughan Williams (1872–1958), distinguished and influential English composer.

96. See Jan. 4, 1940, n. 1.

97. An arrow points to a distortion in the handwriting.

98. This undated letter is found in this position in the original file. Nothing in the content suggests another positioning.

99. See Jan. 4, 1940, n. 1.

100. See Sept. 10, 1941, n. 87.

101. C. E. M. Joad was a Cambridge professor. In C.W.'s review in *Time and Tide* (Mar. 13, 1943) of Professor Joad's book *God and Evil*, he says that a "sense of sin" has led Joad to believe the religious hypothesis is true but that he remains non-Christian and dualistic. "I do not think myself," he writes, "that the 'sense of sin' is wholly explicable without the Incarnation and the Cross, because I do not think that a sense of justice between man and God can exist without the Incarnation and the Cross." See also C.W.'s essay "What the Cross Means to Me," *Charles Williams: Essential Writings in Spirituality and Theology*, ed. Charles Heffling (Boston: Cowley Publications, 1993), 191–203.

102. Mrs. Henry Wood was the author of many popular novels, including *East Lynne*.

103. Eliot's poem *East Coker*. See Oct. 1, 1941, n. 89.

104. The *Periodical* was a small magazine describing the activities and offerings of the Oxford University Press. It contained comments on recent publications, literary chitchat, and advertisements. C.W. took over the editorship in 1941.

105. This is the last letter in the 1941 file. Apparently Michal and Michael were back in the London flat. The next letter is dated February 2, 1942. In the interval of three months a great deal occurred on which we have, however, little specific information.

On November 6, C.W. wrote to Phyllis Potter: "My son is being swept into the Air Force this week, much to everyone's gloom. Fools say 'it will make a man of him;' wiser people like me and his mother, sit agnostically hoping it may not make a beast. . . . He is in a very bad temper. . . . My wife dangerously but beautifully proposes to come to Oxford under my pressure . . . I go to London to-night to fail in saying the right things to Michael. If I were a saint—that is, if I had been different . . . pass, we do as we may."

On 11 December he wrote again to Phyllis: "I am no happier about Michael. He is doing his best in every way, but it is going to be a difficult business—one way or another. . . . We shall be in Oxford over Christmas unless I have to rush down to Weston where my son is. But we are thinking of coming up to London in the New Year."

By the time of the next letter, February 2, 1942, C.W. and Michael, now discharged from the army, were back in Oxford; Michal was in the London flat.

1942

1. See last letter for 1941, undated, n. 105.

2. See Aug. 27, 1941, n. 81.

3. Sampson was an editor at Geoffrey Bles, London, publisher of *The Forgiveness of Sins*.

4. This is the first indication that they are giving up the London flat. On April 21 he wrote to Phyllis Potter that he expected that in two or three weeks the London flat would be vacated. On May 28 he told her that they had abandoned the flat and that they all were in Oxford.

5. For "spoil the Egyptians," see Exod. 3:22.

6. The play *The Three Temptations*. See Aug. 27, 1941, n. 81.

7. The Gloria was Number 4 of a group of sonnets under the general heading "To Michal: Sonnets after Marriage," in Charles Williams, *Windows of Night* (London: Oxford University Press, 1924), 67.

8. The hotel in Canterbury where he and Michal were to go for the enthronement of William Temple as the eighty-eighth archbishop of Canterbury.

9. *The Winter's Tale*, 4.3.144–46:

> So singular in each particular,
> Crowns what you are doing in the present deed,
> That all your acts are queens.

10. Robin Milford. See Jan. 4, 1940, n. 1.

11. The Fellowship of Reconciliation was a passivist organization to which several of C.W.'s friends belonged.

12. St. Anne's was the Williams family's church in London.

13. There are no letters between this one and the one written on September 6. The cause for this long silence, in broad outline, is clear, although details are scarce. In early May they disposed of their flat in London and Michal went to Oxford to join her husband and son. During the period she was often in Lutterworth with her sister, but if there were correspondence between C.W. and Michal during this period—it is difficult to believe there was not—it has not survived. On September 9 C.W. wrote to Phyllis Potter: "Every thing has blown sideways (a) by Michael's having got so worked up that we had to get him away. . . . So they are both at Lutterworth now." Michael finally broke under the tension caused by his increasing frustration over being in Oxford and by his dissatisfaction with his work at Blackwell's. He spent some time in Lutterworth and then with Ursula Grundy in London before the Williamses reestablished a residence of their own in Antrim Mansions, Antrim Road, Hampstead, and Michal and Michael settled there.

14. She had just returned to Lutterworth.

15. *The Forgiveness of Sins.*

16. A favorite image along with "pattern," both summarized in the "Prelude" to Charles Williams, *Taliessin through Logres* (London: Oxford University Press, 1938), 7–9.

> Carbonek, Camelot, Caucasia,
> were gates and containers, intermediations of light;
> geography breathing geometry, the double-fledged Logos.

"Pattern" for C.W. was not to be equated with stasis. Rather, he defined systems, thoughts, and things in terms of their opposites—good with evil, belief with unbelief, restraint with freedom. It is not that one thing is as "true" as the other but rather that we can think of either only in contest with the other. As in "Taliessin at Lancelot's Mass," *Taliessin through Logres*, 49–52.

> That which had been Taliessin rose in the rood;
> in the house of Galahad over the altar he stood,
> manacled by the web, in the web made free;
> there was no capable song for the joy in me: . . .

17. But see Sept. 7, 1942, n. 21.

18. Apparently a "vacation" from Blackwell's.

19. John T. Trevor of the Pilgrim Players.

20. *The Three Temptations.*

21. See Sept. 6, 1942, n. 17.

22. Baron Friedrich von Hügel, a Roman Catholic philosopher and theologian with whom Evelyn Underhill began a friendship in 1911 that was to influence the development of her own Anglican spirituality. C.W. read von Hügel as part of his preparation for editing and introducing Underhill's letters, which were published in 1943.

23. *The Silver Stair*, C.W.'s first book of poems consisting of eighty-four sonnets on the subject of romantic love, for and to Florence Conway who was to become his Michal.

24. *The Three Temptations.*

25. Alicia had died, C.W. had been to Lutterworth, and Michael was with Ursula Grundy.

26. Cumberlege became publisher upon Sir Humphrey's retirement.

27. He had been in Lutterworth for the weekend.

28. A flat in London. See Feb. 9, 1942, n. 4.

29. *The Three Temptations* was broadcast on November 1, 1942. See Nov. 2, 1942, n. 36.

30. No such readings materialized.

31. Evelyn Underhill.

32. Indecipherable word.

33. "Ceremony" is probably a reference to the lecture he was to give at Cambridge.

34. Williams, *Religion and Love in Dante* (London: Dacre Press, 1941).

35. Barnett Freedman, a painter friend of Anne Spalding's who taught at the Ruskin School of Drawing, now a part of Oxford University.

36. This reference would place the broadcast on November 1, 1942.

37. J. G. Wilson was the well-known manager of the Bumpus Book Shop on Oxford Street, at which Michael secured a job in 1943.

1943

1. Wallis was the caretaker of the building in which their flat in London was located. See n. 3 below.

2. He was to be awarded an honorary master of arts degree by Oxford.

3. After having given up their London flat in early 1942, they had become reestablished at 23 Antrim Mansions, Antrim Road, Hampstead, NW 3.

4. See Feb. 14, 1943, n. 9.

5. Charles Williams, ed., *Letters of Evelyn Underhill* (London: Longmans, Green, 1943).

6. The typescript of the Underhill letters from which he had worked.

7. An echo of the famous opening lines of Jane Austen's *Pride and Prejudice.*

8. Barbara Ward of the *Dublin Review.* See Williams, "A Dialogue on Mr. Eliot's Poem," *Dublin Review* 212 (Apr. 1943): 114–22.

9. Named for Edward Bouverie Pusey.

10. Shakespeare, *Julius Caesar,* 2.1.288.

11. *The Letters of Evelyn Underhill.*

12. R. W. Chapman was secretary to the delegates of the Oxford University Press.

13. A distaste for "bodies," "faces," and human society in general, and "wells of hate" were a paradoxical dark undercurrent in C.W.'s psyche, tendencies he struggled to overcome. See June 15, 1943, n. 72; Oct. 15, 1943, n. 122; Oct. 18, 1943, n. 124; Dec. 9[10], 1943, n. 137; Mar. 14, 1944, n. 22; May 17, 1944, n. 45; June 1, 1944, n. 51; June 6, 1944, n. 60.

14. He would be fire-watching.

15. See Sept. 23, 1942, n. 33.

16. See Aug. 14, 1940, n. 167.

17. This letter was found in the Wheaton file among letters dated 1942. The dating is clear; it is, however, also clear that the letter could not have been written so early. That the forthcoming degree was public knowledge in early February 1942 is contrary to the certain chronology of events. That the matter was first made public in early 1943 is clear from the letter of February 12, 1943. The only explanation is that C.W.—once again—erred in dating his letter. This one clearly falls where I have placed it. See, for example, especially Feb. 27[24], 1940, n. 32.

18. He had apparently gone back with her to London for a week after she left Oxford following the ceremony.

19. Alice Mary Hadfield summarizes his heavy lecturing schedule during 1943 as follows: "eight University lectures on Wordsworth and eight on Shakespeare at the Taylorian, as well as 'The Arthurian Tradition in English Literature' at Lady Margaret Hall, 'After Falstaff' to the Oxford

Graduates Society and at Lady Margaret Hall, 'Is there a Christian Literature?' in a series at Pusey House, and 'Religion and Drama' to the Student Christian Movement in the Old Library of St. Mary's the University Church. In 1944 he gave thirteen lectures on Shakespeare and eight on eighteenth-century poetry; in 1945 eight on Milton" (*Outlines of Romantic Theology*, [Grand Rapids, Mich.: William B. Eerdmans, 1990], 188).

20. A paraphrase of the voice St. Paul heard in a vision: "Come over into Macedonia, and help us" (Acts 16:9).

21. This book did not materialize. But see Apr. 6, 1943, n. 36.

22. The ceremony at which he received the degree.

23. He is speaking of her in the new flat in Antrim Road in Hampstead. See Feb. 12, 1943, n. 3.

24. Possibly from "Bors to Elayne: The Fish of Broceliande" (24–26), but more likely to "Bors to Elayne: On the King's Coins" (42–45), both in *Taliessin through Logres*.

25. See "The Departure of Dindrane."

26. He was lecturing at Reading.

27. Any of the four days regarded as beginning a new quarter of the year, when quarterly payments on rents and other obligations are due.

28. Their Hampstead flat at 23 Antrim Mansions.

29. "The Prayers of the Pope," from *The Region of the Summer Stars*, which was published in 1944.

30. Evelyn Underhill. The introduction to her letters.

31. The aunt was a relative of the Spaldings, an occasional visitor at South Parks Road.

32. The book was never written.

33. This style is exemplified in "The Prayers of the Pope."

34. "Taliessin in the Rose Garden," 134–37:

> The roseal pattern
> ran together, and was botched and blotched, blood
> inflaming the holy dark; the way of return
> climbed beside the timed and falling blood. . . .

The same image appears also in "The Founding of the Company" and "The Queen's Servant." The three poems along with "The Prayers of the Pope" all are included in *The Region of the Summer Stars*.

35. See May 5, 1943, n. 55.

36. See Mar. 30, 1943, n. 32.

37. The cauldron especially in Celtic lore symbolizes transformation and rebirth—a process exemplified in the mythical figure of one Gwion Bach through several stages, the last of which is a grain of corn which is swallowed by Ceridwen, who appears in the form of a hen. The corn becomes a fetus in the womb of a goddess and is reborn as Taliessin, the poet (Caitlin Matthews, *The Elements of the Celtic Tradition* [Longmead, Chaftsbury, Dorset: Element Books, 1989], 109–10). Some elements of this myth are made use of in C.W.'s poem "The Calling of Taliessin," *Region of the Summer Stars*, 11.1–70. It must be emphasized, however, that C.W.'s interest is in the process of the transformation itself and not in literal details of its symbolic presentation—details which he changes considerably. In another connection he writes: "There has been much controversy about them—vessels of plenty and cauldrons of magic—and they have been supposed by learned experts to be the origin of the Grail myth. That, in the Scriptural and ecclesiastical sense, they certainly cannot be. Cup or dish or container of whatever kind, the Grail in its origin entered Europe with the Christian and Catholic faith. . . . It was therefore, in the very idea of it, greater than any vessel of less intention could possibly be. If it swallowed up its lesser rivals, it did so exactly because it was greater. . . . It absorbed or excluded all else; *sui generis*, it shone alone" (C. S. Lewis, *Arthurian Torso* [London: Oxford University Press, 1948], 23).

38. *The Figure of Beatrice.*

39. By Edith he perhaps means his sister, in view of letters of April 9, 1943.

40. He would go to Leyton to visit his aunt Edith Wall.

41. *Taliessin* is a reference to the eight poems published in 1944 under the title *The Region of the Summer Stars.*

42. Their wedding anniversary was April 12.

43. Anne Ridler.

44. The image is expanded in "The Founding of the Company," 94–110, one of the poems on which he was working at the time. See Mar. 25, 1943, n. 29.

45. *The Figure of Beatrice.*

46. George Kenneth Allen Bell (1881–1958) was the bishop of Chichester.

47. In the early 1920s C.W. began work on an essay titled "Outline of Romantic Theology." In 1924 he submitted an unfinished version to Sir Humphrey Milford, who, in turn, sent it to the bishop of Ripon for comments. Details of the response are not known but were apparently cautious; at any rate, Sir Humphrey decided he could not publish it. A revised version was sent to the Nonesuch Press in 1925, but it too was rejected. Still further revised, the manuscript was sent to Faber and Gwyer, later Faber and Faber, but put on hold. C.W. continued to feel that theological timidity kept the book from being published. The central concept that the union of man and woman, physically and spiritually, was a means toward union with God became a central theme in all his work that followed. The early work, along with *Religion and Love in Dante: The Theology of Romantic Love,* was edited and introduced by Alice Mary Hadfield in 1990 under the title *Outlines of Romantic Theology.*

48. "The Prayers of the Pope." See Mar. 25, 1943, n. 29.

49. Psa. 87:7: "all my springs are in thee."

50. Possibly a reference to Isa. 12:3: "with joy shall ye draw water out of the wells of salvation."

51. Lord Byron: "She walks in beauty, like the night."

52. "Hand" is an image he uses frequently. He calls hands "love's instruments to love." There is a graphic example of its perversion near the beginning of chapter 5, "The Hall by Holborn," *All Hallows' Eve.*

53. The proposed book on Wordsworth. See Mar. 30, 1943, n. 32.

54. Dr. Robert Havard practiced medicine in the Oxford suburb of Headington. He was a friend of C. S. Lewis and C.W. and a member of the Inklings.

55. See Apr. 6, 1943, n. 35.

56. Lord David Cecil was a scholar and a professor of English literature at Oxford. He edited the *Oxford Book of Christian Verse* in 1940, including C.W.'s poem "At the 'Ye that do truly.'"

57. Wordsworth, *Prelude,* 2.42–44.

58. The poetry reading. See May 5, 1943, n. 55.

59. Kipling, "The Palace":

> After me cometh a builder, tell him
> "I too have known."

60. He means "genius" in the sense of a "particular character or essential spirit or nature," i.e., his poetic gift.

61. He had in mind the great but flawed Achilles as he is depicted in Shakespeare's *Antony and Cleopatra.*

62. "Functions and offices" indicates an aesthetic as well as romantic principle for C.W. On the flyleaf of *Taliessin through Logres* he places a quotation from Dante's *De Monarchia* (1.3) and repeats it with comment in *The Figure of Beatrice* (p. 40). In his translation it reads, "The proper operation (working or function) is not for the sake of being but for the sake of the operation." He comments: "Dante was created in order to do his business, to fulfil his function." As was C.W.

63. Fellowship of Reconciliation was a passivist organization to which several of C.W.'s friends belonged.

64. See July 15, 1941, n. 52; Aug. 1, 1941, n. 57; Aug. 7, 1941, n. 63.

65. The "Figure of Arthur," unfinished at the time of his death, was published in 1948 by C. S. Lewis, along with a commentary on the poems in *Taliessin Through Logres* and *The Region of the Summer Stars* under the title *Arthurian Torso*.

66. "The hill" was a spot outside Hampstead associated in his mind with his courtship of Florence Conway.

67. The lines appear in "The Queen's Servant," 30–31:

> bright as a sudden irrepressible smile
> drive across a golden-fleeced landscape.

68. The novel is possibly *All Hallows' Eve.* n. 170.

69. See June 7, 1943, n. 65.

70. She was obviously his most sensitive, severest, treasured critic. See Oct. 7, 1943, nn. 113, 114; May 23, 1944, n. 49; Oct. 18, 1944, n. 135; Feb. 15, 1945, n. 24.

71. Shakespeare, *Merchant of Venice*, 4.1.228–29:

> An oath, an oath, I have an oath in heaven:
> Shall I lay perjury upon my soul?

72. See Feb. 17, 1943, n. 13.

73. See June 10, 1943, n. 68.

74. St. Hilda's was one of the then four women's colleges on the Oxford campus.

75. A real start, on the novel. See Dec. 17, 1940, n. 206.

76. The Epistle Dedicatory to the Authorized Version of the Bible: "the appearance of Your Majesty, as of the Sun in his strength."

77. Matt. 12:39: "An evil and adulterous generation seeketh after a sign; and there shall no sign be given to it."

78. 2 Sam. 6:6–7: "Uzzah put forth his hand to the ark of God, and took hold of it; for the oxen shook it. / And the anger of the Lord was kindled against Uzzah; and God smote him there for his error."

79. Exod. 5:7. "Ye shall no more give the people straw to make brick, as heretofore: let them go and gather straw for themselves."

80. Although Wordsworth used the word "power" often, C.W. might have had in mind the following, from *Prelude*, 14.189–92:

> This spiritual Love acts not nor can exist
> Without Imagination, which, in truth,
> Is but another name for absolute power
> And clearest insight, amplitude of mind,
> And Reason in her most exalted mood.

81. Unsigned [but by Desmond McCarthy], "Dante's Beatrice: Knower, Known, Knowing," *Times Literary Supplement*, July 24, 1943, 358, a very favorable review. He writes: "According to Mr. Williams's view, the whole of Dante's thought is summed up in her person. In his youth he was struck with the *stupor* of love at first sight; and, as he himself has said, the effect of the *stupor* is, first, to set up the sense of awe, and then to create the desire for full knowledge of the beloved object. Under the influence of the awe of love, the lover sees the very meaning and explanation of the universe in the person of the beloved; and therefore the desire for knowledge cannot be fully satisfied until understanding is gained of the whole order of creation in which she is set, and by virtue of which she exists."

82. See Mar. 14, 1940, no. 58.

83. Alfred Tennyson, "A Dream of Fair Women," 85–88:

> At length I saw a Lady within call,
> Stiller than a chisell'd marble, standing there;
> A daughter of the gods, divinely tall;
> And most divinely fair.

84. Chapter 3 of *All Hallows' Eve.*

85. The last letter containing a poem was the one dated June 20, 1943.

86. "Retreating" in the sense meaning going back to you, finding their source in you.

87. See Jan. 12, 1944, n. 8.

88. Wordsworth, "London, 1802," 9: "Thy soul [Milton's] was like a star, and dwelt apart."

89. Raymond Hunt (see Glossary).

90. The house at 3 Camden Road, Holloway, London N7, where C.W. was born on September 20, 1886. On September 20, 1986, on the occasion of the centenary event, the Charles Williams Society placed a plaque on the outside wall marking the birth spot.

91. John Keats, "Ode to a Nightingale," 15–16: "O for a beaker full of the warm South, / Full of the true, the blushful Hippocrene."

92. Barbara Ward of the *Dublin Review.*

93. "Malory and the Grail Legend," *Dublin Review* 214 (Apr. 1944): 144–53, reprinted in Ridler, *Image of the City*, 186–94.

94. In the sense that he uses the word in the first chapter of *Descent into Hell* when he speaks of "terribly good"—painfully, costly, as in Good Friday.

95. Discarded chapters of *The Noises That Weren't There.* See Dec. 17, 1940, n. 206.

96. See Feb. 14, 1940, n. 31.

97. A biography, *Flecker of Dean Close*, undertaken by C.W. largely for financial reasons. It occupied a great deal of time in preparation and was not published until after his death.

98. *Antony and Cleopatra*, 1.3.88–91:

> Sir, you and I have lov'd, but there's not it;
> That you know well: something it is I would,—
> O! my oblivion is a very Antony,
> And I am all forgotten.

99. Abstractly, the imaginative vision project in *Outline of Romantic Theology;* more concretely, his love for Florence Conway celebrated in his early poetry, particularly *The Silver Stair.*

100. "Mr Williams has written a finer and more important book than can well be indicated in a brief review" *Spectator* 117 (Sept. 3, 1943).

101. Christopher Hollis, "The Figure of Beatrice," quoted by Humphrey Carpenter in *The Inklings: C. S. Lewis, J. R. R. Tolkien, Charles Williams, and Their Friends* (Boston: Houghton Mifflin, 1979), 188: "Dante is perhaps the only great poet of whom one can quite literally say that no man can understand anything who does not understand him, and Mr. Williams's book is not one to pass an idle afternoon, but one to be kept continually at hand until it becomes a part of the furniture of the mind."

102. *All Hallows' Eve.*

103. See Sept. 3, 1943, n. 97.

104. William Cowper, "Verses Supposed to Be Written by Alexander Solkirk":

> Oh, solitude! where are thy charms
> that sages have seen in thy face?

105. *Flecker of Dean Close.*

106. See Dec. 17, 1940, n. 206.

107. Review of *Petrarch and the Renascence*, by J. H. Whitfield, *Time and Tide* 24 (Nov. 6, 1943): 907–8.

108. *All Hallows' Eve.*

109. This letter and the next are dated October 7. I have left them in that order because there is no certain information by which to order them.

110. *All Hallows' Eve.*

111. *The Region of the Summer Stars.*

112. Review of "The Fortunes of Falstaff," by J. D. Wilson, *Time and Tide* 24 (Oct. 1943), reprinted in Ridler, *Image of the City*, 40–42.

113. See note 114 below.

114. She had said that his women were "a man's image of a woman" and, therefore, unrealistic.

115. Of *All Hallows' Eve.*

116. The Flecker book was published after his death.

117. For the American girl, see letter of Oct. 13, 1943.

118. Ben Jonson (1707–1866). These along with C.W. make a rather odd combination.

119. Margaret Sinclair, secretary of the United Church Council for Missionary Education, requested C.W. to write a play which the organization could produce to advance its cause. The result was *The House of the Octopus* about which he said while he was writing it, "I shall make this play as bitter as I know how. It will show them what I think of men." See letter of June 2, 1944.

120. Renée Haynes was the author of *Pan, Cesar, and God*, the third in the I Believe Series of personal statements, published by Heineman. C.W. wrote *He Came Down from Heaven* as the fifth in the series. He met Haynes at a party for contributors and saw her off and on while he was in Oxford.

121. Alfred L. Rowse, poet, biographer, historian, and critic, best known perhaps for his Shakespeare criticism.

122. See Feb. 17, 1943, n. 13.

123. Austin Farrer was a distinguished theologian and brilliant preacher. He became warden of Keble College, Oxford, in 1960. In 1943 he published *Finite and Infinite: A Philosophical Essay.* Obviously, C.W. had not read the book but had heard of it from his Oxford friends.

124. Wordsworth, *The Prelude*, 2.315–18:

> the soul,
> Remembering how she felt, but what she felt
> Remembering not, retains an obscure sense
> Of possible sublimity, . . .

125. Edmund Blunden, critic, biographer, and editor, was involved early in the so-called Georgian Movement, an association which he later renounced. Although C.W. speaks slightingly of him, he became professor of poetry at Oxford in 1966, long after C.W.'s death.

126. See Feb. 17, 1943, n. 13.

127. This is not a direct quotation. It might refer to Rom. 15:8, or 1 Cor. 1:8, or 2 Cor. 2:8.

128. Betty is a character in *All Hallows' Eve.* The event referred to here occurs in chapter 4, "The Dream," about one-third of the way through the novel.

129. Alice Wall, his mother's brother's wife, was instrumental in helping him get his first job at the Methodist Book Store in London in 1904. She was at one time in bad health and in financial difficulties.

130. The writing throughout this letter is almost illegible, and this word is uncertain.

131. In the early 1920s C.W. began lecturing to evening classes sponsored by the London Council, an activity he continued through the years. It was here that he attracted many of his early admirers, some of whom were instrumental in the formation of the Charles Williams Society in 1976.

132. *All Hallows' Eve.*

133. John Keats, "To Sleep":

> Turn the key deftly in the oiled wards,
> And seal the hushed casket of my soul.

134. Margaret Sinclair. See Oct. 14, 1943, n. 119.

135. See Nov. 8, 1943, n. 136.

136. Review of *Paradiso,* by Laurence Binyon, *Britain Today* 95 (Mar. 1944): 27–27). See Nov. 4, 1943, n. 136.

137. See Feb. 17, 1943, n. 13.

138. Alice Wall. See Oct. 29, 1943, n. 129.

139. "His [Lord Lytton's] wife, pointing to a row of dolls of various sizes, replied with pride, 'And I, too, my lord, have not been idle.'" G. W. E. Russell, *Collections and Recollections*, cited in *The Oxford Dictionary of Quotations*, 2d ed. (London: Oxford University Press, 1953), 7.

140. Cambridge Press.

1944

1. C.W.'s review in *Time and Tide* for August 26, 1944, is followed immediately by *Shakespearean Comedy and Other Studies* by George Gordon. The reviewer is Michael Blain. See Jan. 4, 1944, n. 5; Aug. 25, 1944, n. 114.

2. Radley was a well-known school for boys outside Radley, where he was to lecture.

3. Samuel Johnson, "On the Death of Mr. Levett," 27–28.

4. See Oct. 29, 1943, n. 128.

5. See Jan. 3, 1944, n. 1.

6. *All Hallows' Eve.*

7. The Inklings met regularly in C. S. Lewis's room at Magdalen College.

8. See Aug. 20, 1943, n. 87; Oct. 7, 1943, n. 114. She offered the same criticism of the female characters in his novels.

9. "This whipped Jackal [Mussolini] who, to save his own skin, has made of Italy a vassal state of Hitler's empire, is frisking up beside the German tiger with yelps not only of appetite— that could be understood—but even of triumph" (Speech, House of Commons, Apr. 1941).

10. Shakespeare, *The Winter's Tale*, 4.3.144–46. See [Apr. 24/25], 1942, n. 9.

11. A distaste for "bodies," "faces," and human society in general is a dark undercurrent in C.W.'s psyche, a tendency he struggled against. See Feb. 17, 1943, n. 13.

12. Williams, *What the Cross Means to Me: A Theological Symposium* (London: James Clarke, 1942), reprinted in *Ridler, Image of the City*, 132–39; Hefling, ed., *Charles Williams*, 191–203.

13. See Glossary.

14. *Region of the Summer Stars.*

15. A readership position at Oxford became progressively more attractive to him. See especially June 29, 1944, n. 77; Aug. 10, 1944, n. 95; Oct. 14, 1944, n. 132; Feb. 21, 1945, n. 35.

16. See June 29, 1944, n. 77.

17. See especially June 7, 1943, n. 65.

18. On Lewis's brother, see especially *Brothers and Friends: An Intimate Portrait of C. S. Lewis: The Diaries of Major Warren Hamilton Lewis*, ed. Clyde S. Kilby and Marjorie Lamp Mead (San Francisco: Harper & Row, 1982). The book contains valuable material about C.W. during his Oxford years.

19. Mr. Welch, director of religious programming at the BBC.

20. Possibly a restatement of St. Paul in 1 Tim. 2:7: "Whereunto I am ordained a preacher, and an apostle."

21. See *All Hallows Eve*, 147. There is also a poem on page 36 of *Windows of Night* called "A Cup of Water" that may be autobiographical. It illustrates how for C.W. everyday thoughts and actions slip easily into metaphysical proclamations:

> I saw, remote and far in the night,
> Our mother Christendom pausing from war and drinking
> A cup of water,—and sleep came down on the sight.

22. See Feb. 17, 1943, n. 13.

23. Review of *Roman Vergil*, W. Jackson Knight, *Time and Tide* 25 (Apr. 1, 1944): 289–90, reprinted in Ridler, *Image of the City*, 123–26.

24. Alice Wall.

25. "The Figure of Arthur."

26. Their wedding anniversary was April 12.

27. A metaphysical perception from which the part is seen as an epitome of the whole, the microcosm and the macrocosm. For example, in chapter 4 of *Shadows of Ecstasy* Philip, the lover, sees in the outstretched arm of his beloved something greater than the arm itself—that of which the arm is an essential epitome: "He had seen the verge of a great conclusion of mortal things and then it had vanished. Over that white curve he had looked into incredible space; abysses of intelligence lay beyond it."

28. George Bell, bishop of Chichester, for whom C.W. did some editorial work.

29. The new Catholic archbishop was David Matthews.

30. Alfred Tennyson, "The Day Dream, 'The Revival,'" 163–64:

> But dallied with his golden chain,
> And, smiling, put the question by.

31. *Purgatorio*, 30.73–74. Quoted in *The Figure of Beatrice* (London: Faber and Faber, 1943), 180, and there translated: "Yes, look well; We are, We are, Beatrice: How is it you have deigned to draw near the mountain? did you not know that here man is happy?" He also writes: "The Betrician moment is a moment of revelation and communicated conversion by means of a girl" (123).

32. V. H. Collins was a onetime colleague at the Oxford University Press.

33. Review of St. Augustine, *Confessions*, trans. F. J. Sheed, in *The Incarnation of the Word of God, Time and Tide* 25 (June 24, 1944), reprinted in Ridler, *Image of the City*, 89–91.

34. Evelyn in *All Hallows' Eve* refused salvation.

35. *All Hallows' Eve*.

36. C.W.'s prediction was fairly accurate. The invasion began on June 6, and, after almost a year of brutal warfare, the Germans surrendered on May 7, 1945.

37. Herbert Strong was a London printer and publisher of a firm that did considerable business with the Oxford University Press. Strong was involved in the production of *Heroes and Kings* published in 1930. C.W. also read manuscripts for him.

38. Hubert Foss.

39. *All Hallows' Eve*.

40. "Figure of Arthur."

41. See Apr. 24, 1944, n. 33.

42. Shakespeare, *Othello*, 402.56–59:

> But there, where I have garner'd up my heart,
> Where either I must live or bear no life,
> The fountain from the which my current runs
> Or else dries up; to be discarded thence!

43. A better novel than *All Hallows' Eve*.

44. Shakespeare, *As You Like It*, 5.2.36–37: "Caesar's thrasonical brag of I came, saw, and overcame." Derived from the name of the braggart soldier in a play by Terrance.

45. See Feb. 17, 1943, n. 13.

46. He refers, no doubt, to *Seed of Adam, The Death of Good Fortune, The House by the Stable,* and *Grab and Grace*. They were edited by Anne Ridler and published by the Oxford University Press in 1948.

47. Herbert Strong. See May 5, 1944, n. 37.

48. R. M. Leonard, a longtime member of the Press staff and editor of the Press publication *Periodical.*

49. See June 10, 1943, n. 70.

50. See May 5, 1944, n. 37; June 2, 1944, n. 55.

51. See Feb. 17, 1943, n. 13.

52. *All Hallows' Eve.*

53. Song of Solomon 4:16: "Awake, O north wind; and come, thou South; blow upon my garden."

54. Sir John Denham, "Cooper's Hill," 189: "Strong with rage, without o'erflowing full."

55. See May 5, 1944, n. 37; June 1, 1944, n. 50.

56. Thomas Gray, "Elegy Written in a Country Churchyard," 55–56: "Full many a flower is born . . . / waste its sweetness on the desert air."

57. *The House of the Octopus.*

58. D-Day, June 6—the launching of the invasion that was to bring about the total collapse of the German forces and to end the war in Europe.

59. Vivian Ridler.

60. See Feb. 17, 1943, n. 13.

61. Psa. 92:7: "When all the workers of iniquity do flourish; it is that they shall be destroyed for ever."

62. *The Region of the Summer Stars.*

63. John Milton, "On His Blindness," 14: "They also serve who only stand and wait."

64. The invasion. See May 5, 1944, n. 36; June 6, 1944, n. 58.

65. The relationship between Gerry and Phyllis Jones which Hadfield delicately describes: "revealed in his shock and distress a more deadly blow, that he and Phyllis loved each other" (*Outlines of Romantic Theology*, 83).

66. Mrs. Oliver was a neighborhood acquaintance whom C.W. uses as representative of middle-class society and culture. This is one of the best descriptions of what he means by the term.

67. St. Paul uses the epithet in Rom. 11:20, 1 Tim. 6:17, and 2 Tim. 3:4.

68. See [Apr. 24/25, 1942], n. 9.

69. The battle of Blenheim was fought on August 13, 1704, under the Duke of Marlborough and Prince Eugenia of Austria, defeating the Bavarians and the French. The victory, Marlborough's greatest, saved Austria.

70. Tennyson, "The Higher Pantheism," 12.

71. Radley was the location of a well-known school for boys.

72. Brackets in original.

73. Helen Gardner (Dame Helen Louise), an important critic and scholar, is known particularly for her edition of *The Divine Poems of John Donne* and for her work on T. S. Eliot's *Four Quartets*. Both of these works, however, were published years after C.W.'s death.

74. "The Figure of Arthur."

75. Robert Graves was a poet, novelist, critic, and mythologist. C.W. was certainly familiar with his book *The Story of Mary Powell*, which was published in 1943. The book referred to here might be *The White Goddess: A Historical Grammar of Poetic Myth*, which was not published until 1948. Much of his important work on myth came after C.W.'s death.

76. Tolkien was known to his friends as Tollers.

77. The decision about a position at Oxford. See Feb. 5, 1944, n. 15.

78. Shakespeare, *Twelfth-Night*, 1.1.5–6: "O! it came o'er my ear like the sweet sound / That breathes upon a bank of violets."

79. The "silly mistake" was his incorrect memory of the payment date on a contract with Faber.

80. A review that was published in *Time and Tide*. See Jan. 3, 1944, n. 1; Jan. 4, 1944, n. 5.

81. See Apr. 18, 1940, n. 69.

82. See July 6, 1944, n. 78.

83. Bank holiday.

84. The Spaldings were further delayed and had not returned at the time of C.W.'s death.

85. *The Figure of Beatrice.*

86. Shakespeare, *Julius Caesar*, 4.3.9–10: "Let me tell you Cassius, you yourself / Are much condemn'd to have an itching palm."

87. See Feb. 13, 1940, n. 27.

88. Wilfrid Gibson. C.W. wrote the introduction for Gibson's *Solway Ford and Other Poems* (London: Faber and Faber, 1945).

89. Veronica was a member of the *Time and Tide* staff.

90. Margaret Douglas. She typed many of his manuscripts.

91. Review of *Milton, Man and Thinker*, by Denis Saurat, *Spectator* 173 (Aug. 18, 1944): 154.

92. *The House of the Octopus.*

93. He had spent time with Michal in London.

94. *The House of the Octopus.*

95. Das Staatliche Bauhaus was a school formed in 1919 by Walter Gropius to promote the modern movement in painting, sculpture, the industrial arts, and architecture. It was closed in 1933 by the German Nationalist government for its suspect social ideology.

96. See Feb. 5, 1944, n. 15.

97. John Francis Alexander Heath-Stubbs, important poet and critic, was an early member of the Charles Williams Society and author of a short but very good monograph on C.W. He also edited and introduced *Collected Plays by Charles Williams.*

98. Perhaps the contract for "The Figure of Arthur."

99. *All Hallows' Eve.*

100. *Region of the Summer Stars.*

101. Alice Wall.

102. *The House of the Octopus.*

103. Edward Prince of Wales, son of Edward III, became a legendary figure for his prowess in battle. He was called the Black Prince by ancient accounts because of the terror of his arms. Here C.W., consistent with ancient tradition, attributes to him a great devotion to the Holy Trinity. See E. Cobham Brewer, *Dictionary of Phrase and Fable* (London: Cassell, 1899).

104. See Aug. 11, 1944, n. 96.

105. A possible parody of the popular war song "Praise the Lord, and pass the ammunition."

106. Dame Edith Sitwell, *Green Song and Other Poems* (London: Macmillan, 1944).

107. New York branch of the Oxford University Press. The subject was Michael's employment. See Apr. 18, 1940, n. 69.

108. In the original file this letter and the one following were placed in the reverse order to that here. I have rearranged them because the letter referring to the freeing of Paris could not have been written before August 24, the date on which the event occurred. This, however, introduces another problem. There is already a letter in the file dated August 24. It is possible that the two letters were written on the same day, the one in the morning upon first hearing the news and the other after he had reflected on it. It may also be another example of C.W.'s frequent confusion about the date of the day. The sequence of the letters, however, cannot be questioned.

109. *The House of the Octopus.*

110. Review of Raissa Maritain's book in *Time and Tide* 25 (Oct. 28, 1944): 946–47.

111. Review of *Milton, Man and Thinker,* by Denis Saurat, *Spectator* 173 (Aug. 18, 1944): 154.

112. See Aug. 17, 1942, n. 107.

113. Judg. 5:31: "So let all thy enemies perish, O Lord."

114. See Jan. 3, 1944, n. 1; Jan. 4, 1944, n. 5.

115. Letters. Nov. 21, 1944, n. 148.

116. *The House of the Octopus.*

117. *The House of the Octopus.*

118. For a more rational, complex view see the last chapter of *Forgiveness of Sins:* "It is (let it be repeated) the guilty who forgives and not the innocent; not perhaps the guilty in that one act, but guilty of how much else; of how much that led up to that act, guilty even in the very act of mutual pardon—that is, of mutual reconciled love—of how much of weakness, folly, reluctance, pride, or greed. The guilty repents; the as greatly guilty forgives; there is therefore but one maxim for both: 'make haste.' It is one thing to be reasonably intelligent, but quite another to be curiously inquisitive or carefully watchful. We are part of him and he of us; that is the centre; by his death there—his death in that repentance—we live, and he by ours: 'dying each other's life, living each other's death.' It is all a question of whether he and we choose or do not choose."

119. Compare with his description of Taliessin in "The Calling of Taliessin." But see also Nov. 29, 1944, nn. 155 and 156, where he identifies with Bors.

120. John Webster, *The Duchess of Malfi,* with introductions by George Rylands and Charles Williams (London: Sylvan Press, 1945). See Aug. 25, 1944, n. 114.

121. Shakespeare, *Richard III,* 4.4.470: "Is the chair empty? is the sword unsway'd?"

122. Dorothy Sayers.

123. Psa. 59:6: "they make a noise like a dog, and go round about the city."

124. Reunion of Rome and Canterbury.

125. See Sept. 5, 1944, first two paragraphs.

126. Aachen was a symbol as well as a city. Thirty-two Holy Roman emperors and kings were crowned there. Bombed repeatedly by the Allies, it was finally captured October 20, 1944. It was the first large city on German soil to fall to the Allies.

127. See Sept. 7, 1944, n. 118.

128. *All Hallows' Eve.*

129. Dorothy L. Sayers.

130. *The Region of the Summer Stars,* including "The Prayers of the Pope."

131. "To Michal: After Marriage," *The Grasshopper Broadsheets,* ser. no. 10, 1944, edited by Kenneth Hopkins.

132. Review of *Milton, Man and Thinker,* by Denis Saurat, *Spectator* 173 (Aug. 18, 1944): 154.

133. See Feb. 5, 1944, no. 15.

134. Dindrane is a character who represents the idealized woman. He said: "Blessed one, what shall I wish you now but a safe passage through all the impersonalities?" And she: "Most blessed lord, what shall I wish but the return of the personalities, beyond the bond and blessing of departure of personality? I will affirm, my beloved all that I should" (147–52).

135. He refers to the poems in *The Region of the Summer Stars.*

136. See Feb. 17, 1943, n. 13.

137. John Milton, *Paradise Lost,* 8.55–57:

> . . . and solve high dispute
> With conjugal caresses, from his lip
> Not words alone pleased her.

138. Student Christian Movement.

139. Alfred Tennyson, "Tithonus," 1–4:

> The woods decay, the woods decay and fall,
> The vapors weep their burthen to the ground,
> Man comes and tills the field and lies beneath,
> And after many a summer dies the swan.

140. Student Christian Movement.

141. In 1936 C.W. and C. S. Lewis exchanged letters, C.W. admiring Lewis's *The Allegory of Love* and Lewis expressing equal admiration for C.W.'s *The Place of the Lion*. This was the beginning of their close friendship and literary association which culminated during the war years.

142. Dorothy L. Sayers.

143. *Region of the Summer Stars.*

144. Alexander Pope, "An Essay on Criticism," 1.25–27:

> So by false learning is good sense defaced;
> Some are bewildered in the maze of schools,
> And some made coxcombs nature meant but fools.

145. Coventry Patmore, *Amelia*, "Prelude," bk. 2.c.4, Prelude 3, "Valour Misdirected."

146. Matt. 13:45–46: "Again, the kingdom of heaven is like unto a merchant man, seeking goodly pearls: Who, when he had found one pearl of great price, went and sold all he had, and bought it."

147. Prov. 31:10: "Who can find a virtuous woman? for her price is far above rubies."

148. Those who were privileged to hear Williams read generally agreed that his manner of speaking was extraordinary. E. L. Mascall in a brief essay, "Charles Williams as I Knew Him," wrote: "With the Emotional temperament of a Welshman and the accent and sense of humor of a cockney, the impression which an audience received from him on their first meeting could begin with a kind of stunned incredulity, which rapidly passed into wild enthusiasm. I vividly remember the effect which he produced on the students of Lincoln Theological College by reciting the opening lines of Milton's *Paradise Lost*:

> Of man's first disobedience an' the fruit.
> Of that forbidden tree, 'ose mortal tiste
> Brort death into the world and all our wow . . .
> Sing ,'eavenly muse, that on the sicred top . . .

—which was probably much more like Milton's own pronunciation than the etiolated accents of our modern academics" (Horne, *Charles Williams*, 2).

149. See Dec. 21, 1940, n. 209.

150. *The Region of the Summer Stars.*

151. *Silver Stair* was published in 1912.

152. Budgen.

153. See Sept. 15, 1944, n. 120.

154. The Milton script was passages from Milton to be broadcast over the BBC.

155. Percy B. Shelley, "Adonais," 462–65:

> Life, like a dome of many-coloured glass,
> Stains the white radiance of Eternity,
> Until Death tramples it to fragments.—Die,
> If thou wouldst be with that which thou dost seek!

156. But see Sept. 7, 1944, n. 119.

157. See "The Calling of Taliessin," 1–31.

158. See ending of the last chapter of *The Descent of the Dove;* also Sept. 7, 1944, n. 118.

159. See Nov. 29, 1944, n. 154.

160. "The Figure of Arthur."

161. Isabel Duncan.

162. Wilfrid Gibson.

163. "The Figure of Arthur."

1945

1. See chapter 5, "The Coming of the Grail," *The Figure of Arthur,* in Lewis, *Arthurian Toros,* 60–90.

2. See Sept. 15, 1944, n. 120.

3. William Blake, "The Tyger":

> Tyger! Tyger! burning bright
> In the forests of the night,
> What immortal hand or eye
> Could frame thy fearful symmetry?

4. Michael spent a brief time at Weston in the air force.

5. By "parents" C.W. refers to Professor and Mrs. Spalding, who were in America when war was declared and were prevented from returning to England until after the war was over.

6. *Winterset* by Maxwell Anderson.

7. *All Hallows' Eve.* Though he was fearful, actually the reviewers were mainly favorable. See Jan. 30, 1945, n. 10.

8. The manager was a Mr. Walsh, regarding a possible position for Michael in the New York branch of the Oxford University Press. See Apr. 18, 1940, n. 69.

9. Colin Hardie was a fellow and tutor of Magdalen College. As secretary of the Dante Society he was helpful in securing C.W.'s membership in the prestigious group.

10. *All Hallows' Eve.*

11. Evelyn is a confused and misdirected character in *All Hallows' Eve.*

12. Peter Quennell, poet, historian, and biographer, was editor of the influential *Cornhill Magazine* from 1944 to 1951.

13. In the early 1930s a group of writers, most prominent being Ezra Pound and T. S. Eliot, questioned Milton's standing as a great poet. F. L. Leavis was moved in 1936 in *Revaluations* to write, "Milton's dislodgement in the past decade, after two centuries of prominence, was effected with remarkably very little fuss." In 1942, at a time when Williams was strongly defending Milton, C. S. Lewis published *Preface to Paradise Lost,* a strong rebuttal of charges brought by Leavis and his followers. Also in 1957 T. S. Eliot wrote an essay ("Milton II," *On Poetry and Poets*) in which he modified his earlier harsher view of Milton.

14. Robert Browning, "Cleon," 57–58:

> And I have written three books on the soul,
> Proving absurd all written hitherto.

15. "Great deliverance" is a frequent Old Testament expression, e.g., "and the Lord saved them by a great deliverance" (1 Chron. 11:14).

16. See Judg. 5:31: "So let all thine enemies perish, O lord."

17. T. S. Eliot, *Burnt Norton*, 2.16–17:

> At the still point of the turning world. Neither
>   flesh nor fleshless;
> Neither from nor towards; at the still point,
>   there the dance is,
> But neither arrest nor movement.

18. "The first continuation to Cretien's Percival was one attributed to Wauchier de Denain. Then it was shown that the author could not be identified, and scholars during the first half of the twentieth century persisted in naming him Pseudo Wauchier" (*New Arthurian Encyclopedia*, 99).

19. William Wordsworth, *Prelude*, 14.225–27:

> . . . and he whose soul hath risen
> Up to the height of feeling intellect
> Shall want to humbler tenderness . . .

20. Truth comes out of wine. From Pliny.

21. Roosevelt, Churchill, and Stalin met at Yalta on February 4, 1944. The issues discussed dealt with the European Allies, with the termination of the war against Japan, and with the founding of the United Nations.

22. Michael's employment by Oxford University Press in America. See Apr. 18, 1940, n. 69.

23. *All Hallow's Eve.*

24. As did Elijah: "there appeared a chariot of fire, and . . . Elijah went up by a whirlwind into heaven" (2 Kings 2:11).

25. St. John, author of the visionary apocalypse, the *Book of Revelation.*

26. See "Taliessin in the Rose Garden."

27. As he says elsewhere, matter and spirit are two modes of the same substance.

28. Bishop George Bell.

29. *The House of the Octopus.*

30. This outburst was the culmination of Michael's dissatisfaction with Oxford and the tension between father and son that prompted Michael to return to his mother.

31. This may be, in light of Michael's interest, Theater Museum.

32. The piece on religious drama had not been written at the time of his death.

33. *The Figure of Arthur.*

34. Walsh from the American branch of the Oxford University Press. See Apr. 18, 1940, n. 69.

35. See Feb. 5, 1944, n. 15; Aug. 10, 1944, n. 96.

36. "The Figure of Arthur."

37. See Feb. 17, 1945, n. 34.

38. Wallis was the caretaker of the London building in which the Williamses' flat was located.

39. See Feb. 16, 1945, n. 32.

40. *The Figure of Arthur.*

41. Edmund Spenser, *The Faerie Queen*, 7.c.2.131–32:

> For of the soul the body form doth take;
> For soul is form, and doth the body make.

42. Basil Blackwell.

43. See Feb. 5, 1944, n. 15.

44. David Higham was his literary agent in London.

45. See letter of Feb. 28, 1945.

46. James 5:16: "The effectual fervent prayer of a righteous man availeth much."

47. Wordsworth, "Mutability," 1.14.

48. Wilson Knight was a distinguished scholar and critic. He wrote several books of Shakespeare criticism. The one C.W. speaks of was probably *The Crowning Life* (London: Oxford University Press, 1947).

49. Zion was the city taken by David from the Jebusites (2 Sam. 5:7–8); the name came to stand for the Holy City.

50. Sarras is the name of the Holy City in the Taliessin cycle (see Glossary).

51. See first paragraph of letter of Feb. 28, 1945.

52. *English Poetic Mind.*

53. Martin Browne.

54. Tennyson, "Choric Song, 5–6:

> Music that gentlier on the spirit lies,
> Than tired eyelids upon tired eyes.

55. Charles Hadfield was a longtime friend and colleague of C.W. at Amen House. He was married to Alice Mary Hadfield, C.W.'s biographer. His essay "C.W. at Amen House" is a valuable contribution to our understanding of the influence of the Oxford University Press and its staff on C.W.

56. C.W. and Michal were married April 12, 1917.

57. "The Figure of Arthur."

58. President Franklin Roosevelt died on April 12, 1945.

59. On April 25, 1945, President Harry Truman, having succeeded President Roosevelt upon his death, opened the United Nations Conference on International Organization. The result was the launching of the United Nations with headquarters in New York.

60. Hugo Dyson was a lecturer in English at Reading University, a friend of C. S. Lewis's, and a member of the Inklings. After C.W.'s death he became a fellow and tutor in English literature at Merton College, Oxford.

61. *The English Poems of John Milton* in World's Classics Series appeared in 1940 with an introduction by C.W. He had expressed an interest in publishing his Oxford lectures on Milton, but there is no evidence in the letters to indicate such a project was officially under way.

62. The act of surrender was signed May 7 to be effective at midnight May 8–9.

63. If C.W. were planning to write a life of Jesus there is no evidence other than this in the letters.

Works Cited

Bible. Containing the Old and New Testament. Authorized King James Version.

Brewer, E. Cobham. *The Dictionary of Phrase and Fable.* London: Casell and Company, 1899.

Carpenter, Humphrey. *The Inklings: C.S. Lewis, J.R.R. Tolkien, Charles Williams, and Their Friends.* Boston: Houghton Mifflin, 1979.

Charles Williams Society Letter. Vols. 1–90.

Eliot, T. S. *On Poetry and Poets.* London: Faber and Faber, 1957.

Gaskell, G. A. *Dictionary of All Scriptures and Myths.* New York: Gramercy Books, Julian Press, 1960.

Glenn, Lois. *Charles W. S. Williams: A Checklist.* Kent, Ohio: Kent State University Press, 1975.

Hadfield, Alice Mary. *Charles Williams: An Exploration of His Life and Work.* New York: Oxford University Press, 1983.

———, ed. *Outlines of Romantic Theology.* Grand Rapids, Mich.: William B. Eerdmans, 1990.

Heath-Stubbs, John. *Collected Plays by Charles Williams.* London: Oxford University Press, 1963.

Hefling, Charles A., ed. *Charles Williams: The Essential Writings in Spirituality and Theology.* Boston: Cowley Publications, 1993.

Horne, Brian, ed. *Charles Williams: A Celebration.* Herefordshire: Gracewing, Fowler Wright Books, 1995.

———. "The Theological Rhetoric of Vision." In Horne, *Charles Williams.*

Huttar, Charles A., and Peter J. Schakel. *The Rhetoric of Vision: Essays on Charles Williams.* Lewisburg, Pa.: Bucknell University Press, 1996.

Kilby, Clyde S., and Marjorie Lamp Mead. *Brothers and Friends: The Diaries of Major Warren Hamilton Lewis.* San Francisco: Harper & Row, 1982.

King, Roma A., Jr. "The Occult as Rhetoric in the Poetry of Charles Williams." In Huttar and Schakel, *Rhetoric of Vision.*

Lewis, C. S. *Arthurian Torso.* London: Oxford University Press, 1948.

Matthews, Caitlin. *The Elements of the Celtic Tradition.* Shaftsbury, Dorset: Element Books, 1989.

Reynolds, Barbara. *The Passionate Intellect: Dorothy L. Sayers' Encounter with Dante.* Kent, Ohio: Kent State University Press, 1989.

Ridler, Anne. *The Image of the City and Other Essays.* London: Oxford University Press, 1958.

Sutcliffe, Peter. *The Oxford University Press.* London: Oxford University Press, 1978.

Waite, Arthur E. *The Hidden Church of the Holy Grail.* 1909. Reprint, Des Plaines, Ill.: Yogi Publication Society, n.d.

Williams, Charles. *All Hallows' Eve.* London: Faber and Faber, 1945.

———. *The Descent of the Dove: A Short History of the Holy Spirit in the Church.* London: Longmans, Green and Company, 1939.

———. *English Poetic Mind.* London; Oxford University Press, 1932.

———. *The Figure of Beatrice.* London: Faber and Faber, 1943.

_____. *The Forgiveness of Sins.* London: G. Bles, 1942.

_____. *The New Christian Year.* London: Oxford University Press, 1941.

_____. *Reason and Beauty in the Poetic Mind.* Oxford: Clarendon Press, 1933.

_____. *The Region of the Summer Stars.* London: PL, Editions Poetry London, Nicholson and Watson, 1944.

_____. *Shadows of Ecstasy.* London: Victor Gollancz, 1933.

_____. *Taliessin through Logres.* London: Oxford University Press, 1938.

_____. *Thomas Cranmer of Canterbury.* London: Oxford University Press, 1936.

_____. *Windows of Night.* London: Oxford University Press, 1924.

_____, ed. *The Letters of Evelyn Underhill.* London: Longmans, Green, 1942.

Williams, Florence [Michal]. "As I Remember Charles Williams." *Charles Williams Society Newsletter* 78 (Summer 1995).

Index

Flecker, Dr., 170; biography of, 168, 170, 187, 192, 200–201, 205, 209

Flecker, Mrs., 169–70, 174–75, 177, 179, 183, 185, 193, 196, 210–12; mentioned, 225

Forces News Flash, 204

Forgiveness of Sins, The, 9, 108, 121–22, 127–28, 131, 136, 138–40, 185; royalties from, 167, 193

Foss, Hubert J., 15–16, 24–25, 53–54, 88, 96–97, 129, 150, 200, 265; and introduction to *The Duchess of Malfi*, 223, 228, 239; with problems, 4, 118, 132; mentioned, 32, 35, 59, 80, 127

Fox, Adam, 16, 59, 64, 86, 265, 267

Foyle's Book Store, London, 193, 215

Freedman, Barnett, 144

Fry, Christopher, 45, 174, 220, 266

Gardner, Dame Helen Louise, 207

Gardner, Miss, 181, 197, 222

Garvin, Viola, 143

Gibson, Wilfred, 212–13, 237–38

Gielgud, John, 268

Goffin, 33, 221, 234, 257. *See also* Cumberlege, Geoffrey F. J.; Jock

Gollancz, Victor, Publishing Firm, 40, 124, 265

Gordon, George S., 22, 149, 185

Graves, Robert, 209, 266

Greek Orthodox Church, 58

Greene, Graham, 69, 71, 76–77, 266

Grundy, Ursula, 18, 25, 46–47, 55, 58, 62, 93, 146; and Michael, 140, 143–44, 291nn. 13, 25; Michal and, 64, 79; and uncle of, 23, 104

Hadfield, Charles, 119, 254, 270

Hadfield, Mrs., 8, 120

Halifax, Lord, 86, 150

Hampden, John, 250

Harari, Mrs., 144

Hardie, Colin, 243, 249–50, 258, 266–67

Hardson, Canon, 59

Harrington, Mr., 153, 184; and wife, 201

Harris, Jocelyn, 88

Havard, Dr. Robert, 108–9, 158

Haynes, Renée, 25, 32, 175, 177, 212, 266

Heath-Stubbs, John Francis Alexander, 8, 214–15, 301n. 97

Heineman "I Believe" series, 266

Henderson, Lady, 140

Herald Review, 243

Herbert, Auberon, 137

Higham, David, 18, 252, 255, 266

Higham Associates, 266. *See also* Pearn, Pollinger, and Higham

Hill, Rebecca Marion ("the aunt"), 59, 86, 91–92, 94, 134, 152–53, 170, 223; Anne Spalding and, 95, 102, 115, 139, 143; in glossary, 263; and Michael, 132, 139

Hitler, in the news, 38, 49, 81–82, 257

Hoare-Laval Pact, 68, 266

Hollis, Christopher, 169

Hopkins, Gerard Manley, 19, 39, 42, 90, 102, 140, 223, 266, 268, 270; and air raids, 73, 82, 89, 116, 173; and the aunt, 59; away, 16, 41, 70, 85, 105, 136, 152; as a friend, 22–24, 80, 127, 149, 151, 178, 192; in glossary, 266; as a housemate, 16–17, 63, 108, 121, 131, 146, 201; and Michael, 71, 74, 83, 109, 132; and Michal, 20, 46, 62; and new job, 128–29, 183; and Oxford, 7, 26, 28; and the Oxford University Press, 1, 32, 101, 142; review of *The Descent of the Dove*, 26, 135; and wife, 205

Hughes, Mrs., 131

Hunt, Raymond, 8, 21–22, 50–51, 80, 167, 221, 267; and *The Descent of the Dove*, 26, 34

Huttar, Charles, 3

Inge, William Ralph, 34

Inklings, 10, 186, 264–68, 271

Irving, Henry, 81

Jackson, Peter, 114

Joad, Professor C. E. M., 134

Jock, 57, 59, 75, 77, 96–97, 129, 141–42, 217. *See also* Cumberlege, Geoffrey F. J.; Goffin

Jones, David, 4

Jones, Phyllis (Celia), 2, 37, 53, 269, 278n. 95, 280–81n. 58

Julian of Norwich, Lady, 261

Keays-Young, Mrs., 19–20

Kierkegaard, Søren, 139, 169, 281n. 64

Kindersby, Miss, 40

Kinselle, Miss, 20, 122, 124

Knight, Professor Wilson, 253

Kylie, Powell, 240

Lampert, Eugene, 222

Lang-Sims, Lois, 2

League of Nations, 266

Leavis, F. L., 9

Lectures, 48, 173, 200, 202, 215; attendance at, 244, 246, 251; on *Dunciad*, 233; at Ox-

Plays, mentioned, 8; "Courage pamphlet," 49, 69, 74, 76, 78, 81, 280n. 44; *The Death of Good Fortune,* 28, 39–40, 201, 269; "Departure of Dindrane," 152, 228; *The Descent into Hell,* 70, 137, 144, 161–63, 166, 178, 212, 265; *The English Poetic Mind,* 132–33, 171, 176, 253, 271–72; "The Epiphany," 252; *Flecker of Dean Close,* 168, 170, 187, 192, 200–201, 205, 209; *Frontiers of Evil,* 7, 9, 108–9, 114, 122–23, 131; *Frontiers of Hell,* 269; *Grab and Grace,* 201, 269; *The Greater Trumps,* 9, 262, 267; *He Came Down from Heaven,* 25, 96, 97, 103, 266; *Henry VII,* 172; *Heroes and Kings,* 199, 265; *The House by the Stable,* 28, 37, 39–40, 201, 240, 264, 269; *The House of the Octopus,* 7–9, 37, 204, 213, 215, 217, 220–21, 248; "In the Land of Juda," 259–60; introduction to *The Duchess of Malfi,* 223, 228, 231, 234, 237, 239; introduction to *The English Poems of John Milton,* 76–77, 81, 119, 225; "Is There a Christian Literature?" 146, 293n. 19; *The Judgement at Chelmsford,* 8, 41, 267, 270; *The Letters of Evelyn Underhill,* 147; "Outline of Romantic Theology," 294n. 47; *The Oxford Book of Mystical Verse,* mentioned, 8; *The Place of the Lion,* 262, 303n. 141; *Poems of Conformity,* 268, 270; *Poetry at Present,* 221, 271; "The Prayers of the Pope," 152, 156, 205, 226; "Religion and Love in Dante," 117, 121; *Reason and Beauty in the Poetic Mind,* 171, 228, 271; *The Rite of Passion,* 8, 24, 40, 43, 53, 267, 270; *Seed of Adam,* 8, 19, 25, 40, 201, 269–70; *Shadows of Ecstasy,* 144; *The Silver Stair,* 141, 233, 249, 261, 269; *Terror of Light,* 43, 50, 57, 59–61, 64, 269; *The Way of Exchange,* 80; *Thomas Cranmer of Canterbury,* 8–9, 24, 40, 43, 103, 262, 264; *What the Cross Means to Me,* 9, 189. *See also All Hallows' Eve;* British Broadcasting Corporation; *The Descent of the Dove;* "The Figure of Arthur"; *The Figure of Beatrice; The Forgiveness of Sins; The New Christian Year; The Region of Summer Stars; Taliessin through Logres; Time and Tide,* book reviews for; *Witchcraft*

Williams, Michael, 44, 60, 62–63, 92–96, 104–6, 115–16, 189, 214, 243; and air raids, 73–74, 89–90; alias Michael Blain, 185; and the armed forces, 117, 129–30, 136, 241, 304n. 4; and Basil Blackwell, 46, 48–51, 53–56, 145, 170, 263; at Blackwell's, 66, 72, 79–80, 92–93, 98, 102–3; book reviews by, 186, 190, 196, 199, 210, 213, 246; at Bumpus Booksellers, 184, 240; as correspondent, 33–34, 62, 156, 171, 175, 182–83; and father's degree, 146, 148–50; father's interest in, 17, 27, 39–40, 83, 152–54, 166, 179, 201; and London, 82, 99, 167–68; and Michal, 57, 91, 131, 140–41, 176; against Oxford, 172–74; and Oxford University Press, New York, 242, 248; money sent to, 40, 219, 226; social life of, 71, 75, 88, 121, 137–39, 203, 208, 256; at South Parks Road, 43, 59, 78, 89; at the theatre, 85, 96, 108–10, 114, 134, 225, 236; and Ursula Grundy, 143–44, 291nn. 13, 25; mentioned, 1, 7–8

Williams, Ralph Vaughan, 132

Willis, Olive, 20, 26–27, 32, 40, 272

Wilson, J. C., 145

Win, 120, 123–24, 128, 143, 148, 172, 199

Winstanley, 204, 207

Witchcraft, 35, 72, 88, 95, 101, 111, 162, 265; Eliot and, 28, 30, 57, 69; Fabers and, 28, 101, 114; Margaret typing, 27, 39, 55; proofs of, 106, 109; royalties from, 144, 193; writing of, 20, 22–24, 32–33, 40, 42, 45–46, 48, 53; mentioned, 9

Wood, Mrs. Henry, 45, 134

Wordsworth, William, 154, 165, 174, 177, 234, 245, 261; reading, 156–57, 159

Working Men's College, 269

Younghusband, Sir Francis, 227

To Michal from Serge
was designed by Will Underwood;
composed in 10½-point Cycles on
a Macintosh system using
QuarkXpress by Sans Serif, Inc.;
printed by sheet-fed offset lithography on
50-pound Supple Opaque natural stock (an
acid-free paper with 60% recycled content),
Smyth sewn in signatures, bound over
binder's boards in Arrestox B cloth,
and wrapped with dust jackets
designed by Christine Brooks
and printed in three colors
by Thomson-Shore, Inc.;
and published by
The Kent State University Press
KENT, OHIO 44242